Populism and the People in Contemporary Critical Thought

Also available from Bloomsbury

Rewriting Contemporary Political Philosophy with Plato and Aristotle, by Paul Schollmeier
Aesthetics, Arts, and Politics in a Global World, by Daniel Herwitz
East Timor, René Girard and Neocolonial Violence, by Susan Connelly
A Philosophy for Future Generations, by Tiziana Andina

Populism and the People in Contemporary Critical Thought

Politics, Philosophy, and Aesthetics

Edited by
David Payne, Alexander Stagnell,
and Gustav Strandberg

BLOOMSBURY ACADEMIC
LONDON • NEW YORK • OXFORD • NEW DELHI • SYDNEY

BLOOMSBURY ACADEMIC
Bloomsbury Publishing Plc
50 Bedford Square, London, WC1B 3DP, UK
1385 Broadway, New York, NY 10018, USA
29 Earlsfort Terrace, Dublin 2, Ireland

BLOOMSBURY, BLOOMSBURY ACADEMIC and the Diana logo are trademarks of
Bloomsbury Publishing Plc

First published in Great Britain 2023
This paperback edition published 2024

Copyright © Alexander Stagnell, David Payne, Gustav Strandberg and Contributors 2023

David Payne, Alexander Stagnell, and Gustav Strandberg have asserted their right under the
Copyright, Designs and Patents Act, 1988, to be identified as Editors of this work.

For legal purposes the Acknowledgments on p. viii constitute an extension
of this copyright page.

Series design by Charlotte Daniels
Cover image: At the wall of federates. The Paris Commune is an insurrectionary
period in the history of Paris, from March 18, 1871 to the "Bloody Week" from May 21
(© Old Books Images/Alamy)

All rights reserved. No part of this publication may be reproduced or transmitted
in any form or by any means, electronic or mechanical, including photocopying,
recording, or any information storage or retrieval system, without prior
permission in writing from the publishers.

Bloomsbury Publishing Plc does not have any control over, or responsibility for, any
third-party websites referred to or in this book. All internet addresses given in this
book were correct at the time of going to press. The author and publisher regret any
inconvenience caused if addresses have changed or sites have ceased to exist,
but can accept no responsibility for any such changes.

A catalogue record for this book is available from the British Library.

A catalog record for this book is available from the Library of Congress.

ISBN: HB: 978-1-3501-8362-9
PB: 978-1-3501-8528-9
ePDF: 978-1-3501-8363-6
eBook: 978-1-3501-8364-3

Typeset by Deanta Global Publishing Services, Chennai, India

To find out more about our authors and books visit www.bloomsbury.com and
sign up for our newsletters.

Contents

List of Figures	vii
Acknowledgments	viii

Introduction: The People and Populism in Contemporary Critical
   Thought   *David Payne, Alexander Stagnell, and Gustav Strandberg*   1

Part I Political Reflections on the People

1   The People: Proper, Common, Improper. An Interview with
    Jacques Rancière *Jacques Rancière, David Payne, Alexander Stagnell, and
    Gustav Strandberg*   29
2   Demophobia in Politics: Remarks on Liberal Anti-populism and the
    Possibility of a Radical Democratic Populism *Oliver Marchart*   43
3   Logics of Democracy in the Work of Ernesto Laclau and Jacques
    Rancière *Mark Devenney and Clare Woodford*   59
4   Disavowals of Populism: The Political Displacement of
    Homogeneity *Karl Ekeman*   75

Part II Toward an Affectology of Populism

5   The Politics of Resentment and Its Pitfalls *Samo Tomšič*   93
6   "That's Disgusting!": The Shifting Politics of Affect in Right-wing
    Populist Mobilization *Maria Brock and Jenny Gunnarsson Payne*   107
7   The People and the Image of the Leader: Reflections on Mass
    Psychology *Chiara Bottici*   122

Part III The Aesthetics of the People

8   Picturing the People: The Dilemmas of Democratic
    Representation *Paula Diehl*   139
9   Aesthetic Forms of the Political: Populist Ornaments, Cultures of
    Rejection, Democratic Assemblies *Stefan Jonsson*   160
10 The Undivided People: On the Hypothesis of Radical Democracy in
    Peter Weiss' *The Aesthetics of Resistance* *Kim West*   176

Part IV The People beyond the Political

11 Fragmentation of the Idea of the People: The Afro-Brazilian
    Event *Muniz Sodré* 197
12 A Politics of the People and a Politics of the Popular: From the Russian
    Revolution to *Gramsci's Ashes* *Tora Lane* 209
13 Facing People *Ramona Rat* 223

Epilogue 237

14 On "People": Brief Theoretical Notes *Michael Marder* 239

List of Contributors 243
Index 245

Figures

8.1	Unknown, *Matière à reflection pour les jongleurs couronnés*, 1793	142
8.2	Pierre-Antoine Demachy, *Fête de l'Être Suprême au Champ de Mars*, ca. 1794	146
8.3	Thomas Hart Benton, *People of Chilmark*, 1920	151
8.4	Tarsila do Amaral, *Operários*, 1933	152
8.5	Collection of photos from Charlie Hebdo manifestations	154
8.6	Collection of photos from Charlie Hebdo manifestations	155
8.7	Collection of photos from Charlie Hebdo manifestations	155
11.1	Jean-Baptiste Debret, *Vista do Largo do Palácio no dia da aclamação de D. João VI*, 1818	198
11.2	Victor Meirelles, *A primeira missa no Brasil*, 1859–61	199
11.3	Horace Vernet, *Première messe en Kabylie*, 1854	200
11.4	Pedro Américo, *Independência do Brasil ou O Grito do Ipiranga*, 1888	200
11.5	Aurélio de Figueiredo, *O Ultimo Baile da Monarquia ou a Ilusão do Terceiro Reinado*, 1905	201

Acknowledgments

As editors of this volume, we would like to thank the rhetoric department at Södertörn University for financial help in making this anthology possible. We would also like to extend our thanks to the Estate of Tarsila do Amaral, the Hirshhorn Museum and Sculpture Garden, the Musée cantonal des Beaux-Arts de Lausanne, the Musée Carnavalet, the Museu Paulista da USP, and the Trustees of the British Museum for providing us with rights to use their respective images and to Cecilia Schuback for the translation of Muniz Sodré's chapter from Portuguese.

A special and heartfelt thanks to Professor Marcia Sá Cavalcante Schuback for her intellectual and practical support throughout the duration of this project. Without her help, this anthology would never have seen the light of day.

Introduction

The People and Populism in Contemporary Critical Thought

David Payne, Alexander Stagnell, and Gustav Strandberg

The people. A necessary category for political life, even if vexing for critical thought. The famous line from Bertolt Brecht's *Die Lösung*, written in response to popular unrest in East Berlin in June of 1953, would sum up the situation adroitly: after the people had apparently expressed no confidence in the East German government, Brecht wryly commented that the government should "dissolve the people and elect another" (2006: 119). The dissolution of a people, but *only* for another to take its place. For what would a government be without its people? An empty husk? Both needless and useless. This is not simply because politics in its modern form has become coterminous with democracy, with, that is, the notion of "governing *for* the people and *by* the people." After all, where would the aristocrats, the plutocrats, the monarchs, tyrants, and the revolutionary guard be without their people?

It is tempting to see the relationship between government and people in hylomorphic terms, between the "active form" of governing and the "passive matter" of the governed. The two suffixes of *-archy* and *-cracy* bespeak of the defining rule or principle (*archē*) or power (*kratos*) by which a political regime comes to exercise its authority and legitimacy (*princeps*), for example, monarchy as the rule of the One and democracy as designating the power of the Many. Whichever regime we speak about, the source of this power is exercised over the masses as formed matter. They are always subject to an external principle; never, it seems, is the people its own form.[1] Certainly, democracy comes closest: the masses as the *constituent* power at one with the *constituted* power consecrating the legitimacy of its order (Negri, 2009; Rubinelli, 2020). However, as the source of rule and power, the demos remains a quantitative category that does not necessarily equate to the people to whom this rule applies; this is especially so in so-called representative democracies. While popular sovereignty has served as the basis for the legitimacy of a democratic state, famously expressed in the constitutions of the Revolutions of the eighteenth century, with the exception of direct democracy or rule by plebescite, no perfect coincidence exists between the ideal of popular sovereignty as the embodied unity of all members (past, present, and future) of a *politeia*, and the empirical people which, at any given moment, are but a partial and conditioned expounding of this general principle. So, in representative democracy, for example, where the elected government is meant to speak in the name of the all, its policies, legislative priorities, etc. are invariably a reflection of a set of interests that are less than the whole for whom it governs. Likewise, in popular referenda, the popular will can be said to have carried the day even if a vote essentially splits the community in two (as was the case with for instance the Brexit vote). In truth, mass politics (inculcated in the idea of popular sovereignty) would be in excess of any political form (*politeia*) within which a people comes to exist. As Margaret Canovan asks in her oft-quoted study on the people, "[s]hould we perhaps conclude that popular authorization [sovereignty] can never be given adequate *institutional* form because it belongs to a more fluid aspect of politics, in which brief episodes of popular mobilization are encapsulated in myths?" (2005: 7).[2] It could easily be assumed from Canovan's framing of the issue that the people is trapped within an antinomy between its institutional and already constituted form and the protean and ever-shifting matter of collective bodies as they appear and disappear in political history, though several contemporary theorists have sought to overcome this putative opposition with varying degrees of success.[3]

As has been discussed on numerous occasions before, the principle of popular sovereignty is as old as modern democracy, if not democracy, itself—a line that can be traced from Cicero, through Locke, and von Pufendorf, up until modernity.[4] Most famously, it is the work of Jean-Jacques Rousseau from which modern democratic thought proceeds when discussing the people and its sovereign will. In the second book of *The Social Contract*, Rousseau attempts to establish a difference between the people, or "the will of everyone," and the general will, claiming that "the latter is concerned only with the common interest, while the former is concerned with private interests, and is the sum total of individual wants" (2002: 73). He then goes on to explain that the path from the former to the latter can only be crossed if we remove the "excesses and insufficiencies" of each individual desire, constructing out of the shared common ground of each and every individual, hiding behind what appears as an insurmountable divide, a people expressing its general will. The problem here, however, is that issues pertaining to the general will of the people leave unacknowledged the very genesis of a people, a more formative line of questioning that, to his credit, Rousseau had already introduced in the fifth chapter of the first book of *The Social Contract*. Taking issue with Grotius' claim that "a people may give itself to a king," as if a people was preformed, Rousseau insightfully points out that "before examining the act by which a people elects a king, it would be well to examine the act by which people becomes a people" (2002: 162). Rousseau underlines the genetico-constructive operation through which the people come to be. The people is not an accomplished fact, but a fact to be accomplished. The insoluble problem here needs only a passing remark, namely the productive tension between the will to form and the forming of the will. Or, in the imperative form: the people *must* be formed in order for it to be able to assert popular sovereignty. Whence the possible hylomorphism at stake. But things, in Rousseau, are more complicated, since what must be formed is doing the forming. The people must (perhaps) be *per-formed*, existing by virtue of performative or, if one prefers, declaratory acts. In this sense, the people comes to exist by means of the name that supports it, giving it discernibility, distinction, and identity.

This riddle, indexed by Rousseau, returns to us today with the reemergence of different forms of populism and with the figure of the populist demagogue—two less than salubrious images by which contemporary critical thought is confronted. These two concepts, populism and the people, constitute the axis around which this anthology revolves.

The purpose of the volume is threefold. First of all, it is to present a series of reflections on the meaning of the people today, in a world where the material forces of global capital, and the ideological shibboleths of the freedom of movement of goods, services, and peoples that buttress it, have been met with democratic and anti-democratic resistance and contestation, bringing with it appeals to and by the "people" in a variety of different forms and modes of expression. In an era that once was claimed as "post-ideological," today is in fact a time in which the -ism reasserts itself: populism, nationalism, fascism, socialism, democratism, all of which, in contending and incompatible ways, make a stake on the "people," disclosing its real existence as a many-headed hydra. The volume sets out to reflect on its own times by taking cognizance of the notion's complex and overdetermined political, aesthetic, and theoretical histories, not in order to harmonize or synthesize these histories but to present them in their sometimes opposing and contrapuntal dimensions. Third and ultimately, the overarching aim is to show up in what ways the category of the people is today, has been in the past, and will be in the future, both an unsettled and unsettling question for thought. In fourteen chapters, scholars from a wide range of disciplines within the humanities join in order to analyze this phenomenon by drawing upon the history of modern critical thought. In doing so, they seek to respond to a number of distinct but interrelated questions: What is a people and is it still a viable category for emancipatory political thought and practice? Who, and to what end, does the jargon of populism serve? Does populism represent the people or is the people to be saved from populism?

Our specific aims in this chapter will be to lay the groundwork for these questions by first of all attending to the relation between critical thought and the people, both in the context of our own political present, which has not unproblematically been described as "a populist moment" (Mouffe, 2018), and in the wider history of critical thought. In recent decades populism has increasingly become the target of critical inquiry. The first part of this chapter will enquire into how this critical itinerary is carried out in contemporary research on populism, and on what questionable assumptions and presuppositions this critical undertaking is predicated. The second part of our investigation will be to show in what way a certain number of these assumptions can be traced through the development of critical thought, strictly construed as (Post-)Kantian continental philosophy. While populism per se was obviously not a target for the likes of Kant, Hegel, and the Frankfurt School, there has always been a certain reticence surrounding the concrete manifestation of the people, around which a whole series of ambivalences coalesce. In the final section of this introduction we reconstruct a certain understanding of the task of critique that resists the moralizing and normative prejudices of both classical critical thought and its echoes within contemporary populism research, by laying out the possible ways in which critique has entered into a more productive relation with the category of the people. It is this concluding section that sets the parameters within which the individual contributors in this volume operate.

Populism and the Prejudices of the People

If Rousseau draws attention to the co-originarity of the forming of a people and the people that gives form to a certain *politeia*, the category of the people also harbors within it problems of a normative nature. From the outset of this volume, it is normative matters of which we must be mindful; they are a sobering reminder of the risks that lay in wait when critical thought chooses to handle the idea of the people. None more so than today, in a context of emergent populist movements. What then of these normatively inflected problems? First, the distinction between autonomy and heteronomy. If autonomy has been irrevocably tied to the self-legislation of the free-standing individual, then how are we to understand the autonomy and self-legislation of a people composed of a multiplicity of individuals? The autonomous individual, as epitomized in the writings of Kant, is not only a self-legislator but also self-reflective and self-critical, who, by virtue of his or her reason, has the capacity to criticize society at large by way of the free use of public reason. The problem is that the people is allegedly incapable of critical thought, subjected to contingent rules and external factors, whims and inclinations. If the people is deprived of autonomy, it is devoid of reason also, implying that a people does not think, at least not in the way that thinking is normally understood within the critical and philosophical tradition. Second, then, whether as cause or effect of the lack of autonomy, the people is said to be a ferment of irrational and affective desires, drives, and contingent beliefs not grounded in any principle of reason. Not only do these purported "pathologies" bar any rational engagement with the people as such, they also give rise to the therapeutic question of how to "cure" the people from itself. The question then becomes how to extricate the True People from the teeming mass of the multitude?[5] Third, the people is often predicated on a specific *ethos*, though an *ethos* that often surreptitiously glides into an idea of a specific *ethnos*, from which the pathologies of the people reappear once more (in the form of violence against other notions of the good life, other ethnic groups, etc.). These three normative judgments surrounding the phenomenon of the people leave, either in isolation or when taken together, their indelible trace on the history of critical thought.

Interestingly, it is these same normative problems that today permeate much of the contemporary critique of populism. Although initially a self-descriptive term employed by both the Populist Party in the United States and the *Narodniki* in Russia during the end of the nineteenth century, populism has within our own contemporaneity come to designate a specific mode of political practice. There are four generally recognized aspects that are said to characterize populism today.[6] The first is the presence of a clearly demarcated antagonistic frontier between the "we" of a unified people and the "they" of "other" heterogeneous and excluded elements. The latter serve at one and the same time as the obstacle preventing the people from constituting a harmonious whole, as well as the negative condition making possible the contingent appearing of a people. The second defining characteristic of populism is *how* this antagonistic frontier is itself constructed, namely the way in which the dividing line separating the "people" from what does not belong to it is articulated, such that some appeal to the common (e.g., the downtrodden, the hard-working majority, the left behind) against representatives of the status quo (e.g., the elite, corrupt bureaucrats, the beneficiaries of a rigged system) is made. This entails populism's third aspect: its "anti-institutional" character, the fact that it breaks with "politics as usual," aiming at the breakup of political and moral consensus. The fourth and final determination broaches the entire affectology of populism, to wit the forging of a popular identity and the establishing of a stark opposition between "us" and "them" depends on harnessing an indeterminate feeling of discontent, which is then transmuted into a generalized grievance. For there to be a dis-identification with the present social order and an identification making possible a fusion of the many into a people, affects of resentment, frustration, anger, and distrust are often mobilized.[7]

The ruling narrative, from anti-populist politicians and the media alike, is that in the name of the people, a growing number of populist leaders have succeeded in overturning the political system put in place by liberal democracy as purportedly the preservation of true freedom and the rule of law. Populism, on the other hand, is accused of depriving individuals of their autonomy and reinforcing division on the grounds of both *ethos* and *ethnos* by worsening and then exploiting the pathologies of the people in order to be able to dictate what is accepted in terms of both culture and ethnicity, as well as behavior and opinions. And it is understandable that supposedly populist programs and slogans claiming to protect the people, such as Putin's laws against "gay propaganda," Bolsonaro's repeated claim that "a good criminal is a dead criminal," and Erdogan's attacks on those "who think that they defend Western democracy and freedom," while presented as opinions and decisions arising from the will and sentiments of the people, all constitute threats against the rule of law, freedom, and thus the safety of individuals. None of this is new, of course. A general reticence surrounding populism as a specific form of political engagement that directly harnesses the so-called will or views of the people can be traced back to its ignoble origins (cf. Canovan, 1981; Rovira Kaltwasser et al., 2019; Stavrakakis, 2017).

A substantial body of literature on populism today, mainly in the political and the historical sciences, can be construed as empirically orientated.[8] Primarily, this existing research retains a certain indifference toward the Rousseauian problem that every actually existing populism unequivocally poses, namely the transcendental-ontological question concerning the forming of a people. The descriptivist inclination of the empirical sciences has certainly contributed to our contemporary understanding of populism, insofar as such studies offer us analyses of certain characteristics, features, comparisons and draw out the contextual specificity, both in a historical and geographical sense, of the phenomenon (cf. Mudde and Kaltwasser, 2012; de la Torre, 2010; Wayland and Madrid, 2019). However, an onus is often placed on historically situated examples of "populism," the outcome of which is an open and plural set of "apparent" cases lacking any convincing moment of synthesis. While more comparatively inclined studies promise to provide these moments of articulation, often an inevitable double-game is at play, according to which certain *manifest* points of unity are ultimately thrown back onto contextual differences, putting into question the salience of cobbling cases together under a general category in the first place (where talk of "family resemblances" remains the comparativists' fig leaf) (cf. Moffitt, 2016; Mudde, 2007; Ostiguy, 2009).[9]

In an attempt to mitigate these drawbacks, mainstream research on populism often offers a rigorous classification and differentiation of various instances of populism, bringing us to the issue of nomenclature. Here we can regard the procedure as a form of conceptual purification, so that, in spite of its material richness, "populism" can, for the purpose of consistency and applicability, be delineated and defined (cf. Canovan, 1981: 301; Mudde and Kaltwasser, 2017; Taggart, 2000).[10] The problem though is twofold. On the one hand, the study of populism becomes but a scholastic enterprise—either giving rise to a profusion of contending classificatory frameworks that vie for exhaustion over the phenomenon or what is offered is a slight sophistication to an already established classificatory system, which in any case cannot be closed. On the other hand, there is the obverse problem that the very meaning of populism is overextended to the point of accommodating all (geographical and historical) differences and specificities, turning it, as many within the field recognize, into both a hazy and vague notion, and as a paradigmatic case of "an essentially contestable concept" (Gallie, 1956).[11] What ultimately matters, though, is the epistemological task of ensuring the conceptual integrity of the term "populism"—so that the concept can properly function as an organizing and classificatory designator—and not with the ontological concern of examining the very possibility of the formation of popular unity as such.[12]

In the empirical sciences there is, thus, the tendency to superordinate the epistemological question, that is, refining the concepts that adequate to the phenomenon in order to produce knowledge about populism, over issues of an ontological nature. But what of the normative prejudices that are difficult to disentangle from thinking the people and populism? While anti-populist sentiment remains strong in many strands of the public debate, mainstream populist research within the social and historical sciences has gone to great length to distance themselves from what is depicted as its problematic past (cf. Kazin, 2017; Stavrakakis and Jäger, 2018; Tormey, 2019). As is often noted, the pejorative meaning of populism, which emerged around the middle of the last century, was at least partially fueled by academic studies of populism at the time, wherein aims "to 'define' populism" regularly assumed it to constitute a threat against liberal democracies, "haunting" them with a "particular negativism," a "prosecution mania," by worshipping the people (Ionescu and Gellner, 1969: 1–5. See also Hofstadter, 1955; Lee, 1986). Today, such pathologizations are generally shunned, and in particular the Political Sciences have invested great effort into providing a neutral scientific definition of this notoriously ambiguous concept.

Researchers who take as their axiom "fidelity" to the phenomenon in all of its empirical diversity often claim to bracket such normative prejudgments (cf. Cossarini and Vallespín, 2019; Crewe and Sanders, 2020: 3; Mudde and Rovira Kaltwasser, 2017: 1). However, despite all the great effort to dispel current definitions of populism of any pejorative undertones, traces remain clearly legible, festering in the empirical research as unreflected presuppositions. This problem perhaps shows itself most clearly when populist research is forced to take the people as an already formed entity. This means that any description of *actually* existing populism by necessity investigates the people as situated within a constituted *politeia*, often bound to the nation-state.[13] This ends up making any populist "projection" of a unified people a deviation from the liberal-democratic standard, in which "people" are factually comprised from a plurality of individuals—a point that is often jumped on in order to expose populism's infamous anti-democratic tendencies. Admittedly, this can take many forms, from an implicit affirmation of pluralism as the *sine qua non* of liberal-democratic politics (with populism as its antithesis), found most notably in the work of Mudde and Kaltwasser (2017: 1–2), to a more philosophical expounding of the essence of political life arising from "those occasions when many individuals manage to act together [. . .] and where the plural capacity for action [. . .] continually frustrate attempts to predict and control the outcome of projects such as people-building" (Canovan, 1981: 55–6), as well as outright condemnation of populism as "a real danger to democracy (and not just to 'liberalism')" (Müller, 2016: 103. See also Kellner, 2016; Wodak, 2015). And what for the likes of Müller ends up being the defining property of a flourishing democratic polity? "One [that] enables majorities to authorize representatives whose actions may or may not turn out to conform to what a majority of citizens expected or would have wished for [. . .] [that] assumes fallible, contestable judgements by changing majorities [. . .] [and] if anything, a people of individuals, so that in the end only numbers (in elections) count" (Müller, 2016: 77). Nothing other than actually existing representative and parliamentary democracy.

In adumbrating these shortcomings in the empirical sciences, we say nothing that has not been said before. For one, it hearkens back to Max Horkheimer's famous 1937 essay, "Traditional and Critical Theory" (1972). Horkheimer's purpose was to expose how the positive sciences served to reproduce existing social reality by reflecting the ideological precepts of bourgeois class society. *Mutadis Mutandi*, we can see how many of the empirical studies on populism reflect anti-populist sentiments rooted in the basic precepts of liberal democracy that shape received and general opinion about what it means to be political and what is valued in politics today. The irony here is that the prejudices shown against populism in contemporary populist research are in fact very much congenial (and not at variance) with the origins of critical thought itself, meaning that the distinction between traditional (empirical, positivist) sciences and critical thought breaks down. The normative prejudices, which we sketched out earlier, threaten to colonize the openness of the problems associated with the people, by presupposing: (1) that "collective" forms of desire (inculcated in a people) are inchoate and should be treated skeptically, (2) that the people cannot think, and is to be substituted by the individual who can, and (3) that a people is always culturally and historically embedded—a fact that either must be accepted, in its arbitrariness, or it is a fact to be admonished, by exposing how the fragility of a people's own existence is dependent on what it excludes. In what follows, we will provide a short history of critical thought, seeking to ascertain the ambiguous place the people occupy within this history. The aim will be twofold. In keeping with the earlier described twin problematic of the people (i.e., [i] the ontological problem surrounding the conditions under which a people comes into being and [ii] the normative prejudgments that easily infect a proper account of populism and the people), the task will be to show how in critical thought a set of attributes (e.g., autonomy, freedom, reason) ascribed to the task of critique are in constant tension with a thoroughgoing treatment of the people as a central political category. A second aim will be to explore how this irrevocable tension ends up encircling the paradoxes of the people and their genesis in critical thought.

How does a multiplicity of autonomous individuals form itself into a people? How does this form of a people inculcate the principle of autonomy that otherwise operates at the atomic level? Which is to say, how to form an enlightened people? Is this process of forming to be undertaken through a series of pedagogical or educational practices so as to cultivate a sense of collective responsibility? Alternatively, is the formation of a people grounded historically by and through the construction of a shared sense of collective belonging through tradition, heritage, and language? Finally, is the political as such the process by which the forming of an unformed mass into a people is achieved?

Critical Thought: The People as Limit Category

To what extent does the people function as a constitutive outside for critical thought? On the one hand, it can be construed as one of critique's Others. Yet, at the same time, as Other, the people constitutes the identity of critique *via negativa*. This torsion, one could say, is present from the very inception of critical thought up to and including the critical theory of the Frankfurt School.

Let us start this short exploration with a quote from Descartes. While technically part of the prehistory of modern notions of critique, Descartes nonetheless offers one of the founding arguments surrounding the autonomy of critical thought vis-à-vis the people. He writes:

> I was convinced that our beliefs are based much more on custom and example, than on any certain knowledge, nevertheless that the assent of many voices is not a valid proof for truths which are rather difficult to discover, because they are much more likely to be found by one single man than by a people. (Descartes, 1968: 39)

The capacity for deep critical reflection and questioning is located in the individuality of human consciousness, not within the collectivity of the people. Admittedly, this Cartesian gesture is ambiguous, something the history of critical thought will itself exploit. On the one hand, the onus placed on self-doubt as well as an internal circumspection toward the external world brings with it a certain indifference toward others, for example, the people. However, on the other hand, this circumspection was never translated into a critique of the existing society to which Descartes remained a dutiful citizen. Instead, Descartes sought refuge in the inner sanctum of the self. While mindful of the categorial difference between Cartesian doubt and critique proper, this series of articulations surrounding the heteronomy and conventionalism of the people and autonomy and truth of the individual ego (or subject) would become even more pronounced in the work of Kant.

Kant's theoretical revolution, that is, the inauguration of critico-transcendental philosophy, runs parallel with the great revolutions of the latter half of the eighteenth century, where the people as a self-legislating force entered the political stage. For this reason, the following must be accounted for: while Cartesianism laid the philosophical roots for critique, the writings of Rousseau would philosophically express the irruption of the general will of the people in modernity (cf. Althusser, 2019; Pippin, 1997; Villa, 2017). Indeed, the history of critical thought after Rousseau deepens the ambivalence already found in Descartes, inasmuch that the upheavals of the eighteenth and nineteenth centuries made direct critico-philosophical engagement concerning the people unavoidable. No longer was the people a passive background against which the critical inquiry of the individual thinker unfolded (as was the case with Descartes). Now it became a provocation for thought itself. One only has to be reminded of how many of the thinkers associated with Kant's transcendental turn (e.g., Fichte, Schiller, and Hegel) made explicit reference to the French Revolution. In the case of Kant, an underlining of the significance of those events vacillated between almost a sublime fascination with what was unfolding at the time and a deep-seated unease surrounding its anarchic implications. This ambivalence has been noted by many. However, it is worth drawing attention to two basic features of the Kantian position: (i) Kant's proscription of the people's right to revolt against its own constitution;[14] (ii) Kant's recourse to the figure of the disinterested spectator to validate the importance of the revolutionary events in France. Kant's justification for prohibiting the people from rising up, while arguably having many facets, can be brought back to the following basic points: (a) that by rebelling against its imperfect constitution, the people ultimately revolts against itself; (b) that by setting any precedent for rebellion, then power would lie in the act of rebelling, not in the integrity of the constitution. If the first of these points is enveloped within the problem of the constitution as *form* and the people as *formed* matter, the second amplifies the prejudices we have already seen at play in Descartes. Analogous to the child, the people know not what they want. And while Kant acknowledges the formal possibility of a "people of mature rational powers," who would freely will the only rational constitution (namely a republican one), this enlightened people is more of a regulative ideal upon which a ruler should act by already bequeathing to its subjects the perfect constitution that in futurity the people would will for itself (Kant, 1991b: 187). All this boils down to Kant's controversial claim that democracy leads to despotism, while an autocratic regime can remain entirely consistent with both the spirit of republicanism and the principles of the enlightenment. The conceptual equations at play here (autocracy=autonomy=spectator in contradistinction to democracy=despotism=the people) are brought into clear focus in the following passage from Kant's lectures on ethics:

> Man must give the autocracy of the soul its full scope; otherwise he becomes a mere plaything of other forces and impressions, which withstand his will, and is prey to the caprice of accident and circumstance. (1987: 140)

Even with Hegel, whose critique of enlightened thought brings out the violence and terror that absolute autonomy and freedom of consciousness bear within themselves (2017), there is never a doubt that the sublation of self-consciousness and objective spirit must make space within the modern political state for the necessity of *individual* responsibility and autonomy. It should not be forgotten in this regard that, in *The Philosophy of History*, Hegel remains torn in his appraisal of the Athenian city state.

While, on the one hand, Hegel could marvel at the strength of unity holding together the Greek *polis* (in that questions of justice, interest, and truth were entirely bound up with custom, with the Athenian community revealing itself as objective will and substance), he was equally aware that such a political state was not, in the fullest sense, moral; morality for Hegel remained coterminous with subjective conviction and intention. Required was the development and realization of individual self-consciousness (Hegel, 2007: 251). Clearly, before Hegel an antinomy haunts the (non) relation between critical thought and the people. Metonymically, critical thought stands in for the enlightened moral self-consciousness of the individual while the people is either simply a passive background which, disengaged, the critical thinker keeps at arm's length or a people is a hotbed for irrational whims and inchoate desires to be rebuked and admonished. The Hegelian insight puts into question the dogmatic antithesis between critical self-consciousness and collective errancy. Dialectically, the static poles of the singular, particular, and the universal—the individual, the common, the general—are drawn into the historical movement of spirit (*Geist*), for which both individual self-consciousness and the people are its rational (real) moments. Indeed, in the struggle between enlightened reason and popular faith, Hegel goes so far as to say that self-consciousness is not just an attribute of the thinking ego; it can also be cultivated within a people. Through its practices and traditions, a people comes to have consciousness of itself (cf. Hyppolite, 1979: 429; Taylor, 1975). The distinction between critical thought and the people here appears to break down. For, while the moral judgments of individual self-consciousness can still be directed at the irrationality, passions, and desires of the people, these judgments only become effective once it is acknowledged that their source, the individual subject, is historically rooted in the people it criticizes. This means that the very act of critique is mediated by the cultural, historical, and political forms of a given people. Does this, however, imply that the people is finally recognized as a rational, and by extension critical, agent? This would be to overstretch the limits of Hegel's gesture. One only has to look at the *Philosophy of Right* to index how the prejudices haunting critical thought are maintained. Hegel's understanding of the people remains housed within a bivalent structure. He refrains from romanticizing the organicism of popular sentiments. Indeed, on the level of unreflected quotidian practices, *the people are not*. Which is to say, they are a people without history deprived of cultural and historical mediation. What makes a people *qua* people is a certain cultural formation (*Bildung*), and this can take a variety of institutional and historical valences. In the absence of such a pedagogical formation, the unformed people know not what is in their interest, neither do they know their own will nor how to *act* on their will.[15] This particular point surrounding the "wild idea" of the people, which, prior to the constitution of the state and the ethical life that calls it into being, is a "formless mass," will be the object of scathing attack by the young Marx (1992). He takes issue with the congenital mystical-idealism of the Hegelian position that reduces the real concrete people (the subject of civil society) into a predicate of the Idea of the State and a historical corollary of the establishment of a constitutional monarchy (1992: 85–8). Reproachful of the Hegelian idea that the people is the result, rather than the cause, of the constitutional state, Marx continually returns in his critique of Hegel to the factum of the "people" as a preconstituted and empirically given social agent (1992: 87). Interestingly, in so doing, Marx ends up relaxing the very critico-transcendental problem we have been tracing in this introduction. One of the ironies (and complexities) of Marx's position vis-à-vis the people is that, by taking for granted the existence of the people as what is given and what gives, it ends up falling somewhere behind the critical problematic inaugurated by Rousseau and pursued by Kant and Hegel. Ultimately, this is no fundamental problem for Marx, since he quickly leaves behind the category of the people almost entirely, recasting the whole political problematic in class terms: the dialectical figure of the proletariat, as the "class-which-is-not-a-class" will replace the people as the collective name for revolutionary agency and emancipatory change.

The echoes of these ambivalences surrounding the relationship between critical thought and the people are by no means distant, nor are they to be dismissed as bourgeois prejudices. Rather, as unquestioned fundaments, they are carried by the question "What is critique?" This is clear if we consider the work of the Frankfurt School, which in the twentieth century has been instrumental in shaping today's critical sensibilities. The fascism of the Third Reich and its mythologization of the spirit of the German *Volk*, as well as the anonymity of the masses in late capitalist society, forced a certain filiation of thinkers to examine the very possibility of critical thinking once the subject, the locus of critique, was irrevocably damaged. This dismantling of the individual subject as the organon of critique, because the subject is itself a questionable and unreliable paragon of reason and moral conscience, was already set in motion, of course, through the triptych of Marx, Nietzsche, and Freud. The famous "hermeneuticians of suspicion" systematically upended the emancipatory and rational pretensions of the bourgeois individual ego, uprooting critique from its embeddedness as a faculty of human reason and judgment (Ricœur, 1977). From this point onwards, the task of critique becomes nonidentical with the individual ego supposed to press it into action. Here, Theodor W. Adorno offers us the most lucid but extreme set of reflections upon this effacement (2000). While further discrediting the preeminent position of the self-standing, rational, and autonomous subject, Adorno refuses simply (i) to substitute the individual with the collective as the locus of critical judgment and (ii) to relinquish the enlightenment connection between "reason" and "freedom," despite the redoubts surrounding the individual subject. Regarding (i), suffice it to recall how famously Adorno rebukes Brecht for extolling the merits of a collective formation for having "more pairs of eyes" than the individual (Adorno, 2010: 46–7), which, rather than indicating the rational overcoming of the antinomies of bourgeois thought vis-à-vis individual autonomy and the people (as Brecht believed), was, for Adorno, itself a morbid symptom of the liquidation of the individual into the indifferent exchangeability, substitutability, and disposability of human existence, which, in mass society, was beginning to take on all the properties of the commodity-form. As Adorno will write in *Minima Moralia*, "[i]n the age of the individual's liquidation the question of individuality" must not be raised from the ground (*pace* Brecht and orthodox Marxism), but "raised anew" (2005: 129). The possibility of critique will lay at neither pole of the individual ego nor the formed unity of the collectivity or a people. No longer is the possibility of critique secured through the identity (whether individual or collective) of the agent tasked with carrying out critique, but in the questioning of the principle of identity, in the breaking up of identity-thinking, and in the capacities that support this thinking (e.g., "knowing," "willing," and "acting"). One way to interpret the Adornian motto that "the whole is the false" (the *prima principi* of Adorno's negative dialectics) is in taking aim precisely at the formed unities of the indivisible individual and the conforming collective, which in their putative "wholeness," bend what "is" as well as what might be into their own image, into representational thinking (2005: 50). Beyond both individualism and collectivism, social critique remains for Adorno possible only through the augmentation of looser solidaristic ties and collaborative efforts. The relation between the one of the people and the many "Is" of the mass must be kept in dialectical tension, without recourse to any final sublation—neither resolving into the fusion of the One of a collective body or the "We" of a people, nor in the separation of the individual "one" or "I" from the common bond. Critique is now placed in the service of nonidentity, operating within "constellations" comprised of particular elements that have no necessary relation to one another. A loose outline of a unity is formed only through plurality, a unity that is always nonidentical with itself.

If Adorno was able to formulate the nonidentical nature of critical *thought*, then his work can also be said to have shifted the problematic surrounding critique and the people: namely, the possibility of moving from the nonidentical subject as a locus of freedom to an understanding of a nonidentical people as an emancipatory force, and to draw the implications of what the accomplishment of such a shift might mean for thought and practice today. As will be seen later, such a question can be indexed throughout contemporary critical thought and can force us to return to the problem of the formation of a people.

The People and Populism in Contemporary Critical Thought

There is today a general line of research that targets the genetico-constructive question, indexed by Rousseau, of how a people becomes a people. Though, contemporary critical thought engages not with the people within the revolutionary currents of the late eighteenth century (as was the case with Kant and Hegel), nor the fascistic paroxysms of the 1920s and 1930s (Adorno and the Frankfurt School), but within the more nebulous and imprecise arena of populist sentiment, or as Chantal Mouffe has named our particular conjuncture, today's "populist moment" (2018). However, this does not mean that critical thought in the age of populism has been able to radically separate itself from earlier reflections on the limits and possibilities of the people. Albeit less tainted by the prejudices that were part and parcel of the reflections on the people at the time of the French Revolution, contemporary critical thought cannot escape the horrors executed under the banners of a *Volksgemeinschaft*, something that, in turn, completely transformed the very idea of a people. At the same time, since the postwar era, critical thought has greatly expanded in terms of its meaning and practice. While still loosely derived from Kantian, Hegelian, and Marxian provenances, a complex web of other theoretical and philosophical genealogies today provides a highly variegated picture of how critical thought is understood and operates (cf Foucault, 1996; Butler, 2002; Latour, 2004). This is clearly evident from how the category of the people is presently handled by a variety of contemporary thinkers who could be counted as thinking within the broad parameters of critique. Not only regarding how the critical task is carried out in the context of the present conjuncture, but also with respect to a sensibility toward the "people" in an age of "populist" insurgencies. Does populism provide the clearest expression of a politics riveted to the "people"? And if so, how in turn does it inflect one's judgments surrounding the political efficacy of such an idea? Alternatively, does the present irruption of "populist" politics mark a betrayal or a misstep with respect to forming a "people," which, as a category, remains in excess of the real possibilities circumscribed in and through the "populist moment"? In other words, can populism constitute a nonidentical and heterogeneous people, or is populism, by necessity, riveted to ideas of identity and homogeneity?

When contemporary critical thought returns to the vexing category of the people in an age of populism, three delineated positions can be identified: (i) a critical rejection of both "the people" as an emancipatory collective identity and "populism" as one of the people's principal drivers; (ii) a critical task amounting to *separating* out the emancipatory valences of the "people" from its nationalist and exclusivist possibilities, with this resulting in either a rejection or an affirmation of the transformative possibilities of populism; and finally (iii) an affirmation of the "people" as a critical and emancipatory name for which a study of "populism" provides the basic transcendental coordinates for the very possibility of any collective identity.[16]

For those locatable within (i), the critical task is to expose the deficiencies of the people as an emancipatory political category in light of its entailment with present forms of "populism," which are often presented as structural symptoms of the failings of the existing global capitalist system (cf. Brown, 2019; Dean, 2017; Fassin, 2017; Urbinati, 2019; Žižek, 2006).[17] When, for example, Slavoj Žižek speaks against what he calls the populist temptation or when Jodie Dean declares "we are not populists" (2017: 43), they do not only repudiate populism but redirect critical attention to the problem of the strictly cultural-political designation of the category of the "people" as such. The idea of the "people" is easy prey for mythico-nationalist appropriations and, by extension, carries with it the risk of obfuscation, not only by deflecting attention away from the system of capitalist exploitation and expropriation of the commons but also by displacing the primary antagonism between the capitalist and the worker onto an opposition between the unity of a people and its designated Other(s). One problem is that when the "people" is the key operating political term, a zone of indiscernibility opens up between populism and fascism. Both are drawn into a process of substantialization; that is, they require both the substantialization of the people (by way of an appeal to race, territory, language, etc.) and, what ultimately amounts to the same result, the substantialization of the Other, which, in obstructing the unity of the people, must be entirely destroyed. It is for this reason that reactive forces (including, above all else, affects such as ressentiment) become germane once any appeal is made to the "people," which is politically redundant without its excluded Others (cf. Brown, 2019; Fassin, 2017; Gerbaudo, 2021). Thus, this first critical perspective highlights the importance of separating out those critico-emancipatory political categories that are not bound by national and cultural belonging (e.g., the figure of the precariat, the proletariat, the wretched of the earth, the multitude, etc.), and that remain shot through with nonidentity and negativity, from the identity of the people that lends itself to populist opportunism, at best, and fascistic violence, at worst (cf. Mbembe, 2019; Nancy, 2018; Negri, 2017).[18]

If in (i) we find a critical approach that locates in populism the problem of the "people," and thus dismisses both "populism" and the "people" as inimical to understanding the nature of emancipatory collectivities, in (ii) we find those who attempt to recover a notion of the people for emancipatory ends. As Bruno Bosteels remarks in his introduction to the volume *What Is a People?*, in some quarters there is a plea "in favour of the people as a political category" (2016: 1) with contemporary efficacy. Given the premises set out in (i), how is this critical recovery possible? To begin with, one must recall that in many languages, the people carries with it a split designation. While it can be turned into a substantive noun ("the People") in order to designate the specificity of national, cultural, and political belonging, the idea of the people contains also a more quotidian meaning, referring to the commons, the masses, the rabble (cf. Badiou, 2016). Only by focusing on this second sense does the "people" become a category fit for the purveyor of emancipatory ends. Such is the case with the "plebs," the original meaning of the proletarian (which, in Latin, meant those who simply multiply), the demos even. Terms such as these are infused with a popular and common spirit, structurally opposed to the existing order. So, for example, in the work of Jacques Rancière, the "people" ceases to designate a stable identity or unified whole but, rather, refers to the paradoxical figure of the part (of a political community) which nonetheless has no (active) part to play within the political order (1999). Thus the "people" is on the side of those who are excluded (economically, culturally, politically), thereby turning it into a non-substantial and open category that makes possible a plural and "improper" mode of collective subjectivation. If this second approach makes an explicit decision about where it stands vis-à-vis the "people," the same cannot be said for its stance with regard to populism. This is to say that it either results in a rejection of populist politics *tout court* (cf. Balibar, 2013; Butler, 2015; Rancière, 2016; Rosanvallon, 2020) or in a call for a transnational or progressive populism (cf. Arditi, 2007; Devenney, 2020; Fraser and Jaeggi, 2018).

While both of the first two contemporary critical approaches exploit and try to resolve the ambiguity that the category of the "people" harbors, owing to its complex historicity and its semantic latitude, the third strand of contemporary critical thought offers a more formalistic understanding of the notion of the "people." Its first move is to dismiss the ambiguity of the term as, at best, a secondary problem. Now operating as an "empty signifier," the "people" is evacuated of all historical and semantic substance (Laclau, 2005). From this perspective, the category has a formal and constitutive role to play in all possible political mobilizations. The "people" emerges as the result of a strictly politico-discursive operation, according to which a multiplicity of unrelated demands is transformed into the One of a collective identity. The writings of Ernesto Laclau and Chantal Mouffe would, of course, be key reference points here (cf. Laclau, 2005; Mouffe, 2018). The full implications of their understanding of the people emerges precisely out of their analytical and political commitment to populism as "the royal road to understanding something about the ontological constitution of the political as such" (Laclau, 2005: 67). This bold claim admittedly harbors some ambiguity and is liable to mislead. All the same, what Laclau (and Mouffe) point to is that every possible collective formation must pass through the same set of politico-strategic operations, for example, the construction of an antagonistic frontier, the transformation of a multiple set of contingently related demands into a "people" united principally through what it demonstrably opposes, of which populism serves as a formal indicator. Populism now functions as an aperture through which the transcendental riggings of political action as such can be seen in their proper light, and the people becomes the structural placeholder for what must be achieved politically: the discursive construction of unity through plurality. The implication of this is that the nexus of "populism" and the "people" is seen as necessary for rethinking critico-emancipatory transformation today (cf. Biglieri and Cadhia, 2021; De Cleen et al., 2018; Katsambekis and Kioupkiolis, 2019; Panizza, 2005; Stavrakakis et al., 2018).

Although discussed in other terms, and while responding to a completely different conjuncture, contemporary critical thought still circumnavigates the Rousseauian paradox of how a people is formed, seeking to do so without falling foul of the normative prejudices that have hitherto marked the history of critical thought and the empirical sciences. For some, the people is indelibly formed by and through its (national, cultural, linguistic) history, thereby foreclosing the emancipatory potential of the people, while for others the people, as either an "empty signifier" or as the locus of political struggle, offers the principal way of engaging in politics per se. Between these positions, we encounter a field of tensions where contemporary critical thought is played out. It is from within this very field that this volume's contributors take up the question of the relation between populism and the people today.

Presentation of the Volume

Part I: Political Reflections on the People

A general and unquestioned assumption in political thought is the belief that modern democracy marked a profound rupture in, and reconfiguration of, the legitimacy of any political order. As is commonly recited, the breakup of the ancien régime brings to a head the double valence harbored by the meaning of the people, that is, the people as constituting a nation and the popular masses. There is, at the same time, a concomitant split in the way the people as a category *operates*, namely, on the one hand, as the apogee of state power and, on the other, the unruly masses as dissolution and interruption of political (state) order. All the contributors in this section seek to think the ambiguous relationship between the people and democracy, by interrogating the possibilities and impossibilities of the people as, simultaneously, the formed, formless, and forming agent in modern societies. Jacques Rancière's work has thoroughly, though perhaps unilaterally, addressed these questions from the exclusive perspective of the part-of-no-part, which synecdochally presents the every-one and any-one of the demos. In an interview given especially for this volume, Rancière reflects on his own intellectual itinerary over the last fifty years, recontextualizing his archival and philosophical explorations into the category of the people in light of present political circumstances. An indicative feature of our present political circumstances is the trenchant antipopulism that circulates far and wide in media and mainstream public discourse. As Oliver Marchart explores, in the beginning of his investigation into demophobia, antipopulism is consubstantial with the present (neo-)liberal politico-economic order. By way of a critical reading of the work of Nancy Fraser and Chantal Mouffe, Marchart proposes an alternative characterization of the left-populist project by emphasizing a radical democratic ethos of democratizing democracy.

Broadly construed, Jacques Rancière and the tradition from out of which Oliver Marchart's thought originates (the Essex School of Post-Marxism, associated with the work of Laclau) both recognize the political longevity and efficacy of the category of the people *qua* emancipatory practice. Nonetheless, the dividing line that separates them is (i) the contrasting ways they articulate the principle of equality as a defining feature of emancipatory popular struggle and (ii) their position vis-à-vis populism (cf. the prior section entitled "People and Populism in Critical Thought"). By way of a comparative study of the work of Rancière and Laclau, Clare Woodford and Mark Devenney explore these differences, with the purpose of drawing out the implications for thinking both the tasks and the character of contemporary political struggles. The authors resist choosing between the respective positions of Laclau and Rancière, proposing that an intermediary way can be located, which, in actual fact, addresses the possible deficiencies of both a Rancièrian and Laclauian treatment of the meaning of equality and the people in political practice today.

The relationship between democracy and the people casts a longer shadow in times of populist insurgency. In his discussion of discourses on populism, Karl Ekeman critically analyses the liberal prejudices present within contemporary research into populism. While much of this research is critical of the populist turn in political practice today, what Ekeman shows is how these *faux* criticisms only serve as a disavowal of transformative possibilities, leaving the place of capital at the heart of liberal-democratic society unquestioned. The acts of disavowal, explored by Ekeman, show up the *libidinal* investments furnishing so-called rational-liberal inquiries into populism today. The next section of the volume amplifies these psychoanalytic dimensions of the phenomena of populism and the people.

Part II: Toward an Affectology of Populism

As discussed at the beginning of this chapter, classical critical thought can be said to be skeptical toward the people, and the pathologies it harbors, on the bases of its irrationality and heteronomous nature. Not only does this apply to Descartes, Kant, and Hegel, but also to the psychological studies of masses and crowds from the nineteenth and early twentieth century (e.g., Le Bon, Freud). It was a dominant trope in early mass psychology literature to describe the irrational impulses of the people as a freely circulating contagion, infecting the sense and sensibility of the individual subject. By engaging in a critical diagnosis of our present, authors in this section attempt to problematize this simple rejection of the people's pathologies in order to understand the constitutive role that affect play in political mobilizations in general and populism in particular. In his article, Samo Tomšič draws out resentment as a principal means for organizing populist movements, critically analyzing the way in which identification through resentment paradoxically unbinds the social bond, thereby annulling the possibility for transformative and properly collective solutions to social questions. As a counterpoint to this politics of negation, Tomšič offers a politics of negativity, whose principal affect is not resentment but anxiety. If Tomšič draws attention to resentment as the motor for populist identification, Jenny Gunnarsson Payne and Maria Brock approach populism from the vantage point of disgust, proposing that the right's anti-gender discourses, so prevalent today, gain their traction from notions of purity and propriety which are under threat owing to a multiplication of "sexual deviations" and "perversions." While Tomšič provides an aetiology of *ressentiment* which focuses on the asociality of populism, disgust is understood by Gunnarsson Payne and Brock as a way of disciplining the people and maintaining the myth of a full community. In the final chapter in this section, Chiara Bottici returns to the founding texts of mass psychology, problematizing the reductive presuppositions of Le Bon and Freud's pathologization of the people. Ultimately drawing on Adorno's reconstruction and sophistication of Freud's reflections on the libidinal ties binding a crowd together so as to think the continual efficacy of fascist propaganda after fascism, Bottici enquires into the indicative fascist traits of populist movements today.

Part III: The Aesthetics of the People

This section addresses the role that the arts have played in representing the people. Not only does aesthetics designate a subset of practices, experiences, or cultural phenomena (e.g., literary works, poetry, film), but it also pertains to a certain sensibility that belongs to and also frames the appearing and self-forming of a people. This gives rise to a whole series of issues recurring throughout the three contributions comprising this part of the volume. In a wide-ranging essay, Paula Diehl discusses the conditions of possibility and impossibility of the people in visual art by taking her departure in the differences between monarchical and democratic representations of sovereignty. Starting with the iconography of the French Revolution, tracing pictorial representation up to the Charlie Hebdo solidarity marches of 2015, Diehl offers a series of reflections on the problems tied to representing the people as the incarnation of sovereignty in democracy. In the next chapter, Stefan Jonsson looks at the aesthetic dimension of popular movements, opposing two different modes of cultural representation: cultures of rejection and cultures of protest. Through a reading of the work of the German association of worker photographers and the film *An Opera of the World*, portraying the migrant opera *Bintou Wéré: A Sahel Opera*, Jonsson shows how, in these cases, the crowd transforms itself from masses, which are simply seen from afar, into a seeing collective. Finally, in the last chapter of the section, Kim West explores the hypothesis of an undivided people in Peter Weiss' novel, *The Aesthetics of Resistance*. Precisely through forms of literary expression, Weiss explores how an indivisible people can appear as a real but fragile existent. West explores how the idea (in the Kantian sense) of an indivisible people can today operate as a critical counterpoint in times when a divisive and exclusivist image of the people permeates social life (such as in fascist and populist ideological forms). Following Weiss, West analyzes how, in the form of an empty universal, art can imagine a people, whose material content is given by and through its antagonistic relation to the divisions inherent in a capitalist society, within which fascism and populism prosper.

Part IV: The People Beyond the Political

The Rousseauian paradox on the forming of the people brings us back to the dialectical relation between the unformed mass and the formed people. Political thought and practice is condemned to operate within this vicious circle, in the sense that even an emancipatory idea of the people easily reproduces an identitarian and exclusivist logic that subtends its formation. The hylomorphism of the people, as introduced in the beginning of this chapter, is the central way in which the people as a political category has come into being within Western thought. As Muniz Sodré argues, politics takes on the role of giving form to the formless masses, often emanating from heroic deeds, revolutionary events, and the drafting of republican constitutions. But Sodré invites the question: What if the people comes to show itself through a profoundly traumatic event, which is not the origin of unity but rather originates from dispersal, fragmentation, and displacement, and which does not trace out the greatness of political deeds but has its genesis in the slave trade? Such, as Sodré examines, is the case with Brazil. Sodré uses the specificity of the Brazilian case as a way of deconstructing some of the hallowed constructions of Western political thought. In doing so, the author lays the ground for considering whether there is a way to think the people beyond the horizon of politics, at least as politics has come to be understood within the history of critical thought. The remaining two contributions in this section extend and redirect this problematization of the preeminence of politics. No longer satisfied with the directive, central in the 1980s and 1990s, of "returning to the political," these contributions seek to turn away from political thought and action in order to find a vantage point before and beyond politics that can undermine the presuppositions of not only the modern political imaginary, which incubated the great hopes of emancipatory change but the vanquished ground of postmodern irony and reactive nihilism. Taking as her point of departure Pasolini's reflections on the passing of the utopian promise of a revolutionary ideology of the people, Tora Lane retraces the mutations of the people from the French to the Russian Revolution locating a closure in this political history after the Second World War. According to Lane, no longer is it credible to retrieve an idea of the people today, but rather we must think the consequences of the loss of a politics and a collective figure that can positively and transformatively change the course of history. This can only be achieved through literary and poetic experimentation, she argues. Rather than taking recourse to literature as a way of problematizing a politics of the people, Ramona Rat turns to the Levinasian injunction that ethics is *prima philosophia*. With ethics, then, as the foundation for a reflection on the people, Rat sees the possibility of evading the capture of identitarian thinking by redescribing the people as a phenomenon which entails not a fused unity but the concrete exposure to a qualitative multiplicity of others. This shows itself through the dynamic movement of a people facing one another by virtue of the inherent singularity of each individual face appearing as part of a manifold.

In the final contribution, Michael Marder takes a synoptic view on the polyvalence of the category of the people as a grounding term for commonal existence. Presented as a series of theses, the volume concludes with some conceptual glosses on the term that do less to orientate us within the discourse of the people today but serve instead to open up a constellation of contradictory and incompatible meanings indicating the semantic latitude, ideological porosity, and political undecidability that the category harbors for us. Rather than providing a closure, then, the function of Marder's uncertain reflections is to reopen the interpretive latitude and political ambiguities that indicate how the people remain necessary and unavoidable for political life, even if vexing (and a provocation) for critical thought.

That many notable thinkers from within and outside the tradition of critical thought have stressed the ambiguities, paradoxes, and aporias of the ideality and lived reality of the people is testament to its position as a limit category for thought. This is what we have attempted to explore in this chapter, so long that the "limit" is understood in the double sense of what circumscribes the hither side of critical inquiry while also tracing the field of productive possibilities arising from encountering this limit. The people, then, is to be regarded as an unthought that must surrender itself to thought and that to which thought must surrender itself.

If our present conjuncture provokes the ire of critical thought, then this is on account of the jargon of populism, which, often pulled together from inchoate soundbites and a shrill of dog whistles, is the very definition of unthought understood as the absence of thought. Populists of the right, left, and center enter the political stage with their bagatelle of strategies, rhetorical appeals, and substitutable foes, where a ritualized spectacle plays out as the prospect of real emancipatory change appears to have played itself out. At the same time, while populism and anti-populism appear to eclipse all else, it is worthwhile reminding ourselves of a little piece of advice that the French Marxist, Louis Althusser, once gave to an Italian comrade, Maria Antonietta Macciocchi, that "as long as you can't answer the question: what today comprises the people in a given country (today, because the composition of the people varies historically; in a given country, because the composition of the people changes from place to place), you can't do anything in politics" (Macciocchi 1973: 5). Politics and the people: a veritable Möbius strip. This remains our collective starting point today: to move beyond the formalized sophistics of populism so as to return to the people in its manifold as the *locus perennis* of political action and the palimpsest upon which emancipatory hopes have been, and continues to be, etched.

Notes

1. Needless to say, an alternative judgment can be reached. One notable example: The young Marx insists that the "people" has a real existence *prior to* any declaration or constitution that would bring it into being. In "democracy," he writes, "we find the constitution founded on its true ground: real human beings and the real people; not merely implicitly and in essence but in existence and in reality. The constitution is thus posited as the people's own creation" (1992: 87). Marx will be further discussed later in this chapter.
2. Judith Butler makes a similar claim when she notes that "the conditions of democratic rule depend finally upon an exercise of popular sovereignty that is never fully contained by any particular democratic order" (2016: 51).
3. In *The Time of Popular Sovereignty*, Paulina Ochoa Espejo aspires to achieve this when, in a synthetic operation, she finds a position on political sovereignty that acknowledges how "on the one hand, the people requires a set of practices and institutions, some of which are obligatory and constrain individual action [while] it also includes a fleeting community of hopes, expectations, memories, and fraternal feelings, periodically subject to drastic and unexpected changes" (2011: 13).
4. For discussions of the historical origin of the idea of popular sovereignty in antiquity, see Bourke and Skinner (2016) and Canovan (2005).
5. Paradigmatically, this problematic animates the thought of Hobbes (cf. 1983: 104). From within the tradition of critical thought, it is worthwhile recalling how Marx and Engels summarize what can be referred to as the philosopher's conceit in the following way: "The philosopher does not say directly: You are not people. [He says:]: You have always been people, but you were not *conscious* of what you were, and for that very reason you were not in reality True People. Therefore your appearance was not appropriate to your essence. You were people and you were not people" (1998: 267).
6. For a discussion of these defining aspects of populism, see, for instance, Mudde and Kaltwasser (2017), Laclau (2005), Müller (2016), and Moffitt (2016).
7. This final characteristic of populism has only most recently been given a more extended treatment by political scientists studying populism (cf. Cossarini and Vallespín, 2019; Demertzis, 2020; Eklundh, 2020).
8. By empirically orientated we mean investigations that are principally grounded in the analysis of actually existing political practice, events, movements, and electoral behaviour, rather than a form of inquiry that principally functions on a theoretical, speculative, or normative level for which illustrative examples are used as cases for confirming or disproving theoretical claims. Admittedly, this distinction is not a categorical one, and a variety of studies would seek to situate themselves somewhere in between. For our part, our following remarks do not seek to criticize all studies with an empirical orientation. What we wish to point out, however, are the ontological, epistemological, and normative drawbacks that come with much of the literature that deals with issues surrounding populism and the people today.
9. The drawbacks of this descriptivist inclination have been discussed within the field of political science by, for instance, Taggart (2000), Tormey (2019), and Kim (2021) but also from the perspective of political theory by, for instance, Laclau (2005), Marchart (2007), Urbinati (2019), and Katsambekis (2020).
10. Generally, the contemporary research field on populism within political science distinguishes between three different (albeit not entirely distinct) definitions of the concept, going back to Gellner and Ionescu's seminal anthology (1969), namely as

an ideology (cf. Abts and Rummens, 2007; Hawkins et al., 2019; Mudde and Rovira Kaltwasser, 2017), a style or strategy (cf. Taggart, 2000; Weyland and Madrid, 2019), or as a certain rhetorical or psychological mapping of the political (cf. de la Torre, 2010; Ostiguy, 2009).

11 The essential contestability of the concept has today become such a commonplace that it is found in almost every work treating the topic of populism. For a longer discussion surrounding the issue, see Mackert (2019), Mudde and Kaltwasser (2017), and Weyland (2001).

12 This does not go for all empirical studies on populism. There is an emerging divide in populism studies between the so-called ideational and the post-foundational approach, the latter taking inspiration from Ernesto Laclau's political discourse theory (cf. Katsembekis 2020; Kim 2021).

13 This shows itself perhaps most clearly in how different conceptions of populism describe it as a reaction against the status quo or representative politics (cf. Eatwell and Goodwin, 2018; Norris and Inglehart, 2018; Taggart, 2000: 109).

14 "If a people, under some existing legislation were asked to make a judgement which in all probability would prejudice its happiness, what should it do? Should the people not oppose the measure? The only possible answer is that they can do nothing but obey." Further on, Kant says that the prohibition to rebel is "absolute," and that even the most legitimate motivation for resisting the legislator is without Reason (1991a: 80f).

15 In *The Philosophy of Right* Hegel will, for example, write: "The idea with which ordinary consciousness usually begins when it considers the necessity or usefulness of a convention of the Estates will generally be, for example, that delegates of the people, or indeed the people themselves, *must know best* what is in their own best interest, and that their own will is undoubtedly the one best equipped to pursue the latter. As for the first of these propositions, the reverse is in fact the case, for if the term 'the people' denotes a particular category of members of the state, it refers to that category of citizens *who do not know their own will*. To know what one wills, and even more, to know what the will which has being in and for itself—i.e., reason—wills, is the fruit of profound cognition and insight, and this is the very thing which 'the people' lack" (2015: 340).

16 For a recent volume that exemplifies all three of these positions (without specifying them as such), see Kioupkiolis and Katsambekis (2019). Whether these positions are antagonistic and constitute mutually exclusive tendencies within contemporary critical thought, as the title of Kioupkiolis and Katsambekis' volume makes clear, is up for debate.

17 Here one could also mention a tradition of more historiographical inquiry that tries to discover a link between today's so-called Authoritarian Populism and the fascism of the twentieth century, see, for instance, Finchelstein (2017), Morelock (ed.) (2018), and Traverso (2019).

18 Even though these thinkers have not dealt with the question of populism in any extensive way, they nonetheless express similar concerns surrounding the category of the people.

Bibliography

Abts K and Rummens S (2007) Populism versus Democracy. *Political Studies* 55(2): 405–24.

Adorno TW (2000) *Problems of Moral Philosophy*. Cambridge: Polity.

Adorno TW (2005) *Minima Moralia: Reflections from Damaged Life* (trans. EFN Jephcott). London: Verso.
Adorno TW (2010) *Negative Dialectics* (trans. EB Ashton). London: Routledge.
Althusser L (2019) *Lessons on Rousseau* (trans. GM Goshgarian). New York: Verso Books.
Arditi B (2007) *Politics on the Edges of Liberalism: Difference, Populism, Revolution, Agitation*. Edinburgh: Edinburgh University Press.
Badiou A (2016) Twenty-Four Notes on the Uses of the Word "People." In: *What Is a People?* New York: Columbia University Press, 21–31.
Balibar É (2013) Europe : l'impuissance des nations et la question « populiste ». *Actuel Marx* 54(2): 13–23.
Biglieri P and Cadhia L (2021) *Seven Essays on Populism*. London: Polity.
Bosteels B (2016) Introduction: This People Which Is Not One. In: *What Is a People?* New York: Columbia University Press, 1–20.
Bourke R and Skinner Q (eds.) (2016) *Popular Sovereignty in Historical Perspective*. Cambridge: Cambridge University Press.
Brecht B (2006) The Solution. In: D Bowman (ed.), *Poetry and Prose*. London: Continuum, p. 119.
Brown W (2019) *In the Ruins of Neoliberalism: The Rise of Antidemocratic Politics in the West*. New York: Columbia University Press.
Butler J (2002) What is Critique? And Essay on Foucault's Virtue. In: D Ingram (ed.), *The Political: Readings in Continental Philosophy*. London: Basil Blackwell, 212–28.
Butler J (2015) *Notes toward a Performative Theory of Assembly*. Cambridge, MA: Harvard University Press.
Butler J (2016) "We, the People": Thoughts on Freedom of Assembly. In: *What Is a People?* New York: Columbia University Press, 49–64.
Canovan M (1981) *Populism*. New York: Harcourt Brace Jovanovich.
Canovan M (2005) *The People*. Cambridge: Polity.
Cossarini P and Vallespín F (eds.) (2019) *Populism and Passions: Democratic Legitimacy after Austerity*. New York: Routledge.
Crewe I and Sanders D (eds.) (2020) *Authoritarian Populism and Liberal Democracy*. London: Palgrave Macmillan.
De Cleen B, Glynos J and Mondon A (2018) Critical Research on Populism: Nine Rules of Engagement. *Organization* 25(5): 649–61.
de la Torre C (2010) *Populist Seduction in Latin America*. 2nd ed. Athens, OH: Ohio University Press.
Dean J (2017) Not Him, Us (And We Aren't Populists). *Theory & Event* 20(1): 38–44.
Demertzis N (2020) *The Political Sociology of Emotions: Essays on Trauma and Ressentiment*. Abingdon: Routledge.
Descartes R (1968) *Discourse on Method*. Harmondsworth: Penguin.
Devenney M (2020) *Towards an Improper Politics*. Edinburgh: Edinburgh University Press.
Eatwell R and Goodwin MJ (2018) *National Populism: The Revolt against Liberal Democracy*. London: Penguin Books.
Eklundh E (2020) Excluding Emotions: The Performative Function of Populism. *Partecipazione e Conflitto* 13(1): 108–31.
Fassin É (2017) *Populisme: Le Grand Ressentiment*. Paris: Textuel.
Finchelstein F (2017) *From Fascism to Populism in History*. Oakland, CA: University of California Press.

Foucault M (1996) What is Critique? In: J Schmidt (ed.), *What Is Enlightenment: Eighteenth Century Answers and Twentieth Century Questions*. Berkely: University of California Press, 382–98.
Fraser N and Jaeggi R (2018) *Capitalism: A Conversation in Critical Theory*. Medford, MA: Polity.
Gallie WB (1956) Essentially Contested Concepts. *Proceedings of the Aristotelian Society* 56(1): 167–98.
Gerbaudo P (2021) *The Great Recoil: Politics after Populism and Pandemic*. Brooklyn: Verso Books.
Hawkins KA, Carlin RE, Littvay L, et al. (eds.) (2019) *The Ideational Approach to Populism: Concept, Theory, and Analysis*. London: Routledge.
Hegel GWF (2007) *The Philosophy of History* (trans. J Sibree). New York: Cosimo Classics.
Hegel GWF (2015) *Elements of the Philosophy of Right* (ed. AW Wood; trans. HB Nisbet). Cambridge, MA: Cambridge University Press.
Hegel GWF (2017) *The Phenomenology of Spirit* (trans. TP Pinkard). New York: Cambridge University Press.
Hobbes T (1984) *The Cive: The English Version*. Oxford: Oxford University Press.
Horkheimer M (1972) Traditional and Critical Theory. In: *Critical Theory: Selected Essays*. New York: Continuum, 188–243.
Hyppolite J (1979) *Genesis and Structure of Hegel's Phenomenology of Spirit* (trans. S Cherniak and J Heckman). Evanston, IL: Northwestern University Press.
Hofstadter R (1955) *The Age of Reform*. New York: Vintage Books.
Ionescu G and Gellner E (1969) Introduction. In: G Ionescu and E Gellner (eds.), *Populism: Its Meanings and National Characteristics*. London: Weidenfeld & Nicolson, 1–8.
Kant I (1987) *Lectures on Ethics* (trans. L Infield). Gloucester, MA: Peter Smith.
Kant I (1991a) On the Common Saying: "This might be true in theory, but it does not apply to practice." In: HS Reiss (ed.), *Kant: Political Writings*. 2nd ed. Cambridge: Cambridge University Press, 61–92.
Kant I (1991b) The Contest of Faculties. In: HS Reiss (ed.), *Political Writings*. 2nd ed. *Cambridge Texts in the History of Political Thought*. Cambridge: Cambridge University Press, 176–90.
Katsambekis G (2020) Constructing "the people" of Populism: A Critique of the Ideational Approach from a Discursive Perspective. *Journal of Political Ideologies* 27(1): 53–74.
Katsambekis G and Kioupkiolis A (eds.) (2019) *The Populist Radical Left in Europe*. Routledge Advances in European Politics. London: Routledge.
Kazin M (2017) *The Populist Persuasion: An American History*. Ithaca: Cornell University Press.
Kellner D (2015) *American Nightmare: Donald Trump, Media Spectacle, and Authoritarian Populism*. Boston, MA: Sense Publishers.
Kim S (2021) Taking Stock of the Field of Populism Research: Are Ideational Approaches "moralistic" and Post-Foundational Discursive Approaches "normative"? *Politics*. doi:10.1177/02633957211007053.
Laclau E (2005) *On Populist Reason*. London: Verso.
Latour B (2004) Why Has Critique Run out of Steam? From Matters of Fact to Matters of Concern. *Critical Inquiry* 30(2): 225–48.
Lee R (1986) The New Populist Campaign for Economic Democracy: A Rhetorical Exploration. *Quarterly Journal of Speech* 72(3): 274–89.

Macciocchi M A (1973) *Letters from Inside the Italian Communist Party to Louis Althusser*. London: Verso.
Mackert J (2019) Introduction: Is There Such a Thing as Populism? In: G Fitzi, J Mackert, and BS Turner (eds.), *Populism and the Crisis of Democracy*. London: Routledge, 1–14.
Marchart O (2007) In the Name of the People: Populist Reason and the Subject of the Political. *Diacritics* 35(3): 3–19.
Marx K (1992) Critique of Hegel's Doctrine of the State. In: K Marx (ed.), *Early Writings*. London: Penguin, 57–199.
Marx K and Engels F (1998) *The German Ideology*. New York: Prometheus Books.
Mbembe A (2019) *Blacks From Elsewhere and the Right of Abode*. South Africa: Johannesburg. Available at: https://journalism.co.za/blacks-from-elsewhere-and-the-right-of-abode/ (accessed January 21, 2021).
Moffitt B (2016) *The Global Rise of Populism: Performance, Political Style, and Representation*. Stanford, CA: Stanford University Press.
Morelock J (2018) *Critical Theory and Authoritarian Populism*. London: University of Westminster Press.
Mouffe C (2018) *For a Left Populism*. London: Verso.
Mudde C (eds.) (2007) *Populist Radical Right Parties in Europe*. Cambridge: Cambridge University Press.
Mudde C and Rovira Kaltwasser C (2012) *Populism in Europe and the Americas: Threat or Corrective for Democracy?* Cambridge: Cambridge University Press.
Mudde C and Rovira Kaltwasser C (2017) *Populism: A Very Short Introduction*. New York: Oxford University Press.
Müller J-W (2016) *What Is Populism?* Philadelphia: University of Pennsylvania Press.
Nancy J-L (2018) Populisme et démocratie. *Libération*. Available at: https://www.liberation.fr/debats/2018/11/04/populisme-et-democratie-par-jean-luc-nancy_1689861.
Negri A (2009) *Insurgencies: Constituent Power and the Modern State*. Minneapolis: University of Minnesota Press.
Negri A (2017) Antonio Negri: "The Central Banks are Today's Winter Palace." Available at: https://global.ilmanifesto.it/antonio-negri-the-central-banks-are-todays-winter-palace/ (accessed January 21, 2021).
Norris P and Inglehart R (2018) *Cultural Backlash: Trump, Brexit, and the Rise of Authoritarian-Populism*. New York: Cambridge University Press.
Ochoa Espejo P (2011) *The Time of Popular Sovereignty: Process and the Democratic State*. University Park: Penn State University Press.
Ostiguy P (2009) The High-Low Political Divide: Rethinking Populism and Anti-Populism. *Committee on Concepts and Methods Working Paper Series* 35(360). Available at: https://kellogg.nd.edu/documents/1670.
Panizza F (ed.) (2005) *Populism and the Mirror of Democracy*. London: Verso.
Pippin RB (1997) *Idealism as Modernism: Hegelian Variations*. Cambridge: Cambridge University Press.
Rancière J (1999) *Disagreement: Politics and Philosophy* (trans. J Rose). Minneapolis: University of Minnesota Press.
Rancière J (2016) The Populism That Is Not to Be Found. In: *What Is a People? New Directions in Critical Theory*. New York: Columbia University Press, 101–6.
Ricœur P (1977) *Freud and Philosophy an Essay on Interpretation* (trans. D Savage). New Haven, CT: Yale University Press.
Rosanvallon P (2020) *Le Siècle Du Populisme: Histoire, Théorie, Critique*. Paris: Éditions du Seuil.

Rousseau J-J (2002) *The Social Contract: And, The First and Second Discourses* (trans. S Dunn). New Haven, CT: Yale University Press.
Rovira Kaltwasser C, Taggart PA, Ochoa Espejo P, et al. (2019) Populism: An Overview of the Concept and the State of Art. In: C Rovira Kaltwasser, PA Taggart, P Ochoa Espejo, and P Ostiguy (eds.), *The Oxford Handbook of Populism*. Oxford: Oxford University Press, 1–26.
Rubinelli, L (2020) *Constituent Power: A History*. Cambridge: Cambridge University Press.
Stavrakakis Y (2017) How did "populism" Become a Pejorative Concept? And Why is This Important Today? A Genealogy of Double Hermeneutics. *POPULISMUS Working Papers* 6: 25.
Stavrakakis Y and Jäger A (2018) Accomplishments and Limitations of the "new" Mainstream in Contemporary Populism Studies. *European Journal of Social Theory* 21(4): 547–65.
Stavrakakis Y, Katsambekis G, Kioupkiolis A, et al. (2018) Populism, Anti-Populism and Crisis. *Contemporary Political Theory* 17(1): 4–27.
Taggart PA (2000) *Populism*. Buckingham: Open University Press.
Taylor C (1975) *Hegel*. Cambridge: Cambridge University Press.
Tormey S (2019) *Populism: A Beginner's Guide*. London: Oneworld Publications.
Traverso E (2019) *The New Faces of Fascism: Populism and the Far Right* (trans. D Broder). London: Verso.
Urbinati N (2019) *Me the People: How Populism Transforms Democracy*. London: Harvard University Press.
Villa DR (2017) *Teachers of the People: Political Education in Rousseau, Hegel, Tocqueville, and Mill*. Chicago, IL: The University of Chicago Press.
Weyland KG (2001) Clarifying a Contested Concept: Populism in the Study of Latin American Politics. *Comparative Politics* 34(1): 1–22.
Weyland KG and Madrid RL (eds.) (2019) *When Democracy Trumps Populism: European and Latin American Lessons for the United States*. Cambridge: Cambridge University Press.
Wodak, R (2015) *The Politics of Fear: What Right-Wing Discourses Mean*. London: Sage.
Žižek S (2006) Against the Populist Temptation. *Critical Inquiry* 32(3): 551–74.

Part I

Political Reflections on the People

1

The People

Proper, Common, Improper. An Interview with Jacques Rancière[1]

Jacques Rancière, David Payne, Alexander Stagnell, and Gustav Strandberg

Editors (E): We would like to begin proceedings by reflecting on the idea of "logical revolts," taken from Rimbaud's poem "Démocratie" (2003: 264), but significantly the name of the journal, *Les Révoltes Logiques*, for which you were the main editor during the 1970s.[2] Your work, for us, follows a quite unique trajectory in setting out how to think the relation between "the people" and "revolt," and the intimate logic or rationality entailed therein. For some, the very triptych of "the people," "revolt" and "logic" would make for a rather strange admixture. We only have to look at recent events to be reminded of how the notion of "popular revolt" is held in general contempt: the masses are irrational, fickle, unreasonable, illogical, etc. Against this prejudice, a central part of your investigations has been to show quite the opposite: namely, that a certain logic or rationality can be traced within historically situated figurations of politics. It is on the bases of these cases that, in your later work, you have even managed to redefine how we are to think politics in general. Consistent throughout your work is the idea that there is a logic *to* and *of* revolt, a "raving with (and not against) reason" (Rancière, 1991: 94). At the same time, the way you approach this logic is by eschewing the standard procedures by which an inquiry into "the logic of popular revolt" has often been demonstrated. About this, it could be said, you are engaged in a revolt of your own, in the form of a renunciation of "ontology," "sociology," "politology," "anthropology," that is, all the "logical" pathways that are possible to embark upon in order to "donate" to the masses what is rightfully theirs (admittedly, a most disingenuous double-gesture). As a way of beginning this conversation, we were wondering whether you could reflect upon the reversibility of terms at play between "logic" and "revolt" in your thinking, and the shifting emphases and reordering these terms undergo in your work.

Jacques Rancière (JR): We must begin with the torsion within which I introduced all these terms. I borrowed the term "logical revolts" from Rimbaud who himself put it in the mouths of those who massacred these revolts—that is, "democrats" of a very specific kind, namely the soldiers recruited among villagers in order to crush urban rebellions (the Paris Commune) and national revolts (in Algeria). Performing it in this manner allowed me to distinguish myself effectively from those who begin with some substantial identity of a people—as it is empirically or even "ontologically" manifested—and who then from this deduce the right to revolt. Here, my operation was the complete inverse: I started from the division inherent in all the terms used to identify these popular subjects. For example, in *Proletarian Nights: The Workers' Dream in Nineteenth-Century France* (2012), I demonstrated how the signifiers of the "workers movement" were created by workers who precisely refused the identity of the worker bestowed on them by the existing system. In *Disagreement* (1999), to offer another example, I recalled that "democracy" was not, originally, the name of a political regime but an insult that the aristocrats of Athens ascribed to a regime in which those people (*gens*) of nothing, people of no account, claim to decide the community's affairs. I have also shown that the political animal of which Aristotle speaks is a divided subject and that what gives place to politics is not the fact that man is a speaking being but rather a quarrel about knowing who speaks and those who only make noises with their mouths.

On the matter of "logical revolts," I did not introduce any relationship between the identity of a popular subject and the reasons that he or she might have for revolting. On the contrary, it is a revolt that first emerges by deviating from an identity to which a group of human beings is assigned, and that creates the subject. This also means a deviation (*écart*) from the sociological essentialism of Marxism that founded the classical distinction between revolt and revolution. This essentialism in actual fact redeploys the Aristotelian opposition between voice and *logos*, according to which revolt would simply be the fact that those people who suffer are unable to do more than voice their pain, while the revolution is the effective transformation of the whole situation, founded on a consciousness of the reasons behind that situation. In this way, the disqualification of the "spontaneous" revolt reproduces the positivist determination of social identities. I had, on the contrary, wanted to say that social subversion begins with the struggle against these identities. It begins when those who are supposed to be capable of only making noise affirm themselves as speaking and reasoning subjects, doing so as "people," "workers," "proletarians," as well as under other names. The point is that these names are the names of subjects in action, not pre-given identities.

E: There seems to be two ways of reading the coincidence between your continual return to the people, as a disavowed politico-philosophical category, and today's resurgence of politics that putatively speaks in the name of the "people." On the one hand, it is as if finally we have the actualization of a politics that returns to the people its central role as a political operator (irrespective of the indeterminate and contradictory forms in which this populist politics manifests itself). On the other hand, it seems as if, despite appearances, the recent emergence of populist politics is the latest and most pernicious form of the denigration of the people, where the people is in fact kept in "its place." In light of your own work, how are we to understand this renewed interest in the category of the people with the conflagration of so-called populisms in Europe today?

JR: It should doubtless be clear that my usage of the term "people" runs precisely counter to the common usage of the term "populism." The People is, for me, the name of a political subject, that is, a subject constituted by those who have no particular title to govern. This political subject is a supplement to every count of social identities, a supplement that divides the police order, which conversely puts every identity in its place. I have termed "consensus" the will to suppress this supplement so as only to have to deal with clearly defined social groups and the negotiation of the redistribution of goods and powers between them, and I have also said that politics cannot dispense with the operator of the "people" and that any attempt to suppress the people as a supplement necessarily ends up with stirring up a figure of the *substitutive* figure of the people: the people as *ethnos*, as a substantial reality constituted in its opposition to the stranger, to those who are not from here. In my writings, I had in mind principally the French *Front National* which had succeeded in playing the role of the contemptuous people [*du peuple profond dédaigné*] neglected by the elites and subjected to an invasion of immigrants. Since then, the same cause has produced the same effects in a growing number of countries, with the difference being that some racist or xenophobic parties and leaders have succeeded in seizing power. The term "populism," which is used to designate this phenomenon, is equivocal. It substantializes a people to which it then lends primitive racist and xenophobic drives, although this "people" in question is, itself, constructed by our consensual governmental system. It is the logic of consensus that, by making politics into an affair of evaluations and negotiations between experts of economic management and professionals of state management, automatically generates its own antibodies. So, this consensus creates the figure of a substantial people, forsaken and despised, which must then make its voice heard thanks to "populist" leaders, the self-appointed men of the "anti-system" even though they are products of this system.

E: When rereading the final chapter from your book, *The Hatred of Democracy* (2006), there is an especially prescient claim you make, when you write: "The ignorance that people are being reproached for is simply its lack of faith. In fact historical faith has changed camps. Today's faith seems to be the prerogative of governors and their experts" (Rancière, 2006: 81). One is struck by how recent events show ("Brexit" in the United Kingdom, Trump in the United States, along with the recent travails in Italy, etc.) that "the chickens have come home to roost." The oligarchic system that has presided over the empty husk of our so-called western liberal democracies for so long now—where both the people and politics have been entirely evacuated of function and purpose, and where the economic experts and psephologists are meant to carry the day—has had its sense of fideism in technocracy and deregulated markets exposed as a mockery; it has underestimated the profound sense of agitation present today. However, while we see, for example, the liberal establishment reel in disapproval about Brexit in the United Kingdom and the election of Trump in the United States, is there not a pyrrhic victory in all this?

JR: The Marxist belief in a historical evolution steering us toward the socialist triumph has in fact been reversed into a belief in a historical evolution moving toward the triumph of the free market. It is clear that the financial and state elites, their experts and their intellectuals, must maintain this belief. When they want to rely on the victims of the system, it is not their active enthusiasm but rather their fear that they arouse. The risk, of course, is that they are not able to control this fear. This creates an equilibrium of rather peculiar affects, and neither the experts of economic rationality nor the professionals of consensus are well equipped to manage it. On the other hand, the public amusers, much simpler than they, succeed better in finding the right formula. The case of Trump is instructive in this regard. It is clear that Trump is not exactly the kind of dynamic expert, pragmatist, and man of business as his colleagues wish to see in that post. But he knew how to represent the simplest recipe containing a mix of laisser-faire neoliberal, protectionist state measures, and the unleashing of racist passions. And, since this recipe has the *air* of working, the financial elites and the elites of the Republican Party perceive him today in a better light.

E: In a situation in which most of the so-called populist movements in the West are dismissed as racist, sexist, authoritarian, etc. France's president, Macron, holds an interesting position. Macron has been accused of representing what the French sociologist Michel Wieviorka has called *populisme d'en haut* (2017). There is a certain irony that the arch-insider, both a member of the political, financial, and academic elite, has now rebranded himself as the political embodiment of change, enjoining us all to take the "forward march" (*En Marche!*). We all know what this means: further neoliberal reform, a continued breakup of the social settlement, workers' rights, championing of entrepreneurism, etc. Macron has called for an era of "democratic" or "political heroism," the restoration of great metanarratives against the destructive nature of postmodern incredulity. What is your understanding of Macron's call and how do you make sense of the relationship between him and *Front National*, are they (as you have written elsewhere) just different satellites "that profit from the strategies of the state and the distinguished intellectual campaigns" (2004: 104)?

JR: This notion of "populism from above" particularly demonstrates the inanity of the concept "populism," lending itself to any and all uses. The principal fact is, under a diversity of names and forms, the tendency, throughout the world, is a reinforcing of the power of the state and the personalization of power. They want to make us believe that this reinforcement derives from the demands of a "people from below" that calls for stronger authority. But it emanates first and foremost from the will of the ruling elites wishing to have a free hand. The financial oligarchs wish that we already went further in the destruction of public services and social rights. It is effectively what they call *se mettre en marche*: to progress as far as possible in the domination of the capitalist logic over every aspect of life. The question is just knowing what the best way is to go about it. There is, on the one hand, a direct power grab. This is what Macron represents: the man who represents nothing other than the financial powers, whose hands are not tied by any ideological pact and who governs with people coming directly from the business world. It is clear that this, despite everything, is a fragile base. There is, on the other hand, another solution, which consists of giving a "popular" base to financial power: we have here the owners of commercial empires, such as Berlusconi and Trump, presenting themselves as representatives of the little people despised by the elites. Even further we have the case of Brazil, where the capitalists have chosen to find support in an officer reminiscing about military dictatorship.

E: We would now like to focus on your specific intellectual trajectory, going back to what appears as a formative intellectual and political experience, both with respect to your break with Althusser and your engagement with *La Gauche prolétarienne*:[3] the events associated with May '68. To what extent can we today reflect on these significant political events as reawakening the problem of the people? We guess that, at the time, the connection between emancipatory politics and the people still harbored a great deal of obscurity (given the previous protracted conflict in Algeria, in Vietnam, alongside the hegemonic position of Gaullism at the time, etc.). At the same time, there was the growing suspicion surrounding Soviet Marxism due, for example, to the Prague Spring and the *Partie Communiste Français* (PCF)'s complicity with Stalinism, as well as the way that the Chinese Cultural Revolution found political sustenance in French emancipatory politics at the time. All of this points to a highly complex, fragmented, and overdetermined political situation. Yet evidently, May '68 opened up political possibilities that had otherwise been foreclosed to the Left before then. Looking back, what was your understanding of the political situation at the time and how do you assess May '68 with respect to the category of the people today?

JR: It is clear that May '68 in France was marked by a fundamental ambiguity between political subjectivation and a sociological identification of the people. The triggering element was a phenomenon of *dis-identification*:[4] the students denouncing the logic that forced them to become managers in the service of exploitation. This in turn created, between the street and the university, a new people, a constituted people: a people of equality everywhere questioning the hierarchical order—in the ateliers, the shops, the offices; but also a people created by the very dynamic of the moment, by the disturbance in the distribution of spaces and the creation of an autonomous temporality. This was a properly political people, detached from sociological identities. And it was a form of action which no longer obeyed the strategic model of calculated actions that followed the objective of "taking power." In the same way that equality was no longer an objective to achieve but a form of effective action, the meaning of action was no longer ruled by an instrumental logic of means and ends, but by the present reality of the expansion of an autonomous collective power effectively exercised. But, at the same time, this movement understood itself from within a Marxist worldview. Thus, the student struggle was seen as being in the service of the objectives of revolutionary strategy and placed in the hands of a force that had the right to lead the revolution, that is, the force of the workers incarnated in the Communist Party and its union. Since then, this force to which the May movement showed its reverence has been weakened. And the identification of the working masses and the revolutionary force has become impossible. It has appeared with even more clarity that there were no other revolutionary people than the one constituting itself in the struggle against the oligarchy and, more precisely, in the struggle against the "neoliberal" enterprise of destroying social rights. But this people is like an orphan of the social force that would serve as a real or imaginary support. In 1968, the occupation was the weapon used by the working collective to block the production process at its very location. In the more recent case of "Occupy Wall Street," occupation has become one means by which a people of equality attempts to constitute itself next to those spaces belonging to the financial and state powers.

E: Clearly your understanding of the people puts into question the logic of the "proper," a notion that has been part of political philosophy from its very inception. The predilection of the political philosopher is to define the properties that must be possessed by those subjects (as well as the spaces and objects) which end up circumscribing the strictly political. Today, a somewhat antiquated discussion surrounding the "proper" of the people returns to us in the form of the interrogative question: "What is a people?," that is, what is proper to, what belongs to, a people *qua* people? For you, on the contrary, "politics has no proper place nor any natural subjects" (2010a: 39). By extension, this means that there is no "people" to discover, to found, to realize. The people is rather an "empty operator" (a mechanism of subjectivation) that helps to stage a dispute between the police order and the "part of those who have no part." And yet, your discourse does not entirely disown "the proper." At the same time as you draw attention to the anti-political inclinations of political philosophy (which seeks to suppress the scandal of impropriety), there is another risk to which you are sensitive, namely the narrative surrounding the "end of politics," its "loss," its "eclipse." What is striking is how, in order to keep the specificity of politics in play, the "proper" out of necessity returns in your work, albeit displaced. What is "proper" is displaced from the field of objects and subjects claimed to belong to political life (defining the order of the "police") to, we could say, the very form of politics as a distinct operator. This means that for you, there is something that *properly* defines politics after all. That for politics to be identifiable as such it must contain (albeit) a minimal set of properties. What *defines* the singular stagings of politics is the redistribution of the sense of who and what counts as political. Textually, this can be traced in your text

"Ten Theses on Politics." There, on the one hand, you speak of an "interrogation into what is 'proper' to politics" (2010a: 27) but also you choose to speak of "the litigiousness *proper* to politics" (2010a: 35). What of this trace of the "proper" in your work? What is its "status" or "function," for want of some better terms?

JR: I do not believe that we here have to look for a return of the repressed. It is rather a problem of translation. The "Ten theses" were written in French and "proper" was used in the two examples that you are quoting to translate the French adjective *propre* even though in the latter it should have been translated as "characteristic." The question of *propre* and of *l'impropre* has effectively a crucial role in my reflection, but this only becomes understandable if one takes into account the three different meanings that the adjective *propre* has in French and that English translates by a number of different adjectives (own, proper, suitable, appropriate, characteristic, etc.). Even when putting to one side its more usual meaning in French (clean), the adjective varies between several significations that are appreciably different: from "that which belongs to" all the way to "is characteristic of," passing through "that which is suitable for." The critique of Hannah Arendt presented in "The Ten Theses" should be understood with this as a starting point. I critique the idea that politics should be the realization of a proper quality pertaining to one particular group of human beings or to a specific form of life. I claim, on the contrary, that what is characteristic of a political act is the act of putting into question the idea that there are proper forms of life belonging to politics, on the one hand, and forms that are excluded from the political sphere, on the other. I rediscover, in this idea of a proper "political life" belonging to a particular group of human beings the classical Platonic thesis that ascribes to each group a specific quality, thereby endowing it with a determinate task proper to its own occupation.[5] If there is something "proper" to politics—that is, some characteristic that differentiates it—then for me it is to be found in the sense of "impropriety," that is, a disorder brought about within the police partitioning/distributing of forms of life by those subjects who start doing things other than the tasks and the roles assigned to them. Here, one must also think about the role I give to words in subverting forms of life. In fact, *propre* relates to the use of words and has, in French, two significations: the "literal" as opposed to the "figural"; and also the "correct" in contrast to "incorrect." To this question I dedicated my book *The Names of History* (Rancière, 1994): the subversion of the order of things takes place when one makes improper use of certain words—the poor, people, the proletariat, the bourgeois, etc.—that is, by means of their metaphoric or metonymic usage, which separates them from their identity function. Faced with this, the social sciences, often seconded in this task by philosophy, tasks itself with bringing back these names so that they designate clearly identifiable social categories or properties. Thinking the *propre* in an activity or a sphere or experience to me means thinking the specificity of operations of dis-identification or of de-classification that makes it exist: politics exists in and through the struggle against the identities that define the police order. Likewise, art began to exist as a specific sphere of experience once the frontiers delimiting the domains of the fine arts, which separated out the "liberal" arts from the "mechanical" arts, had become blurred. Finally, literature was made possible by sundering the properties and distinctions that had defined the "belles-lettres."[6]

E: On this subversion of the logic of the proper in your work, sometimes, in certain formulations you make, one detects a "playfulness" bordering on an ironic distance, forcing us not to take things too literally. Would this sense of ironic distance be present in how you deploy the "proper"? Is there an intentional paradox at play in your retention of the term? If for you politics coalesces around the "the part that has no part," "the count of the uncounted," then are we to read you as presenting a relation of torsion here, for example, an idea of the "improper proper" or the "proper improper" that says something about the peculiar logic of worker's emancipation and popular revolt?

JR: With respect to my "distance" surrounding the literal sense of words, it is also an attentiveness to the work that made the words move and to the way in which these displacements of words displace bodies in relation to their "normal" place. There are people who desire that one give a strict definition to words and notions, in fear of falling into "relativism." But this putative rigor is itself perfectly relativist. It imposes a particular meaning and usage to words as their proper sense and their valid use. On the contrary, I have always been attentive to the way in which speech acts make words move, and through these displacements, how they sediment and form a shared common power of the possibilities of language.[7] The part that has no part, in one sense formal, is the empty property of men without qualities. But this "empty" property also constructs itself by means of appropriating the language of others. I underlined, in the "Ten Theses," that the first occurrence of the word "demos" can be found in Homer, where it signifies the condition of those that do not have the right to speak. In *Proletarian Nights*, I commented on a particular letter penned by a tiler and addressed to a floor worker. In the letter, the worker speaks of a verse by Victor Hugo ("Mes jours s'en vont de rêve en rêve" ["My days go from dream to dream"]). My point here was to highlight how the worker, captured in the obscurity of work, appropriates this verse that had otherwise seemed to describe the time of the idle bourgeois dreamer. At the heart of emancipation much work is dedicated to the reclaiming [*réappropriation*] of words, which also means reclaiming a common sensible world. It is this work that takes place in the play of the proper and the improper.

E: Looking around at our own political present, the "left" has increasingly accused "right-wing" populists of having stolen certain ideas, symbols, historical sites. There is nothing new in this type of accusation, of course. Though nonetheless it is a claim that has become increasingly prevalent in the wake of the instrumentalization and appropriation of women's rights and worker's rights (an integral part of the history of emancipatory struggle) by less than salubrious sources. This is particularly significant since your work has often (and rightly) highlighted how the political process of emancipation is about the "equality of intelligence" (see, for example, 1994, 1999, 2007), where, and this is especially significant, "the logic of the egalitarian assumption is radically opposed to the aggregation of social bodies" (1999: 34). Which is to say, for you the politics of emancipation is in "no way a form of culture" (1999: 36). Nor does it amount to a collective ethos of "finding its voice." "Speaking out," you write in *Disagreement*, "is not awareness of a self asserting what belongs to it" (1999: 37). How are we, then, to understand or interpret those who see themselves as somehow acting and thinking within the long history (stronger still, the "tradition") of emancipatory struggle but regard themselves as victims of a certain "expropriation" (both infelicitous and improper) by certain right-wing populists? Is there a trace of *ressentiment* in such accusations made by those on the left or can we say that there is a legitimate sense of wrong (*le tort*) being experienced today on the side of those groups and movements who feel dispossessed of the sense and lived political history of the emancipatory struggle to which they belong, and believe to be their own?

JR: My experience, in the French context, is a little different. It is not really the "populists of the right" that are "stealing" from the left its formulations and its arguments. The problem comes from part of the so-called left, and which has itself reversed the meanings of yesterday's words and struggles in order to turn them into a cultural and national property that excludes foreigners. This left which calls itself "republican" has claimed the universalism of the French tradition of human rights against every particularism and communitarianism. First, they opposed this "universalist" tradition against all demands formulated on the basis of particular groups and most notably against the feminist struggle for equality. Now, however, they have reversed the situation, weaponizing the universal *French* values of equality between men and women against Muslim particularism and the inferior role it ascribes to women. Furthermore, it meant reclaiming the word *laïcité* which, in the nineteenth century, meant the struggle to free schools from the religious grip in order to turn it into a great battle against the Islamic veil. It has also provided the extreme-right with an alternative ideology in which anti-maghrebian or anti-Black racism has become the struggle against Muslim communitarianism in defense of the universal values of the *laïcité* of the republic. For me, this inversion inscribes itself in a larger process than that of the overturning of revolutionary traditions in Europe. In *Althusser's Lesson* (2011a) I showed how Marxism had become a philosophy of order, condemning certain uprisings as "petit-bourgeois deviations" and purely "ideological." Later, in *Hatred of Democracy* (2006) and *The Emancipated Spectator* (2009), I showed how the critiques of the commodity-form, of consumer society, and of the society of the spectacle were soon transformed into critiques of "democratic individualism" and thus put into the service of an antisocial politics of the right. There is a whole ressentiment of the left in relation to the disappointment of revolutionary hopes, which has succeeded in creating a reactive ideology servicing both the "neoliberal" right and the "populist" extreme-right.

E: In the concluding passages from a paper you gave at a colloquium on the "Division of the Sensible" in 2004, you write: "Philosophy as I conceive of it is placed under the sign of disagreement . . . that is, as a conflict over homonyms, a conflict between one who says white and another who says white" (2010b). Through this quote, we would like to address the homonymic status of the category of the "people." We are entirely accepting of the presuppositions of your discourse. Nonetheless, today when we look at the United States, France, Britain, and Sweden (for that matter), we see the people as an empty operator that opens up for spaces of dissensus and contestations and that "undermines" the established ways of being, belonging, and thinking within a given regime of the sensible. However, these invocations of the people come from a variety of political positions and sources, some are a lot more desirable than others. This, in turn, raises the question (undoubtedly more political than philosophical) of how to separate out the good from the bad—the emancipatory from the reactionary—uses of the homonym the people, which seem to coexist within the same police order. Through recourse to the presupposition of equality, recurrent in your work, it would appear that homonyms are not so empty and indeterminate. Even in your own thought, are you not—however "guarded" and "careful" you otherwise are to avoid such claims—forced into making such a separation? Can we really be content with affirming the floating and indeterminate nature of the taxonomy of political ideas and names that furnish political action?

JR: First, let me remind you that I have never founded my vision of politics on any idea of empty or floating signifiers! Even the lack of quality of the demos is a *determined* lack of quality. It is an active negation of the hierarchical distribution of identities, capacities, and places. This negation might be expressed in simply a formal manner, as a lack of any principle for the distribution of roles. I have emphasized this formal aspect in my "Ten Theses" (2010a). But I have also searched throughout the modern thinking and history of emancipation, for a positive content regarding the implementation of equality: emancipation is the work of those that show their equal capacity to participate in all forms of experience of a common world. It is effectively the presupposition of equality that according to me distinguishes the democratic people from its homonyms. This means that the affirmation of difference from the dominant oligarchy (the people against "the elites") is not enough to define a democratic people. The democratic people is a people constituted by acts that draw out the implications of the presupposition of equality. It is this aspect which was at the forefront of the recent movements in the squares, even if at times it has taken on a bit of a caricature in assemblies where everyone is allotted an equal amount of time to say what he or she wants to say. This is diametrically opposed to how the figure of the people operates under the banner of "populism": the people is supposed to exist as a substantial reality, and this substance is defined through its difference with those who are not from here, who do not have the same skin color, the same history, the same values, etc.

E: Today, when everyone appears to be playing the populist game, claiming to speak in the name of the people against the established political regime, one is inclined to ask about an emancipatory alternative, which in a more incisive manner redistributes the sensible and breaks from the deadlock of the pseudo-struggle between the so-called populist and the liberal establishment internal to the oligarchic system. For us, the difficulties today seem to coalesce around the problem of "naming." We ask this because in *Disagreement* you reformulate the famous Marxian thesis regarding class struggle as the motor of history. In Marxism: slave and free man, serf and lord, proletarian and bourgeois, but also for you, demos and the oligarchs, the plebeians and the patricians, the *tiers état* and ancien régime, etc. would be the placeholders for these names. We do not want you to identify the nominal candidates that appear today to circulate as possible placeholders for emancipatory change. Rather, we would ask you whether today there is in fact a problem with nomination as such, that is, of thinking the appropriate names that are "supernumerary" to "the calculated number of groups, places, and functions in a society."

JR: Let us first say that class struggle is not a specifically Marxist notion. I recall in *Disagreement* that it is Aristotle who first made class struggle into the motor of politics.[8] Books III and IV of his *Politics* are devoted to the struggle of the poor and the rich which, in every city, gives content to politics. But precisely these notions of "rich" and "poor" designate ways of constructing a space for the political community instead of simply designating economical groups. Politics is not the consequence of a class struggle existing on a more profound level. It is a direct exercise of this struggle that displaces social identities. As I discussed earlier, I have tried to show how this displacement is performed by an "improper" use of names. Those political subjects who name themselves the "people," "workers," or "proletarians" separate themselves from their homonyms, at least as they come to be defined within the police order. But this separation remains always liable to a possible re-identification, thereby turning people into a figure of being a collective already there or identifying the working class as a political subject with the working class as a sociological *reality*. For a long time one has been able to identify under the same name—worker or proletarian—a political subject with the reality of a social group and the power of a world-to-come. This has, however, opened up the space for several confusions. Today, in fact, we find ourselves in the reverse situation where it appears impossible to name a political subject, even at the cost of homonymy. The figure of the "precariat" has not taken the place of the "proletarian," even though it designates the dominant form of work under which, in our countries, the exploitation of living work takes place. This is because precarious labor has not been granted a power to symbolize the common. *Indignés* has designated the motivation of a revolt but could not become the name of a community. The 99 percent have presented a disembodied form of identity between the people of militant equality and the substantial reality of a population. The movements of the squares or the Occupy movement has singularized acts and places without being able to relate it to subjects. Maybe it is time to recuperate the word "proletarian" which today no longer is identifiable with the sociological reality of factory workers. I don't believe that one could say much more.

E: While the people has been a recurrent topic in your work, a number of other political theorists and philosophers have, during the last decades, turned their attention toward concepts and ideas that seem to have a certain "family resemblance" with your conception of the people. Here we are thinking of concepts such as "community" and "multitude" (among others). However, these concepts seem at the very least to respond to a shared sense of urgency for the Left when it comes to defining the "operator" for emancipatory change. At the same time, these concepts also bring other philosophical traditions to the discussion, such as phenomenology and existential thought, and a certain Spinozist understanding of Marxism. How would you characterize your own work in relation to this wider debate? Can we speak of a certain "family resemblance" here or are there any specific differences that you would like to highlight?

JR: I don't believe that the idea of community could play the same role as that of the people. In fact, it oscillates between two different uses: on the one hand, there *are* communities, that is, the concrete groups defined by a shared ethnic origin, a religion, or a common culture that our epoch tends to value are willing to valorize by opposing their concrete ties to the abstraction of the "people." On the other hand, there is *the* community that is readily opposed to egoistic solitude by which one characterizes today's social life. This idea of being together has been greatly valorized in the squares of the occupy movements, especially in the form of the assembly. Personally, I have always thought that the opposition that structures politics is not the opposition between individual and community but between antagonistic ways of doing community. It is this that I want to point to with the opposition between politics and the police. Every community defines itself within this tension of opposites. Regarding the idea of the "multitude," this also appears to me torn between two understandings. On the one hand, it might be seen as closely related to my conception of the people as a community of equals constructed through the struggle against a system of places and identities. On the other hand, it reappropriates the Marxist vision of a subject of communal action identified with a power defined by and through economic processes. This has always been the problem of Toni Negri: to provide a contemporary equivalent of the Marxist logic which deduces the agents of political combat from the transformations taking place within relations of production. The "multitude" is still heir to the Marxist theme of the "revolt of the productive forces." It is now fifty years since I first saw Marxists use Spinoza as a way of remedying the impasses of historical Marxism and the relative effacement of the worker-subject. I cannot see that these struggles have gained even one iota of more power.

Notes

1 This interview was conducted through written correspondence with the editors of this volume (Payne, Stagnell, and Strandberg) and Jacques Rancière between September

2018 and March 2020. Rancière responded in French, and all responses have been translated by the editors.
2 For some translations of Rancière's early work, which originally appeared in *Les Révoltes Logiques*, please see *Staging the People* (2011c).
3 In the mid-1960s, he was a student of Louis Althusser, the notable French Marxist, at *L'école normale superieur*. Famously, Rancière contributed to *Reading Capital* (Althusser et al., 2015), a book emerging out of a series of seminars that Althusser held with his students. By the time of 1968, the young Rancière became increasingly disillusioned with the political positions that Althusser, as an intellectual within the PCF, took up vis-à-vis May 1968. Althusser (and the PCF) was blindsided by the sheer magnitude of the student-worker uprisings. Rancière would subject Althusser to blistering and public critique, drawing a straight line between Althusser as maître-philosophe of "order" and his politico-revolutionary orthodoxy. See *Althusser's Lesson* (2011a).
4 The idea of dis-identification is discussed by Rancière in *Disagreement* (1999: 36–7).
5 For Rancière's reading of Plato, please see *Philosopher and His Poor* (2004).
6 See in particular Rancière's *Mute Speech: Literature, Critical Theory, and Politics* (2011b).
7 For a more extensive treatment of this matter, the reader should refer to Rancière's essay "The Use of Distinctions" (2010b).
8 Rancière is specifically referring to Chapter 1 of his *Disagreement* (1999).

Bibliography

Althusser L, Balibar É, Establet R, et al. (eds) (2015) *Reading Capital* (trans. B Brewster and D Fernbach). London: Verso.
Rancière J (1991) *The Ignorant Schoolmaster: Five Lessons in Intellectual Emancipation*. Stanford, CA: Stanford University Press.
Rancière J (1994) *The Names of History: On the Poetics of Knowledge* (trans. H Melehy). Minneapolis: University of Minnesota Press.
Rancière J (1999) *Disagreement: Politics and Philosophy* (trans. J Rose). Minneapolis: University of Minnesota Press.
Rancière J (2004) *The Philosopher and His Poor* (trans. A Parker, J Drury, and C Oster). Durham, NC: Duke University Press.
Rancière J (2006) *Hatred of Democracy* (trans. S Corcoran). London: Verso.
Rancière J (2007) *On the Shores of Politics* (trans. L Heron). London: Verso.
Rancière J (2009) *The Emancipated Spectator* (trans. G Elliott). London: Verso.
Rancière J (2010a) Ten Theses on Politics. In: S Corcoran (ed.), *Dissensus: On Politics and Aesthetics*. London: Continuum, 27–44.
Rancière J (2010b) The Uses of Distinctions. In: S Corcoran (ed.), *Dissensus: On Politics and Aesthetics*. London: Continuum, 205–18.
Rancière J (2011a) *Althusser's Lesson* (trans. E Battista). London: Continuum.
Rancière J (2011b) *Mute Speech: Literature, Critical Theory, and Politics* (trans. J Swenson). New directions in critical theory. New York: Columbia University Press.
Rancière J (2011c) *Staging the People: The Proletarian and His Double* (trans. D Fernbach). London: Verso.

Rancière J (2012) *Proletarian Nights: The Workers' Dream in Nineteenth-Century France* (trans. J Drury). London: Verso Books.
Rimbaud A (2003) Democracy. In: *Rimbaud Complete. Volume 1*. New York: Modern Library, p. 264. Available at: http://search.ebscohost.com/login.aspx?direct=true&scope=site&db=nlebk&db=nlabk&AN=739669 (accessed October 6, 2021).
Wieviorka M (2017) Michel Wieviorka : Le populisme est "un discours qui prétend parler d'en bas pour dénoncer le monde d'en haut." Available at: https://www.touteleurope.eu/vie-politique-des-etats-membres/michel-wieviorka-le-populisme-est-un-discours-qui-pretend-parler-d-en-bas-pour-denoncer-le-monde/.

2

Demophobia in Politics

Remarks on Liberal Anti-populism and the Possibility of a Radical Democratic Populism

Oliver Marchart

Liberal Anti-populism as a Case of Demophobia

How wonderful democracy would be without the people! The refrains of liberal anti-populism can be heard from politicians of all stripes. The lament resounds from the top of the EU, where Commission president Jean-Claude Juncker, in his own self-created format of a "State of the European Union Address" in September 2016, warned of "galloping populism," repeating what former EU Council president Herman Van Rompuy had already called the "storms of populism" in 2012, all the way down to local politics. It is echoed in the analyses, reports, and commentaries of the media, where the term "populism" is almost universally associated with the threatening scenario of an irresponsible seduction of the people, if not of an incendiary popular sedition. In public discourse, the term "populism" primarily serves the purpose of political denunciation of parties and movements that either do not come from the traditional spectrum of the political center or, where they do, turn against it. The pejorative use of the term indicates that anti-populist discourses, while seemingly neutral in their defense of liberal values, draw a political line of conflict—an antagonism—between "us liberal democrats" and the "populist anti-democrats." This "axis of *populism* and *anti-populism*" is aptly described as the dominant split over which political meaning is organized in our current political conjuncture (Stavrakakis, 2016: 110). "The rift," according to Wolfgang Streeck, "between those who call others 'populists' and those who are called such by them is the dominant line of political conflict in the crisis societies of finance capitalism today" (2017: 261).[1]

It is remarkable, however, that in the discourse of the critics of populism, opposing parties of extremely different political orientations can be given the stigma of populism, so that the concept of populism seems strangely devoid of any specific content due to its sweeping overextension. In this regard, the political use of the derogatory signifier "populism" overlaps with populism as defined in political analysis. There is now widespread agreement among researchers that populism does not represent a specific political worldview or is characterized by any distinct content or by typical demands. While, for example, socialism at its core stands for social justice or liberalism for individual liberties, no such ideological core, it seems, can be found in populism—except in the injunction that politics is to be made "for the people" or "in the name of the people," a claim ultimately made by all democratic parties as far as they are not strictly clientelistic. Thus the development in populism research has moved away from impressionistically designed catalogs of characteristics of populist politics and toward minimal definitions. According to the currently most relevant definition by Caas Mudde, populists divide society into two homogeneous and antagonistic camps—a "pure people" and a "corrupt elite"—whereby politics does not only express the *volonté générale* of the people, but the populist distinction between people and elite becomes primarily a *moral* distinction of "good"/"evil" or "pure"/"corrupt" (2004: 543). At its core, this minimal definition coincides with the second important theory of populism, which emerged from the Marxist tradition and was introduced by Ernesto Laclau in the 1970s and later developed into a post-foundational theory of populism. Laclau, too, does not understand populism as a specific political ideology but, rather, as a *logic* of simplifying the political space around a central antagonism between the "people," or the underdog, and the "power bloc," or the elite (Laclau, 2005; Marchart, 2018).

These minimal definitions can help to classify the sweeping criticism of populism by liberal mainstream parties and media. For if it is true that populism in itself has no particular ideological content, then such sweeping criticism of populism is equally devoid of content. This is because the liberal attack is directed against a certain *form* of mobilization, while the specific *whys* and *wherefores* mobilized in the respective case remain secondary. The general criticism of populism thus remains empty, not because the anti-populist phalanx of centrist politics and the mainstream media adheres to a scientific minimal model of populism, but because liberal anti-populism denounces everything that could appear as a political alternative to the neoliberal dogma to which the parties of the entire traditional spectrum—including the social democratic and green parties—for decades adhered with only slight variation: unhindered rule of the markets in all areas of life; the sell-off of public goods; constitutionalization of the austerity regime (e.g., the constitutionalization of debt brakes); the dismantling of social security systems, the expansion of the low-wage sector in favor of global competitiveness together with the harassment of the unemployed, etc.[2] As Wolfgang Streeck has aptly, if polemically, remarked, populist parties

> are therefore perceived and fought as a mortal danger to "democracy" by the state-bearing parties, which have long since conspired with each other and merged with the state apparatuses. The combat term used in this context, which was quickly introduced into the post-factual knowledge, is that of "populism," which is used to describe right-wing and left-wing currents and organisations that oppose the TINA logic of "responsible" politics under conditions of neoliberal globalisation. (Streek, 2017: 260)

Against the background of the TINA principle, the critique of populism by the media and traditional parties thus turns out to be a critique of every politically articulated—and thus potentially dangerous—demand for alternatives to a neoliberal status quo. Liberal anti-populism must remain abstract and empty in order to denounce such alternative demands regardless of their content and on the basis of their populist form of articulation alone. In the night of liberal anti-populism, all populists are grey.[3] In this night, it is no longer possible to make out differences between left or right, inclusive or exclusive, democratic or authoritarian varieties of populism.[4] For it is not only authoritarian or even fascist movements that use the semantics of "people" versus "elite," but also genuine democratizing movements such as *Podemos* in Spain, the global Occupy movement, *Syriza* in Greece, and *La France insoumise* in France. Although these movements also formulate an antagonism between "the people" and the "corrupt elite" (e.g., in Spain between *la gente* and *la casta*), they do not oppose the political elite with an ethnically pure body of the people, nor do they pursue a project of authoritarian transformation of the state. Rather, the political project of such progressive variants of populism consists in the *democratization of democracy*—a formula that encapsulates the main idea behind radical democratic thought and practice.

It follows that, even when retaining the minimal definition of populism in academic research, we need to clearly distinguish between progressive and reactive versions of populism, for otherwise we end up playing the game of mainstream liberal anti-populism. In the following, I will thus propose to have a closer look at Nancy Fraser's and Chantal Mouffe's respective proposals for a progressive or left populism. For the future development of a synthetic theory of radical democratic populism, however, two additional steps are required: first, the sweeping assault on any kind of populism by the "spontaneous ideology" of mainstream liberal anti-populists will have to be countered. I will argue that anti-populists, by virtue of being "anti," remain themselves locked within the populist problematic. This is not an accident that could easily be remedied with an ever-greater dose of liberal pluralism. Rather, it attests to the shared problematic of an antagonism between populism and elitism, if by the latter we understand a demophobic ideology with roots in both liberalism and conservatism. If democracy is conceived to be the rule of the people, rather than the rule of traditional, functional, or economic elites within an oligarchic power bloc, elitism in both its outmoded conservative and current (neo) liberal variants is by definition anti-democratic. It is therefore important, second, to locate liberal anti-populism within the tradition of anti-democratic sentiment. This, in turn, necessitates not only a critical engagement with the history of demophobia; it also demands an engagement with populism as democracy's "shadow," as Margaret Canovan famously put it (1990). Is populism an intrinsic dimension of democracy or is it, as liberal anti-populists hold, anti-democratic *eo ipso*? Is populism a legitimate corrective attempt at counterbalancing elite control of the political process; or, is it a pathological aberration of democracy itself? There is no space within the frame of this chapter to elaborate on the historical dimension of demophobia, so I will restrict my argument to the systematic task of relating populism, anti-populism, and democratic populism.[5]

Why Liberal Anti-populism Is the Problem, not the Solution

In liberal anti-populism, the derogatory use of the concept of populism is employed to delegitimize any demands that could mobilize the interests of broader sections of the population against policies that systematically bypass these very interests. In this regard anti-populism is a particularly disingenuous ideology, as it is employed by neoliberal ideologists to fight a phenomenon that was inflamed by their policies in the first place: "The implemented neoliberal policies become increasingly *unpopular* and trigger *popular* mobilizations, which in turn are denounced as *populist*" (Stavrakakis, 2016: 110). If populist movements resonate with the population—and this also applies to far-right parties that make use of populist strategies—it is above all because, after three decades of neoliberal politics, there is a not entirely unfounded mistrust of a functional elite that is impossible to be irritated even by a full-blown world economic crisis that flies in the face of neoliberal dogma. Indeed, since the beginning of this crisis in 2008, the neoliberal restructuring of the European welfare states has gained enormous momentum before being, for now, decelerated by the Covid-19 pandemic. The costs of bailing out "distressed" banks have been passed on to the population rather than back to the banks, and the neoliberal credo has been enforced more vehemently than before by increasingly authoritarian means, even as it has become clear that the social foundations of liberal democracy are being undermined. In most European countries, however, the social devastation left behind by these policies is not so much becoming a breeding ground for democratization movements such as *Podemos*, but for right-wing extremist movements which—following the failure of the European center-left parties—are now in many places the only political force giving, or claiming to give, a voice to the real or perceived losers. The conflicts that are emerging in this way are much more dramatic than the usual competition between different political ideas. For since an alternative to the neoliberal generalized precarization of all areas of work and life cannot be formulated within the established party spectrum of liberal democracy, there is a danger that it will be formulated by forces seeking to supplant liberal democracy by some form of nativist, yet partially redistributive, ethnocracy.

That is why any critique of those far-right parties which are typically lumped together under the heading of right-wing populism must be *substantive* in the sense of not restricting its view to the purely formal definitional criterion of a "people" being invoked against the power bloc. For sure, the authoritarian turn of countries like Hungary and Poland poses a manifest danger to liberal democracy. But this is precisely why liberal anti-populism—as an arsonist in the uniform of the fire brigade—is so dangerous. For in those Western European countries where no authoritarian Bonapartists have yet come to power, liberal anti-populism obscures the causes of the current misery, which are to be found in precisely those policies that it so vehemently defends against "the populists." Liberal anti-populism thus promotes a misleading diagnosis of the problem. For example, the much-discussed crisis of political representation, which has created a vacuum that is now being filled from the right in many countries, is due to the conversion, above all of center-left parties, to the tenets of neoliberalism. The unprecedented decline of European social democracy bears witness to the consequences of this conversion. In some countries, social democracy has lost its former core constituency almost entirely to nonvoters and far-right parties—in the 2016 Austrian presidential election, for example, 85 percent of workers voted for the extreme right-wing FPÖ candidate Norbert Hofer—while in others it has been virtually wiped out: in 2017, the Socialist Party came to a stand of 7.4 percent in the French parliamentary elections, losing nearly 22 percent, and in the Netherlands, the Party of Labour was reduced to a voter share of 5.7 percent, losing 19 percent. Social democrats would be ill-advised to blame racist demagogues for their own decline. Most often, Social Democrats are the architects of their own misfortune. But evidence to the contrary can also be provided by some social democratic parties which are currently proving successful where they oppose dogmatic neoliberalism. Even if Bernie Sanders ultimately lost in the party primaries, his "democratic socialism" has proven significantly more popular than Hilary Clinton's "progressive neoliberalism" (Fraser, 2019). Jeremy Corbyn's program of re-nationalizing key businesses, especially the railways, and the promised protection of the National Health Service allowed him to break the Tories' absolute parliamentary majority and almost win the election in 2017 before becoming the victim in 2019 of a "Get Brexit Done!" jingoist populism combined with some redistributive offers to Labour constituencies designed to beat Labour on its own terrain. A minimal wage of 12 euro and the promise to keep pensions safe were key in securing Olaf Scholz a winning lead in the 2021 elections to the German *Bundestag*. And in Portugal, a minority social democratic government under António Costa, supported by radical left-wing parties, was able to escape Greece's fate and kick-start an economic recovery precisely because it resisted the austerity *Diktat* by Germany's then finance minister Wolfgang Schäuble, who had deceptively predicted the apocalyptic collapse of Portugal.

In all these cases resorting to the usual refrains of liberal anti-populism offered no solution. In truth, in day-to-day political struggle liberal anti-populists turned out to be in need of a certain dose of populism themselves. The political world of anti-populism turns upside down when mainstream parties of the center-right and even liberal parties resort to mobilization strategies and ideologemes of populists. Emmanuel Macron who, as a former investment banker and economy minister, is himself part of "the system" against which he opposed his seemingly anti-systemic movement can at least formally be described as a liberal populist, even when running on a purportedly anti-populist ticket.[6] In the Austrian parliamentary election campaign of 2017, Austrian foreign minister Sebastian Kurz, a sort of Austro-Macron who fell from grace due to a corruption scandal in 2021, had successfully disguised the old conservative party ÖVP as a new "movement" purporting to oppose that outmoded system to which he himself had belonged for six years as a member of the government and where his own party had uninterruptedly served for thirty years. The neoliberal mainstream, having encountered a massively dwindling following in the electorate, has little choice but such labeling fraud. But anti-populism, of course, becomes a farce as soon as the neoliberal elite starts to engage in a mock battle with itself. This may still be democratically acceptable as long as only the *logic* of populist mobilization is adopted. But what happens when the ideological *content* of populist far-right parties is adopted? It can be observed on a broad front that parties of the political center, after years of adopting neoliberal ideologemes, started to adopt racist and ethno-nationalist ideologemes. In taking on board positions of the far-right Austrian Freedom Party on migration policy, the aforementioned Sebastian Kurz succeeded in gaining massive ground on the FPÖ, thus turning the conservative party ÖVP into a xenophobic populist party. Comparable events are the Danish general elections of 2019, which saw the Social Democrats running a xenophobic campaign imitative of the populist Danish People's Party, and the 2017 Dutch parliamentary elections. The outcome of the latter was greeted with relief by anti-populist commentators, as Geert Wilders fell short of expectations with a voter share of 13 percent. The fact that the liberal-conservative party under Mark Rutte secured its election victory by adopting Wilders' ideas seemed largely irrelevant to most observers. However, now that these ideas were formulated by liberal anti-populists, were they suddenly no longer "populist"? Does racism only count as racism when it comes from populists, but not when it is adopted by liberal anti-populists? Once again it becomes apparent: liberal anti-populism increasingly adopts, even implements, the authoritarian and racist demands of its ostensible opponents, while at the same time blocking the urgently needed democratization of liberal democracy.

That elitist anti-populism, especially of the center-right, turns out to be crypto-populist may come as a surprise, since the elite and the people are supposed to appear as opposites in populist discourse. But the quandary dissolves when it is understood that they are also mirror images. As Mudde observes: "Populism is the mirror-image of elitism, which is based upon the same, essentially moral distinction between 'the' elite and 'the' people, but considers the former pure and the latter corrupt." And he adds: "Elitism was the main world-view until the early 1920s, informing most prominent ideologies (such as conservatism) and religions (like Catholicism)" (Mudde, 2015: 433). At this point, Mudde fails to mention that elitism, of course, did not disappear from the face of the earth. A thoroughly elitist mood dominates postwar democratic theory and contemporary neoliberalism, and it also motivates liberal anti-populism. What the anti-populist elite sees, when looking into a mirror, is the Medusa's head of its opponent. One strategy to cope with the frightening image of its Other is to simply change places by taking up the structural position of the enemy, the "populists." As Thomas Frank remarked in his history of US anti-populism: "This imagined struggle of expert versus populist has a fundamental, almost biblical flavor to it. It is a battle of order against chaos, education against ignorance, mind against appetite, enlightenment against bigotry, health against disease" (2020: 3). In other words, what researchers have always made out as a defining criterion of populism—the dichotomic worldview and a struggle between the forces of good and forces of evil—is as much a criterion of many strands of elitist anti-populism, only under the opposite sign. In the ideological discourse that Frank calls "Democracy Scare," it is of course not the elite, but it is the people who are corrupted: "If the people have lost faith in the ones in charge, it can only be because something has gone wrong with the people themselves" (2020: 3); and he goes on to quote the telling headline of an article from *Foreign Policy*: "It's Time for the Elites to Rise Up Against the Ignorant Masses." Perhaps, what can be described as the *reverse populism* of the elite might best be illustrated—in a clear case of performative self-contradiction—by the main title of Yascha Mounk's abysmal book: *The People vs. Democracy*. Mounk (2018) constructs the very same antagonism constructed by populists, only from the other side of a mainstream liberalism as defended by Mounk's ideological mentor Tony Blair, with "the people" as the enemy of democracy.

Obviously, these are not isolated cases of demophobia; they are symptomatic of the "spontaneous ideology" of liberal anti-populists. In the mirror of a deeply demophobic elite, "the people" appear as a threatening mass or as an easily seducible child, or in any case as deeply irrational, immature, and acting against their own interests—which are, of course, much better perceived by neoliberal technocrats. Indeed, one of the regular responses to populism is paternalism, which we still encounter even in such seemingly innocuous phrases as "one must take the fears and concerns of the people seriously," even if, according to the unspoken postscript, one considers them to be unfounded. Yet such paternalism only adds insult to injury by demeaning the disenfranchised. What is more, anti-populist discourse—as a modern offshoot of demophobic discourse—obscures the actual causes of social insecurity, propagates bogus solutions, and drives economically weak sectors of the population into the arms of far-right parties.

Progressive and Left Populism

While ochlophobia can be traced back to the discursive denigration of the masses so typical for the bourgeois imaginary of the nineteenth century and, for instance, the mass psychology of that age, it remains operative in elite and pluralist theories of democracy. That populism could be more than merely a disease and pathological aberration of democracy seems to be inconceivable for many liberal approaches to democracy. But how to envisage a democratic or radical democratic kind of populism that aims at the integration of the masses rather than marginalizing them. I shall discuss the suggestions of Nancy Fraser and Chantal Mouffe, before ending with a short synthetic view of the contours of a radical democratic populism.

Both theorists follow a Gramscian approach in political analysis. Correspondingly, their conceptions of a progressive or left populism are based on a Gramscian analysis of the current historical conjuncture. Hegemony is defined by Nancy Fraser, following Gramsci, as "the process by which a ruling class makes its domination appear natural by installing the presuppositions of its own worldview as the common sense of society as a whole" (2019: 9). Organizationally, hegemony is condensed in a hegemonic or, with Gramsci, "historical bloc" through which the ruling class secures its hegemony by allying with other social forces. Hegemony in the Gramscian sense of persuasion, consensus, and unforced consent is located on the axis of, in her lexicon, *recognition*, conceived as the way in which status hierarchies are organized in a given society. But Fraser seeks to supplement this axis by proposing that it needs to be combined with an axis of *distribution*, that is, with an economic dimension. Only in the combination of recognition and distribution can a given hegemony be fostered. I very much doubt that this point constitutes a true amendment to Gramsci, because that hegemony needs to be supported, in the long run, by distributive effects is exactly what Gramsci himself said. Hence, this would open a discussion of merely academic relevance. Now, Fraser bases her plea for a progressive populism on the analysis of the current crisis of the hegemonic bloc, a crisis described, again with Gramsci, as an interregnum between a dying hegemonic formation and a new one that cannot be born. The nature of the old hegemonic bloc is captured by Fraser's powerful and influential concept of "progressive neoliberalism."

If we translate her account of progressive neoliberalism into the Essex school framework of discourse analysis (Marchart, 2013), the following picture emerges: the hegemonic bloc of progressive neoliberalism combines an economic axis of neoliberal distribution with a progressive, that is, liberal politics of recognition. Each one of these axes constitutes what in the Essex paradigm would be called a chain of equivalence. The axis of recognition consists of "mainstream liberal currents of the new social movements." The chain of equivalence reads: /feminism/=/antiracism/=/multiculturalism/=/environmentalism/=/LGBTQ+ rights/ (Fraser, 2019: 11). And a few pages onward, Fraser presents the equivalential chain of progressive neoliberalism in terms of social groups: /entrepreneurs/=/bankers/=/suburbanites/=/"symbolic workers"/=/new social movements/=/Latinxs/=/youth/=/African Americans/ (2019: 15). Now, in progressive neoliberalism the mainstream, or "mainstreaming," version of all these movements and social groups enters into an alliance with neoliberal actors, described by Fraser as the "most dynamic, high-end, 'symbolic,' and financial sectors of the US economy," that is, Wall Street, Silicon Valley, and Hollywood (2019: 11). Fraser insists that the progressive chain stands in a subordinated relation to the capital factions of the neoliberal chain. Yet what emerged from this unholy alliance, in which, as Fraser insists, the progressive chain stands in a subordinated relation to the capital factions of the neoliberal chain, was what Boltanski and Chiapello (2005) have called the New Spirit of capitalism, which found its political expression in the governments of Clinton, Blair, or Schröder.

To the extent that progressive neoliberalism superseded the New Deal hegemonic bloc of previous decades, the articulatory effort of combining these chains of equivalence went necessarily hand in hand with an effort to disarticulate the postwar hegemonic bloc that had fostered an equivalential chain between /organized labor/=/immigrants/=/African Americans/=/the urban middle classes/=/some factions of big industrial capital/ (Fraser, 2019: 15). While the upper middle class seemed to profit from their alliance with neoliberalism, financial deregulation and de-industrialization left behind large sectors of the New Deal hegemonic bloc, which consequently disintegrated. Two decades of the effective hegemony of progressive neoliberalism ensued, and forces that would not succumb to the latter were marginalized. When the devastating results of the neoliberal agenda made itself felt, the lower-income sectors were without a political home. A "hegemonic gap" opened in the political universe and given "the accelerating pace of deindustrialization; the proliferation of precarious, low-wage McJobs; the rise of predatory debt; and the consequent decline in living standards for the bottom two-thirds of Americans, it was only a matter of time before someone would fill the gap" (2019: 19). This was the hour of what Fraser calls "reactionary populism." Donald Trump moved in and filled the political vacuum left behind by progressive neoliberals. So did Bernie Sanders in his primary campaigns. What became visible in both cases, according to Fraser, was the contour of a potential, non-neoliberal hegemonic bloc, only that in Trump's case this bloc consisted of a reactionary chain of equivalences: /racism/=/misogyny/=/Islamophobia/=/homophobia/=transphobia/

=/anti-immigrant sentiments/ (2019: 22). Trump did, however, construct rhetorically a "working-class" base for his hegemonic project, yet in Trumpian discourse this base was "white, straight, male, and Christian, based in mining, drilling, construction, and heavy industry." In this respect, the subject positions of the "working class" addressed by Trump were decidedly different from those entering the "broad and expansive" equivalential chain constructed by Sanders: /Rust Belt factory workers/=/public sector and service workers/=/women/=/immigrants/=/people of color/ (2019: 22). The hegemonic bloc envisaged by Sanders was to be constructed through a strategy of *progressive populism*: "He sought to join an inclusive politics of recognition with a pro-working-family politics of distribution: criminal-justice reform plus Medicare for all; reproductive justice plus free College tuition; LGBTQ+ rights plus breaking up the big banks" (2019: 23).

So far, both hegemonic projects failed, but they attest to the historical possibility of fostering a large anti-neoliberal consensus against the neoliberal politics of redistributing economic resources from the bottom to the top of the social ladder. Still, Fraser insists that only a progressive populism can be powerful enough to lead us out of the interregnum. Such populism should be premised, if it is to be successful, on an inclusive form of recognition that allows for the integration of more traditional sectors of the working class and the middle classes:

> Combining egalitarian redistribution with nonhierarchical recognition, this option has at least a fighting chance of uniting the whole working class. More than that, it could position that class, understood expansively, as the leading force in an alliance that also includes substantial segments of youth, the middle class, and the professional-managerial stratum. (2019: 30–1)

In turn, this would also imply that mainstream progressive positions need to be disarticulated from the neoliberal chain of equivalences. In Fraser's words: "less privileged women, immigrants, and people of color have to be wooed away from the lean-in feminists, the meritocratic antiracists and the mainstream LGBTQ+ movement, the corporate diversity and green-capitalism shills who hijacked their concerns, inflecting them in terms consistent with neoliberalism" (2019: 32). Equally, the traditional sectors of the working class need to be wooed away from reactionary populism and convinced that the latter will not be able to deliver. A counter-hegemonic bloc, as Fraser concludes, can only be built "by joining a robustly egalitarian politics of distribution to a substantively inclusive, class-sensitive politics of recognition" (2019: 39–40).

Chantal Mouffe, who shares with Fraser a Gramscian background, bases her plea for a left populism both on her previous work in *Hegemony and Socialist Strategy*, cowritten with Ernesto Laclau (Laclau and Mouffe, 1985), and on Laclau's theory of populism as developed in his *On Populist Reason* (2005). While in *Hegemony and Socialist Strategy*, a project of radical and plural democracy—consisting of a chain of equivalence between new social movements that would partially retain their autonomy without surrendering it to struggles over class—was commended in order to revive the left and construct a progressive hegemonic formation, a path followed by Mouffe in her subsequent work on radical democracy and agonistic pluralism (2013), her book *For a Left Populism* (2018) marks a certain shift in the argument. As her diagnosis goes, we are living through a "populist moment" where the old is dying and the new cannot be born due to a crisis of hegemony.[7] Democracy, in our historical conjuncture, can only be radicalized by means of a left populism through which a frontier is constructed between "the people" and "the oligarchy." Such a project was hardly visible in *Hegemony and Socialist Strategy* but clearly follows from Laclau's work on populism. Due to the post-foundational design of Mouffe's hegemony theory, the people, of course, is not something objectively given—it is not congruent with a particular segment or the whole of the population—but has to be constructed *as a people* through precisely such a strategy of populist antagonization. This does not imply that one should abandon the diverse struggles of the new social movements, but they are now to be reassembled in a populist mode, that is, they need to be inscribed into a larger chain of equivalence and rallied around the signifier of "the people" and democracy.

In what sense can Mouffe's populism be located on the Left of the political spectrum? Mouffe is very clear about the fact that populist forms of mobilization can take many different political directions, which is why one needs to leave behind a merely formal definition and *give content* to populism: "It needs to be qualified as a 'left' populism to indicate the values that this populism pursues" (2018: 6). These values are the democratic values of equality and popular sovereignty, as opposed to liberal values such as individual liberty, the separation of powers, and the rule of law. In the neoliberal era of "post-politics," an imbalance occurred between democracy and liberalism, as the two pillars of equality and popular sovereignty began to crumble. Interestingly, though, Mouffe does not want her preferred idea of a populist project—purportedly the only chance to revitalize democracy—to relinquish the liberal side of what she calls the "democratic paradox" (2000): "The democratic logic of constructing a people and defending egalitarian practices is necessary to define a demos and to subvert the tendency of liberal discourse to abstract universalism. But its articulation with liberal logic allows us to challenge the forms of exclusion that are inherent in the political practices of determining the people that will govern" (Mouffe, 2018: 15). A left populism, then, can be distinguished from a right-wing populism not by the mere fact that a people is constructed, but with respect to the way in which the people are constructed, and, equally important, how their political adversary is articulated:

> Right-wing populism claims that it will bring back popular sovereignty and restore democracy, but this sovereignty is understood as "national sovereignty" and reserved for those deemed to be true "nationals." [. . .] Left populism on the contrary wants to recover democracy to deepen and extend it. A left populist strategy aims at federating the democratic demands into a collective will to construct a "we," a "people" confronting a common adversary: the oligarchy. This requires the establishment of a chain of equivalence among the demands of the workers, the immigrants and the precarious middle class, as well as other democratic demands, such as those of the LGBT community. The objective of such a chain is the creation of a new hegemony that will permit the radicalization of democracy. (Mouffe, 2018: 23–4)

Fraser and Mouffe seem to agree on many points. They share the Gramscian framework of analysis, and they both plea for an expansive progressive populism that would not simply focus on an orthodox idea of the working class but integrate the demands of other sectors of the population. On a closer look, however, their ideas about a progressive left populism diverge. To begin with, while Donald Trump's "enemies" are more than obvious to anybody who has ever heard him speak, it is not entirely clear who "the enemy" is that would give coherence to Fraser's progressive-populist chain of equivalences. The candidate that comes closest to this role is "financialized capitalism," since Fraser holds that "a progressive-populist bloc must highlight the shared roots of class and status injustices in financialized capitalism" (2019: 35). While this may be true, it raises both theoretical and practical questions. In terms of day-to-day political struggle—and especially in comparison to reactionary forms of populism—"financialized capitalism" remains much too abstract. While many people are indeed critical of "capitalism," a sign of hegemony shifting, the signifier may still remain too vague and indeterminate to mobilize significant affective investment beyond the card-carrying left. And theoretically, it is debatable whether financialized capitalism should be conceived of, as Fraser argues, as "a single, integrated social totality." Progressive populists are supposed to raise awareness of that totality which supposedly "links the harms suffered by women, immigrants, people of color, and LGBTQ+ people to those experienced by the working-class" (2019: 36). With this idea of "financialized capitalism" constituting a "single, integrated social totality," Fraser seems to fall back into a rather simplistic version of economic theory. Mere cognitive awareness of shared objective conditions, if it is to be achieved at all, has rarely led people to enter into an alliance. And what, on a theoretical plane of argumentation, if capitalism, financialized or not, does *not* constitute a single, integrated totality? What if it is much more heterogeneous, much more precarious than we think? What if capitalism is only a name for the contingent confluence of multiple and incongruent practices? What if there is not one capitalism, and certainly not "finance capitalism" as the only game in town, but many? And what if capitalism, rather than infiltrating the totality of social relations, does have an outside where other modes of production persist? Fraser's residual economism may also be the cause for her rather unconvincing idea that it should be the working class that takes the lead in a hegemonic alliance. For sure, this will be an open-ended, expansive, and pluralistic working class. And while it is true that the new social movements in the age of progressive neoliberalism tended to outshine labor struggles, it would be theoretically unfounded and politically premature to assume that it can only be the signifier of the "working class" that can take up the role of the empty signifier that holds together a progressive populist alliance. Fraser tends to smuggle into the discourse on progressive-populism what Laclau had tried to disentangle from his earliest articles onwards: an economic definition of the working class which, in Fraser's case, still serves as a foundation for any political construction of the people.

While Fraser's progressive populism, hence, is more socialist than democratic in the strict sense, Mouffe's left populism is partially democratic, but at the same time exceedingly liberal. She insists, correctly I think, that it is the democratic imaginary that serves as the precondition for challenging relations of subordination and oppression.

Yet, the left populism she defends appears to be subordinated to the rules of the game of liberal democracy, redescribed by Mouffe as agonistic pluralism. What constitutes an *agon*, as a rule-based competition, is the fact that the opponent is considered a legitimate adversary (as long as she plays by the rules of the game) rather than an enemy to be destroyed, as in the case of antagonism. Despite its Greek roots, the agonistic model comes very close to the standard idea of politics in Western pluralist democracy. And left populism, as defined by Mouffe, is not supposed to break the rules of this game. It is unclear, however, how a pluralist view of liberal-democratic agonism can be compatible with the populist injunction to establish a single line of confrontation between the people and the power bloc. Would this not be a clear case of antagonism, rather than agonistic pluralism? What is more, the "outside" of a populist chain is much closer to the figure of an enemy that needs to be *politically* (not physically) destroyed than to the figure of an adversary that requires respect. What sense does populism make, if a "corrupted elite" to be fought is at the same time considered a perfectly respectable and legitimate adversary? And, to make a very blunt and certainly over-simplifying point, are not the rules of the liberal agonistic game not rules established and defended by those who have a vested interest in liberal democracy remaining stuck forever in the status quo? While Mouffe, of course, does acknowledge the ever-present possibility of antagonism in all politics, thus adhering to a dissociative (rather than an associative) view thereof, her understanding of *populist* politics strikes me as not dissociative enough. In Fraser, to conclude, a residual economism seems to predetermine the empty signifier that comes as the only true candidate for a progressive populism: the working class, with the enemy position filled, by virtue of an economic analysis, with "financialized capitalism" as a single, integrated totality. On the other hand, by Mouffe embedding left populism within agonistic pluralism, the political enemy is reduced to a legitimate adversary, as if corrupted elite rule could ever appear as legitimate and the rules of the game as impartial in populist discourse. Such an argument runs the danger of bereaving populism of its antagonistic edge—and, in which case, why then talk about populism?

Toward a Democratic Populism

The reasons for Mouffe's skepticism are clear, though. Should the democratic side of liberal democracy ever emancipate itself from its liberal side, then all dams may break and we could face the ultimate nightmare of all liberals: the "tyranny of the majority." But apart from simply defending the liberal side of liberal democracy to avoid popular tyranny (which is quite unlikely to occur any time soon, given the current balance of forces in Western democracies), we have another option: we can see whether resources are available within the *democratic* tradition that would allow for protecting minorities and individuals. Too easily the democratic tradition is often reduced, mostly by its enemies, to banal and uniform collectivism. Even for Marx, the free development of each is the condition for the free development of all. Liberalism has effectively managed to monopolize not only the idea of the individual but also many institutions, even if some, such as the rule of law and *Rechtsstaat*, are much older than liberalism itself—as if everything that is good and honorable was invented by liberals. Similarly, the ethico-political principle of freedom—located by Mouffe in the liberal camp—was historically perceived to be the defining principle of *democracy* long before liberalism existed (the Greek *eleutheria*), while, ironically, equality was not the most important slogan of nineteenth-century socialism (which were, in fact, solidarity and, again, freedom), because in the view of the time it was associated with the merely formal equality of liberal rule. So, the very principle of freedom was itself monopolized by liberalism (Dijn, 2020). What is more, the democratic revolution that invented the motto of freedom, equality, and fraternity, first proposed by Robespierre, did not envisage any trade-off or incompatibility between these components. They were seen as perfectly compatible within a democratic, Jacobin frame of reference. My point is simply that liberalism has largely managed to rewrite history and define our own frame of references, so that it becomes difficult for democratic theorists to think out of the liberal box. Hence, why should an anti-liberal populism that at the same time integrates, for instance, a defense of human rights be impossible? It simply depends on the concrete articulation and historical conjuncture. As Laclau reminds us regarding the Latin American case:

> In Latin America during the 1970s and 1980s, for instance, the defence of human rights was part of the popular demands and so part of the popular identity. It is a mistake to think that the democratic tradition, with its defence of the sovereignty of the "people," excludes liberal claims as a matter of principle. That could only mean that the "people's" identity is fixed once and for all. If, on the contrary, the identity of the "people" is established only through changing equivalential chains, there is no reason to think that a populism which includes human rights as one of its components is a priori excluded. At some points in time — as happens today quite frequently in the international scene—defence of human rights and civil liberties can become the most pressing popular demands. (Laclau, 2005: 171)

Let us add to this that human rights do not have an exclusively liberal history either. Already, at the moment of their invention, they come with either a "liberal" spin, for example, the declaration of 1789, or a democratic spin, as in the Jacobin version of 1793 (Tomba, 2019). It should therefore be possible to find within the democratic revolution the resources that may allow for developing a democratic *ethics of self-interrogation* that is not simply liberal. Claude Lefort's account of the democratic revolution can be read, as Laclau sometimes does, as a liberal redescription of democracy's founding moments, but it can also be read as an account of the self-reflexive and self-critical dimension *intrinsic* to democracy (Lefort, 1988). In this reading, democracy is not domesticated by its outside enemy, liberalism, but, rather, by the way in which its own ungroundable nature is registered within democracy itself. Modern liberalism, then, only grafts itself onto a democratic horizon that is neither closed nor grounded. As Ernesto Laclau has argued in the footsteps of Lefort: "A democratic society is not one in which the 'best' content dominates unchallenged but, rather, one in which nothing is definitely acquired and there is always the possibility of challenge. [. . .] There is democracy only if there is the recognition of the positive value of a dislocated identity" (1996: 100).

Democracy, in other words, puts a demand on us to abandon our phantasmatic beliefs in fully fledged identities, including the phantasy of a fully established positivity of the people. The logic of democracy then runs counter to the prevalent ideas of a technocratic administration of the status quo or, at the other end of the scale, to identitarian versions of populism. The same will apply a fortiori to any politics of *radical* democracy, if by the latter we understand the political project of deepening and expanding democratic revolution, that is, of democratizing democracy. A radical democratic populism does require us to recognize the emptiness of the place of power, the impossibility of absolute and limitless sovereignty, and the unavoidable recurrence of social conflict: in short, the self-alienated nature of the democratic order. No doubt, such an ethics of democratic self-alienation stands in an antinomic relation to an antagonistic politics of self-assertion, but this democratic ethics has its roots not in liberalism, but in the democratic revolution which, at the same time, gave birth to antagonistic politics and, thus, to populism. A radical democratic populism would accept, or even affirm, the impossible nature of the people without renouncing the claim for popular sovereignty. It would be based on an inclusive rather than exclusive outlook and would accept the heterogeneous nature of the people—heterogeneous precisely because of its unfounded and unfoundable nature. Yet at the same time a radical democratic populism would seek to politically establish what democracy is about: the rule of the people, even if the people—and Mouffe is entirely right on this point—needs to be constructed through populist articulation. There is no easy way out of the antinomy between the ethical and the political. Liberal anti-populism is as political as right-wing populism; and, from a democratic perspective, it is equally unethical.

Notes

1. On anti-populism see Ostiguy (2009), Stavrakakis (2017; 2020), Markou (2021). For an overview see Moffit (2018).
2. While there is currently much talk about a return of the State during the pandemic and a "great recoil" (Gerbaudo, 2021), optimism would be premature. It is likely that neoliberalism will adapt by following a double strategy of transformism and authoritarianism.
3. In view of the denunciatory treatment of left-wing parties that in the last decade have emerged from social protest movements—or of left-wing populist currents in older parties—one could almost believe that anti-populism has inherited the ideological tradition of Cold War anti-communism.
4. On populism and nationalism see De Cleen and Stavrakakis (2017)
5. From the course of my argument, however, it will become clear that liberal anti-populism, which condemns any political alternative to the neoliberal status quo and, in its current phase, transforms itself into populism, acts no less anti-pluralistically.
6. That a part of the power bloc seemingly turns against this very power bloc from within it is, as studied by Stuart Hall on Thatcherism, a typical feature of what Hall called "authoritarian populism" (Hall, 1988). This leaves us, in the peculiar case of Macron, with a case of liberal "authoritarian populism."

7 The populist moment is defined by Mouffe as follows: "We can speak of a 'populist moment' under the pressure of political or socioeconomic transformations, the dominant hegemony is being destabilized by the multiplication of unsatisfied demands. In such situations, the existing institutions fail to secure the allegiance of the people as they attempt to defend the existing order. As a result, the historical bloc that provides the social basis of a hegemonic formation is being disarticulated and the possibility arises of constructing a new subject of collective action—the people—capable of reconfiguring a social order experienced as unjust" (2018: 11).

Bibliography

Boltanski L and Chiapello É (2005) *The New Spirit of Capitalism*. London and New York: Verso.
Canovan M (1999) Trust the People! Populism and the Two Faces of Democracy. *Political Studies* XLVII: 2–16.
De Cleen B and Stavrakakis Y (2017) Distinctions and Articulations: A Discourse Theoretical Framework for the Study of Populism and Nationalism. *Javnost – The Public* 4(24): 301–19.
Dijn A de (2020) *Freedom. An Unruly History*. Cambridge, MA: Harvard University Press.
Frank T (2020) *The People, NO. A Brief History of Anti-Populism*. New York: Metropolitan Books.
Fraser N (2019) *The Old Is Dying and the New Cannot Be Born*. London: Verso.
Gerbaudo P (2021) *The Great Recoil. Politics after Populism and Pandemic*. London: Verso.
Hall S (1988) *The Hard Road to Renewal. Thatcherism and the Crisis of the Left*. London: Verso.
Laclau E (1996) *Emancipation(s)*. London: Verso.
Laclau E (2005) *On Populist Reason*. London: Verso.
Laclau E and Mouffe C (1985) *Hegemony and Socialist Strategy*. London: Verso.
Lefort C (1988) *Democracy and Political Theory*. Minneapolis: University of Minnesota Press.
Marchart O (2013) *Die Prekarisierungsgesellschaft. Prekäre Proteste. Politik und Ökonomie im Zeichen der Prekarisierung*. Bielefeld: transcript.
Marchart O (2018) *Thinking Antagonism. Political Ontology after Laclau*. Edinburgh: Edinburgh University Press.
Markou G (2021) Anti-Populist Discourse in Greece and Argentina in the 21st Century. *Journal of Political Ideologies* 26(2): 201–19.
Moffit B (2018) The Populism/Anti-Populism Divide in Western Europe. *Democratic Theory* 5(2): 1–16.
Mouffe C (2013) *Agonistics. Thinking the World Politically*. London: Verso.
Mouffe C (2018) *For a Left Populism*. London: Verso.
Mouffe C (2000) *The Democratic Paradox*. London: Verso.
Mounk Y (2018) *The People vs. Democracy: Why Our Freedom Is in Danger and How to Save it*. Cambridge, MA: Harvard University Press.
Mudde C (2004) The Populist Zeitgeist. *Government & Opposition* 3: 541–63.
Mudde C (2015) Conclusion. Some Further Thoughts on Populism. In: C de la Torre (ed.), *The Promise and Perils of Populism. Global Perspectives*. Lexington, KY: The University Press of Kentucky, 431–52.

Ostiguy P (2009) The High-Low Divide. Rethinking Populism and Anti-Populism. In: *Political Concepts*. Committee on Concepts and Methods Working Paper Series. Instuto de Ciencia Política, Universidad Católica de Chile.

Stavrakakis Y (2016) Die Rückkehr des "Volkes": Populismus und Anti-Populismus im Schatten der europäischen Krise. In: A Agridopoulos and I Papagiannopoulos (eds.), *Griechenland im europäischen Kontext. Krise und Krisendiskurse*. Wiesbaden: Springer, 109-37.

Stavrakakis, Y (2017) How did "populism" become a Pejorative Concept? And Why is This Important Today? A Genealogy of Double Hermeneutics. *Populism Working Papers No.6*.

Stavrakakis Y (2020) Krise, Linkspopulismus und Antipopulismus in Griechenland. SYRIZA von der Opposition zur Macht und zurück. In: S Kim and A Agridopoulos (eds.), *Populismus, Diskurs Staat*. Baden Baden: Nomos, 51–78.

Streeck W (2017) Die Wiederkehr der Verdrängten als Anfang vom Ende des neoliberalen Kapitalismus. In: H Geiselberger (ed.), *Die große Regression. Eine internationale Debatte über die geistige Situation der Zeit*. Frankfurt/Main: Suhrkamp, 253–74.

Tomba M (2019) *Insurgent Universality. An Alternative Legacy of Modernity*. Oxford: Oxford University Press.

3

Logics of Democracy in the Work of Ernesto Laclau and Jacques Rancière

Mark Devenney and Clare Woodford

Ernesto Laclau and Jacques Rancière both inspire contemporary radical democratic thought and politics. Yet, despite sharing a strikingly similar intellectual heritage, they never engaged in any prolonged debate about their respective accounts.[1] Instead, their projects have long been interpreted by others—and even by Laclau himself in *On Populist Reason*—to be broadly similar though divergent in the smaller details. In this chapter, we read them together to trace the intersections between them rather differently, but also productively for thinking the people and the project of radical democracy today.

We first demonstrate that Laclau and Rancière's projects are distinct. Where Laclau focuses on political strategy, building movements and parties, and taking power, Rancière's focus is on how changes in our everyday ways of life alter our perceptions of the possible. Despite these differences, there are points of intersection. In order to map these, we situate their works in a wider context. Their works replay a key division that has plagued the left since its inception—whether to focus on strategies for taking power or on enacting equality in the way we live here and now. Each tradition mobilizes the left's commitment to equality differently. We track the intersections between Rancière's and Laclau's works across three key differences: equality, ontology, and radical democracy. We contend that Laclau's work poses questions for Rancière and Rancière's for Laclau in ways that complement rather than undermine their respective projects. Rather than resolve the differences, our approach recognizes in them an irreconcilable but productive tension for a democratic politics of equality. As Rancière himself notes, despite the perpetual need to keep our perceptual horizons open, we can only ever live in police orders (2011). Critics thus demand a focus on the workings of police orders (see Norval, 2007; Davis, 2010; Bosteels, 2009; Citton, 2009: 139; Dillon, 2003) rather than on so-called radical moments of rupture. We suggest instead that such disagreement demonstrates a need for politics to avoid confusing instrumental actions with democratic enactment but to attend to both tasks *together*: the institutionalization of orders alongside moments of break and change, with neither eclipsing the other. We conclude by summarizing how this juxtaposition brings into focus tasks needed to build a radical (populist in Laclau's sense) democratic politics of the left.

The chapter begins with their different interpretations of equality. We demonstrate that their accounts of what counts as political stem from this disagreement and note the consequences for political action. Second, we analyze the place of ontology in these accounts. A persistent critique of Rancière (see Laclau, 2005; Badiou, 2006; Žižek, 2008: 199–288) holds that he presupposes an unacknowledged ontology. We test this argument against Laclau's reliance on an ontology of lack, an ontology definitive of the political in his reading. With Rancière, we argue that this ontology limits a politics of equality. Last, we focus on their respective understandings of radical politics. We agree with Rancière that equality should not be equated with any regime, even those labeled democratic. However, Laclau is right to insist that radical democratic politics requires forms of institution and order designed to realize a politics of equality. We conclude by detailing a politics that begins to rethink the relationships between states, parties, people, and democracy.

The Politics of Equality

The starting premise for any politics of the left is equality. However, what this means in practice has always been in dispute. The hegemonic Marxist left of the twentieth century viewed equality as a substantive promise that would be realized in time. An insistent alternative—both in theory and in practice—demands that we enact equality here and now, rather than strategize for its future realization. The strategic approach delays equality to a future date. The discordant history of the left always concerned this contretemps between the deferral and the enactment of equality. Laclau and Rancière are contemporary proponents of these different approaches. For Laclau hegemony concerns the strategic articulation of oppositional politics through parties, organizational forms, and planning—requiring that equality is delayed for strategic reasons and becomes a project to be realized through radical democratic institutionalization. In contrast, rather than thinking of the strategic articulation of a better regime, Rancière insists on the immediate enactment of the equal capacity of all. Laclau characterizes this account of equality as dangerously idealistic, since Rancière refuses to actively think of an alternative political order. He writes that Rancière "identifies the possibility of politics too much [. . .] with the possibility of emancipatory politics" (Laclau, 2005: 246). He does not recognize that the uncounted could construct their uncountability in a fascist direction (Laclau, 2005: 246) and may not enact equality at all. However, this is a misreading of the place of equality in Rancière's work. Rancière does not see equality as substantive. Rather, equality is a presupposition enacted by those who do not accept the place assigned to them within any social order. Politics takes place when equality is enacted against police orders—but subjects often act in ways that confirm, and conform with, a dominant distribution of the sensible.

Rancière (perhaps rather too mysteriously for many readers) insists that politics is the moment that the part that has no part becomes the demos. An excluded minority asserts that they are in no way substantively different from the whole of society—from the rest. Laclau agrees that this asymmetry is at the root of popular action (2005: 93).

Populism plays on the double meaning of *populus* in Latin, referring both to the entire community and the poor, the *plebs* excluded from much of social life.

To understand how this works for Laclau, recall that he theorizes populist politics as the articulation of populist unity from multiple demands. Although demands (e.g., for electricity, or the vote, or for higher wages) may not have anything in common, they share the fact that demands are made to the hegemonic order, to the state. If unmet, this shared failure of the governing powers unites different demands in opposition to a regime. A successful populist movement articulates such demands into a precarious "chain of equivalence." In order to build this chain into a movement, one key demand associated with the movement functions as an "empty signifier" that symbolically represents the chain—equality is an example that Laclau often invokes.

In a populist politics, the people presents its collected demands not as those of a particular disadvantaged group (the *plebs*) but as the demands of everyone (the *populus*). Populist politics arises when social demands are unmet and coalesce into an oppositional movement against "the [elites] who are responsible" for failing to respond to demands and who "cannot be a legitimate part of the community" (Laclau, 2005: 86). Laclau argues that the *plebs* present themselves as the only legitimate *populus*. In this hegemonic moment the universal and particular fuse—what were initially particular demands come to be seen as unified demands, the particular is linked to a universality that it can never fully incarnate (Laclau, 2005: 226).

Laclau's reading of Rancière subtly reformulates the moment of politics. This is not as with Rancière when the part with no part "identifies its name [. . .] with the name of the community itself" (1999: 8–9). Rather, it is when the plebs "claim [. . .] to be the only legitimate populus" (Laclau, 2005: 81). This reformulation is in fact rather more significant than Laclau allows.

Rancière emphasizes that any such moment demonstrates the "miscount" of democracy (1999: 8). Any regime necessarily allots places, names, and distinctions to subjects. Politics demonstrates the contradiction between this order and democracy as the simple equality of all, in the sense that no substantive difference is recognized between people. For Rancière this is not one group with a given identity acting as the stand-in for the whole of society. Rather, the differentials between groups are shown to be contingent. In that moment all that can be perceived is the lack of criteria with which to distinguish between people—not rather a new criterion that supplants the old.

In his examples, Rancière insists that such a moment occurs when those unrecognized as political—such as the plebs of the Aventine hill, Blanqui's proletarians of nineteenth-century France, and segregated groups in 1960s United States—suddenly appear not as equal to other groups because of some substantive identity but as no different from the rest. At that point criteria used to exclude and categorize people no longer function.

The plebs cannot remain the plebs and simply claim to be the *populus*. Such a claim does not enact a miscount. Rather it enacts a recount, but the parts remain intact. For it to be a miscount, the dominant understanding of *plebs qua plebs* has to be dissolved such that there are no conceptual means to distinguish any "proper" people from the rest, from "the indistinct mass of men" (Rancière, 1999: 9). The plebs have to not just *represent* the *populus*, but to be no longer distinguishable from the populus (this is not the same as *essentially* being the *populus*). The dissolution of any criteria to distinguish those who rule enacts the equality of the *demos* (for Rancière), or *populus* (for Laclau), of all people, without distinction. For Rancière, all politics emerges from playing off this definition against any attempt to define the people or *demos* as a particular group. It emerges as a challenge to *any* attempted ordering of the people. He writes:

> the people appropriate the common quality as their own. What they bring to the community strictly speaking is contention. (Rancière, 1999: 8–9)

This is an apophantic politics with no requirement for justification. In fact it is the lack of justification and the disintegration of the justifications that have been given in the past, that is the point: "The people are nothing more than . . . those who have no positive qualification—no wealth, no virtue—but who are nonetheless acknowledged to enjoy the same freedom as those who do" (Rancière, 1999: 8). Equality is axiomatic rather than substantive. It is the equality of those who do not accept the place assigned to them within a police or a hegemonic order.

Laclau misses this detail in his overinterpretation of Rancière's assertion that the demos emerges from the "freedom of the people" (1999: 8–11). He reads this freedom as a shared "attribute," the only common feature of the part that has no part (Laclau, 2005: 245). For Rancière, the freedom of the people is not a "positive property" nor is it "proper to the demos" (1999: 8). It emerges *in spite* of the people not having any "shared attribute" or "communitarian function" (Laclau, 2005: 245). It is a freedom in opposition to property and properties (see Devenney, 2020; Devenney and Woodford, forthcoming). Rancière understands politics as the enactment of equality. This can never be fascist. It challenges all social orders that require partition, division, and distinctions between people, places, and roles. It rejects the allotment of all to appropriate ways of being, doing, and saying. Laclau assumes that freedom is a positive attribute because he reads Rancière's demos as a "part that functions simultaneously as the whole" (Laclau, 2005: 245). As we have argued, this misreading means that Laclau cannot imagine a politics without hegemonic ordering of parts to their appropriate place, and thus misses the axiomatic logic of democratic equality that is distinct from populist reason. Rancière's is not a theory of representation but a rupture of our everyday order.

This everyday order, referred to by Rancière as the "order of domination" (1999: 12), "police order" (1999: 28) or later, the distribution or "partage" of the sensible, is what Gramsci termed the order of "common sense" to delineate the set of accepted ideas and practices which are hegemonic. Indeed, for Rancière, any hegemonic order attempts (and always fails) to discipline subjects, partition, and then allot a place and a name to all parts. It is with regard to order that the distinctions between Laclau's and Rancière's projects become most stark. Laclau's concern is how to articulate and enact a counter-hegemonic order. Rancière has little interest in accounting for how such orders are built or maintained. He recognizes that there are worse and better police orders but insists that regimes are not equivalent to democratic practices (Rancière, 1999: 31). Rancière does begin to outline how we might distinguish these orders, but this is not his primary interest (2006: 72–3). Instead, the success of a police order in no way entails that it is natural or legitimate—although to ensure their own stability we might assume that they will operate as if there is no contingency. Rancière's concern is not to establish a counter-hegemonic police order. Rather, he focuses on the moment of politics when a break with police order takes place, a moment when equality is taken and ruptures common sense.

The point is not that scandalous democratic practices of equality are antipathetic to a new counter-hegemonic regime as detailed by Laclau. Rather, Rancière's focus is on how these moments of equality break, albeit momentarily, with common sense. Alternatives that seemed impossible become possibilities. Any new common sense that arises from such a moment will have its own problems. Rancière's concern is not with "[t]aking over power" which he surprisingly suggests "is not such a big problem" (1999: 118). The issue is how any power can be broken with and protected from its own hegemonizing impulses. Laclau's theory of the "political" focuses on the hegemonic articulation of an alternative common sense against the existing hegemony. For Laclau a radical democratic politics would have at its center practices of equal liberty that are inclusive, enact equality, and foster participation. Yet Laclau, unlike Rancière, will insist that any radical democratic politics requires exclusion and antagonistic frontiers. There is no way to resolve this difference—and it would be foolish to propose a queasy compromise that would paper over the differences. We can, however, acknowledge that in political struggles for equality, the strategic questions Laclau poses will come to the fore. There is no way to extend equality without addressing these strategic questions. Simultaneously, we accept Rancière's insistence that equality cannot be institutionalized or disciplined—that all orders will face challenges in the name of a democracy they cannot police.

Laclau's account of hegemony, which is part of a longer left-wing tradition, insists on the strategic articulation of oppositional politics through parties, organizational forms, and planning. This will aim to bring about a society in which equality is instantiated in the face of their radical contingency. Rancière too accepts that any form of ordering is contingent. However, rather than strategizing the building of a better regime, Rancière equates this contingency with equality. It opens the opportunity to enact an equality that is possessed by no one.

Both authors agree then that the articulation of a counter-hegemonic politics demands a shift in the ruling logics of a social order. If Laclau too quickly equates equality with radical democratic order, potentially missing the opportunity for more radical change, Rancière too quickly dismisses strategic questions from his account of the relationship between police orders and politics. For Laclau, hegemonic stability is ensured as long as an extant order is organized in terms of a *logic of difference*. Demands are resolved one at a time without being articulated as equivalent or oppositional (Laclau, 2005: 125–8). However, when multiple demands fail to be met, they are articulated in opposition to an existing regime. Remember that the role of equivalence here is that of a negative shared attribute—all the claims are unmet, not because they share any underlying positive feature. In these cases a chain of equivalential (unmet) demands can be used to form an antagonistic frontier pitting the people against the regime. This is what Laclau refers to as a "populist movement."

Such populist movements aim to take power, establish a new common sense, and reorder the social in such a way that equality and liberty are enacted by a democratic regime. They are organized according to a *logic of equivalence*: "the rules or grammars of a practice as well as the conditions which make the practice both possible and vulnerable" (Glynos and Howarth, 2007: 136). These logics of equivalence and difference are political: they concern the institution and de-institution of social relations and help to detail how established social practices can always be subject to challenge.

Our discussion here suggests that the logic of equivalence differs from the logic of equality central to Rancière's work. For Rancière neither the logic of difference nor the logic of equivalence is political. They are police logics which accord with one of two ways in which a social order might give an account of itself. Indeed in *Disagreement* Rancière describes an arithmetic order that fragments the people into unrelated units and a geometric order that incorporates all as part of a wider whole (1999: 1-20). Both of these logics have an *arche* (equivalence or difference). They are both opposed to politics for each describes a way in which the social order can be instituted and challenged. Rancière adds a third logic, that of equality. This logic is strictly political. It undermines all other logics. Crucially, equality is not equivalence—it does not assume that differences can be reduced to an overarching geometric logic. Nor is equality about the equal worth of different units. Instead, it is a presumption put to work against the logics of any order, all of which will always rely on domination. It may seem that at this point we have simply sided with Rancière. In fact, Laclau too conceptualizes this logic—but does so in terms of a fundamental contingency that is the condition of possibility and impossibility for any political order. Contingency, like equality, has no *arche*. The difference then is simple—for Laclau contingency is not in itself akin to equality. For Rancière, it is the place of equality. What we propose then is that a radical democratic politics must recognize this third logic—that Laclau's account requires this third logic. If hegemonic orders always require some form of articulation between the arithmetic and the geometric, radical democratic equality as a logic cannot be reduced to either of these orders. Contingent equality opens up a new way to consider the politics of radical democracy proposed by Laclau.

All orders then ascribe to people and things their proper place. The logic of equality is oppositional. It is the irregular logic of emancipation that loosens without reordering. It unsettles ordained distinctions playing instead on the emptiness of the non-place and the no-name. Such axiomatic equality is only possible because of an underlying contingency. It is this contingency that equality as axiomatic exploits. It is "the logic that disrupts this harmony through the mere fact of achieving the contingency of equality" (Rancière, 1999: 21-42). Unlike Laclau's logic of equivalence, the logic of equality is not an equivalence rooted in contingency—it is contingency itself. Rancière does not claim that any political or ethical necessity arises from the fact of contingency. In that moment of rupture the people *are* rendered equal. Yet Rancière gives little sense as to the relation between different police orders and equality. One might think that all police orders are equivalent in failing to appreciate this contingent equality. Laclau's focus on radical democracy and hegemony details how we might organize a society in which the emergence of such contingency is more likely. This was at the center of the radical democratic politics of *Hegemony and Socialist Strategy*.

Rancière's politics enacts equality for all, even the antagonists, in a hegemonic struggle. Rancière is not concerned then to strategize the symbolic framing of political order—what Laclau views as the groundless ground of the political. Instead, politics takes place when the contingency of such orders is foregrounded through the staging of equality. Laclau reinscribes equality in his account of hegemonic politics. In reinscribing and potentially neutralizing the logic of democratic equality within any hegemonic order, Laclau confuses one inscription of alternative politics from the logic of equality. But, Laclau is right. There is no way to extend equality beyond its contingent eruption if we do not begin to conceptualize a radical democratic politics that can become hegemonic.

Before we turn to consider Laclau's account of ontology, let us summarize the different projects outlined in this section. First, for Rancière, politics is not equivalent to a regime and to the gathering of people together either in terms of birth or of wealth. It occurs as an exception to the normal order of things. Politics is not exceptional or rare in temporal terms as certain critics mistakenly assume (see Rancière, 2009: 114–23; and a recent clarification in Rancière, Jeanpierre and Zabunyan, 2016). Rather, politics occurs as an exception to the norm and to the conventional forms of police order. It involves the inscription of that which is unaccounted for against police orders, which partition the sensible and structure the field of the visible and the invisible, the audible and the inaudible, what is recognized as having sense, against what cannot even be seen. Police orders prescribe our normal ways of being, doing, and saying (Rancière, 1999: 29). They are equivalent to what Laclau terms a hegemonic order. If the police order maintains the sphere of circulation as it already exists, political in(ter)vention reconfigures space, the visible, the sayable, and the sensible.

For Laclau equality is one aim of a radical democratic politics. Laclau's understanding of the political coheres around how political movements can create fertile conditions for the enactment of such equality. If Rancière's notion of equality is a necessary corrective against the authority claimed by parties, leaders, and movements, it is also essential (as Laclau argues) that radical democratic movements extend equality through forms of institutionalization that will police the limits of equality. There is no way beyond this disjunctive synthesis that embeds contingent equality in any radical democratic politics.

Ontology and Identification

Rancière irritates those who insist that he harbors an unacknowledged ontology (Badiou, 2006; Žižek, 2008: 199–288). Indeed, the assumption that his work is ontological is behind Laclau's argument that the demos identifies with the whole of the community as the part that has no part in terms of representation (2005: 94). For Laclau, because society is an impossible object, hegemony is the battle between particularities to occupy the empty place of the universal. Laclau contends that this structural impossibility must find some means of representation. In hegemonic struggles a particular signifier comes to represent the system itself, but the outcome of such struggles is always contingent. For Laclau, although equality may emerge in some struggles as an empty signifier, this is the result of a hegemonic struggle and cannot be guaranteed in advance. Equality is an achievement that cannot be presupposed.

In contrast, for Rancière freedom and equality do not require or imply a struggle to hegemonically occupy the place of the universal. Representation is not an issue for Rancière. It is unrepresentability—the impossibility of inscription in the current order of things—that is the strength of any emergent movement. The freedom of the demos exists *despite* not being representable. The enactment of equality in the name of the demos, the demonstration of the contingency of all order, puts any ordering of a people (the people as "ethnos, with shared attributes or common functions") into question (Rancière, 2011: 5). Acts of equality are contingent and depend on specific interventions in particular circumstances—the modes of verification for equality cannot be predetermined by a political ontology, even a negative one. Rancière's response to theorists who invoke ontology to found, if not to ground, their politics is pointed:

> I think it is necessary to set aside any original determination of difference, excess, or dissensus. [. . .] I do not ground political dissensus in an excess of Being which would make any count impossible [. . .] the demos does not embody the excess of Being. (Rancière, 2011: 12)

Laclau equates the political with the impossibility of "Being" and the struggle to represent the impossible universality of the community. Indeed, Laclau and Mouffe argued that societies are constituted "as a repression of the consciousness of this impossibility that penetrates them" (2001: 127). Hegemony is the momentum for perpetually repressing this impossibility, and while this allows the possibility of counter-hegemony, they do not envisage that hegemony itself may too be contingent rather than ontologically given (which means that we have to fight for it rather than assuming it will occur). Laclau conceptualizes politics in terms of competing hegemonic attempts to fix the infinite play of signification, rather than as an extension of this play. Rancière helps us see that any attempts to fix are forms of discipline and domination that will always be opposed to the ruptural emergence of politics. Rancière too denies that we do ever move beyond police orderings (2011: 5). However, in refusing to give his claim ontological status it remains simply descriptive. It is not that living beyond order could never be the case, simply that it has not been the case in all the examples we have available to us.

Laclau further argues that Rancière's axiomatic approach to equality hinders the fight against oppression because it is too closely allied with a sociological account of class. He suggests that Rancière develops an incomplete account of "the incipient movement, in Gramsci, from 'classes' to 'collective wills'" relying in the last instance on a sociological rather than an ontological account of politics and the political (Laclau, 2005: 249). In contrast, Laclau's ontological account of the social as comprised by antagonism asserts that identifications are formed in and through the hegemonic struggle over what the social is. Initially, isolated demands are united into a chain of equivalence under a shared empty signifier. This requires the formation of "an identity that does not precede but results from the process of representation" (Laclau, 2005: 161). The group that comes together to form the counter-hegemonic frontier can thus no longer be assumed to be defined by a pre-given fixed sociological identity such as class. Instead, every struggle constitutes the contending group anew within the limits of a sedimented order, so while it may at one time unite people together under the auspices of a working-class identification, it may at other times constitute trade unionists alongside feminists, gay rights activists, environmentalists, and peasants. This means that for Laclau, the identifications that comprise populist politics are articulated in struggle rather than given in advance (Laclau, 2005: 159).

Consequently, hegemonic politics is not just a matter of pledging political allegiance to a preexisting camp but a more radical, affective investment on the part of subjects engaged in an alternative hegemonic project. Here Laclau follows Freud insisting that signification is intimately tied to the affective dimension:

[A]ffect is not something that exists alone independent of language; it constitutes itself only through the differential cathexes of signifying chains. This is exactly what investment means [...] the complexes which we call discursive or hegemonic formations [...] would be unintelligible without the affective component. (2005: 111)

Note the stages that link affective identifications with ontology: a structural void is read in ontological terms as a lack of being. The structural void determines a lack in all identity, which demands repeated identifications in the articulation of counter-hegemonic projects. These objects of identification (empty signifiers) function in the manner of Lacan's account of the *objet petit a*: they are impossible objects of identification, which nonetheless make identification possible although never permanent.

Rancière too refuses a sociological account of class. Rather, class signifies the wrong of political regimes which are unequal (Rancière, 1999: 8–11). Yet their reasoning differs. For Laclau, we have seen that any sociological accounting is not political because it falsely limits identities to a given antagonism, namely, class. For Rancière it is not political because politics does not emerge from identifications *at all* not even looser ones, but from dis-identification. It does not matter what category is initially problematic (class, part, race, sex) for in the moment of dis-identification *any* partition into labels and names dissolves.

For Rancière, the moment of politics is about dis-identification with one's allotted place rather than identification with an alternative hegemonic formation. His theorization of dis-identification as a moment of dislocation that is not yet a relocation draws attention to the way in which politics *disrupts* without *necessarily* indicating any direction for the resolution of this disruption. Laclau's ontological reading of contingency overemphasizes the necessity of identification with "the emergence of a new [counter-hegemonic] order" (2005: 228). He proposes new forms of affective investment and identification which limit the potential social change that emerges from politics. This is a slightly different point from the one we noted earlier. We accept that social orders can instantiate equality and make space for a disruptive politics of equality in different ways. However, we reject the ontological reduction that confuses contingency with the impossibility of an ontological grounding of the social. The groundless ground of any social order does not demand or indeed require a politics of identification. In fact, it opens a range of possibilities that may not require the establishment of hegemonic forms of political order. Laclau's implicit philosophical anarchism is too quickly disciplined into a call for political ordering—but this theoretical articulation is not necessary.

There is a further and important detail in the divergence between Laclau and Rancière regarding disagreement and antagonism. In their seminal text *Hegemony and Socialist Strategy* Laclau and Mouffe argue that political antagonism is not predetermined by class position. They rethink antagonism as the limit of social objectivity, rather than as the inevitable outcome of a clash between predefined classes. In Marxist theory antagonism had been conceptualized either in terms of real opposition or in terms of logical opposition. Real opposition occurs in the natural world. In a physical collision, for example, one or both objects may be destroyed. However, such collisions are not inherently antagonistic.[2] Logical contradiction, in turn, is conceptual according to Laclau (Laclau and Mouffe, 2001: 124). In the cases of both logical and real oppositions the identity of the constituent units is presupposed. What the objects already are, conceptual or real objects, is not put into question. In antagonistic struggle the authors contend that the very "being of the antagonists" is at stake. The subjects and objects at stake are themselves modified in the dispute, and what they are assumed to be can no longer be taken for granted. Antagonistic struggles take place in the context of a set of relations, where what is crucial to the identity of subjects and objects is the relational complex within which they have a place.

Antagonism does have a place in Rancière's work. However, it does not emerge from a desire for a fullness that we lack. It does not require identification or affective ties of identification. We have seen already that politics takes place when dominant ways of being, doing, and saying are appropriated and a new political subject emerges (always referred to as subjectivation for Rancière). This entails dis-identification with allotted ways of being. At the core of this account of politics is Rancière's notion of disagreement. Disagreement is in many respects similar to Laclau's notion of antagonism, but there are important conceptual differences. Rancière develops the notion of disagreement in the context of what might be termed a retreat of the political, and its deliberate delimitation to particular spheres—"its limitation to the realm of discursive public justification for the state" (1999: viii) and thus consensus. Disagreement is not about misunderstanding—this can be corrected through clarification of the subject or object which causes the disagreement. Nor is it about the misconstrual of words—which might be clarified through "language medicine" (Rancière, 1999: x–xi). Rather it occurs when there is a contention over speaking—when, for example, the words of one speaker are not recognized as words, or when a speaker is deemed incapable of speaking or understanding. In these cases there can be no common object shared between interlocutors. The scandal is that disagreement, like antagonism, cannot finally be resolved. We cannot presuppose a moment of perfect communication between rational subjects, nor a perfect language, which is transparent to all. Disagreement is the very site of politics. Political theorists, Rancière contends, mask this ineradicable disagreement and in doing so police the domain of politics. Policing limits equality and freedom, restricting them to their proper domain.

This sounds in many respects similar to Laclau's writing about antagonism and hegemony. A hegemonic order does its best to appear harmonious, to appear inclusive, and to not rely on antagonistic exclusions. Yet once again the divergence over ontology is here pertinent. Disagreement for Rancière is not linked to an ontology of the political—it is politics itself, the site of a dispute over the equality of all. For Rancière, politics enacts the presupposition of equality in the context of police orders that throughout history order the social world unequally. The institution of disagreement is in Rancière's words a "reasonable-unreasonable idea, which disrupts the ascription of identities, of appropriate spaces, of whose speech can be recognised" (1999: 124). Politics as disagreement stages conflict that goes all the way down, over the subjects, objects, and the places of politics.

Perhaps the key difference between these theorists concerns ontology. As we have noted, Rancière rejects the ontological rendering of antagonism, thinking of a politics of disagreement that upends accepted hierarchy. We accept this critique of the politics of ontology but note that Laclau does not in fact need an ontology. Antagonism indicates the impossibility of any police order finally displacing politics. However, there is no need to render such contingency in ontological terms. Such a reading disciplines politics—and potentially undermines the radical democratic commitments central to Laclau.

Radical Democracy

For Rancière the lack of an *arche*, the absence of any entitlement to rule (2007: 64, 1999: 15), always undermines any particular distribution of the sensible. The demos is not proper to rule and represents the mere rule of chance. Importantly, equality is not equivalent to the institutionalization of a new radical democratic order. Rather it is disruptive of any order. The verification of equality is a democratic assertion *against* police or hegemonic orders. Such orders cannot see, hear, or understand the part that has no part: "Policing is not so much the 'disciplining' of bodies as a rule governing their appearing" (Rancière, 1999: 29). Politics is in contrast the appearance of that which has no part.

For Laclau democracy is a particular type of regime rather than the enactment of equality in contexts that may have nothing to do with a particular regime. At one point in *On Populist Reason* Laclau suggests that populist movements may be democratic but need not be liberal. As a regime, however, "democracy [. . .] is [. . .] an order, in which the logic of difference prevails, and demands are addressed separately and so remain in isolation" (Laclau, 2005: 74, 77). Such regimes share a set of common features. First, they aim to institutionalize equality and conflict. Second, and following Lefort, in a democracy "there is a fundamental indeterminacy as to the basis of power, law and knowledge" (Laclau, 2005: 164). Third, democracy is not simply about competition over the empty place of power. Rather it concerns the very struggle to institutionalize an order in which power may be competed over. Fourth, Laclau argues that the link between liberalism and democracy is contingent, rather than natural, and as a consequence popular democratic subjects may be articulated in a number of different ways. There are a "plurality of frameworks which make the emergence of a people possible" (Laclau, 2005: 167). Such popular articulations, as Gramsci recognized, cut across the distinction between state and civil society. In the context of an irreducible pluralism, the creation of a people as democratic requires that different groups, demands, identities, and sectors are rendered contingently equivalent. Hegemony is a democratic logic because it recognizes this plurality. Laclau concludes that

> [D]emocracy is grounded only on the existence of a democratic subject, whose emergence depends on the horizontal articulation between equivalential demands. An ensemble of equivalential demands articulated by an empty signifier is what constitutes a "people." So the very possibility of democracy depends on the constitution of a democratic people. (2005: 169)

Yet for Rancière this is too quick. The demos of democracy is not equivalent to "a distinct people"; it assumes the equality of all regardless of whether or not they are of the people. In fact, it might well be that the articulation of a distinct people undermines a democratic politics of equality. He thus reserves the name democracy for ruptures with a hegemonic regime. While most regimes justify rule on the basis of some exclusive virtue, Rancière argues that democracy is based on the absence of qualification, the rule of chance, and no predetermined principle for the allocation of roles. Democracy names those who have no right to rule, those who are deemed not proper to rule, who do not count. "The people is the supplement that inscribes the count of the unaccounted for, or the part of those who have no part" (Rancière, 2010: 33). This is not equivalent to the regime often referred to by the same name of democracy. Contemporary democratic regimes are in fact oligarchies, characterized by the rule of wealth.

The key claim here is that for Rancière, democracy is based on the absence of qualification to rule, on chance. The constitution of a people, premised on the drawing of antagonistic boundaries, introduces qualifications which determine who is proper to rule and who is a legitimate representative or member of the people. As a result we are led to emphasize that all regimes remain to be further challenged by democracy—democracy is a set of practices through which equality is enacted and taken (Woodford, 2019). Laclau's account is indicative of a tradition that focuses on strategic articulation of oppositional politics through parties, organizational forms, and planning. Despite Laclau's post-Marxist intentions, the ghost of Lenin's *What Is to Be Done?* haunts this account of the political. Lenin argued that workers will not develop a political consciousness simply by fighting battles over wages. Instead, a political party acts as a vanguard of the revolution, teaching workers about their place in the broader struggle. Class consciousness, Lenin argued,

> [C]an be brought to the workers only from without; that is, only from outside the economic struggle, from outside the sphere of relations between workers and employers. The sphere from which alone it is possible to obtain this knowledge is the sphere of relationships (of all classes and strata) to the state and the government, the sphere of the interrelations between all classes. (Lenin, 1963: 48)

Laclau rejects what he views as the essentialism of Lenin's account—and indeed of Marxism in general, which assumes that the struggle between classes defined in terms of their relation to the means of production drives history (Laclau and Mouffe, 2001). The revolutionary theorist claims privileged access to this knowledge, as does Lenin for the vanguard party. Laclau recognizes with Rancière that a key stage in moving from Marxism to post-Marxism is a critique of knowledge and its relation to power such as that found in Rancière's *The Ignorant Schoolmaster* (1991) and *The Philosopher and His Poor* (2004). Drawing on the experience of revolutionary exiled teacher Joseph Jacotot who fled from France to Flanders during the French restoration, Rancière emphasizes the importance of self-education for emancipation. It is only through self-education that the subject avoids capture within the existing hierarchies of the social order. Rather than mimicking the stultifying forms of education and knowledge, a left politics needs to create conditions for emancipatory auto-didactism. This is impossible when the privileged knowledge of a revolutionary party justifies its role as a vanguard. Vanguardism justifies inequalities of knowledge and leadership and refuses the instituting of a politics of equality in the here and now. Laclau and Rancière agree about this.

While rejecting the substantive claims made by Lenin, Laclau's commitment to ontology retains the unequal relations of its political logic: on the one hand, the theorist knows that all politics is contingent, knows that the claim to identity is always false, a covering up of the essential lack constitutive of all social orders; yet it is on this basis that the theorist can define the political, as well as the forms of political struggle (hegemonic) which count as political. The ontological account of the political very soon appears as a privileged account of knowledge, although now the political theorist—unlike Lenin—is absolved of all responsibility for engaging in political struggle. They have already disclaimed the ultimate futility of all forms of political identification. What appears as a minor dispute about the politics that follows from an acceptance of a fundamental contingency is in fact a disagreement about the very possibility of politics as such. This discussion of Lenin may seem a distraction, but it allows us to focus on one key issue. Laclau's politics is always strategic—and strategy must always privilege revolutionary knowledge, as well as the suspension of equality until a later date—when the conditions are ripe. Democracy is always delayed in the interests of winning the hegemonic battle. Yet Laclau himself thinks of the contingency of all social order. He knows that in dismissing the people, anti-populists rely on knowledge, power, and privilege. His politics begins with the reality of bodies caught in struggle, with the demands made by those that regimes tend to dismiss and ignore. He vests a power of equality in the demands and the actions of the excluded plebs—those who comprise the majority of the global population. Perhaps the reality of strategic and hegemonic struggle is the introduction of new forms of hierarchy. However, we can take from Rancière a recognition that equality begins with the enactment of those demands. The plebs, who for Laclau are the particular that come to embody the universal through enacting demands, are the site of an unqualified equality regardless of the outcome of any hegemonic struggle.

Post-Marxist Radical Democracy

We have argued that Rancière and Laclau's respective works are indicative of a wider division on the left regarding the politics of equality. These are often interpreted as a division between spontaneity and organization, hierarchy and verticalism.[3] This has perpetuated division between those who could otherwise work together. Instead of reading these traditions as opposing, we conclude that they allow us to identify different *but complimentary* tasks for a leftist politics.

Let us begin with the question raised by Laclau about how to conceptualize those regimes named democratic and how to differentiate between regimes. The strength of Laclau's account lies in sketching how a better order might be instituted. His theory of hegemony details the precise logics at work behind any political mobilization. However, it is Rancière's third logic of emancipation—axiomatic equality—which allows us to distinguish leftist forms of political articulation from those of the right.

How then do we propose to combine a theory of hegemonic construction with a logic of emancipation that ruptures via the emergence of an axiomatic equality; an ontological account of the political with conceptual dissolution which entails a refusal of any ontology's division of knowledge; and the central role for identifications necessary to build political movements with dis-identification and rejection of institutionalized political regimes? Laclau and Rancière's work treat different objects. Laclau theorizes how counter police orders might be constructed. They can never be built in isolation, but they always emerge in antagonistic opposition to that which already exists. Rancière focuses on the moment when the order of the sensible is ruptured. Laclau works in the order of the sensible, theorizing how to readjust the balance of power by exploiting this rupture in the most egalitarian way.

We contend that any substantive concept of equality on the left must always be acknowledged as temporary and incomplete, local and established anew in each particular struggle. It should never be muddled with the axiomatic equality that is never finally substantiated. For us even a negative understanding of equality undermines the potential scope of a democratic politics of equality. Radical democratic forms of politics extend equality, by recognizing that they never finally instantiate the equality that renders all orders contingent.

Yet what are the implications of combining Laclau and Rancière in this way for left politics today? First, the contrast between Rancière and Laclau's work has been productive because it articulates in a new way how democratic politics is in tension with property and property regimes—regimes that believe they can properly police the limits of the proper. This allows us to reframe radical democratic theories of property in order to rethink the contingency of the properties that structure political order. The disjunctive synthesis of these theorists indicates that post-Marxist politics needs to rethink democratic politics, but such a thinking does not require internal consistency in either logical or geometric term. In fact it is the disagreement that is most productive. In this account of democratic theory, we focus on how equality is enacted and taken and play this back against the political science of democracy as a regime. Finally, this leaves the question of how we can distinguish between different types of political regimes. Our discussion indicates that we should not assume that a democratic regime is hostile to enactments of equality and vice-versa. Regimes may foster conditions in which equality can be enacted. In turning to these tasks the respective works of Rancière and Laclau are invaluable. Laclau forces us to attend to better regimes. Rancière forces us to recognize that equality will always emerge to undermine, challenge, and overturn such orders.

Notes

1. The only such event in print was a meeting in Buenos Aires in 2012, but sadly Laclau was late and missed Rancière's talk (O'Connor, 2015). However, Rancière did engage in dialogue with Laclau on the Argentinian TV-show *Diálogos con Laclau* in 2011 (the episode of which is unfortunately not readily available today).
2. Class struggle is not antagonistic because a policeman hits a worker, for example.
3. Current ramifications of this play out in disagreements between thinkers such as Hardt and Negri, Badiou, Deleuze, Foucault, and Žižek, Dean, Laclau.

Bibliography

Badiou A (2006) *Metapolitics* (trans. J Barker). London: Verso.
Bosteels B (2009) Rancière's Leftism, Or, Politics and its Discontents. In: G Rockhill and P Watts (eds.), *Jacques Rancière: History, Politics, Aesthetics*. Durham, NC: Duke University Press, 158–76.
Citton P (2009) Political Agency and the Ambivalence of the Sensible. In: G Rockhill and P Watts (eds.), *Jacques Rancière: History, Politics, Aesthetics*. Durham: Duke University Press, 120–39.
Davis O (2010) *Jacques Rancière*. Key Contemporary Thinkers. Cambridge: Polity.
Devenney M (2020) *Towards an Improper Politics*. Edinburgh: Edinburgh University Press.
Devenney M and Woodford C (forthcoming) *Democratic Theory Beyond the Pale*.
Dillon M (2003) (De)void of Politics?: A Response to Jacques Rancière's Ten Theses on Politics. *Theory & Event* 6(4). doi:10.1353/tae.2003.0011.
Glynos J and Howarth DR (2007) *Logics of Critical Explanation in Social and Political Theory*. London: Routledge.
Laclau E (2005) *On Populist Reason*. London: Verso.
Laclau E and Mouffe C (2001) *Hegemony and Socialist Strategy: Towards a Radical Democratic Politics*. 2nd ed. London: Verso.
Lenin VIU (1963) *What Is to Be Done?* (trans. P Utechin and SV Utechin). London: Oxford University Press.
Norval AJ (2007) *Aversive Democracy: Inheritance and Originality in the Democratic Tradition*. Cambridge: Cambridge University Press.
O'Connor K (2015) "Don't They Represent us?": A Discussion Between Jacques Rancière and Ernesto Laclau. In: *Verso Blog*. Available at: https://www.versobooks.com/blogs/2008-don-t-they-represent-us-a-discussion-between-jacques-ranciere-and-ernesto-laclau (accessed October 22, 2021).
Rancière J (1991) *The Ignorant Schoolmaster: Five Lessons in Intellectual Emancipation*. Stanford, CA: Stanford University Press.
Rancière J (1999) *Disagreement: Politics and Philosophy* (trans. J Rose). Minneapolis: University of Minnesota Press.
Rancière J (2004) *The Philosopher and His Poor* (trans. A Parker, J Drury, and C Oster). Durham, NC: Duke University Press.
Rancière J (2006) *Hatred of Democracy* (trans. S Corcoran). London: Verso.
Rancière J (2007) *On the Shores of Politics* (trans. L Heron). London: Verso.
Rancière J (2009) A Few Remarks on the Method of Jacques Rancière. *Parallax* 15(3): 114–23. doi:10.1080/13534640902982983.

Rancière J (2010) Ten Theses on Politics. In: S Corcoran (ed.), *Dissensus: On Politics and Aesthetics*. London: Continuum, 27–44.

Rancière J (2011) The Thinking of Dissensus: Politics and Aesthetics. In: P Bowman and Stamp R (eds.), *Reading Rancière*. London: Continuum, 1–17.

Rancière J, Jeanpierre L and Zabunyan D (2016) *The Method of Equality: Interviews with Laurent Jeanpierre and Dork Zabunyan* (trans. J Rose). Cambridge: Polity Press.

Woodford C (2019) Hatred and Democracy: Ernesto Laclau and Populism in Europe. In: C Flesher Fominaya and RA Feenstra (eds.), *Routledge Handbook of Contemporary European Social Movements: Protest in Turbulent Times*. London: Routledge, 112–26.

Žižek S (2008) *The Ticklish Subject: The Absent Centre of Political Ontology*. 2nd ed. London: Verso.

4

Disavowals of Populism

The Political Displacement of Homogeneity

Karl Ekeman

Populism research generally asks what is populism and from there proceeds to ensure that there is an adequation between the "what" of populism and the concepts used to understand it. This research is often coupled with a disavowal of populism that echoes mainstream discourse, claiming that populism is a dangerous or illegitimate form of politics. Scholars who on the other hand problematize and critique this very disavowal tend to ask not what populism is, but what the academic and mainstream discourse on populism itself does: in particular, the way disavowals of populism enforce or maintain specific kinds of political practices or imaginaries (see Rancière, 2016; D'Eramo, 2013; Laclau, 2007). This chapter follows a similar route, asking what is involved when populist ideas are disavowed as fictitious, imaginary, or illusionary. I will turn to Koen Abts and Stefan Rummens' "Populism Versus Democracy" (2007) as an example of such research and discuss the idealization of populism through which the disavowal is justified—centered on the populist notion of the people as a homogeneous unity. The discussion will be undertaken in dialogue with the philosophy of Claude Lefort, whose work also constitutes the main inspiration for Abts and Rummens' analysis.

"Populism Versus Democracy" is a recurring footnote in populism research and provides an exemplary critique of populist logic (briefly restated in Rummens, 2017). The purpose of the present inquiry is not to disprove the pertinence of the authors' critique or to better explain populism, but to show how the idea of a homogeneous or substantial unity—dismissed as illusion, myth, and fiction, and thus exempted from any explanation—in fact can be understood, following Lefort, as related to the introduction of an unconditional reference point for society that makes processes of homogenization possible. Theoretically, this suggests that the invocation of a homogeneous "people" is not only a proto-stage for future homogenization (and, as such, a danger to be kept at bay) but a symptom of already existing homogenizing processes consequently obscured through the disavowal of popular homogeneity *as* a fiction. The concluding section of this chapter will seek to concretize the point by drawing on Michel Foucault's analysis of neoliberalism to suggest ways in which homogenizing processes might be in play.

"Politics" and "the Political"

When W. B. Gallie (1955) introduced the idea of essentially contested concepts—often invoked to explain the contested nature of populism (Mudde, 2017)—he did so by providing an artificial example. In the example, Gallie posits a championship without fixed end, without fixed judges, and without fixed rules for determining the winning team. Supporters of the different teams all herald their own team as "the champions" (the example's contested concept). What is pertinent for our purposes, while not emphasized by Gallie, is how the contestation among different supporters and teams implies not merely a bickering about who plays the game best but also a contestation about the nature of the game itself. What the supporters and teams aspire to is not merely to alter the status of a team within the parameters of the game (a first-order question), but to align the parameters of the game with the style of play of the preferred "champions" (a second-order question). It thus stands to reason that, approaching the concept of populism as essentially contested, we are required to think of the discourse on populism as involving both a first- and second-order contestation. In so doing, we approach Claude Lefort's distinction between "politics" and "the political."

Lefort's discussion of "politics" and "the political" distinguishes between the former as an instituted and recognized particular sphere where "politics" takes place (i.e., political campaigning, debates, elections, parliamentary deliberation, etc.), distinct from other equally recognized and instituted spheres (such as economic, judicial, and epistemic); and "the political" as the generation and configuration of these spheres as such: the institution of forms through which these spheres appear and which gives these spheres their particular intelligibilities, meanings, rules, and ways of appearing. In short, whereas "politics" might be taken as a given, "the political" is what in each case gives "politics" its *"what" and "how"*.

Lefort proposed this distinction as part of a critique of political science. The point of the critique regards the failure to see that the categories by which political scientists analyze their specific phenomena are given by their insertion in a particularly instituted social life and consequently conditioned by its historically determined framework. "The fact," Lefort writes, "that something like *politics* should have been circumscribed within social life at a given time has in itself a political meaning [. . .] [and] raises the question of the constitution of the social space, of the *form* of society" (Lefort, 1988: 11).

The element of the "political" does not necessarily appear in the familiar sphere of instituted "politics" but in the uncanniness of the formative process by which society is ordered and reordered. In modern democracy, this formative process is often obscured, since the obviousness of "politics" tends to hide the originary forming process that gives rise to it. The problem of "populism" in which I am interested here has to do with the tendency to misrecognize the way the convulsions surrounding "populism" signify not merely a question of "politics" but also that of the "political" which gives to "politics" its determinate content ("what") and its specific ways of operating ("how").

At the core of many projects called "populist" lies an attempt not to do "politics" but to change its "what and how"—all the while the rejection of "populism" tends to be undertaken from the point of view of "politics" *such as it is*, and as if how it is, is the only way for it to be. In this back-and-forth movement, "the political" both appears and is concealed: "the political" appears, since what so-called populists often do is to invoke the arbitrariness of the presently given "what and how," thus indicating "the political" as that from which instituted politics is given; and it is concealed, in the reactions toward those labeled populists, since the latter are taken as particular deviations from normality, and not as projects that, in their own way, question the formative principles that establish normality as "normality."

While there are many accounts of what the present "normality" is, in which the game of formative principles is being played out, the present inquiry subscribes to the explanatory value and critical potential of "neoliberalism" as a descriptive operator, and I will turn to a critical analysis of neoliberalism in the concluding section of the chapter. For now, suffice it to say that depending on what kind of normality is at stake, the first-order rejection of populism amounts to different kinds of second-order implications. The point of this investigation is to show where, in the rejection of populism, a second-order issue (i.e., the political as such) tends to be obscured, while its first-order anchor point (i.e. politics) is emphasized.

The Philosophy of Claude Lefort

Central to Claude Lefort's political thought, employed by Abts and Rummens, is the notion of modern democracy as determined by an emptiness in the place of power. However, modern democracy is merely one form of society, and in order to understand the specificity Lefort gives this form, it is necessary to turn to his wider political philosophy.

The work of "the political" consists in a shaping of society (*mise-en-form*), which in turn involves both giving particular *meanings* to social relations (*mise-en-sens*) and *staging* those relations (*mise-en-scène*). The meaning-giving aspect of the political concerns the institution of conditions of intelligibility, whereas the staging aspect consists in allowing society to arrive at a self-representation by which it can be something for itself—which, in turn, is one of the conditions under which society is instituted (Lefort, 1988: 219).

Modern democracy bears witness to a specific shaping and a specific configuration of the place of power. However, for Lefort power is not merely localized in established authorities. First and foremost it arises through a representation of an Other in which society sees itself: the symbolic pole which makes society's self-externality manifest (Lefort, 1988: 225). As such, the place of power is a liminal position neither wholly internal nor external to society, from which power signifies in two ways. First, power forges a representation of the internal divisions of society, which Lefort regards as constitutive (Lefort, 2000: 215; 2012: 139ff; Marchart, 2007: 92 ff). While internal division itself amounts to society's condition of possibility, the form and meaning given to this division follow from the configuration of power. Second, power "makes a gesture towards something *outside*, and [. . .] defines itself in terms of that outside" (Lefort, 1988: 225). This liminal aspect of power in its gesture toward an outside can be seen in the way premodern princes took up a position as mediator between mortals and gods or, in secularized contexts, "between mortals and the transcendental agencies represented by a sovereign Justice and a sovereign Reason" (Lefort, 1988: 17). Lefort writes:

> Being at once subject to the law and placed above laws, [the prince] condensed within his body, which was at once mortal and immortal, the principle that generated the order of the kingdom. His power pointed towards an unconditional, other-worldly pole, while at the same time he was, in his own person, the guarantor and representative of the unity of the kingdom. The kingdom itself was represented as a body, as a substantial unity, in such a way that the hierarchy of its members, the distinction between ranks and orders appeared to rest upon an unconditional basis. (Lefort, 1988: 17)

Power was in the ancien régime thus embodied in the king, and the body of the king constituted the point of intersection between society and its outside: its legitimacy in a supersensible sovereign—whether Reason or God. Through this dual signification of society's Other, the kingdom was represented for itself as a homogeneous body and substantial unity—as One—in the sense that the divisions of society appeared as resting on an unconditional basis. Similarly, by virtue of constituting the point of intersection between society and its outside, the monarch managed to gather all spheres of society (economic, judicial, cultural) in his body, since the unconditional outside which this body mediated was the common origin in which they all coincided.

Understanding the king as an embodiment of power gives a special significance to the advent of modern democracy, which can be understood as the disincorporation of both the king and society (Lefort, 1986: 302 f). With democracy, the figure of the Other disappears, as does the One, or society's substantial unity. The place of power nevertheless remains, in terms of the otherness in which society sees itself—only that it now holds merely the *mechanisms* of power, signifying in ways rather different than the figure of the king: society is no longer unified through an Other gesturing toward unconditional principles (God, Reason, Justice), but through the unity of a political stage where the mechanisms of power continue to be played out. The arc of the gesture has shifted from a limit in the supersensible (an "unconditional, other-worldly pole") to the impossibility of full legitimization as such: hence, a "dissolution of the markers of certainty" (Lefort, 1988: 11).

Thus, Lefort writes that democracy "is the only [regime] to have [. . .] maintained a gap between the symbolic and the real" (Lefort, 1988: 225). While division is constitutive of society, it can never be saturated with a meaning that entirely undoes its eruptive potential (such as an account that legitimizes division by recourse to dictates of a supreme reality). It thus remains as that "real" which cannot be fully grasped by the symbolic; not as a positive content but as an impossibility of full symbolic saturation. This gap between, on the one hand, the mechanisms of power and the divisions of society, and, on the other, their legitimacy, is what is retained in democracy. In the empty place of power, society is represented for itself as *this* society, but if there is a gesture toward an outside, it is not toward a foundation in the supersensible but toward the impossibility of fully giving meaning and ground to social division. Division and strife are not legitimized by way of a reference to something unconditional. Instead, they are played out symbolically in contests where different protagonists seek to lay claim to authority while recognizing that nobody can entirely embody that authority. In a similar way, power no longer gathers the spheres of society within itself, since with the disappearance of a common point of origin in which all spheres coincide, each sphere is subsequently referred to as having their respective internal functioning—enabling, among other things, a distinct sphere of "politics" to emerge.

This provides sufficient background to engage with Abts and Rummens' diagnosis of the populist logic, beginning, first, with the outlines of the ideational approach to which they belong, and second, the specific position taken in the text with regard to the "democratic paradox"—both central in understanding Abts and Rummens' critique of populism.

Ideational Approaches to Populism

Within studies of populism, especially in political science, the ideational approach constitutes an increasingly dominant strand of literature. Approaches of this kind often center on how populism transposes the democratic ideal of popular sovereignty into a moralized ideational framework. According to this framework, the virtuous and homogeneous "people" needs to reclaim power from the vicious "elite" and restore popular sovereignty by turning politics into an immediate expression of the general will of the "people." Cas Mudde thus defines populism as a thin-centered ideology "that considers society to be ultimately separated into two homogeneous and antagonistic groups, 'the pure people' versus 'the corrupt elite', and which argues that politics should be an expression of the *volonté générale* (general will) of the people" (2017: 30). Jan-Werner Müller presents a similar notion through two definitional distillates. First, he claims that populism is "a set of distinct claims" with an inner logic that constitutes a "permanent shadow of representative democracy, and a constant peril" (Müller, 2016:10 f). Second, that populism is "a particular moralistic imagination of politics," at the heart of which lies the claim that "only some of the people really are the people" (Müller, 2016: 19 f). The key concern for Müller is thus populism's anti-pluralism, and its disavowal of both legitimate opposition and constitutional checks and balances.

While in "Populism vs Democracy," Abts and Rummens agree with Mudde's definition, they argue that the antagonistic relation between the people and the elite is already contained in populism's advocacy for popular sovereignty. Hence, they define populism as "a thin-centered ideology which advocates the sovereign rule of the people as a homogeneous body" (Abts and Rummens, 2007: 409). While Mudde argues that populism is compatible with democracy—but a potential threat to *liberal* democracy—Müller, Abts, and Rummens claim that populism poses a danger to democracy *tout court*. This indicates an element central to the different evaluations of populism, in the way democracy is understood in relation to either the recognition or refutation of the so-called democratic paradox.

The Democratic Paradox

The democratic paradox refers to the idea that liberal democracy is predicated on two pillars that constitute an irreconcilable contradiction: the liberal or constitutive pillar, stressing the need for the rule of law to be the locus of authority, over and against arbitrary exercise of power by the state or other citizens; and the democratic pillar, stressing the need for supreme authority to reside with the people, in order to stave off rules of law that despite their universalistic claims might institute the dominance of particular interests. The paradox lies in the way these two "pillars" allegedly undermine one another, such that liberal democracy consists of a vacillation between these two principles.

For many who agitate for a fundamental change in the coordinates of actually existing democracy, the idea of a democratic paradox is central. Chantal Mouffe, for instance, claims that a present imbalance in this uneasy relationship must be remedied and the democratic pillar rectified. Referring to the historical works of C. B. MacPherson, she stresses that liberal democracy is the result of a contingent historical articulation of two distinct traditions: the liberal tradition, advocating individual liberty and property rights; and the democratic tradition that advocates equality and popular sovereignty (Mouffe, 2018: 14 f; 2000: 3 f). Neoliberalism—as the present hegemonic formation—has in Mouffe's analysis increasingly redefined political life in ways that erode democratic ideals. In short, it has led to a situation of "post-politics," where the alternatives available to voters at the ballot box are so alike that they fail to effectively constitute a political choice at all. Without any effective choice, the antagonistic dimension of politics disappears, and popular sovereignty—minimally conditioned upon a selection between alternatives—is eroded: politics has become "a mere issue of managing the established order, a domain reserved for experts" (Mouffe, 2000: 17). Populism is in her eyes a reaction to such a situation. As a form of reaction, it can, however, be articulated in a number of ways, and Mouffe's political concern regards how to articulate it in a manner consistent with progressive politics.

In works that point to the dangers of populism, the idea of a democratic paradox is instead often disavowed. For Müller, liberal democracy *is* democracy, and the idea that "liberal democracy involves a balance where we can choose to have a little bit more liberalism or a little bit more democracy is fundamentally misleading" (2016: 11). While Müller grants Mouffe a point in raising concerns about an emerging technocracy, he declines the idea that democracy would still be democracy without the liberal pillar (2016: 60). As we shall see, Abts and Rummens' argument is of a piece with Müller, and it is through their engagement with the question of the democratic paradox that their critique of populism is articulated.

From Two Pillars to Three Logics: Abts and Rummens' Critique of Populism

While Müller, Abts, and Rummens are dissatisfied with the idea of a paradox, they nevertheless retain the notion of two logics and claim that what is called a liberal and a democratic pillar—if taken in their "pure" forms—in fact constitutes two pathological degenerations of one original democratic logic. Hence, in contradiction to a paradox of two pillars, they propose a theory of three logics: the democratic, the populist, and the liberal logic respectively.

The authors understand the democratic logic in Lefortian terms, stressing the empty place of power and the symbolic staging of conflicts representing society as "unified-in-diversity" (Abts and Rummens, 2007: 416). Their point is that this requires both "pillars": liberal individual rights guarantee diversity *and* the democratic sovereignty of the people refer not only to the possibility of constitutional reform but to the continuous reinterpretation of the identity of the people also (Abts and Rummens, 2007: 413). In this regard, their position is akin to Mouffe's, who views the tension between liberalism and democracy as constitutive, serving to retain the real possibility of an ongoing "agonistic" negotiation between them. In contrast to Mouffe, however, Abts and Rummens argue that the paradox is merely apparent, and that the democratic logic is not so much a constant renegotiation between the two conflicting "pillars," as a unified whole where the two pillars are reconciled (cf. Abts and Rummens, 2007: 413). Hence, rather than an irreconcilable contradiction, there is co-originality and mutual interdependence, and the risk identified by Abts and Rummens lies in two possible and pathological degenerations of this original unity: the "liberal" and "populist" logics. The passage is worth quoting in full:

> The major problem with the liberal logic is that it fails to grasp the way in which the political stage allows for the symbolic integration of society, by representing social conflicts in such a way that differences are recognized while at the same time political unity is maintained. When this process of representation fails, there is a risk that the empty place of power is perceived as an *effective emptiness* and that society is threatened with disintegration. This possibility is all the more dangerous, as it might engender susceptibility for the second and opposite illusion of *unity-in-itself*, where the need for a representation of the unity of society is met with the imaginary fiction of the *people-as-one* [. . .]. The phantasmal image of the organic unity of the political community tries to provide the security of a clear and well-defined collective identity, which eliminates the need for the laborious democratic construction of temporary interpretations of this common identity. This fictional belief in the homogeneous unity of the political community generates a logic which disregards the idea of otherness at the heart of democracy and aims at the suppression of diversity within society. This logic thus implies the closure of the locus of power and imposes the sovereign rule of the people-as-one. (Abts and Rummens, 2007: 413f)

While the dangers of the liberal logic are epitomized in such a way that its degeneration possibly provides a hospitable milieu for its populist counterpoint, the dangers of the populist logic lay in eliminating the gap that represents the empty place of power. Here, the authors raise a possible objection to their own claim, since Lefort himself took this act of elimination as the starting point for his analysis of *totalitarianism*. While Abts and Rummens acknowledge that "the fictitious image of the people-as-one is a defining characteristic that populism shares with totalitarianism," and hence that populism follows "a proto-totalitarian logic" (2007: 414), they point to an important difference: Lefort's analysis of totalitarianism involves a homogenization of all spheres of society, while populism, in their eyes, accepts the relative autonomy of politics, restricting homogenization to "the people." And since Lefort's analysis is insufficient to cover the specificity of the populist danger, they turn to a reading of Carl Schmitt in order to formulate their understanding of the logic of populism.

In their reading, Schmitt's theory of democracy rests on a substantial identification between rulers and ruled. The problem they point to is the resulting disavowal of democratic representation (since the people must be *presented*), the delegitimization of political opponents (since those that do not belong to the people have no legitimate part in power), and the rise of authoritarian rule (since leaders who make present the people can only find in constitutional checks an obstruction of the will of this people). At the heart of the analysis lies the need to preserve the "fictitious image of the people-as-one" that brought populism to power, which in turn requires a continuous process of pointing out new enemies of the people. Consequently, populist regimes can only be sustained as "authoritarian and despotic" (Abts and Rummens, 2007: 421).

While they argue that populism risks overstepping the bounds of constitutional checks and balances, they also claim that such balances are in themselves insufficient to safeguard democracy. Democracy "ultimately depends on the integrity of the democratic ethos of the people and is, therefore, threatened as soon as citizens are lured by the fictitious image of a substantive collective identity" (Abts and Rummens, 2007: 422). Since populists do not "share the symbolic framework that defines the political stage for democratic political struggles [. . .] populists are no longer ordinary adversaries, but *political enemies* who hold an incompatible view of the symbolic structure of the locus of power itself" (Abts and Rummens, 2007).

What is interesting in the accounts of Müller and Abts and Rummens is not only the way democracy is conceived differently (from, for instance, that of Mouffe) but how historical perspectives on democracy seem to be obscured in the refutation of the democratic paradox. Mouffe's claim regarding the two traditions is thus not only a claim about the parts of a democratic machine but of the different sociohistorical processes that were involved in the articulation of democracy as a historical form of political institution. In doing so, Mouffe not only advances with respect to the parameters of the game (what we called a first-order question) but brings into question the formation of the game itself (a second-order question). Müller, Abts, and Rummens, on the other hand, offer a normative account of democracy, which, as normative, seems predicated on the minimization or even exclusion of second-order questions. The latter point is made explicit: "constitutional democracy should not be analyzed as a historically contingent and paradoxical mixture of two pillars" (Abts and Rummens, 2007: 412), and the need to sustain a belief in a specific idea of democracy and popular identity is required from citizens if the populist threat is to be kept at bay.

In a critical overview of recent populism scholarship, John Abromeit (2017: 182) points to how such approaches posit liberal democracy as the most perfect form of government possible, which Abromeit argues makes it difficult to understand why anti-democratic populist forces develop within liberal democracies—leading him to suggest that it may indicate the limits of political science itself to provide an explanation. For this reason, I will seek to push one such limit of explanation, found in Abts and Rummens' disavowal of the idea of homogeneous unity as "fictional belief" (Abts and Rummens, 2007: 414).

On Limits and Delimitations of Explanation

The belief in a homogeneous unity is a flashpoint in understanding populism as a threat. Thus, social dissatisfaction engenders susceptibility for an "imaginary fiction" that in turn closes the gap in the empty place of power. One question to be asked is how the text positions the reader in relation to this fiction, and what this relation reveals and obscures.

As we have seen, "Populism versus Democracy" proceeds through a methodological idealization of populism where certain essential ideas are identified. The relation between these ideas constitutes populism as a logic. The question is: What kind of understanding of the ideas inherent to this logic is prescribed by the logic as such? What are the limits of this logic in providing an understanding of populism, and what takes root and grows at that limit? Let us now look into these questions, starting from Abts and Rummens' methodological idealization.

Abts and Rummens define populism as a "thin-centered ideology which advocates the sovereign rule of the people as a homogeneous body" (2007: 409). We had discussed this definition earlier. At this point, I would like to highlight how their definition (what I have called "idealization") is built on three ideas often referenced in the literature on populism:

(1) The antagonism between "the people" and "the elite,"
(2) The idea of restoring popular sovereignty, and
(3) The idea of "the people" as a homogeneous unity.

How are we to understand the rationality of these ideas in terms of an explanatory *ratio* between them?

Abts and Rummens state that (1) is already contained in (2)—"the sovereign rule of the people." The idea of "popular sovereignty" is a central part of the democratic imaginary, and the origin of this idea can thus be located not internal to the logic (as simply made up by populists) but externally, in the actual political imagination of our time. In this way, to borrow a phrase from Müller, it seems as if this aspect of populism comes "from within the democratic world," from where it emerges as "a degraded form of democracy that promises to make good on democracy's highest ideals" (Müller, 2016: 6).

Remaining with the idea of populism as originating from within democracy, populism can thus be understood as a negativity in need of positive articulation. If (1) is already contained in (2), we might presuppose that this aspect of the logic of populism emerges once the democratic promise of popular sovereignty is at variance with the political experience of its unfulfillment. It provides a way of understanding the first half of Abts and Rummens' idealization with respect to the promise of democracy and allegations surrounding its failure to deliver. But what are we to make of the second half of the definition, the last (3) element in the idea of "the people" as a homogeneous unity? First, it cannot be said to originate in the democratic notion of "popular sovereignty" or be equated with the idea of a democratic "people," for the simple reason that if it did, it would undo the difference between "democracy" and "populism" maintained in the theory of the three logics. Second, the claim that it somehow emerges from an experienced lack is difficult to maintain, since this fact alone does not account for how it is awarded the legitimacy and rhetorical potency that allows for it to be experienced *as* lack. History shows no shortage of invocations of substantial popular unity, but the sheer fact of historical precedents does not in itself explain the phenomenon. (In fact, recognizing the historical failures and ever-present dangers of such invocations is a part of the educational and ideological structures of many liberal democracies, to the extent that examples from history should, in all likelihood, make present-day affirmations of this idea *within* liberal democracies seem futile, rather than a persuasive appeal.) Neither does it seem plausible to claim that the idea of a homogeneous unity stems from an experience of such unity. (Times when such unity is said to be lacking, as well as when invocations of such unity are raised, are equally times when critics rightly claim that such unity has never existed.) This is stated not to imply that there is no way to explain the phenomenon, or to suggest that this limit of explanation stems from an inability to explain what is at stake. I say all this in order to focus on an apparent simplicity in Abts and Rummens' reference to a seemingly self-evident attraction of opposites: a process whereby an appearance of society as "diversity-in-itself" engenders susceptibility for the *opposite illusion*, that is, "unity-in-itself" (Abts and Rummens, 2007: 414). How are we, as readers, positioned within Abts and Rummens' text, such that we might understand and relate to this leap between illusions that they proffer?

To recapitulate: according to the authors, the notion of a "homogeneous unity" is a necessary condition for the notion of populism, but in order to be explained, it requires something that neither the experience of a fulfilled or unfulfilled democratic life nor the ideas available in the provided logic of ideas seem to provide. In other words, while the notion of "homogeneous unity" seems to be what is most in need of explaining—given its centrality in the populist threat—it is also this idea that is least explained in the text. In this light, it is curious that rather than being explained or examined, it is doubled down upon as imagined, fictional, and phantasmatic. "Doubled down upon" in a very literal sense—as if a single reference to its fictitious nature is not enough but solicits a multiplication of pleonasms, repetitions of repetition: "the imaginary fiction," "the fictitious image," the "fictional belief," and the "phantasmal image" of the people-as-one (Abts and Rummens, 2007: 414). It is almost as if here, when faced with the spearhead of populist danger, we turn from rational discourse to morality, reminding us to enforce the "democratic ethos" upon which democracy depends, and not to be "lured by the fictitious image of a substantive collective identity" by which it is ultimately threatened (Abts and Rummens, 2007: 422). The way the text positions us to understand "homogeneous unity" suggests that we have a democratic responsibility not to understand it but to reject it as a dangerous and pathological fantasy. But what if, instead of pathologizing, we would try to rationalize the notion of "homogeneous unity" by the very means that their text itself enables?

Where There Is Materialization of the Other, There Is One: A Rationality of Homogenesis

Abts and Rummens refer to populism's idea of "homogeneous unity" in terms of what Lefort calls the image of the "People-as-One" and locates it at the foundation of totalitarianism. Totalitarianism was for Lefort an answer to the indeterminacy of modern democracy, involving the attempt at achieving full social self-organization— merging the image of the body with that of the machine. While modern democracy arrives with the dissolution of markers of certainty, and thus with a constitutive inability to provide a foundation for its justification, power in totalitarianism points to the social itself as such a foundation (Lefort, 1986: 297–306; 1988: 13 f). In this way, totalitarianism is coupled with the attempt at letting technical rationality be the grid of intelligibility to which complex social relations are made to fit, in order for the social to be completely amenable to organization (1988: 234). This also fosters the idea of a "People-as-One," insofar as the internal divisions of society are denied and transposed to an Other in the enemy of that "people" which thus constitutes popular identity (1986: 287). However, since Abts and Rummens have clearly distinguished between populism and totalitarianism, it is important to note that Lefort's notion of "substantial unity" is not restricted to totalitarianism—nor is it warded off simply as a baseless fiction—but explained in relation to the gesture of power toward an unconditional basis. This gesture is what I will now highlight. Lefort's discussion of the turn from monarchy to modern democracy serves to elucidate it:

> It is because the division of power does not, in a modern democracy, refer to an *outside* that can be assigned to the Gods, the city or holy ground; because it does not refer to an *inside* that can be assigned to the substance of the community. Or, to put it another way, it is because there is no materialization of the *Other*—which would allow power to function as a mediator, no matter how it were defined—that there is no materialization of the *One*—which would allow power to function as an incarnation. (Lefort, 1988: 226)

What constitutes the specificity of modern democracy is the fact that there is no materialization of the Other (here emphasized in its gesture to the unconditional) and, hence, no One (as a symbolically substantive unity of society subject to the unconditioned). As we saw in the first section on Lefort, it was the monarch's reference to "an unconditional, other-worldly pole" that enabled (a) the representation of the kingdom as a substantial unity—allowing the divisions in society to be seen as resting on an unconditional basis (1988: 11). The point here concerns the mirroring of the unconditional, substantial, or phrased otherwise, the *ultimate*: the markers of certainty that are dissolved with the advent of modern democracy. The same structure was involved in the closing of the gap, whereby (b) all spheres of society collide into one, insofar as their principles were deemed to have one and the same origin. The two processes are, if not analogous, then linked, in the sense that the gesture toward the unconditional forges both (b) a representation of the homogenesis of the different spheres of society and (a) the homogeneity of society as a substantial unity.

If this is true, then a clue as to the rationality of "substantial unity" could be given by removing Lefort's double negation in the abovementioned quote, and instead state: *where there is materialization of the Other, there is One*. Seen in this light, it seems—far from having its roots in myth, fiction, or illusion—the roots of "substantial homogeneity" originate from the gesture of power, formative in society, toward an unconditional externality by virtue of which the notion of homogenesis is given political rationality and rhetorical potency. While the disavowal of populism in the analysis of Abts and Rummens affirms the democratic importance of not being lured by the fictitious image of homogeneity, Lefort seems to suggest that the fiction and fixation of homogeneity, rather than a first stage (a "proto-totalitarianism"), might in fact be co-original with wider homogenizing processes, in turn related to second-order "political" transformation in how society is instituted. Of course, this does not prove the actual existence of such processes, but it shows that the theoretical framework employed by Abts and Rummens in fact indicates their possibility. Their disavowal of "homogeneous unity" *as a dangerous fiction*, however, risks obscuring this indication. While further development of the specific mechanics and real processes undergirding "homogeneous unity" far exceeds the confines of the present chapter, I will here only seek to show in what way such an inquiry could be fruitful—drawing on and restricting my account to Michel Foucault's analysis of neoliberalism (2008).

Homogeneity in Neoliberalism

While Foucault and Lefort differ not least in their view of power, they both stress the ways in which the workings of power are related to the formative processes of society, which in turn are connected to the institution of meaning and staging of social relations (what Lefort called *mise-en-form*, *mise-en-sens*, and *mise-en-scène*). What Foucault can add here, as well as those following his line of research (e.g., Brown, 2015; Dardot and Laval, 2014), is a precise understanding of our present political moment. The question is whether or not we are in the midst of a regime where power again makes a gesture toward something unconditional, providing a symbolic homogenesis for society's spheres and divisions. This section, although condensed, will seek to show that—when read through Lefort—Foucault's analysis of neoliberalism indicates that we are, in fact, living through such a change (see also Braeckman, 2015, for a similar reading of Lefort and Foucault, although centered on the question of the role of state).

Central to Foucault's analysis of neoliberalism is the extension of a specifically neoliberal market rationality (centered on "competition" rather than "exchange") throughout the social field, encompassing the "formative power of society" (Foucault, 2008: 148). This extension has taken place through the multiplication of the "enterprise form" as a grid of intelligibility in whose terms an increasing number of previously noneconomic spheres are to be understood. Seen through this grid, states and individuals alike are first and foremost enterprises, and while they are expected to act as such, social reality is also shaped to enable this acting-as-such—from the level of the individual to the level of state. Reading Foucault through Lefort, it is possible to understand this process as having consequences for both forms of homogenization mentioned earlier: (a) the homogeneity of society as a substantial unity and (b) the homogenesis of social spheres. The following discussion of Foucault will be limited to remarks relevant to these forms.

First, as a consequence of this extension, the relation between state and market has changed. Instead of the state interfering to counter negative market effects, the state in Foucault's analysis of neoliberalism interferes so as to secure the sufficient conditions for market competition. Whereas the former configuration enforces the distinctness of the economic sphere vis-à-vis other spheres (tasking the state with regulating the effects between them), the latter takes market rationality as the governing principle for all spheres, allowing not only for the economic domain to be left governed by economic principles but for the increasing economization also of noneconomic domains (Foucault, 2008: 242 f). With Lefort, we can say that power here makes a gesture toward an outside in terms that the market itself defines—only this outside is now a Market comparable to sovereign Reason. In neoliberalism, government action is judged less on how well it regulates market effects, but more on how well it allows for market rationality to settle questions of division and organization throughout society at large (Foucault, 2008: 246f). Foucault here, for instance, points to how neoliberals conceived of the economic grid as a means by which governmental validity can be tested. A consequence of his analysis is, however, also that if social life in general—from family life to education to penal practices and onwards—is understood in economic terms, even judgments that are drawn from previously noneconomic spheres come to rely on an economic, instrumental rationality as their standard. Economic principles thus increasingly assume the ultimate reference point for society, not as something to be judged by power but as something according to which power itself is judged, and toward which power, when justifying itself, makes a gesture—allowing for (b) an increasing homogenization of social spheres.

Second, this extension has consequences for how social relations are staged and are given meaning, and for the representation of social division. On the level of the individual, the enterprise form allows for the cultivation of a subjectivity of *homo oeconomicus*—"economic man" who, in neoliberalism, understands him- or herself first and foremost as an *entrepreneur*, simultaneously her own capital, producer, and consumer of the satisfaction produced. As such, the individual approaches the whole of the social environment according to economic rationality and conducts herself through calculations of efficiency, minimization of risk, and maximization of profit. While social division might remain, inequalities are represented as equalized, in the sense that where they exist they are articulated as stemming from equal and free participation in entrepreneurial competition, and from *individual* failures in management of risk. Everyone is, as Foucault allegedly put it, "equally unequal" (quoted in Hamann, 2009: 50). While this might seem far from the idea of the homogeneous "people" often ascribed to populists, the defining characteristic of the People-as-One in Lefort is less the form of its articulation (who or what we say the "people" are), and more the denial or elision of social division that allows for its homogenization. From this perspective, the neoliberalism here described can indeed be understood as producing the conditions of (a)—the homogeneity of society as a substantial unity—in the sense that the divisions of society are represented as if resting on an unconditional basis: following from individual engagements within a game of immutable rules and parameters, rather than from the formation of the game as such.

Now, "Populism vs Democracy" bracketed the question of totalitarianism (understood as involving both kinds of homogenization, (a) and (b), mentioned earlier) and argued that populism as a kind of "proto-totalitarianism" merely homogenizes "the people." The fiction of homogeneous unity is thus given the role of a potential first stage of homogenization that must not be made actual, and—importantly—its actualization is cast in terms of people being seduced by the myth of "the people"; citizens being "lured by the fictitious image of a substantive collective identity" (Abts and Rummens, 2007: 422). When we, instead, inquire into the rationality of this fiction, it however points—in theory and in the above reading of Foucault—to precisely the kind of wider social homogenization that was bracketed in Abts and Rummens' analysis. In short: the invocation of a homogeneous unity might not be the seed of a coming homogenization, but at least coincidental with, if not a symptom of, homogenizing processes already in play. By disavowing the invocation of homogeneity as pathological and dangerous fiction, one, however, risks pathologizing also the recognition of homogenizing processes of which the invocation might be understood as a symptom.

Abts and Rummens point to the idea of a homogeneous unity as the element constituting the primary danger of populist logic. They repeatedly stress this element as fictional, fictitious, imaginary, and illusory and exhort democratic citizens to sustain the democratic ethos by not being lured by it. The reading of Lefort I have sought to offer has, however, indicated that this element can be understood as relating to the gesture of power toward an unconditional reference point, enabling (a) the notion of a homogeneous or substantial unity insofar as the divisions of society thereby are revealed as if resting on an unconditional basis and (b) the homogenization of social spheres, which are referred back to one and the same origin for the generation of their respective principles. Where Abts and Rummens thus close off an important line of inquiry (disavowing the idea as dangerous fiction), the reading of Lefort proposed here indicates a question worth pursuing. The last section, in which Foucault's analysis of neoliberalism was read through Lefort, has served to show in what way this question is meaningful, given the way neoliberalism seems to provide the conditions of both kinds of homogenization discussed in this chapter.

This does not explain populism. Nor does it show that Abts and Rummens' critique of the "populist logic" misses the mark. The question has rather been to show what the disavowal of populism *does*, in terms of a second-order relevance related to the opening or closing of the "political." What I have sought to argue is that a devout rejection of the fiction of homogeneous unity *as fiction* risks directing the attention away from second-order questions of political institution and, more specifically, from the question of homogenizing processes related to the current institution of social forms. Above I have sought to show that there is a strong argument to be made for paying attention to such wider processes in relation to appeals to homogeneity, which in turn generates other questions for future research. For example, where Abts and Rummens suggest an oppositional relationship between the "liberal" and the "populist logic," might we not inquire into their continuity (in general, or specifically in neoliberalism)? In other words, if a liberal logic amounts to the totalization of difference, does not totalization of difference result in equivalence? On the one hand, this is akin to what writers who have inspired right-wing populists argue (cf. Benoist, 2017: xvii), and for whom the call for particular identity is being made in (genuine or strategic) opposition to homogeneity. At stake would then be not the alleged fact of identity, but the forms identities are given, and the mode of repoliticization of the divisions in society coupled with these forms—which in turn could serve to show the natures and dangers of the specifically populist modes of repoliticization (see Gambetti, 2018, for such a critique, although of Alt-Right writers).

On the other hand, it can also foster a sensitivity to the way mainstream politics have increasingly invoked the very figure of homogeneity it rejects, from George W. Bush's ultimate dichotomy ("either with us or with the terrorists") to Hillary Clinton's explicit reference to the politics of Donald Trump as "hate" (and implicit self-ascription as champion of "love"). The very concept of populism here seems to do the same, since uses of the concept often bring about the very distinction that the referents of the concept are feared to produce: the distinction between legitimate and illegitimate participants in politics; political friends and enemies ("populists are no longer ordinary adversaries, but *political enemies*," Abts and Rummens, 2007: 422). As Ernesto Laclau (2007; 2015) has so often shown, the continuous emptying of political signifiers (the endpoint being a radical opposition between pure good and evil) signals a process of equalization whereby internal differences are elided. Radical dichotomy is the other side of indistinctness and meaninglessness. If this is the case, appeals to "homogeneity"—be they of Trump or of Clinton—should perhaps not be met by mere disavowal. Instead, they should be confronted with the question of what lurks behind the meaninglessness that nonetheless heralds the introduction of something absolute—and how that meaninglessness is politically instituted.

Bibliography

Abromeit J (2017) A Critical Review of Recent Literature on Populism. *Politics and Governance* 5: 177–86.

Abts K and Rummens S (2007) Populism versus Democracy. *Political Studies* 55: 405–24.

Benoist Ad (2017) *View from the Right – Volume I: Heritage and Foundations*. London: Arktos.

Braeckman A (2015) Neo-Liberalism and the Symbolic Institution of Society: Pitting Foucault against Lefort on the State and the "Political." *Philosophy & Social Criticism* 41: 945–62.

Brown W (2015) *Undoing the demos: Neoliberalism's Stealth Revolution*. New York: Zone Books.

Dardot P, Laval C and Elliott G (2014) *The New Way of the World: On Neoliberal Society*. Brooklyn, NY: Verso.

D'Eramo M (2013) Populism and the New Oligarchy. *New Left Review* 82: 5–28.

Flynn B (2005) *The Philosophy of Claude Lefort: Interpreting the Political*. Evanston, IL: North Western University Press.

Foucault M. (2008) *The Birth of Biopolitics: Lectures at the Collége de France, 1978–1979*. Basingstoke: Palgrave Macmillan.

Gallie WB (1955) Essentially Contested Concepts. *Proceedings of the Aristotelian Society* 56: 167–98.

Gambetti Z (2018) How "Alternative" is the Alt-Right? *Critique & Praxis 13/13*. https://blogs.law.columbia.edu/praxis1313/zeynep-gambetti-how-alternative-is-the-alt-right/. First published November 10, 2018.

Hamann TH (2009) Neoliberalism, Governmentality, and Ethics. *Foucault Studies* 6: 37–59.

Laclau E (2007) *On Populist Reason*. London: Verso.

Laclau E (2015) *Ernesto Laclau: Post-Marxism, Populism, and Critique*. London: Routledge.

Lefort C (1986) *The Political Forms of Modern Society: Bureaucracy, Democracy, Totalitarianism*. Cambridge, MA: MIT Press.

Lefort C (1988) *Democracy and Political Theory*. Cambridge: Polity.

Lefort C (2000) *Writing: The Political Test*. Durham, NC: Duke University Press.

Lefort C (2012) *Machiavelli in the Making*. Evanston, IL: Northwestern University Press.

Marchart O (2007) *Post-foundational Political Thought: Political Difference in Nancy, Lefort, Badiou and Laclau*. Edinburgh: Edinburgh University Press.

Mouffe C (2000) *The Democratic Paradox*. London: Verso.

Mouffe C (2018) *For a Left Populism*. London: Verso.

Mudde C (2017) Populism: An Ideational Approach. In: Kaltwasser CbR, Taggart P, Espejo PO, et al. (eds.), *The Oxford Handbook of Populism*. Oxford: Oxford University Press.

Müller J-W. (2016) *What is Populism?* Philadelphia, PA: University of Pennsylvania Press.

Rancière J. (2016) The Populism That is Not to be Found. In: A Allen (ed.), *What is a People?* New York: Columbia University Press, 101–6.

Rummens S. (2017) Populism as a Threat to Liberal Democracy. In: P Taggart, P Ostiguy, CR Kaltwasser, et al. (eds.), *The Oxford Handbook of Populism*. 1 ed. Oxford: Oxford University Press.

Part II

Toward an Affectology of Populism

5

The Politics of Resentment and Its Pitfalls

Samo Tomšič

A System Running Amuck

I would like to begin my account of the populist politics of the present with a reference, which seems somewhat remote from the issue: Hannah Arendt's diagnosis of the global political turmoil in her essay "On Violence." Going through the forms of government, Arendt supplements the classical series—monarchy and oligarchy, aristocracy and democracy—with the properly modern form, bureaucracy, or "the rule of an intricate system of bureaus in which no man, neither one nor the best, neither the few nor the many, can be held responsible, and which could be properly called rule by Nobody" (1972: 137). The speculative scope of the term "Nobody" must be taken seriously. While monarchy and oligarchy localize power in "some-body," aristocracy in a multiplicity of bodies, and democracy in "every-body," bureaucracy disentangles power from corporeality. Arendt's description responds to the rising authority of anonymous experts in Europe and the United States during the Cold War period, but its validity reaches beyond these historical framings.[1] For the decades of financialization and neoliberal deregulation—a process that fully unfolded what Proudhon and Marx already called "bankocracy"—only sophisticated the bureaucratic governance and unleashed its crisis-driven character. In this decentralized regime power cannot be localized *despite* its visibility. The greater the number of experts and bureaus, the more disembodied and uncontrollable power becomes. "Nobody" makes itself felt in everybody in a most destabilizing manner:

> If, in accord with traditional political thought, we identify tyranny as government that is not held to give account of itself, rule by Nobody is clearly the most tyrannical of all, since there is no one left who could even be asked to answer for what is being done. It is this state of affairs, making it impossible to localize responsibility and to identify the enemy, that is among the most potent causes of the current world-wide rebellious unrest, its chaotic nature, and its dangerous tendency to get out of control and to run amuck. (Arendt, 1972: 138–9)

Even though today's combination of authoritarian neoliberalism and right-wing populism creates the impression that power descends back to individual bodies,

Arendt's accent on the link between disembodied power and the amuck run can be extended to our present. One could argue that populists such as Donald Trump are both administrators of systemic violence and players in the broader anarchic scenario, in which the capitalist system indeed increasingly runs amuck. From this perspective, the populist becomes a symptomatic personification of the tendency of capitalism to unfold its out-of-control, antisocial character.

Both the notion and the phenomenon of populism are marked by vagueness. We can differentiate between populism as a label of political disqualification, populism as semblance of antiestablishment politics, and populism as a symptom of the left's failure. It can hardly be overlooked that in liberal parlance "populism" serves for dismissing opponents left and right from the political center. This liberal use actively blurs the notion, stretching it to mutually exclusive phenomena such as democratic socialism, nationalism, and neofascism. Populism as a semblance of antiestablishment politics can be for the most part associated with the right. This aspect of populism will be discussed in the present chapter. Right-wing populism stands for a politics, which mobilizes the masses by means of negative affects such as hate, anger, and rage. This affective efficiency is one of the reasons why many on the left take populism seriously, to the extent that they strive to invent its leftist version.[2] This brings us to the third meaning of populism. Here the incapacity of the left to introduce an affect politics of its own is at stake: it remains questionable whether imitating the populist organization of affects will allow the left to beat the right at its own game.[3] The common denominator of these aspects is the coupling of semblance and affect. Populism is less about political content than it is about the form of social mobilization, which organizes an "affective economy"[4] in accordance with the "dangerous tendencies" of the capitalist system. For this reason it makes sense to insist that populism is a contemporary symptomatic expression of capitalism running amuck.

The problematic of populism comes with a reminder that the division between reason and affect does not contribute to our understanding of politics. This brings us back to the liberal deployment of the term for discrediting political opponents. Such use indeed departs from the opposition between reason and passions, thinking and affect, normality and normativity of the law, on the one hand, and abnormality and anarchism of affects, on the other. Liberalism remains astonishingly blind to its own confrontations with the problematic of social passions, not least in the work of its founding figure, Adam Smith. While the dichotomy of reason and passions must be rejected as false, another distinction can be made in the field of affects themselves: between the social and the antisocial affects, or differently, between affects, which allow for the construction and sustaining of social bonds, even if only in a precarious manner, and affects, which actively dismantle these bonds.[5] Contemporary debates on left and right populism seem to turn around the fact that affects appear both as the means of social organization and as a means of social dissolution. The latter marks the rule of right-wing populism, but this should not mislead us into believing that under liberalism social bonds were less unstable or endangered, on the contrary.

As discussions have evolved around populism, one particular notion has undergone a renaissance: resentment (*ressentiment*). Along with this affect the problem of the antisocial fully enters the picture. The antisocial, too, can be understood in three different manners. Its most obvious meaning is the negation of the social, dismantling the bonds that hold society together. The second connotation concerns what is at stake in the populist mobilization of resentment, the turn away from structural contradictions of the capitalist mode of production, their mystification through aggressive politics of spectacle, the fabrication of scapegoats, and conspiracy theories barely accounting for the present social condition. The third meaning relates to the appearance, according to which whatever operates as antisocial disrupts the otherwise uncorrupted social relations and regulated economic order. This third meaning overlooks that resentment is a *systemically* induced affective economy, a manner in which the power of "no-body" actualizes in "every-body." While the vulgar figures of right-wing populism are a rude reminder that "politics [. . .] essentially stands in the element of affects" (Lordon, 2016: 12),[6] this still requires that affects be considered in structural rather than psychological terms. Only a structural view allows us to understand resentment as a bodily manifestation of systemic resistance against social and economic transformation. Needless to add, the urgency of such systemic change only increases in our times of accelerated climate breakdown; what equally intensifies in response is the overt aggressiveness of the global capitalist system.

The enforced antisocial affective turn in contemporary capitalism did not emerge out of nowhere. It stands in continuity with the political development of the past two decades, the breakdown of the last grand narrative, which in the late twentieth century seemingly solidified the capitalist social bond: the justifiably ridiculed liberal idea (spelled out by Francis Fukuyama) according to which history culminated in the global triumph of capitalist parliamentarism. The myth of the end of history replaced the notion of progress with the idea of growth, comprising the virtually endless economic growth, or rather a fantasy thereof, and a post-historical expansion of the liberal model. With the breakdown of this ideological tale humanity progressively entered an epoch that could be characterized as the implosion of history. More precisely, if the decade of the end of history (the 1990s) was followed by one in which it was possible to speak of a return of history (the 2000s), then the second decade of the twenty-first century moved in the direction of an overtly catastrophic introversion of capitalism.[7] The climate emergency shows not only that the pursuit of economic growth encountered its limits; it also demonstrates that the fantasy of perpetual growth can now only be sustained by means of a systemic running amuck. It is hardly surprising that contemporary capitalist ideology comes with a sort of negative version of capitalist self-naturalization, a capitalist naturalism recycled for catastrophic times: the effort of identifying the end of capitalism with the end of the world, the conviction that climate breakdown, accompanied by the conditions of a global civil war, is the only way for capitalism to end.[8] By imposing this identification of the end of capitalism with the end of the world, capitalism enforces the old view of pessimistic political philosophies, according to which violence is the very DNA of human nature.

The Anti-sociality of Neoliberalism

The populist organization of antisocial affects should in any case not seduce us in believing that this development stands for some kind of negative reaction to the decades of neoliberal deregulation and austerity. Political figures like Donald Trump and Jair Bolsonaro, to name only two examples with global impact, personify the antisocial tendencies of neoliberalism and signal the renewed, undisguised embrace of colonial and sexual violence. Wendy Brown pointed out this continuity between neoliberalism and the new authoritarians by breaking their shared political project down to the overtly antisocial slogan "society must be dismantled" (Brown, 2019).[9] According to Brown, Margret Thatcher explicated this perspective in her notorious remark: "There's no such thing as society. There are individual men and women and there are families." In denying the existence of society, Thatcher expresses the neoliberal conviction, according to which society is an artificial and restrictive construction at odds with the "self-evident" existence of individuals, their "natural" inclination to self-love, and, most crucially, the assumed market capacity of self-regulation and auto-correction. The only symbolic space, in which individuals and their families operate in accordance with their interests, is the market, which for neoliberalism most certainly exists,[10] and the only "social" relation worth pursuing is that of economic competition. Thatcher's political axiom, then, suggests that there is no such thing as independent social bonds outside economic exchange, and consequently, there is no society of humans, only a society of markets, where individuals are nothing more than units of economic calculus and where constant interplay of private interests takes place: an antisocial society, driven by mutual exclusion through competition.

However, this deregulated vision of the social does not constitute a total break with previous capitalist modes of organizing the social; it remains supplemented with "tradition" (Thatcher mentions the nuclear family and binary sexual difference). Consequently, it remains haunted by the all too familiar forms of violence that have been constitutive of capitalism throughout the centuries.[11] When reflecting on the combination of neoliberal deregulation and "traditional morality" in Thatcher's remark, Brown quite tellingly speaks of the "neoliberal dream":

> The neoliberal dream was a global order of freely owing and accumulating capital, nations organized by traditional morality and markets, and states oriented almost exclusively to this project. Nailed to the requirements of markets that are neither self-stabilizing nor enduringly competitive, the neoliberal state, with its commitment to freedom and legislating only universal rules, would also protect the traditional moral order against incursions by rationalists, planners, redistributionists, and other egalitarians. (Brown, 2019: 82)

It was the Austrian-born economist Friedrich von Hayek who most vigorously insisted that traditional moral codes and modern market rules stand in mutual symmetry to each other. At first glance this symmetry may appear paradoxical, since tradition imposes itself as a sphere of seemingly invariable laws, conducts, and identities, whereas the market repeatedly reveals itself as the register of structural instability and recurring crises. Neoliberal orthodoxy strives to overcome this apparent tension by conceiving the market as a symbolic space capable of self-regulation. In a similar manner, Adam Smith deployed the metaphor of the Invisible Hand and Providence in order to name the market's spontaneous regulation of individual and corporate private interests. For Smith, the function of the market ultimately comes down to guaranteeing the social embedding of the otherwise antisocial tendencies of private interests. But while Smith strived for a metaphysically grounded economic doctrine,[12] the neoliberal discourse on market spontaneity, self-regulation, and self-correction displays all the features of superstition, camouflaged by the reference to traditional morality. Society may not exist, but traditional morality does, and this morality must join forces with the market in order to unfold its value-generating potentials. Hayek was one of the loudest proponents of such a combination. His dream was to install "markets and morality where society and democracy once were, through the principle of freedom from state regulation" (Brown, 2019: 108),[13] targeting a thorough realization of the economic Nobody in everybody. However, this aim required the combination of economic violence (market deregulation and precarization of labor) and social violence (neo-patriarchy and neo-colonialism). In this precise regard contemporary authoritarian populism is nothing more than a violent offspring of neoliberalism. By striving to roll back the precarious results of emancipatory struggles (feminism, anti-colonialism, LGBTQI+ struggle, environmentalism, etc.), it continues to combine regulation of subjectivities and deregulation of the markets, no longer concealing that the truth of tradition is violence and obscenity. Right-wing populists may create the impression that they do away with morality, and thus with the presumably stabilizing perspective that Hayek's attempt of uniting social regulation and economic deregulation relied upon. But their political practice shows that they draw their affective capital from the toxic core of tradition: masculine supremacism, religious fanaticism, and conspiracy thinking.

The populist radicalization of neoliberalism can be exemplified in the way it engages in the construction of the people that it claims to merely represent.[14] Because the populist vision of the people rests on the rejection of enemy figures and menacing others, their attempt in constructing a unified people's body is underpinned by aggressivity. In this scenario, the people comes down to a bifurcated mass, which directs its resentment both outwards and inwards, combining rejection of cultural, racialized, and sexual others with economic competition. In the end the ideal people of right-wing populism finds its realization in an autoaggressive mass tied together by negative affects and embedded in a gradual process of self-dissolution.[15] Despite claiming otherwise, right-wing populism is a politics that is ultimately geared to dismantling the people. In doing so it perpetuates the neoliberal antisocial contract and strives for a social bond, which is ultimately an "un-bond," a paradoxical, antisocial social bond grounded on destructive impulses and actively working on dissolving the social.

What seems to unite left and right populism is that the construction of the people in both cases depends on the operation of *homogenizing division*, which is supposed to draw a clear and univocal border between the body of the people and a host of supposedly foreign bodies. The obvious difference is that left populism for the most part delimits the people from the more or less abstract elites, whereas its right-wing counterpart always targets concrete bodies: migrants and foreigners, women and homosexuals, Muslims and atheists, etc. While in the left appropriation of populism the body of the people remains an open set of different subjectivities, the right-wing construction of a homogenous body of tradition unsurprisingly stands in the sign of masculinity (and masculine fantasies of femininity). Every attempt at imposing the unified vision of *the* people (which is to say: the fantasy of an uncastrated, phallocentric people's body without inner differences) requires a libidinal economy of resentment as its foundation. Although there are certainly enormous differences as to the question of the social, the process of unification in both cases follows the familiar scheme of the friend-enemy-divide, which unsurprisingly sustains the ongoing generation of resentment. In other words, resentment is the inevitable affective surplus of the homogenizing division, the affect that logically results from the determination of the other as a threat of the people's consistency or one's own identity. For this reason the left succumbing to the populist temptation always encounters the same affective deadlock, in contrast to the populist right, which hardly wants to be anything more than a (neoliberal) politics of resentment.

There is yet another truth that populists hardly fail to make clear, namely that they are ultimately nothing more and nothing less than a politics of negation, directed against the unified enemy, either the abstract and indeterminate elites, as in the case of left populism, or against every political subjectivity embodying difference (again beginning with women via racialized subjects to refugees and beyond), when it comes to right-wing populism. Here, an important detail from Wendy Brown's formulation of the neoliberal project can be recalled, "Society *must* be dismantled." The dismantling of social bonds is a political imperative, an obligation of politics toward the market. Needless to recall, neoliberalism is an open call for the subversion of the social through the antisocial tendencies of capitalism. It is therefore hardly surprising that the advocates of neoliberal orthodoxy hasten to protest on behalf of the markets, these suprasensual beings, who, in the words of their political and economic administrators, "react in panic" whenever an emergence or solidification of the social is on the horizon. It is in the moments of intensified instability that the disembodied capitalist Nobody demonstrates its problematic anchoring in corporeality, as disturbance and disruption that violates subjectivized bodies.

The populist politics of negation must not be conflated with something that could be called a politics of negativity. Despite the legitimate critique that can be addressed to Marx for privileging the white industrial proletariat as the agent of revolutionary change,[16] his political and economic work continues to exemplify the effort of uniting multiple emancipatory struggles in a common political aim of overcoming the resistance of capitalism against social change and, more fundamentally, against the existence of society. Politics of negation and politics of negativity comprise two incompatible visions of political subjectivity. While populism can pursue its unification of the people only under the condition that it negates its others, the politics of negativity has to construct an inwardly heterogeneous subject, whose main feature is precisely difference. Rather than recognizing the subject's immanent nonidentity, populism stands for its exteriorization. The people is presumably without the negativity of difference and thus without the potential for transformation, given that difference is the driving force of movement, change, and becoming. To the populist logic of homogenizing division, one could contrast something like the logic of *immanent differentiation*. The latter no longer pursues the task of reestablishing a presumably lost or corrupted imaginary unity and instead strives to construct an "unbordered" political subjectivity, which is no longer defined through the rejection of difference but, rather, through its mobilization. Immanent differentiation suggests that political subjectivity is more than a mere collection of different identities. Because it comprises a multiplicity of identities, which moreover all undergo historical transformations and are therefore never completely constituted as identities, the "trans-differential subject" that is supposed to unify them is equally nonidentical.

Resentment between Systemic Violence and Systemic Enjoyment

The distinction between the politics of negation and the politics of negativity gives us reason to reconsider a controversial polemical notion in Marx, the rabble (*Lumpenproletariat*). This category may provide another way of addressing the continuity between neoliberalism and today's proliferation of antisocial affects, enforced by the populist turn in politics. A closer look at Marx's ambiguous remarks on the *Lumpenproletariat* may reveal that he describes a social formation, which strikingly resembles the mass mobilized by right-wing populists, with the increasingly significant role of conspiracy thinking.[17] Moreover, the main function of today's populism may indeed consist in the transformation of what political liberalism promotes under the notion of the people into the *Lumpenproletariat*. This affective metamorphosis or mutation of the people further exemplifies Brown's point regarding the neoliberal dismantling of society.

Marx's attitude toward the *Lumpenproletariat* is anything but unproblematic: "The 'dangerous class,' the social scum, that passively rotting mass thrown off by the lowest layers of old society, may, here and there, be swept into the movement by a proletarian revolution; its conditions of life, however, prepare it far more for the part of a bribed tool of reactionary intrigue" (Marx, 2000: 254). One detail is nevertheless worth retaining: the *Lumpenproletariat* is bribed. The specification *lumpen* contains its share of semantic lessons, suggesting that we are dealing with a negative double of the proletariat. Furthermore *lumpen* is metonymically linked with "pseudo," suggesting that the *Lumpenproletariat* can be understood as a proletariat without truth—above all without the truth about the contradictions in the presumably free and equal economic exchange. For Marx, the proletariat is a symptomatic product of the valorization of living bodies, the perfect counterpart of the political-economic fiction of *homo oeconomicus*. It is not unimportant that the proletariat is bought (participates in relations of exchange), whereas the *Lumpenproletarian* is bribed (participates in systemic corruption). Economic relations transform living bodies into producers of value and labor-power, while bribing turns them into an extension of systemic resistance against emancipatory political organization. The *Lumpenproletariat* is "bought" in order to "make violence"—violence being its specific "surplus-product"—and in doing so incite fear of the masses, creating the appearance that all political masses are ultimately violent mobs.[18] The populist politics of resentment actively pursues the *lumpenproletarization* of political subjectivity in order to continue dismantling the social; it constructs a "dangerous class" that will contribute to the perseverance of capitalism in catastrophic times.

The association of *Lumpenproletariat* with the lower and disorganized social groups is not Marx's ultimate word on the topic, nor is it the most interesting aspect of the problematic. Another feature of the *Lumpenproletariat* is that it stands for the point of contact between the lowest and the highest, social abject and financial capital: "The finance aristocracy, in its mode of acquisition as well as in its pleasures, is nothing more than the rebirth of the *Lumpenproletariat* on the heights of bourgeois society" (Marx, 2000: 316).[19] In this line, the *Eighteenth Brumaire* declares Louis Bonaparte the "*chief of the lumpenproletariat*, who here alone rediscovers in mass form the interests which he personally pursues, who recognizes in this sum, offal, refuse of all classes the only class upon which he can base himself unconditionally" (Marx, 1975: 75). The *Lumpenproletariat* must not be reduced to what seems to be its predominant appearance, poverty. Beyond this appearance the term describes a structural position, covering the refuse of *all* classes. The word *Abfall*, closely associated with the *Lumpenproletariat*, must be taken seriously. What is at stake is production of the social abject, the flipside of the predominant antisocial production taking place in capitalism, production of surplus-value, or "production for the sake of production" (Marx, 1990: 742). Just like surplus-value is deprived of social value—its sole "social" value being tied to the self-valorization of capital, another name for antisocial economic activity—there seems to be no inherent social bond between abjects. Contemporary right-wing populism offers itself as a politics, which claims to provide a social bond to this unbound systemic product. It forms abjects into a coherent group, using precisely resentment as the affective binding material. In doing so the figure of the populist accomplishes a paradoxical achievement, pushing for a social bond that inherently unbinds and dissolves the social.

Although it would be tempting to associate it with the meanwhile dismantled working class, resentment is not a class affect. Rather, its organizing function, that is, its importance in the process of *lumpenproletarization* of political subjectivity explains why today's right-wing populism attracts workers, middle class, and financial elites alike. Nietzsche's critique of resentment has its share in the false attribution of this antisocial affect. In turn, we can find an important reformulation of the problem in Max Scheler, who thoroughly questioned Nietzsche's association of resentment with "slave morality." While adopting Nietzsche's focus on the subject's impotency in the generation of resentment, Scheler at the same time demonstrates that its actual causes must be sought in the economic sphere. The conditions for resentment to proliferate are given in a society, "in which everyone has the 'right' to compare himself with everyone, and yet factually cannot compare himself" (Scheler, 2017: 9). Scheler's observation can be supplemented with Marx's remark that "commodity exchange [. . .] is the exclusive realm of Freedom, Equality, Property and Bentham" (1990: 280), yet behind this social façade we find exploitation, inequality, expropriation, and violence. It is the constant experience of the gap between appearance and structure that gives ground for the generation of resentment—an affect that Scheler explicitly links with the rise of liberalism, its social implementation of a universal law of private property, and its restriction of social bonds to the system of mutual competition and exclusion.

The system of resentment was not introduced by some fictitious "slave morality," which according to Nietzsche's narration reached its organizational peak in Christianity; it was indeed an effect of the capitalist organization of production, and more specifically the shift from finite exchange to virtually endless production of value:

> The structure of motivation becomes Money-Commodity-Money, whereas before it was Commodity-Money-Commodity (K. Marx). The enjoyment of qualitative values of course does not cease, but this enjoyment—yes its possibility—now itself moves within the limits of goods, which are at first perceived as units of commodity values. (Marx, 1990: 15)

One could say that in the circulation C-M-C, the economic sphere is still organized around the satisfaction of needs. Although this activity is incomplete, repetitive, and accompanied by enjoyment, it remains a finite process, in which no surplus functions as the main structural motive. M-C-M' changes this by organizing the entire social and subjective sphere around the demand for uninterrupted and virtually endless quantitative increase of value. With this shift, satisfaction becomes indistinguishable from dissatisfaction: "The modern ascetics shows itself in the fact that enjoyment of the pleasurable, to which all useful is related, undergoes constant displacement" (Scheler, 2017: 95). It is crucial that Scheler recognizes in the "constant displacement" of enjoyment, hence in satisfaction *qua* dissatisfaction a key feature of ascetics. Capitalism is a moral order, grounded on "renunciation of enjoyment"; it is this ongoing renunciation that according to Lacan conditions production of what he calls "surplus-enjoyment" (2006).

Lacan recognized the paradigm of this renunciation in Pascal's wager. To recall the point in question, in his *Pensées*, Pascal engages in a thought experiment, where he must convince the libertine to abolish his pursuit of earthly pleasures in favor of belief in God, adding that this renunciation will in any case be rewarded. If it turns out that God exists, the libertine will gain infinite amount of pleasure beyond pleasure— precisely surplus-enjoyment—and should the libertine's skepticism be proven right, he will have to concede that he ended up losing nothing, for life in accordance with morality is in any case more valuable than life in pleasure. What at first glance appears to be a win-win-situation embeds the subject of wager in a compulsive system of moral imperatives and rituals, in which the feeling of loss and the chase for an unattainable surplus condition and intensify each other. No "enjoyment of the pleasurable" is any longer possible, no use-value unmarked by uselessness. Dissatisfaction becomes the main general feeling: "The modern ascetics formed an ideal, whose ethical sense is the exact *opposite* of the old one: the *'ideal' of minimum of enjoyment in face of the maximum amount of pleasurable and useful things!*" (Scheler, 2017: 96–7). By sabotaging satisfaction, and moreover by imposing that the satisfaction of needs be sacrificed for the impossible satisfaction of systemic demand for surplus-value, capitalism pursues the imperative of uselessness.[20] Scheler's point regarding the interdependency between the minimum of enjoyment and the maximum of enjoyable things can be further complicated. The feeling of resentment exemplifies a libidinal economy, in which the lack-of-enjoyment and surplus-enjoyment, dissatisfaction and satisfaction are fused together, turning the subject's impotency into a source of surplus-enjoyment.

It is hardly surprising that such libidinal economy is marked above all by aggressivity toward others: "Resentment is the idea that there are others who enjoy instead of me; if I do not enjoy it is because of them. And such impotent rage itself becomes enjoyment" (Fassin, 2017: 76). Rage signals that the person in question obeys the capitalist imperative to renounce enjoyment. He misidentifies the lost enjoyment in others, thereby assuming that they have direct access to it or that they did not respond to the systemic imperative to renounce enjoyment: migrants who "parasite" on social welfare, homosexuals who "corrupt" the youth, women who emancipate themselves from "tradition," etc. presumably enjoy without deprivation. In his assumption of the other's enjoyment, the raging subject overlooks that in his rage he is himself enjoyed by the system. The raging subject is bribed, and the currency is surplus-enjoyment. He is allowed to release aggression, while being kept in the position of impotency.[21]

Another affect that is repeatedly thematized in relation to the antisocial affective turn in contemporary politics is anxiety. With it, political commentators try to grasp the affective motivation of white Europeans and US-Americans to vote *against* their interests, for political figures, which personify the problematic features of the capitalist system, while successfully delegating the cause of social misery to minoritarian social groups. But do minoritarian groups really cause anxiety? Is the main achievement of populism not in blocking anxiety with resentment, thereby mystifying the systemic causes of the subject's impotency? Anxiety, too, is an affect embedded in a libidinal economy. But contrary to resentment, anxiety does not comprise any projection of enjoyment onto the other. Instead, the intrusion of enjoyment into the subject is at stake, and consequently, the confrontation with an enjoyment that the subject cannot recognize as her own—because it is not. In anxiety the subject confronts the actual foreignness of enjoyment, enjoyment of the system (what Lacan somewhat enigmatically called "enjoyment of the Other"), and recognizes herself in the position of *enjoyed* subject. No theft or loss of enjoyment is assumed or projected to some imaginary or real other. Furthermore, in anxiety the subject finds herself in the position of impossibility, rather than impotency, directly confronting her real status in the social bond—the material, from which surplus-value, this Marxian name for enjoyment of the system, is extracted to the point of the subject's exhaustion or destruction. It is because of this confrontation that anxiety can motivate the subject to social rather than antisocial action, even if this action consists merely of escape or flight. In difference to the violent outbursts of resentment, in anxiety the subject can articulate the demand for constructing a nonexploitative social bond. However, this does not mean to suggest that the politics of resentment should be contrasted by a politics of anxiety. Rather, the point is that, no matter how we turn it, the subject of resentment always aims at annihilating the other and more or less overtly demands that the system and its reactionary political representatives accomplish this task. In turn, the subject of anxiety demands a bond with the other or at least finds herself in the position, in which organized work on such bond can be initiated. For this reason, Lacan occasionally remarked that an important component of psychoanalysis consists in careful dosage of anxiety in order to motivate the analysand to work through her traumatic history and counteract the resistance against the analytic cure. In contrast to this scenario, populism does not cease to prove that it is engaged in converting anxiety into resentment in order to continue demolishing the bonds that hold society together. Resentment is *the* affect needed in order to put this neoliberal antisocial program into practice.

Finally, the opposition of anxiety and resentment may explain why so-called left populism risks getting caught in the structure defined by the populist right. If the existential condition of populism is the reduction of politics to the antagonistic relation between friend and enemy, then the production of resentment returns at the very core of the left's attempt to beat populism at its own game.[22] Even if this opposition is reformulated in the struggle of "us down here" (people) against "them up there" (elite), this displacement remains within the conditions, in which competitive and ultimately antisocial affects proliferate. According to Éric Fassin, who uncompromisingly rejects the idea of left populism, the leftist flirt with the populist paradigm adopts a discursive form, which has a wide-reaching impact on the very content of leftist politics:

> In fact, replacing "socialism" (or "communism," or every other substantial project of social transformation) with "populism" means to move on from a full definition of the left to another, empty one; from positive to negative version. [...] In face of neoliberalism it is certainly easier to oppose than to propose, to resist than to invent. (2017: 83–5)

The populist discourse thus desubstantializes the left, threatening to reduce it to mere affected speech devoided of content. The point here is not that the left should pursue the liberal fantasy of disaffected speech, but that in its struggle it must implement its own notion of the political, rejecting foremost the framework imposed by vertical politics, competition, and the friend-enemy divide. Communism already on the level of its name implies a horizontal politics, in which the construction of a "we" without a "them," a collectivity without exclusion remains crucial. In contrast to the populist resentment directed either against abstract "elites" (the capitalist-bureaucratic Nobody) or against subjectivities embodying difference (every-body), the communist organization of politics would require an affective term, which reflects the horizontal organization of differences in a collective body without border or identity. The French Revolution proposed one such affective term, "fraternity," which remains problematic, because it connotes both masculinity and closed society (and one should not underestimate the affective force of these connotations). Although today such affective terms seem to be lacking, political signifiers such as "community" and "solidarity" can at least fulfill the function of its placeholder.

Notes

1 As a side note, at the same moment around 1970, Jacques Lacan and Michel Foucault issued a similar diagnostic, when they spoke of the university discourse and the regime of power-knowledge. In doing so, they drew attention to the epistemic aspects

of bureaucratic rule and more generally to the role of scientific knowledge in the detachment of power from corporeality. However, it should be added that Arendt's formulation equally targets the tendency of bureaucracy toward the installment of a regime founded in paranoia. Therein lies its core danger.

2 For the same reason the liberal-centrist critique deliberately equates affect politics of the left with populism. The most recent example is Pierre Rosanvallon (2020). For a critical reply to Rosanvallon, see Chantal Mouffe's "The controversy over left-wing populism" (2020). Caught between the hegemony of liberalism and the resurgence of right-wing populism, the left often enough remains split between repeating the liberal denouncement of affective politics and the populist efficiency in mobilizing the masses by means of negative affects.

3 Another distinction between both populisms is that the left "celebrates the weak as the exclusive embodiment of moral excellence" (Losurdo, 2016: 327), whereas the right fetishizes them as the embodiment of danger to the presumably homogenous social body.

4 For the notion, see Sara Ahmed, "Affective Economies" (2004: 117–39). The systemic aspect of resentment will be addressed in the third section of this chapter.

5 Similarly, Sigmund Freud distinguished between the binding power of Eros and the dissolving power of death-drive. Lacan argued that these two names describe two contradictory tendencies in one and the same force.

6 Lordon's work exemplifies the structural take on affects.

7 In her bestseller *The Shock Doctrine* (2008), Naomi Klein used the term "disaster capitalism," which in its own way marks the historical shift in capitalism toward the full realization of its antisocial tendencies. Meanwhile right-wing populism presents itself as *the* politics for catastrophic times.

8 Echoing Fredric Jameson's well-known proverb that it is easier to imagine the end of the world than the end of capitalism, regarding the self-naturalization of capitalism, I can only recall the rightly famous lines from Marx: "When the economists say that present-day relations—the relations of bourgeois production—are natural, they imply that these are the relations in which wealth is created and productive forces developed in conformity with the laws of nature. These relations therefore are themselves natural laws independent of the influence of time" (2000: 226–7).

9 The formula is an inversion of Foucault's seminar title *Society Must Be Defended*, in which Foucault began preparing the terrain for his preoccupation with the genesis of biopolitics.

10 In the neoliberal scenario, deregulated market is the best exemplification, as well as the perfect disembodiment of decentralized power, the Nobody par excellence. In Lacanian terms, the market is the economic version of the big Other, the symbolic order, by means of which humans establish intersubjective relations.

11 "When the claim 'society does not exist' becomes common sense, it renders invisible the social norms and inequalities generated by legacies of slavery, colonialism, and patriarchy" (Brown, 2019: 42). By imposing its self-naturalization, capitalism perpetuates the naturalization of racial, sexual, and economic violence.

12 It has been argued that Smith's use of the Invisible Hand and Providence stands for the afterlife of metaphysical theodicies in the economic sphere (Vogl, 2015).

13 The development of a moral framework that accompanied the implementation of neoliberalism is further examined in Jessica Whyte, *The Morals of the Market* (2019).

14. "It is a populist illusion, symmetrical to the illusion of consensus, that it knows and recognises only one single people, as if political work consisted in expressing the people rather than constructing it" (Fassin, 2017: 61). In contrast to democratic representation, where an abstract people is constructed on the basis of election calculus, populism constructs its people by implementing a divisive affective economy. The populist procedure only appears less abstract, as long as we do not adopt the structural view, which helps recognizing in resentment the very much corporeal actualization of an excluding structure.
15. With the exclusion of the other, the social bond as such is rejected, since a social bond is always a bond with, rather than against, the other. Furthermore, it is a bond with otherness, which is not only located outside the subject but is also an inner otherness.
16. See, for instance, Silvia Federici, *Caliban and the Witch* (2004: 12). Such critique does not necessarily imply the rejection of Marx's thought. Rather, it expands the field of critique of political economy and in the same move exposes the complex structure of political subjectivity.
17. Conspiracy theories stand in a similar relation to knowledge as populism does to politics. Rather than simply relativizing knowledge and negating truth, conspiracy theories target some kind of esoteric "surplus-knowledge" and remain faithful to the doctrine of "hidden truth."
18. This was Trump's move when Black Lives Matter protesters took the streets. By trying to present them to his white base as an exemplification of violent *Lumpenproletariat*, he in fact *lumpenproletarianized* his own voters and ultimately revealed himself as a leader of the *Lumpenproletariat*. For a detailed reading of Trump in relation to the problematic of the *Lumpenproletariat*, see Clyde Barrow, *The Dangerous Class* (2020).
19. The crucial point is that the notion of *Lumpenproletariat* describes a mode of acquisition and a mode of enjoyment, thus leading to a problematic feature of capitalism, the link between value, enjoyment, and violence.
20. Here the Lacanian extension of Scheler's point concerning the structural features of capitalism comes in. Production of surplus-value is the paradigm of useless production and surplus-value *the* useless object par excellence. The connotation of uselessness and redundancy is built in the very semantic of "surplus." Surplus-value serves no purpose, except for keeping the capitalist machinery running. In this feature surplus-value touches upon Lacan's occasional definition of enjoyment (1999: 3).
21. Right-wing populism exploits the frustration resulting from the systemically imposed renunciation of enjoyment (labor being the paradigmatic example of this renunciation). As "substitute satisfaction" it offers aggressive enjoyment, which obtains its systematized expression in racism and sexism, but also in conspiracy thinking, rejection of science, etc. Because they are bribed with surplus-enjoyment, the subjects of resentment rarely move on to action themselves. For the most part they cast their vote for those who promise to act in their behalf. The mass shootings in the Unites States may be an exception to the rule. But these individuals running amuck at the same time perform the action that the subject of resentment otherwise demands from the system.
22. For this criticism, see Fassin (2017: 83–5). Of course, the friend-enemy-divide comes from Carl Schmitt. The very same divide conditions the hypothesis of "enjoying subject" that was mentioned earlier.

Bibliography

Ahmed S (2004) Affective Economies. *Social Text* 22(2): 117–39. doi:10.1215/01642472-22-2_79-117.
Arendt H (1972) *Crises of the Republic.* Harmondsworth: Penguin Books.
Barrow CW (2020) *The Dangerous Class: The Concept of the Lumpenproletariat.* Ann Arbor, MI: University of Michigan Press.
Brown W (2019) *In the Ruins of Neoliberalism: The Rise of Antidemocratic Politics in the West.* New York: Columbia University Press.
Fassin É (2017) *Populisme: Le Grand Ressentiment.* Paris: Textuel.
Federici SB (2004) *Caliban and the Witch.* New York: Autonomedia.
Klein N (2008) *The Shock Doctrine: The Rise of Disaster Capitalism.* London: Penguin Books.
Lacan J (1999) *The Seminar, Book XX: On Feminine Sexuality: The Limits of Love and Knowledge, Encore, 1972–1973* (ed. J-A Miller; trans. B Fink). New York: W.W. Norton & Co.
Lacan J (2006) *Le séminare, book XVI: D'un autre à l'autre, 1968–1969* (ed. J-A Miller). Paris: Seuil.
Lordon F (2016) *Les Affects de La Politique.* Paris: Seuil.
Losurdo D (2016) *Class Struggle: A Political and Philosophical History.* New York: Palgrave Macmillan.
Marx K (1975) *The Eighteenth Brumaire of Louis Bonaparte.* New York: International Publishers.
Marx K (1990) *Capital, Vol I: A Critique of Political Economy* (trans. B Fowkes). London: Penguin Books.
Marx K (2000) *Selected Writings.* 2nd ed. Oxford: Oxford University Press.
Mouffe C (2020) The Controversy over Left-Wing Populism. *Le Monde Diplomatique.* Available at: https://mondediplo.com/2020/05/14populism (accessed October 18, 2020).
Rosanvallon P (2020) *Le Siècle Du Populisme: Histoire, Théorie, Critique.* Paris: Éditions du Seuil.
Scheler M (2017) *Das Ressentiment im Aufbau der Moralen.* 3. Auflage. Frankfurt am Main: Vittorio Klostermann GmbH.
Vogl J (2015) *The Specter of Capital.* Stanford, CA: Stanford University Press.
Whyte J (2019) *The Morals of the Market: Human Rights and the Rise of Neoliberalism.* Brooklyn, NY: Verso Books.

6

"That's Disgusting!"

The Shifting Politics of Affect in Right-wing Populist Mobilization

Maria Brock and Jenny Gunnarsson Payne

During a plenary debate at the European Parliament regarding an alleged criminalization of sex education in Polish schools in 2019, EMP for the German right-wing populist party Alternative für Deutschland (AfD) Christine Anderson not only equated sex education with teaching primary school children "sexual practices such as oral and anal sex, and encouraging them to do it with whomever" but also referred to such education as the "*disgusting* attempt to sexualise our children as prematurely as possible," the driving force behind which she identifies the "disgusting left-green ideology" (*links-gruene Ekelideologie*). Invoking the affect of disgust in order to express moral outrage about current political matters is a trope increasingly used in conservative, nationalist, and populist discourses, especially (but not exclusively) in relation to issues of gender and sexuality. More significantly still, the trope is swiftly making its way into the political mainstream.

This chapter centers on the increasing prevalence of such public expressions of revulsion in relation to feminists and LGBTQ subjects by public figures, especially in the context of what Chantal Mouffe (2018) has called "the populist moment," as well as the more recent "turn to gender" in the radical populist right and the increasing influence of anti-gender politics in Europe and beyond (see, for example, Gunnarsson Payne, 2019; Sayan-Cengiz and Tekin, 2019; Korolczuk and Graff, 2021). We argue that the latter has paved the way for a shift whereby not only issues of gender and sexuality have come to constitute a central battlefield in the so-called culture wars but also for an "affective shift," whereby the affects of anger, *ressentiment*, and fear increasingly coexist alongside that of disgust as a form of moral outrage—and that this has serious consequences for issues of gender equality and reproductive and sexual rights. Although it is not possible, or even desirable, to offer a "taxonomy" of these affects and their exact relationship to each other, we argue that any theoretical discussion on current populism and its affective force needs to take such expressions of disgust seriously. As we demonstrate in the following discussion, while relying on stereotypes and preexisting forms of stigma, these sentiments of *moral disgust* and revulsion are carefully engineered to create new political alliances and coalitions at a time when general support for LGBTQ rights, gender equality, and reproductive rights for women are seemingly higher than at any other point in modern history.

The aim of this chapter, then, is to investigate the psychic and discursive (or psycho-discursive) work performed when something is denoted as disgusting, especially within the context of the radical right's "turn to gender" and the increasing influence of anti-gender politics. We will investigate the ways in which expressions of disgust serve a mobilizing function in uniting a range of right-wing populist and conservative groups, and how this mobilizing function feeds on longer political traditions of stigmatization and abjection of women and sexual minorities—traditions that have not only proven to be politically effective in the creations of "enemies" to fear but that have also, as we shall see, served important disciplinary functions in keeping the people in place. To this end, we will begin with a brief discussion of the relationship between right-wing populism, sexuality, and gender. Second, we will examine the affects that characterize the "populist moment," especially in its right-wing instantiations, and third, we turn to disgust, from its origins to its targets and the psychic and socio-legal implications thereof. In the conclusion, we shall discuss possible responses to the effects of disgust entering the political and discursive arena.

Anti-gender Mobilization in the Populist Moment: Gender, Sexuality, and "the People"

The beginnings of the "anti-gender narrative," which today has grown into a transnational political formation on a global scale, are well documented. Its emergence can be found in the mid-1990s conservative Catholic initiative offering resistance to the integration and implementation of reproductive and sexual rights into human rights discourse and policy documents. The perceived risk at hand was that of the global normalization of homosexuality and abortion, as well as the disintegration of the "traditional" family and "traditional" motherhood. The two UN conferences in 1994 and 1995, the Conference on Population and Development in Cairo and the Fourth Conference on Women in Beijing respectively, have been pointed out as important events for what would later grow into today's so-called *anti-gender politics*.

Indeed, the formulation of the antiestablishment narrative against "gender" is evident already in the 1997 book *The Gender Agenda: Redefining Equality* where Dale O'Leary, a conservative Christian US journalist and "anti-gender public intellectual," described the polarization around "gender" during these conferences in terms of an antagonistic struggle between left and right, arguing that "[i]n the culture wars, the Left generally supports sexual liberation, sexually explicit entertainment, abortion on demand, homosexual rights, contraceptive-based sex education, quotas, and affirmative action, while the right supports marriage, the family, life, chastity, and equality of opportunity" (1997: 24).

Against this enemy stand "normal" men and women, united "not by adherence to a particular religion, but by a commitment to the family and a belief in human nature"

(1997: 24). O'Leary's narrative quickly caught on in conservative Christian circles, as well as Orthodox and Evangelical ones, and, as we shall see, subsequently in more secular contexts. In this narrative the very concept of gender is associated with danger, not just to individual religious men, women, and children: it is said to threaten the "basic unit of society" ("the family") and, as a consequence, human civilization as such; its teachings are said to rely on a distorted ("ideological") understanding of "nature" and "science," the methods used to impose it onto "common" people are understood as a form of Soviet-style social engineering (Gunnarsson Payne, 2019; Kuhar and Patternotte, 2017). The quest for anti-gender proponents, then, is to counter this oppressive "gender regime" by spreading the words of "truth."

This proselytization has indeed been successful. Through effective mobilization, through petitions, on- and offline media, lobbying organizations, think tanks, publishers, and conferences with their own movement intellectuals as keynote speakers, the message has spread far outside the rather narrow circles in which it was first formulated and is today embraced and reproduced by other right-wing populist and extreme-right parties and organizations. The most well-known organizations and platforms for mobilization include World Congress of Families; Political Network for Values; *LifeSite*; Tradition, Family and Property; CitizenGo, and Agenda Europe (Datta, 2018, Gunnarsson Payne and Tornhill, 2021). The influence of the increasing number of radical conservative organizations lobbying for a "return" to "traditional values" at the level of UN and EU should not be underestimated (e.g., European Centre for Law and Justice (ECLJ), Alliance Defending Freedom, European Federation for Life and Human Dignity), and neither shall the growing numbers of national organizations working for this cause (the Ordo Iuris Institute in Poland, the Clapham Institute in Sweden, etc.) (Korolczuk and Graff, 2021, Gunnarsson Payne, 2019). In other words, the turn to (anti-)gender politics in nationalist right-wing populism and authoritarian illiberal political projects is by no means a coincidence, but must rather be understood as the result of a successful mobilization to articulate their ideas of "traditional family values" with nationalist understandings of the people.

Gender, Sexuality, the People, and Its Enemies

While the "anti-gender turn" in nationalist right-wing populism and authoritarian, as well as the so-called illiberal democracy, must be analyzed in light of active anti-gender mobilization, its current status also has to be understood in the context of what Chantal Mouffe has described as a "populist moment" (2018). "The happy marriage" between right-wing populism, "illiberal democracy," and anti-gender politics—or what Elżbieta Korolczuk and Agnieszka Graff (2021) call their "opportunistic synergy"—thrives off the same neoliberal hegemony of the last few decades, its failure to live up to its own promises, and especially the disastrous austerity politics after the financial crisis in 2008 (Mouffe, 2018). What these in part overlapping political projects offer is both a critique of the democratic deficit in neoliberal global governance whereby power has been removed from democratically elected bodies and handed over to global corporations and supra-national organizations and an alternative to the rampant individualism, elitism, and self-responsibility proscribed by neoliberal ideals. Taken together, the responses offered—if only on the level of rhetoric—promise to restore the sovereignty of the nation and its people and the autonomy of (heterosexual nuclear) families, against the (real and imagined) cultural, political, and financial elites. In other words, the fact that both follow a populist logic of articulation, constructing an antagonistic frontier that divides "society into two camps and calling for the mobilisation of the 'underdog' against 'those in power'; 'the people' against 'the elite'" (Mouffe, 2018: 11) provides another key for understanding their "easy fit." Hence, although there is no *intrinsic* compatibility between the two political projects, their formal similarities have eased their mutual articulation.

In some contexts, such as Poland and Hungary, anti-genderism has made its way into the governing parties and influenced public policy. In other countries, such as Sweden and Germany, the right-wing populist parties Sverigedemokraterna and AfD manage to combine femo- and homonationalist discourse with anti-gender politics, sometimes in seemingly incompatible ways (see also Sayan-Cengiz and Tekin, 2019). Such different (though sometimes combined) articulations of gender, sexuality, and "the people" are continuously used to establish and guard national and regional, physical and symbolic borders, not least with regard to imagined moral geographies of "East" and "West" (see, for example, Edenborg, 2020; Graff and Korolczuk, 2021). In this new geopolitical moral landscape, "the East" (e.g., Russia and Poland) has often come to represent "the last bastion of Christian civilisation," as opposed to a "morally corrupted and degenerated West."

Right-wing Populist Affect: Fear, Anger, Disgust

As Renata Salecl observed already in the years after the disintegration of the Soviet Union, the then rising nationalism in several regions of the former Eastern Bloc consisted of creating "a specific version of the 'moral majority' (in Poland, Slovenia and Croatia etc.), which conceives Christian values as the ideological 'cement' holding together the Nation, demands the prohibition of abortion etc" (Salecl, 1994: 20). In this way, this construction of a moral majority, then as well as now, "have built their power by creating similar fantasies of a threat to the nation and so put themselves forward as the protector of 'what is in us more than our selves'—our being a part of the nation" (Salecl, 1994: 20). As Salecl argues, such nationalist identifications are

> based on the fantasy of the enemy, an alien who has insinuated himself into our society and constantly threatens us with habits, discourse and rituals which are not of "our kind." No matter what this Other "does," he threatens us with his existence. (1994: 20-1)

The common political rhetoric of "threats"—to the nation, to civilization, to the family, to "our" women and children—in contexts of right-wing populism and anti-gender politics has often been described as a "politics of fear" that feeds on citizens' concerns, in particular in times of crisis (Wodak, 2015: 2). Indeed, both anti-immigration and anti-gender rhetoric consistently point out minority groups as scapegoats (e.g., immigrants and queers) that are held responsible for the destruction of the nation. Metaphors of war, extinction, disease, and even genocide are used: "the culture war," "ebola from Brussels," "worse than nazism and communism put together," "the plague" (e.g., Korolżuk and Graff, 2018; Gunnarsson Payne, 2020).

In the literature on right-wing populist and radical mobilization, particular attention is often also paid to the politics of grievance or *ressentiment* (Hoggett, 2018; Canovan, 1999; Demertzis, 2006). These affects are regarded as amplifying the resurgence of reactionary and right-wing populist movements in the mid- to late 2010s. While this resurgence is at least in part facilitated by increasing economic and social inequalities, it frequently seeks to identify unconnected objects or others as targets of their anger. In the wake of the election of Trump and the Brexit vote, Pankaj Mishra went as far as calling the current time the "age of anger." While he is more concerned with the roots of the specifically *nationalist* anger he views as dominating the contemporary spectrum of political emotions, he also speaks about the (perceived) facets of those who become targets of this anger, namely "an allegedly cosmopolitan and rootless cultural elite," members of which "conveniently embody the vices of a desperately sought-after but infuriatingly unattainable modernity" (Mishra, 2016). Importantly, in a politics of *ressentiment*, there is a palpable investment in the status of victim, and the "moral narcissism" associated with that (Hoggett, 2018: 400). The sense of injury—often connected to a perceived loss of an ideal—is sustained and offers a kind of narcissistic satisfaction. Like in disgust, one's perceived opponents are frequently deprived of their humanity, which in turn is the result of envy stemming from a sense that the other has what one is entitled to (or as commonly phrased in the psychoanalytical literature, "they are stealing our enjoyment"). However, and importantly, the negative affect at the heart of these grievances is a hatred of authority or authority figures that have failed subjects. They nevertheless submit to authority, and the repression of these feelings due to a sense of powerlessness can lead to their targeting other objects in expressions of "social ressentiment."

The charge of cosmopolitanism and elitism which is so characteristic of expressions of populist grievance, and the privilege associated with this, is often applied to feminists and LGBTQ subjects, perhaps in part due to popular ideas and representations of their lives, imbuing them with an economic, intellectual, and social capital that distorts lived reality and neglects continued inequalities and dangers facing many women and queers. At the same time, moral panics such as the "Lavender Scare" in McCarthy's America also demonstrate that there is an at least latent suspicion of a lack of "loyalty" to the nation, whereby a "cosmopolitan" orientation can be reinterpreted as potential acts of betrayal of one's fellow citizens. The recent rise of "pink economics," "business feminism," and other forms of "progressive neoliberalism" (see, for example, Fraser, 2017) has offered further support for forces seeking to articulate feminism and LGBTQ-issues with powerful global economic interests (Gunnarsson Payne and Tornhill, 2021).

A more psychosocial reading of the anger experienced in relation to such rootless, "immoral" others would focus on the work of the defenses, and the ways in which those we resent are also intimately connected to the self; how we may in fact need them as a way of expelling unwelcome parts of ourselves. In a move that synthesizes these affects, Barry Richards speaks of the interrelation between fear and anger in their manifestation of a specifically populist affect, especially in relation to the resurgence of nationalism around the Brexit campaign:

> The defence of projection enables us to deal with unwanted feelings by experiencing them as present in others, not in ourselves. [...] Like all defences, however, it deals with an internal problem only by creating another: the externalisation of parts of the self creates an "other" with whom one cannot live, and who must be avoided, feared—or in the worst case—attacked and destroyed in order to defend the self from attack or contamination. (Richards, 2019: 176, authors' italics)

For the current discussion, it is the fear of contamination by parts of ourselves we believed we had managed to expel that is particularly relevant, along with the strict need to police boundaries between the self and those undesired "others." In other words, while it does make sense to speak of a politics of fear in this respect—all of these metaphors and comparisons do indeed connote various threats—the analyses of a politics of fear or *ressentiment* do not tell the whole story. For example, when, in the summer of 2019, the archbishop of Kraków Marek Jędraszewski called the rainbow flag a "neo-marxist plague with roots in Marxism and bolshevism," the metaphorical plague does not merely connote an external threat, but also an immanent risk to the national body contaminating it with an "illness" displaying gruesome, and indeed "disgusting," symptoms. What is at stake here is not only "safety" but also "purity" (see also Gunnarsson Payne, 2020). Although metaphors of illness and contagion (Sontag, 1978), ideals of moral and ideological purity or expressions of disgust are not unique to conservative and right-wing politics, we argue that in order to understand the affective grip of anti-gender discourse, its consequences for targeted groups, and its political utility for contemporary right-wing populism, we need to better understand their psychosocial effects. To this end, we thus need to turn to disgust and its "close cousins," shame and contempt.

Disgusting Others: The Sociopolitical Workings of Revulsion

William Ian Miller has claimed that disgust is above all "a moral and social sentiment" which "plays a motivating and confirming role in moral judgement in a particular way," thereby ranking "people and things in a kind of cosmic ordering" (1997: 2). Disgust is related to the *particular* danger intrinsic to pollution, contamination, and defilement and, according to Miller, "involves particular thoughts, characteristically very intrusive and persistent thoughts" about its object (1997: 8).

> Some emotions, among which disgust and its close cousin contempt are the most prominent, have intensely political significance. They work to hierarchize our political order: in some settings they do the work of maintaining hierarchy; in other settings they constitute righteously presented claims for superiority; in yet other

settings they are themselves elicited as an indication of one's proper placement in the social order. Disgust evaluates (negatively) what it touches, proclaims the meanness and inferiority of its object. (Miller, 1997: 8–9)

Disgust is sometimes used to justify making an act illegal—a move of which, Martha Nussbaum argues, we should be inherently suspicious. And while she concedes, like Miller, that there may be evolutionary reasons for disgust's prominence in the human repertoire of affects, we should refrain from making a sense of disgust the arbiter of a society's civilizational level, whereby "feeling disgusted" with a group of people or set of practices could be seen as a form of refinement or even societal progress. Instead, the problematic cognitive content of disgust can be likened to a form of magical thinking, which equates human vulnerability and mortality with animality and looks for ways to rid itself of this state.

According to Nussbaum, such fantasized acts of purification of the community are adjacent to a "highly dangerous and aggressive xenophobia" (Nussbaum 2004: 107). Her examples include the anti-semitism of National Socialist Germany, racist legislation in the United States, and the misogyny and homophobia that are at the root of the type of disgust we detailed earlier. As with moral panics, contemporary preoccupations with specific groups or practices point to recurrent fears of societal disintegration and instability, and the need to manage this fear. There is nothing "natural" about homophobia, and using disgust as a vantage point teaches us nothing about LGBTQ+ individuals. However, it "shows us that this group is currently a focus of our desire to cordon ourselves off from the viscous, the all-too-animal" (Nussbaum, 2004: 134).

Boundary work that makes an appeal to disgust is particularly evident in contemporary conservative and right-wing populist mobilization. The ultraconservative news site *LifeSite*, for example, uses a type of trigger warning, cautioning their readers about "disgusting contents" in articles on topics such as pornography, pedophilia, prostitution, sado-masochism, and pride. Expressions of revulsion are common in the site's posts which concerns sex and minors. One blog post by recurring author Jonathan Van Maren (2019) has the long and telling title: "'Pride' Celebrations: A Disgusting Month of Naked Men Twerking for Innocent Kids." In another text, his colleague Peter La Barbera (2017) criticizes an article in *Teen Vogue* for describing how to perform anal sex (or as he calls it, anal "sodomy") safely. Like in the initial example of AfD, a point of concern for him is anal sex.

Appeals to a sense of disgust as a foundation for specific legislative or more broadly political measures often follow similar scripts, whereby the focus is placed on, say, the alleged qualities of gay men that might inspire disgust. In Nussbaum's example, the proponents of a referendum in Colorado in 1992 to prevent gay and bisexual citizens from being recognized as a protected class "circulated pamphlets in which it was stated that gay men eat feces and drink human blood" (Nussbaum, 2004: 101). In fact, disgust's preoccupation with orality, anality, other forms of incorporation, and the imagined contamination that results from this can potentially explain the recurrent topics of food and sex in the instantiations of revulsion described in this text.

> So sex is a site of anxiety for anyone who is ambivalent about having an animal and mortal nature, and that includes many if not most people. Primary-object disgust therefore plays a significant role in sexual relations, as the bodily substances people encounter in sex (semen, sweat, feces, menstrual blood) are very often found disgusting and seen as contaminants. Therefore, it is not surprising that projective disgust also plays a prominent role in the sexual domain. In almost all societies, people identify a group of sexual actors disgusting or pathological, contrasting them with "normal" and "pure" sexual actors (prominently including the people themselves and their own group). (Nussbaum, 2004: 17)

A common feature in analyses of the origin and function of disgust has been precisely the fear of contamination, which may have evolutionary origins, as well as the transference of this affect onto other objects which are seen as reminders of human mortality and animality. The workings of the defenses can mean that disgust is projected onto others. As Nussbaum insists, disgust may be a sign of ambivalence, but, or rather *because* of this, it is never ambivalent about its object. Sianne Ngai, in her examination of *Ugly Feelings*, reiterates this argument. The result is that "[w]hereas the obscuring of the subjective-objective boundary becomes internal to the nature of feelings like animatedness and paranoia, disgust strengthens and polices this boundary" (Ngai, 2007: 335). It is this very strict policing between self and other out of a fear of the collapse of this boundary that fuels the virulent expressions of disgust and revulsion against certain groups or populations.

From Ambivalence to Virulence: Disgust as a "Disciplining Affect"

Discussions of disgust often feature comparisons with anger. While both are characterized by a virulence of expression, Nussbaum argues that there is something "reasonable" about anger's thought content—and we may say the same about the origins of *ressentiment*. Disgust, on the other hand, always has at its core "magical ideas of contamination, and impossible aspirations to purity, immortality, and nonanimality, that are just not in line with human life as we know it" (Nussbaum, 2004: 14). While we are not entirely convinced by this distinction between "reasonable" anger and "irrational" disgust, we agree that the social consequences of anger and disgust can be similar, as they rely on demands to expel members deemed unwanted from a community, on the basis of specific criteria. In the manifestations of right-wing populist anger discussed earlier, there is a preoccupation with "privilege" that is perceived as unearned. Disgust centers on the body, sexuality, and life and death (though often in veiled form). Feminists and LGBTQ subjects, through their association with, on the one hand, the body, sexuality, and/or femininity and (the politics of) reproduction—as well as, on the other hand, their status of something of a "cultural elite"—in effect represent an uneasy amalgamation of the two.

Monstrous Women, Disgusting Truths

In fact, feminists have long argued that the resistance experienced to their taking a public stance goes beyond any rational objection to specific arguments; this resistance is in fact *pre-rational*. Imogen Tyler writes how "women who speak out" have attracted stigma and punishment throughout history (Tyler, 2020; see also Beard, 2014). Indeed, a woman is never allowed to be separate from her body and all the "trouble" and troubling associations this evokes in a patriarchal structure.

Women's bodies are seen as sites of suspicion and danger, "intrinsically unpredictable, leaky and disruptive" (Shildrick and Price, 1999: 2). In the already familiar move of policing the boundaries between self and other, and in order to exert (a semblance of) control, the male body becomes the one that is clean and proper, "sealed and self-sufficient," while "it is women who are marked by the capacity of that which leaks from the body—menstrual blood is the best exemplar—to defile and contaminate" (Shildrick and Price, 1999: 7). The cultural archetype of the "monstrous" woman, according to Barbara Creed (1993), is associated with such images of monstrous wombs, menstruation, castration, and *vagina dentatas*. Adrienne Massanari and Shira Chess' (2018) work on "memes" produced by members of alt-right communities and which mock and denigrate so-called SJWs or "Social Justice Warriors" is full of such images evoking the sick, leaky bodies and perverse, feeble minds of women. In this chain of association, women are always associated with the biological, and the biological with the monstrous "other."

This "cultural unease" (Shildrick and Price, 1999) with the feminine and the female body is enhanced when the female-bodied take up the "masculine" position of speaking up and making (political) demands, as this could further disrupt the carefully set up separation between feminine and masculine order, with fears of "leaky" femininity spilling over into and destabilizing self-contained masculinity/society. In Imogen Tyler's earlier work on "social abjection" (2013), she reworks Kristeva's original notion as the sense of horror when experiencing a breakdown in the separation between self and other, or that which has been cast off the self and been made abject (Kristeva, 1982), in order to describe the ways in which neoliberal Britain (mis)treats migrant and working-class mothers, marking them as "revolting subjects" (Tyler, 2013).

Returning briefly to evolutionary psychology, disgust emerged as a mechanism put in place in order to distance oneself from possible sources of contamination. The scope of this system was gradually extended to include others not only when they represent clear sites of infection but also when they come to be associated with actions or attributes seemingly ("irrationally") threatening the "health" or stability of the social order. Disgust is thus both a seemingly inevitable (though not ahistorical) response to certain "conspecifics" and it also operates as a "cheap form of punishment that does not carry the likely costs associated with angry displays of aggression" (Curtis and de Barra, 2018).

While Curtis and de Barra refer to the greater *danger* to the individual person who opts for physical displays of anger or threats over those of merely opting for a rhetoric of disgust, we argue that disgust may come at a lower cost *overall* for the person(s) expressing it. Not only is the rhetoric of revulsion easily available, and increasingly becoming so (BBC, 2011), it offers a sense of protection of the self, and the social as an extension thereof. At the same time, like anger, it offers up specific scapegoats, thereby avoiding complicated demands of a more complete (and destabilizing) restructuring of society, as it works *within* existing (gendered, capitalocentric) logics. Thus, the "disgust with egalitarianism" expressed by the aforementioned supporters of the AfD displaces the true source of rising inequalities in Germany: "[i]nstead of condemning the exploitative structures of patriarchal (as well as racist and classist) capitalism, women's liberation, gay marriage, drag queens and divorce rates are the subject of outrage" (Schutzbach, 2016: 594, authors' translation).

At the same time, disgust can come at a higher psychic cost for the "accused," as well as, we argue, for the "potentially accused." As Nussbaum has argued, disgust is "not the only mechanism of stigmatization" but "a powerful and central one" (2004: 16–17). Its power, we argue, lies on the one hand, in its strong connection to our bodily selves; it is aimed at the bodies we *are*, thus having the capacity to instill shame in a way few, if any, other affects can. Its potency in producing abject bodies can be seen in, among other things, its use as a tool to control and discipline sexuality, from the phenomenon of slutshaming to so-called conversion therapies for people with nonheterosexual desires. While, as Nussbaum has shown, it has played a role in criminalizing certain behaviors, its disciplining effects in the absence of criminalization are today far more widespread, and the speed and logic of online publishing and social media have amplified this tendency. In Helen Wood's examination of the case of the "Magaluf Girl," the young woman becomes "as an object of disgust, while her own subjectivity (deliberately or not) was erased" (Wood, 2018: 634).

Through its connection to stigma and abjection, disgust operates to expel the targeted subject from the category of those "deserving" of rights, respect, and protection. Following Butler, abjection is a discursive process related to "all kinds of bodies whose lives are not considered to be 'lives' and whose materiality is understood not to 'matter'" (Costera Meijer and Prins, 1998: 281). The production of women's and LGBTQ bodies and desires as abject effectively expels subjects from the normal, thereby depriving them of the status of full personhood and acknowledgment of rights to bodily autonomy (see Butler, 2004: 20–1). The concrete devastating effects of this can be seen not only in discriminatory policy and practices but also in overtly violent practices such as domestic, psychological and sexual abuse, sexual harassment, "gay bashing," and rape. Oftentimes, however, not least when abjection takes place through the use of illness metaphors and pathologization, such violence is concealed as care. Indeed, Dale O'Leary herself has, for a long time, argued that feminists (especially lesbian radical feminists) are likely to suffer from attachment disorders in need of therapy (1997). Promotion of conversion therapies for nonheterosexual people follows the same rhetorical logic, as do anti-gender mobilization against sex education as a way to "protect the young."

When dressed up as care, the recipient may ultimately end up grateful for the "help" to overcome their previously "disgusting" behaviors, like the woman in another narrative from LifeSite: "I don't think any woman in this world is as disgusting and vile as I am because you see I didn't have one abortion, I had THREE! . . . I was the scum of the earth—the most vile and disgusting human being, so unworthy of good"

(*LifeSite*, May 3, 2017). Or, in another example provided in a publication by the Swedish Evangelical Alliance, in the voice of a homosexual Christian man describing how he after having confessed his "struggle [with same-sex attraction] as a sin [. . .] finally ended up in a crisis": "I felt dirty and false—like I could not continue serving God unless I was freed from my thoughts and feelings" (2019: 136). Both of these examples clearly show how potent projective disgust can be: when internalized in the form of guilt, shame, and self-loathing, the targeted subject is likely to police and condemn themselves, ultimately making external disciplinary measures unnecessary.

Importantly, however, and of more overarching significance for the ongoing hegemonic struggles of how to construct "the people," projective disgust serves a disciplinary function not only for those immediately and explicitly targeted by it. Rather, every (more or less) public display of it simultaneously constitutes a warning for each and everyone, a moral imperative not only for how to behave but also how to *be*, in order to be included in "the people." But while Nussbaum argues that projective disgust serves "a deep-seated human need [. . .] to represent oneself as pure and others as dirty" (2004: 16), with Salecl, we argue that such a need will never be fully met, not even for the "purest of citizens." The reason for this is that projective disgust always operates on both the level of *ideal* and on the level of *fantasmatic* identification; that is, on the one hand, on the level of identification with (and desire to be acknowledged as) a member of the "pure," respectable, and "righteous people" and, on the other hand, on the level of identification with the "potential enemy in every individual" (1994: 50). As a consequence, expressions of revulsion will necessarily play a more fundamental function, not only in "defining" the people but in disciplining it to hide or suppress the potential "inner enemy" ("dirty deeds," animal bodies, forbidden desires).

In this chapter, we have attempted to grapple with the trend of right-wing populist, authoritarian, and conservative Christian political actors invoking the affect of disgust in discussions of those they have constructed as their political enemies—in this case, those proffering the "ideology of gender," feminists, LGBTQ subjects, as well as those sympathetic or associated with their causes. Even though nationalist right-wing populism and anti-gender politics shall not be reduced to one another, and their coexistence to a great extent can be described as an "opportunistic synergy" (Korolczuk and Graff, 2021), their ideological and psychosocial compatibility shall not be underestimated.

Although some expressions referred to in this text might seem "too extreme" to trigger strong concern, or might even seem comical, the political consequences of the increased normalization of this rhetoric are no laughing matter. On the contrary, we already see the devastating effects not only in the ongoing withdrawal of basic health care and rights for women and LGBTQ-people in many countries but also in the more general political instrumentalization of its affective force. As Agnieszka Graff has commented about Poland, where the ruling party *Prawo i Sprawiedliwość* and the Catholic Church have consistently mobilized against "gender" and "LGBTQ ideology" as a way to articulate a broader "enemy of the people" (EU, UN, the opposition, the protesters): "For those for whom the essence of politics is men being real men, branding one side as fishy, as something that arouses distrust, if not disgust, can actually work" (Ostolski and Graff, 2019).

The question remaining is how one might counter the strong affective force of a politics of disgust. For, if, following Ernesto Laclau and Chantal Mouffe's theory of hegemony and populist mobilization, the *form* of the alliances between right-wing populist, authoritarian-minded leaders, and movements can be explained by the construction of an "empty signifier" of "gender and LGBTQ-ideology," to understand its *force* it is necessary to turn to the affects that support them. As we have argued, this cannot be done by limiting the analysis to investigating this as a straightforward example of the "politics of fear" of various "others" (see, for example, Wodak, 2015). Although a "politics of disgust" is similarly used in the creation of scapegoats and others that threaten and contaminate "the nation and its people," its particular force lies in the way in which disgust, or what is "abject," is inscribed on our bodies and in our innermost desires. Hence, we argue, any counter-hegemonic attempts by leftwing or other progressive political actors to invoke disgust against their political opponents will also come at a high price; for example, mocking Donald Trump for being overweight or "unmanly" might be both tempting and effective, but its stigmatizing effects are bound to "spill over" onto anyone whose body by these criteria can be deemed "disgusting."

Instead, feminist and queer activists have often attempted to meet the charge of being "revolting" head on. The use of more or less explicitly sexual performances in pride parades (nakedness, S/M-gear) is one example of this, as are so-called naked protests and feminist artistic use of menstrual blood (see, for example, Devenney, 2020; Guitérrez-Albilla, 2008). The Russian punk collective Pussy Riot, for example, tried to confront the "woman-as-biology-as-disgusting" tendency directly by making their very name evoke female genitalia, as well as the disturbance caused by this association. Although such confrontational strategies have indeed contributed to challenge assimilatory struggles for equal rights that are often conditioned on "respectability," they can—especially when authoritarianism is on the rise—come at another high price. The Pussy Riot action, for instance, triggered a surge of negative reactions deeming them mentally ill and perverse, asking for their punishment, as well as eventual imprisonment (Brock, 2016). Any political articulation beyond that very disruption (Chehonadskih, 2012) was, however, forestalled. At the same time, shifting or reorienting the affective charge of disgust by appealing to reason is something of a discursive dead end, as disgust successfully bypasses the rational, which is also what makes it such an effective strategy in discrediting one's opponents.

In the meantime, those opposing the increasing right-wing presence in politics which places its emphasis on the validity of so-called traditional values have to continue their insistence on taking up space in politics, while being denoted as disgusting, perverse, or sick. This bears its own costs: apart from the obvious injurious nature of these terms, it also leads to what we describe as the continued strain of having to overcome the self-disciplining and punishing aspects of disgust and shame. Therefore, in order to disarm and defuse the affective force of revulsion, a politics countering it would necessarily need to target not just the formulation of "external enemies" but also its "inner targets," reformulating that which is "within us," our animality, our desires, our vulnerability, as something other than disgusting—and most certainly as something other than issues of "liberal tolerance" and "protection of minorities." In other words, an alternative formulation of "the people" must be able to effectively rearticulate these "abject" and vulnerable dimensions of our psychic and bodily existences not as something "other" but as something we have in common (see also Butler, 2004b), thereby placing them as an intrinsic part of our mutual vulnerability and interdependence, at the very center of political life.

Bibliography

Beard M (2014) The Public Voice of Women. *London Review of Books*, March 20. https://www.lrb.co.uk/the-paper/v36/n06/mary-beard/the-public-voice-of-women. (accessed November 30, 2020).
Blech N (2019) Höcke: "Gender-Gaga" entsorgen wir auf "Müllhaufen der Ideologie-Geschichte." *Queer.de*, October 27. Available: https://www.queer.de/detail.php?article_id=34764 (accessed November 30, 2020).
Brock M (2016) A Psychosocial Analysis of Pussy Riot: Velvet Revolution or Frenzied Uteri. *Subjectivity* 9(2): 126–44.
Butler J (2004a) *Undoing Gender*. London: Routledge.
Butler J (2004b) *Precarious Life: The Power of Mourning and Violence*. London: Verso.
Canovan M (1999) Trust the People! Populism and the Two Faces of Democracy. *Political Studies* XLVII: 2–16.
Chehonadskih M (2012) What is Pussy Riot's "idea"? *Radical Philosophy* 176: 2.
Costera Meijer I and Prins B (1998) How Bodies Come to Matter: An Interview with Judith Butler. *Signs: Journal of Women in Culture and Society* 23(2): 275–86.
Creed B (1993) *The Monstrous-Feminine: Film, Feminism, Psychoanalysis, Popular Fiction Series*. London: Routledge.
Curtis V and de Barra M (2018) The Structure and Function of Pathogen Disgust. *Philosophical Transactions of the Royal Society B* 373: 20170208.
Datta N. (2018) *"Restoring the Natural Order": The Religious Extremists' Vision to Mobilize European Societies against Human Rights on Sexuality and Reproduction*. Brussels: the European Parliamentary Forum on Population & Development.
Demertzis N (2006) Emotions and Populism. In: S. Clarke, P. Hoggett, and S. Thompson (eds.), *Emotion, Politics and Society*. Basingstoke: Palgrave Macmillan, 103–22.
Devenney Mark (2020) *Towards an Improper Politics*. Edinburgh: Edinburgh University Press.
Disgust: How Did the Word Change so Completely? *BBC News*, November 15, 2011, https://www.bbc.co.uk/news/magazine-15619543 (accessed November 30, 2020).
Edenborg E (2020) Saving Women and Bordering Europe: Narratives of "Migrants' Sexual Violence" and Geopolitical Imaginaries in Russia and Sweden. *Geopolitics* 25(3): 780–801.
Fiano C (2017) "Nothing has Ever Hurt Me This Bad": 15 Women who Regret Their Abortions. *LifeSite*, May 3, 2017. Available at: https://www.lifesitenews.com/pulse/15-women-on-why-they-regret-their-abortions-nothing-has-ever-hurt-me-this-b (accessed November 30, 2020).
Fraser N (2017) Progressive Neoliberalism versus Reactionary Populism: A Choice that Feminists Should Refuse. *NORA - Nordic Journal of Feminist and Gender Research* 24(4): 281–4.
Guitérrez-Albila JD (2008) Abjection and the Politics of Feminist and Queer Subjectivities in Contemporary Art. *Angelaki: Journal of Theoretical Humanities* 13(1): 65–84.

Gunnarsson Payne J (2019) Challenging "Gender Ideology": (Anti-)Gender Politics in Europe's Populist Moment. *The New Pretender*, February 10, 2019. Available at: http://new-pretender.com/2019/02/10/challenging-gender-ideology-anti-gender-politics-in-europes-populist-moment-jenny-gunnarsson-payne/ (accessed November 30, 2020).

Gunnarsson Payne J (2020) Kulturkrigets kultursjukdomar: patologisering som politik och problemet med diagnostikens retorik. In: Anders Burman and Shamal Kaveh (eds.), *Demokratin och det politiska: essäer om samtidens politiska tillstånd*. Huddinge: Södertörns högskola: 97–114.

Gunnarsson Payne J and Tornhill S (2021) The Enemy's Enemy: Feminist Anti-Capitalist Politics at the Crossroads of Neoliberal Cooptation and Anti-Gender Conservatism. *Journal of Political Ideologies*: 1–21.

Hoggett P (2018) Ressentiment and Grievance. *British Journal of Psychotherapy* 34(3): 393–407.

Korolczuk E and Graff A (2018) Gender as "Ebola from Brussels": The Anticolonial Frame and the Rise of Illiberal Populism. *Signs: Journal of Women in Culture and Society* 43(4): 797–821.

Korolczuk E and Graff A (2021) *Anti-gender Politics in the Populist Moment*. London: Routledge.

Kristeva J (1982) *Powers of Horror: An Essay on Abjection*. New York: Columbia University Press.

LaBarbera P (2017) Activist Burns Piece of Trash Teen Vougue over Anal Sex Article. *LifeSite*, July 17. Available at: https://www.lifesitenews.com/news/activist-burns-piece-of-trash-teen-vogue-over-anal-sex-article (accessed November 30, 2020).

Massanari A and Chess S (2018) Attack of the 50-Foot Social Justice Warrior: The Discursive Construction of SJW Memes as the Monstrous Feminine. *Feminist Media Studies* 18(4): 525–42.

Miller WI (1997) *The Anatomy of Disgust*. Cambridge, MA: Harvard University Press.

Mishra P (2016) Welcome to the Age of Anger. *The Guardian*, December 8. http://www.theguardian.com/politics/2016/dec/08/welcome-age-anger-brexit-trump (accessed November 30, 2020).

Mouffe C (2018) *For a Left Populism*. London: Verso.

Ngai S (2007) *Ugly Feelings*. Cambridge, MA: Harvard University Press.

Nussbaum MC (2004) *Hiding from Humanity: Disgust, Shame, and the Law*. Princeton, NJ: Princeton University Press.

O'Leary D (1997) *The Gender Agenda: Redefining Equality*. Lafayette, LA: Vital Issues Press.

Ostolski A and Graff A (2019) Gender Ideology and the Crisis of Care in Poland. *Green European Journal*, December 17, 2017. Available at: https://www.greeneuropeanjournal.eu/gender-ideology-and-the-crisis-of-care-in-poland/ (accessed November 30, 2020).

Patternotte D and Kuhar R (2017) Gender Ideology. In Movement: Introduction. In: D Patternotte and R Kuhar (eds.), *Anti-Gender Campaigns in Europe: Mobilizing Against Equality*. London: Rowman & Littlefield International, 1–22.

"Peter" (pseudonym) (2019) Sann frihet. In: Edsinger and Baker (eds.), *Bekänna färg: Kyrka och hbtq i en regnbågsfärgad värld*. Stockholm: Apologia förlag, 135–9.

Richards B (2019) Beyond the Angers of Populism: A Psychosocial Inquiry. *Journal of Psychosocial Studies* 12: 1–2, 171–83.

Salecl R (1994) *The Spoils of Freedom: Psychoanalysis and Feminism After the Fall of Socialism*. London: Routledge.

Sayan-Cengiz F and Tekin C (2019) The "Gender Turn" of the Populist Radical Right. *Open Democracy*, December 16. Available at: https://www.opendemocracy.net/en/rethinking-populism/the-gender-turn-of-the-populist-radical-right/ (accessed November 30, 2020).

Schooyans M et.al. (2006) *Lexicon: Ambiguous and Debatable Terms Regarding Family Life and Ethical Questions*. Virginia, Rome and Miami: Human Life International.

Schutzbach F (2016) Der Heidi-Komplex: Gender, Feminismus und der Ekel vor der Gleichmacherei. *PROKLA. Zeitschrift für Kritische Sozialwissenschaft* 46: 185, 583–97.

Shildrick M and Price J (1999) Openings on the Body: A Critical Introduction. In: J Price and MShildrick (eds.), *Feminist Theory and the Body: A Reader*. New York: Routledge, 1–14.

Sontag, Susan (1978) *Illness as Metaphor*. New York: Farrar, Straus & Giroux.

Tyler I (2013) *Revolting Subjects: Social Abjection and Resistance in Neoliberal Britain*. London: Zed Books.

Tyler I (2020) *Stigma: The Machinery of Inequality*. London: Zed Books.

Van Maren J (2019) "Pride" Celebrations: A Disgusting Month of Naked Men Twerking for Innocent Kids. *LifeSite*, June 20. Available at: https://www.lifesitenews.com/blogs/pride-celebrations-a-disgusting-month-of-naked-men-twerking-for-innocent-kids (accessed November 30, 2020).

Wodak R (2015) *The Politics of Fear: What Rightwing Populist Discourses Mean*. London: Sage.

Wood H (2018) The Magaluf Girl: A Public Sex Scandal and the Digital Class Relations of Social Contagion. *Feminist Media Studies* 18(4): 626–42.

7

The People and the Image of the Leader

Reflections on Mass Psychology

Chiara Bottici[1]

There is a much talk today about whether contemporary forms of right-wing populism represent a new political formation or whether fascism has returned to us.[2] This discussion often fails to take into account that, in some important ways, fascism has never gone away. To be sure, history never repeats itself, and there are characteristics of the regime that created the term, and explicitly embraced fascism in the 1930s, that will not return. But how do things look if we, as philosophers and social scientists, treat "fascism" as an ideal-type, as an heuristic tool that can be used to think about and compare different forms of power?

Consider for a moment some of the features that characterize the regime that reigned in Italy between 1922 and 1943 and gave fascism its name: hyper-nationalism; racism; sexism; machismo; the cult of the leader; the replacement of history and empirically formulated notions of truth fused with political myths; the cult of the state; extreme conceptions of enemies: perceived as existential threats to the nation, and the consequent endorsement of violence against them.[3] We can thus see how different aspects of that form of power, after its formal fall in 1943, continued to exist in different guises and shapes not simply in Europe but also elsewhere.[4] We can point to how fascist parties continued to survive in Italy and elsewhere, how fascist discourses were kept alive, and how different postwar regimes emerging worldwide exhibited some, or even many, of the fascist traits listed earlier, even when they did not formally embrace fascism in its entirety. When a regime exhibits a critical mass of the traits characteristic of historical fascism, we can then usefully speak of neofascism. Similarly, when focusing on a single trait of a political ideology, such as, for instance, its underlying mass psychology, we can speak of a fascist mass psychology, without thereby implying that the state or the government under which that happens is fascist in its entirety.[5]

If we use the concept of fascism as a polyhedral heuristic tool, we can see how Trumpism, for instance, as an ideology, embodies a form of neofascism that presents its own peculiar features, including some respect for the formal features of representative democracy, the combination of free-market ideology and populist rhetoric, and the paradox of a critique of the state and its "corrupt" elites accompanied by the massive recourse to its institutions. But Trumpism also exhibits features, such as an extreme form of nationalism, systematic racism, macho-populism, and an implicit legitimation of violence against enemies that are indeed typical of fascism. Therefore, I propose to consider fascism here as a tendency of modern power and its sovereign logic, a tendency that, like a Karstic river, can flow underneath formal institutions but can also always erupt in its most destructive form whenever the structural conditions allow that to happen. Although some authors differentiate between historical fascism and contemporary forms of right-wing populism, because the former tends to produce dictatorships while the latter is compatible with democratic legitimacy (cf. Finchelstein, 2014), I will argue in this chapter that the mass psychology upon which they rely can be very similar, if not the same. This, in my view, is in agreement with the statement that right-wing populism is the contemporary reformulation of fascism, which rejected some of its extreme forms such as the systematic use of violence, in order to make it compatible with democratic legitimacy.

In this chapter, I would like to explore the psychological ties that bind fascist followers to their leaders and then move on to argue that Trumpism, as a psychological and political phenomenon, relies precisely on such a fascist libidinal bond. After briefly discussing Freudian mass psychology, I will explore the insights provided by Adorno's work and feminist reinterpretations of it, in particular as it concerns the specific type of mass psychology that we can designate as fascist and neo-populist.

Back to Freud's Mass Psychology

In order to discuss the features of the mass psychology that sustains fascist leadership, I would like to focus on a text written by Theodor Adorno in the 1950s to address US-American fascist agitators, "Freudian Theory and the Pattern of Fascist Propaganda" (1991). Although written in reference to the American fascist leaders of that time, this text provides key insights into fascist mass psychology and thus helps us to illuminate the type of libidinal bond that links fascist leaders to their followers more generally. Certainly, the rise of Nazism was also present in Adorno's mind when he wrote this text. But the fact that this text directly addresses American fascist agitators of the 1950s, and not Hitler or Mussolini, is in my view already an indication that fascist propaganda did not stop with the dismissal of fascist regimes of the 1940s.

Adorno's "Freudian Theory and the Pattern of Fascist Propaganda" is a strange text. It presents itself as a dynamic interpretation of Freud's *Mass Psychology and the Analysis of the Ego*, which in its turn is, also, according to Adorno, a "dynamic interpretation" of Gustave Le Bon's description of the mass mind (Adorno, 1991: 134). It is, therefore, technically speaking, a dynamic reinterpretation of an already dynamic interpretation. Despite Adorno's pledge to adhere to Freudian theory, he departed from Freud on crucial points, and, precisely by doing so, he provided particularly incisive insights as to the nature of fascist propaganda, including the type we have recently witnessed with Trumpism. Hence the image of fascism as a Karstic river I proposed: a tendency of modern political power that can erupt here and there, in specific political movements or even single agitators, like little rivulets that do not change the general landscape, but that can also occasionally erupt like a virulent torrent that reshapes what it finds in its way.

Despite Adorno's dynamism, Freudian theory remains the starting point of his approach, and his text cannot be understood without reference to Freud's reflections.[6] Let us therefore briefly recall the structure of Freud's *Mass Psychology*, as well as its main insights. In the first few chapters, full of long quotations from Le Bon and other theorists of mass psychology, Freud considers both stable and unstable masses, emphasizing the existence of all kinds of groups (1949: 52). Much emphasis is placed on the exaltation and intensification generated by imitation and by the affective contagion that members of a mass exert on each other. In Chapter III, Freud insists that the most noteworthy and important phenomenon in a collective formation is the intensification of affects created by participation in a mass. Freud subsequently defines our tendency to imitate the affective state of a person with whom we are in contact as an "incontestable fact" (1949: 26). The varieties of the affects imitated, we may add, can thus also explain why Freud insists so much on the diversity of possible collective formations. In Chapter III, by means of a beautiful metaphor, he states that there are different types of masses, some temporary and open like high waves, others fixed and closed, which are more like a groundswell in the open sea, as well as all other forms that situate themselves in between them.[7]

However, after reconceptualizing such affectivity in terms of his general theory of the libido, Freud suddenly shifts to the question of whether the presence of a leader is a *conditio* sine qua non for the existence of a mass (1949: 53).[8] And his affirmative answer is consequently based on the observation that followers identify with one another through the idealization of the figure of the leader, which comes then to provide the cement that keeps the crowd united. It is at this point that Freud also explicitly shifts to his two main examples, the church and the army, which, as Adorno among others noticed, are in fact two peculiarly hierarchical groups (1991: 149). Not only do the church and the army depend on defined ranks; they are also highly institutionalized social structures, which set them apart from other types of masses, such as spontaneous, open crowds.[9] Yet, it is via these examples along with the analysis of the process of identification via idealization that Freud arrives at the analogy between the mass and the primal horde that then becomes central to this text and to his mass psychology more generally.

Notice, however, that it is late in the text, to be precise in Chapter X, that this analogy is introduced: Freud states that the head of the mass is the psychological equivalent of the father of the primal horde, the archaic phantasy that mass psychology revives in the midst of civilization.[10] Interestingly enough, though, there is here no sustained argument for why this analogy between mass and primal horde would be justified. Quite the contrary, Freud seems to be aware of possible criticism and the lack of a robust argument in favor of such an analogy. For instance, at the beginning of Chapter X, Freud himself mentions those who have criticized his theory of the primal horde as a "just so story," and yet he continues to insist on this "just so story" by stating that it should not be discarded because it can be applied to so many different fields—as if the variety of possible applications would by itself be a justification of its validity (1949: 90).

On the other hand, the analogy between the mass and the primal horde with its powerful male figure remains the major reply offered to the question of whether masses need a leader in order to come into being and to persist over time. All the different types of masses that were mentioned at the beginning of the text seem to be reduced to just one type: the cephalic type, which is held together by identification with the leader, and which feeds on the reactivation of the archaic father figure of the primal horde. Note here the gendered element introduced by the analogy itself: the primordial horde analogy revolves around the figure of the patriarchal father, the cis-male who is presented as both the head of the family and the head of the horde, very much in keeping with the patriarchal tropes of that time.

Freud operates here the same sort of *reductio ad penem*[11] that has been observed in many other parts of his work—from his writings on feminine sexuality to his writings on religion and culture—where everything revolves around the figure of the father and where the mother is persistently marginalized.[12] The Freudian theory of the libido reflects this bias, which is also clearly visible in his incapacity to explain female sexuality without using male sexuality as the yardstick for assessing sexuality and the development of the libido more generally.[13] Apart from Freud's biography, this certainly reflects the patriarchy of the epoch, which Freud embodies so well, but which—it should be remembered—he also provides important tools to understand and to unpack.[14] This I take to be the virtue of an intellectual genius: transforming one's own sickness into a medicine for it; in the case of Freud, this means transforming the cure for his own neurosis into an entire discipline that can potentially treat it.

And yet, because it reduces all types of masses to the cephalic type, on the basis of the story of the primal horde and the omnipotent father, Freud's approach to mass psychology is misleading in a number of ways, beginning with the fact that it can, at best, only account for certain types of masses. Besides the hierarchical cephalic masses, held together by identification with the leader, there are other types of masses, most notably those that Elias Canetti termed "open crowds." Canetti, like Freud early in his text, insists on the importance of the *imitation of affects*, which is the cement for all types of masses. Canetti even concludes, on that basis, that the open crowd is the true crowd: "The open crowd is the true crowd, the crowd abandoning itself freely to its natural urge for growth. An open crowd has no clear feeling or idea of the size it may attain; it does not depend on a known building which it has to fill; its size is not determined; it wants to grow indefinitely and what it needs for this is more and more people" (1973: 20). Open crowds are thus the true crowds because they are not held together by a leader or a closed, hierarchical structure but, rather, by the pure desire to be part of the crowd, free to just follow its own immanent size and its inclination to grow. These are very different crowds from those identified by Freud via the examples of the church and the army. Yet, for Canetti they are the true crowds because they show why people in general come together—through the imitation of affects, which is itself contagious and which generates that special pleasure arising from overcoming the fear of touch. Only certain types of crowds are cemented together via cephalic forms of identification with the "head" of the crowd.

Beyond Freud, with Adorno: On the Fascist Libidinal Tie

It is here, precisely, that Adorno's reflections enter the picture. Certainly Adorno did not live in a less patriarchal environment. Yet, in contrast to Freud, he manages to avoid any simplistic *reductio ad penem*. The reason he does so is because, despite his reference to the story of the primal horde with its omnipotent father, he limits that diagnosis to fascist masses. Adorno openly states that the type of psychology described by Freud in his mass psychology is the psychology of the *fascist* masses and explicitly denies that it could be applied to other types of masses. As Adorno puts it:

> Furthermore, one may even ask: why is the applied group psychology discussed here peculiar to fascism rather than to most other movements that seek mass support? Even the most casual comparison of fascist propaganda with that of liberal progressive parties will show this to be so. Yet, neither Freud nor Le Bon envisaged such a distinction. They spoke of crowds "as such" similar to the conceptualizations used by formal sociology, without differentiating the political aims of the group involved. [. . .] Only an explicit theory of society, by far transcending the range of psychology, can fully answer the questions raised here. (1991: 149)

Adorno's argument here is twofold. First, Freud's reconstruction of the formation of masses via identification with the leader does explain the peculiar psychology that sustains the fascist community of the people, although this should not be mistaken as the psychology of all masses per se: it only applies to fascist masses. Second, however, fascism is not solely a psychological issue, because an entire theory of society is needed to explain it. The two claims may appear to be in tension with one another, so let us unpack them further.

Despite the fact that, as Adorno observes, both Freud and Le Bon had in mind early socialist masses when they wrote (rather than the fascist crowds that followed them), Freud does not share with Le Bon his reactionary contempt for the mass movements of the time. From the perspective of Freudian psychoanalysis, we are all to a certain extent sick. And this more neutral attitude leads him to a far deeper understanding of its mechanism of formation: the cement that holds them together is a specific type of libidinal tie, that is, narcissistic identification. The members of the mass can identify with one another as members of the same group because they have substituted one and the same object, which is the image of the leader, as their ego ideal (Adorno, 1991: 99–100). They are, so to speak, equal in the image of the leader. This, in turn, explains why the leader has to appear as the big narcissist and why he can actually do so while also appearing as a rather average person.

As an example of such narcissism, consider Trump's declaration on January 23, 2016, during his first presidential campaign: "I could stand in the middle of Fifth Avenue and shoot someone and I wouldn't lose any voters" (January 23, 2016). As Jay Bernstein noted, it is in reference to this type of declaration that Adorno's essay is particularly insightful and can indeed help us understand the kind of libidinal bond with his supporters that Trump is thereby presupposing (2021). And I would say, also creating at the same time. Who is this big narcissist who can claim that he could be shooting people in the street and still get elected?

In order to explain the role of narcissism, Adorno quotes Freud, once again, who stated that "the leader himself needs to love no one else" (1991: 141).[15] But then Adorno rephrases the same sentence by saying that "the leader can be loved *only if* he himself does not love" (1991: 141). The issue of love, as Jamieson Webster underlines, is crucial in this chapter (2017). But notice how Adorno goes beyond Freud by adding that little qualification: "only if." By doing so, Adorno further emphasizes a feature that is not only typical of, but I would even say essential to, fascist propaganda: the emptiness of the fascist agitator's speech, the absence of anything they may actually "give," and the consequent prevalence of the register of threat and violence.

This is what Adorno calls hatred and aversion for others as a "negatively integrating force," which, in fascism, according to Adorno, takes the peculiarly empty name of race (1991: 144). Race and bourgeois individualism go hand in hand. As we read in the *Dialectic of Enlightenment*, the enigmatic text that Adorno coauthored with Max Horkheimer, trying to make sense of the failed promises of modernity: "Race today is the self-assertion of the bourgeois individual, integrated into the barbaric collective" (2002: 138). It is important to remember that, despite the rhetoric of the melting pot, race-based segregation has been a crucial feature of the United States from its very inception: as a country built through a settler-colonial project, its very history is inseparable from the recourse to race-based negative integration.

As an example of the "empty character" of race and the way it has helped the self-assertion of the bourgeois individual in the history of the United States, consider for instance the differential roles assigned to Blackness and redness. Whereas the one-drop rule in the case of Black bodies assured that slaves remained at work in the plantations and that their labor force could be exploited, the project of annihilation of Native Americans was carried out in the name of the myth of the "vanishing Indian" so much so that for them the opposite rule applied: only a full-blooded Indian could reclaim their right to the land and their entitlements under the treaties. The law established in most cases stipulated that having even a single drop of non-Indian blood would be sufficient to deny Native American origins and thus the right to the land (Grand, 2018: 92; see also Schmidt, 2011: 9). This is a clear example of how "empty" the notion of race is by itself, and how, even in the same context, it can fill up with the most contradictory elements.

There is an intimate link between the US settler-colonial history and systemic racism, a link that has been a source of inspiration for other racist regimes.[16] It may be worth remembering, for instance, that the genocide of Native Americans was highly praised by Hitler as a major source of inspiration for the Holocaust, that is, for the physical annihilation of a people based on their racial belonging. As he imagined his expansion toward Eastern Europe, Hitler made explicit reference to the example of the elimination of Native Americans, hoping that Nazism would deal with the Slavs in the same way the United States dealt with Native Americans in its Westward expansion.[17]

The 1950s fascist agitators, as well as today's neo-populist and neofascist leaders, can draw from a long history of racialization. Certainly, history does not determine the future but, rather, presents possibilities and, in this case, a powerful symbolic reservoir of myths, images, and symbols of racialization from which any newly appointed neofascist agitator can draw. Particularly in settler-colonial histories, such as the United States, Adorno's insights apply very well: race can function as an "empty" space that defines the group negatively ("we are *not* them") and can thus take form by pointing to all different kinds of targets; we see this today in Trump's propaganda, Mexican people,

Chinese people, Muslims, but also those who do not conform to the idealized image of the leader, including, as we will now see, sexual and gender minorities who do not conform to the heteronormative patriarchal family embodied in Trump's propaganda and his mythical "America."

Trump's Neo-populist and Neofascist Propaganda

Although Adorno does not specifically focus on sexual and gender minorities in his essay on fascist propaganda, he stressed how hatred for others as a negatively integrating force is indeed one of its distinctive features, and thus one that unifies the 1950s American fascist agitators that Adorno refers to at the beginning of his essay with Hitler and the other fascist agitators of the 1930s, who are also central to Adorno's thinking in this essay. With an operation similar to Adorno's, we can extend his analysis of 1950s fascist leaders to Donald Trump and the other authoritarian agitators of our time and see a very similar type of group formation via narcissistic identification with the image of the leader. Certainly, Trump is not Hitler. And while we did not live under Nazism during Trump's presidency, as Judith Butler, among others, has emphasized, the rhetoric that Trump uses and the libidinal ties that bind his followers to him are nonetheless fascist (Butler, 2016, 2017).

So many features of Trump's propaganda correspond to those enumerated by Adorno: from the rigid distinction between the "beloved in-group" and the "rejected out-group" to the technique of personalization centered on the "great little man" figure; from the "sheep and goat" device to the repetition and standardization of slogans, so typical of stereotypical thinking, and so on. So many features that Adorno ascribes to the American fascist agitators of the 1950s read like a description of the American fascist agitators of our own times, so much so that, as Jay Bernstein has noted, while reading Adorno's text now one has the impression it was literally written to describe Trump (2017).

Many features of Trumpism that have left commentators astonished and unprepared could indeed be summarized with Adorno's succinct formula: the paradox of the fascist leader, who appears at the same time as a superman and as an average person, "just as Hitler posed as a composite of King Kong and the suburban leader" (1991: 141). Since, for most of his followers, their ego ideal is not very distant from their ego, the fact that Trump appears as simply a little bit better than they are, just richer and more audacious, facilitates the process of identification. As Adorno explicitly puts it:

> The category of "phoniness" applies to the leaders as well as to the act of identification on the part of the masses and their supposed frenzy and hysteria. Just as people do not really believe in the depth of their hearts that Jews are the devil, they do not completely believe in their leader. They do not really identify themselves with him but enact this identification, perform their own enthusiasm, and thus participate in their leader's performance. It is through this performance that they strike a balance between their continuously mobilized instinctual urges and the historical stage of enlightenment they have reached, and which cannot be

revoked arbitrarily. It is probably the suspicion of this fictitiousness of their own "mass psychology" that makes fascist crowds so merciless and unapproachable [transl. mod.]. (Adorno, 1991: 150)

The distinction between "identifying with the leader" and "enacting this identification" is crucial: the point is not so much hatred for others as the performance of it, which explains the ambivalence and irony of such performances.

While reflecting on Adorno's contributions to understanding contemporary neofascism, Vladimir Safatle has introduced the notion of "the fascist laugh": what is typical of contemporary forms of fascism, according to this account, is that they embody a form of power that laughs at itself, thus enacting a form of "ironic" identification with the leader, a falsehood that affirms itself ironically.[18] As an example of such a "fascist laugh," consider a tweet that Trump wrote in March 2018: "Lowest rated Oscar in HISTORY. Problem is, we don't have Stars anymore—except your President (just kidding of course!)" (Donald J. Trump, March 6, 2018 @realDonaldTrump).

"HISTORY," written in capital letters, registers the absence of stars from the scene: "except your President," also written with a capital letter. Whereas all other US presidents before Trump used social media as a way to announce the result of a policy that had been discussed for a long time or some other formal public announcement, Donald Trump uses social media, and Twitter in particular, as a tool to express his own opinions and state of mind, *as if* he were one of his followers, which, at its height, reached 88.8 million (Mathers, 2020). With his incendiary and passionate communication reaching such an astronomical number of users, he can thus literally appear as "one of us," while signaling himself out as exceptional: if you are one of his 88.8 million followers, you participate in a performance with "@realDonaldTrump" as both one of the many people you interact with daily on social media *and* the "only Star" available at this moment in history, a Star who is even able to laugh at himself.

This, according to Safatle, is something that Adorno had already understood as typical of the production of ideology in the age of television; ideology is not simply false consciousness but, through the culture industry, becomes a falsehood that knows itself to be such, and yet nevertheless affirms itself ironically (2021). Although this is certainly a feature of media images ever since the invention of television, I do think that social media adds a further dimension to this logic. To begin with, social media have exacerbated both the quantitative and the qualitative change in the nature of images that mediate contemporary politics. As I have argued at length elsewhere, virtualization has changed the phenomenology of the image, the way in which we relate to images by suspending their reality. At the same time, the increase in the competition for our attention has exponentially increased their spectacularization: while in the case of the big screen, or the movie theaters that Adorno considered, one could count on a spectator committed to sitting down for a certain amount of time, in the case of individual media, consumed by distracted spectators on the subway, at the park, or in the barbershop, images have to compete for attention with many more sources of distraction and thus fight for access to people's imaginations through much tougher competition.[19] Hence, the increased recourse to the register of the spectacular and its concomitant virtualization and suspension of truth: because of this affective surcharge, images are no longer simply what mediates our way of doing politics but also what threatens to do politics in our stead.[20]

While pushing the register of the spectacle and changing attitudes toward the truth of the image, the imaginal politics triggered by social media also turn all of their users into equal actors within the performance: this deeply subverts the logic of the spectator/audience that television, to which Adorno referred, still implied. It is not just that a personality like Trump, with his (largely delusional) narrative of the self-made man, fits the new social media; it is consubstantial with them, because it is inseparable from the type of performance that these new technologies enable (Cammaerts, 2020; Fuchs, 2018: 197, 2020: 278). By interacting on Twitter with their leader and his followers, Trump's supporters do not simply feel but literally become protagonists of the performance of "rebirth-in-greatness" that Trump's invocation to "Make America Great Again!" triggered. They do not even have to imagine what their president looks like or what he would think about X and Y and Z in this moment in space and time. These thoughts are constantly there, buzzing on mobile phones. And some of them even become unexpected stars of the spectacle: like the fire lieutenant in Tuscaloosa, who on the evening of April 29, 2019, tweeted to his scant followers: "Granted I am in Alabama but most of the firefighters I talk to are voting @realDonald Trump" (Ben Rawls, April 30, 12:10 a.m. @firemanbrawls), and then woke up the morning after to discover he had become a Twitter celebrity with 14,000 likes in a few hours, just because he had been retweeted by the president himself.

Social media such as Twitter, Facebook, and Instagram are a crucial component of today's resurgence of authoritarianism worldwide, and their power can hardly be overestimated: when navigating on social media, with their promise of friendship and community, you are literally navigating a certain form of mass psychology. In order to emphasize how much authoritarian capitalism feeds today on such media, Christian Fuchs helpfully labels them "digital demagogues."[21] It is not just that authoritarian personalities, such as Trump, can skillfully manipulate their followers; these media have themselves such a manipulative logic because they deeply feed on and exacerbate affects circulating in the social unconscious.

Think, for instance, of how the algorithm that decides on which tweet, which Facebook post to show next on a newsfeed, works: by selecting the image and content that is most likely to keep you glued to the media itself, the one able to capture your imagination and your emotions. Hence, the tendency to produce emotionally laden and polarized versions of reality that progressively alienate those who literally see it and feel it differently: by reading only the news that confirms your own opinion and that fuels the emotions that the algorithm expects from you, some of Trump's 88.8 million followers ended up living in a true "society of spectacle," one that, in contrast to what Guy Debord expected, now lives on the palm of your hand. By selecting content that elicits similar emotional responses, the algorithms regulating social media feed on the performance of the friend/enemy divide and the psychological symbolic reservoir that sustains it. The point is not deeply believing that the enemies are evil, but performing that hate, except that that hate then becomes the algorithm that builds the reality you live in and thus your own emotional constitution. This, in turn, shapes the content that adept users decide to post, and it does not therefore come as a surprise to learn that Trump has attacked someone or something in more than half of his tweets (Shear et al., 2019).

And yet, as Adorno observes in the passage quoted earlier, the performance of identification, which lies at the basis of the psychology of fascist masses, and which is exponentially increased by the new social media, cannot explain fascism per se. Psychology can at best describe the mechanisms triggered by fascist propaganda, but it does not explain why they are triggered in the first place. We need an entire theory of society in order to explain why such propaganda arises in the first place and what kinds of interests sustain it. To begin with, as Nancy Fraser observed, we need to connect the new forms of authoritarianism with the current crisis in the capitalist mode of production; although crises are endemic to capitalism, what characterizes the ongoing current one is that finance and financialization play a much weightier role than it did in previous crises. A crisis at the structural level, with a more and more predatory financialized capitalism, is accompanied by one at the hegemonic level, leading to a widespread feeling of disorientation and disconnection (Fraser, 2019).

This is the juncture where "speculative communities" proliferate: the enormous success of contemporary social media is indeed inseparable from the emergence of financialization, that is, from the incredible polarization of wealth produced by the abstraction of capital from materiality, and the feeling of uncertainty created by lives that are structured by debt and financial uncertainty (Komporozos-Athanasiou, Forth.). For Aris Komporozos-Athanasiou, financialization facilitates (and at the same time relies on) the widespread circulation of a speculative imagination, and social media are key "nodes" for that circulation, as an increasingly anxious society relies on them to "cope" with the uncertainty of everyday life. So the forces of finance work in tandem with new social media to cultivate (from the ground up, as it were, rather than merely from the top down) such a "speculative imagination," which is often populist, nationalist, and regressive in its nature. The axis of inequality here forms precisely as a result of uneven exposures to uncertainty, which yields huge profits for finance (and political gains for the authoritarian right worldwide), while it sows further anxiety for those without resources to play the game of speculation effectively (and who therefore can only participate in speculation through social media activity).

Thus by ideologically depicting such uncertainty as the result of those evildoers who dare to question "American values and tradition," digital demagogues such as Trump can protect their own interests, those of corporate capital, while pretending to protect those of all everyday Americans. The feeling of uncertainty is there, but its sources are fundamentally displaced through the spectacular performance of scapegoating.

To sum up, mass psychology can help us understand the *how* of neofascism but not yet the *why*. For that, like Adorno and with Adorno, we need to go beyond mass psychology and certainly beyond Freud. Even more so: if we remain confined to the level of the psychology of the masses in our understanding of fascism, Adorno argues, we may end up reinforcing the very same ideology that sustains it. In a puzzling passage Adorno states:

> Fascism as such is not a psychological issue and [...] any attempts to understand its roots and its historical role in psychological terms still remains at the level

of ideologies such as the ideology of "irrational forces" promoted by fascism itself. Although the fascist agitator doubtless takes up certain tendencies within those he addresses, he does so as the delegate of powerful economic and political interests. Psychological dispositions do not actually cause fascism: rather, fascism defines a psychological area which can be successfully exploited by the forces which promote it for entirely non-psychological reasons of self-interest [transl. mod.]. (1991: 151)

Whether Adorno is right in saying that self-interest is not also a psychological issue is a tricky question that goes beyond the scope of this chapter. But we can certainly agree with him when he says that fascism defines a certain psychological area and that is precisely this that we see mobilized both by the American fascist agitators of the 1950s and their contemporary versions. Yet remaining at the level of pure psychological and psychoanalytic explanation could be very dangerous, because this risks reproducing the ideologies that justify fascist mass psychology itself.

Adorno's formulation, in the passage just quoted, is very synthetic and leaves space for different interpretations, but it also hints at a number of further questions we may want to raise while rereading Adorno's text today: What kind of ideology do we end up reproducing when we remain exclusively at the level of psychoanalytic explanations? Is it the patriarchal ideology that, as we have seen, is reflected in Freudian theory or, perhaps much more radically, in psychoanalysis itself? Can we understand the nature of the psychology that sustains fascism today by applying the psychoanalytic tools elaborated by Freud to unpack the foundations of the European bourgeois family structure, centered as it is on the triad of mom, dad, and child, without reproducing this structure? To what extent can psychoanalysis be exported to non-Western contexts, for instance, if it is true that, Frantz Fanon argues, some people, like the Antillean, do not have the Oedipus complex? (2008: 130).

By uncritically applying Freudian theory to such different contexts, there is indeed the risk of Eurocentrism, of implicitly reproducing the very same European bourgeois family model as *the* model whereby to measure all others. We may think that, through our own psychoanalytic investigation, we are reaching out to the "childhood of the world," but in the process we may also end up discovering that we are reaching only down to the European unconscious (Fanon, 2008: 166). The danger is not just Eurocentrism, and thus a bias based on a peculiar history that may prevent us from understanding radically different contexts, such as those with a very different family structure. By making the European bourgeois family structure implicitly appear as the normal family structure, centered as it is on the mother-father-child relations, we risk indeed presenting a historically situated social arrangement as a natural one, which is indeed the typical operation of ideology. Even worse: while trying to understand fascism, together with the racist and patriarchal ideology that sustains it, we may even end up reinforcing its very conceptual foundations.

If that is the case, then in our attempt to understand contemporary fascism, we, too, should proceed with Adorno, but also beyond him, thereby adding to his mass psychology not only an entire theory of society but also a rethinking of the potential patriarchal and racist biases that Freudian theory carries within itself.

Notes

1. I am grateful to Lucas Ballestin for his invaluable research assistantship in the preparation of this chapter. For reading and commenting on earlier drafts of this piece, as well as for the many conversations on this topic, I wish to thank Amy Allen, Aris Komporozos-Athanasiou, Benoit Challand, Judith Butler, Simona Forti, and Jamieson Webster. An earlier version of a part of this chapter appeared in Public Seminar in 2016, https://publicseminar.org/2016/11/the-mass-psychology-of-trumpism/.
2. See, for instance, the edited volume *Global Resurgence of the Right* (Pereyra Doval and Souroujon, 2021), which, through its collection of different voices, ponders the usefulness of different categories, such as "neofascism," "right-wing populism," and even "neo-liberal totalitarianism" to describe the resurgence of the right on a global scale. As an example of a journalistic approach, see "How Far Is Europe Swinging to the Right?" (Aisch et al., 2016).
3. I am here implicitly drawing from Federico Finchelstein's definition of fascism, which, very usefully, provides an approach that takes into account the Latin American historical examples of fascism (2017: 7).
4. For instance, Matteo Albanese and Pablo del Hierro reconstruct the way in which, through the Italian-Spanish connection, a global fascist network of ideas, movements, and leaders built up transnationally over the course of the twentieth century. The authors thereby provide a very useful map for understanding the ramification of fascist ideas and movements in the last century (Albanese and Del Hierro Lecea, 2018).
5. Among those who have rejected the concept of neofascism to describe Trumpism, see, for instance, Slavoj Žižek, who has asserted provocatively that the fear that Trump could turn the United States into a fascist state is a "ridiculous exaggeration," and that we should rather look at Trump's election as a great opportunity to reinvigorate the left (2018). Four years into Trump's presidency, we can now say that Žižek's idea that having Trump as a president could help the consolidation of the left was itself a "ridiculous exaggeration." The left did not prosper under Trump as much as it did under Obama; the eruption of the Occupy Wall Street movement, the most significant nonviolent episode in the history of the United States left since the 1960s, did not happen under Trump but under Obama. Similarly, in European history, we saw that the left did not prosper under the fascist and authoritarian regimes of the 1940s but, rather, under the liberal democracies of the 1960s.
6. Mass psychology has a much broader history than what I can reconstruct in the brief space of this chapter. For a useful reconstruction of the history of mass psychology, from the point of view of its possible application to an analysis of Trumpism, see Eli Zaretsky's essay on "The Mass Psychology of Trumpism" (2018).
7. Freud writes: "The opposite opinions owe their origin to the consideration of those stable groups or associations in which mankind pass their lives, and which are embodied in the institutions of society. Groups of the first kind stand in the same sort of relation to those of the second as a high but choppy sea to a ground swell" (1949: 21).
8. This important shift happens in Chapter V, after chapter IV's introduction of his theory of the libido, thus suggesting that it is in the latter chapter that a bias toward a certain type of libido is introduced.

9. As we will see, other authors, such as Elias Canetti, also took distance from such a view and insisted on the substantial difference existing between two types of crowds, the "open" and the "closed" ones, and even went so far as to state that open crowds are the true crowds (1973: 20).
10. "Thus the group appears to us as a revival of the primal horde. Just as primitive man virtually survives in every individual, so the primal horde may arise once more out of any random collection; in so far as men are habitually under the sway of group formation we recognize in it the survival of the primal horde" (Freud, 1949: 70).
11. The operation is indeed a form of *reductio ad unum*, that is of reduction to the one, but with the important qualification that the one is the development of the libido in bio-males.
12. Feminist psychoanalysts have emphasized this aspect of Freudian theory for a very long time. See, for instance, Karen Horney (1924); Luce Irigaray (1985: 23); Julia Kristeva (1984: 46); more recently, see Jill Gentile (2019).
13. For instance, in his (in)famous essay on female sexuality, which he begins to address with reluctance and which he concludes is a "puzzle to be left to poets" (Freud, 1965: 167). Freud nevertheless presents an entire reconstruction of female sexuality done from the point of view of the development of the libido in bio-males, leading to his very controversial statements about women's supposed penis envy.
14. Recently Joel Whitebook, in his very innovative intellectual biography of Freud, adduces new historical evidence as to why Freud himself could not really deal with feminine sexuality (2017: 52). According to Whitebook, Freud's mother suffered from a chronic depression that left little beloved Sigmund in an emotional vacuum, only partially filled by his Czech nanny (2017: 43).
15. It is worth noting that, according to a *New York Times* study of Trump's usage of Twitter, published on November 2, 2019, "the person he most often singled out for praise was himself" (Shear et al., 2019). Note also that he has repeated this feat apropos the Covid-19 pandemic (Peters et al., 2020).
16. On whiteness and the settler-colonial property regime, see Aileen Moreton-Robinson, *The White Possessive* (2015: xi–xxiv); for a more general take on the role of labor control in the history of colonization of the Americas, and how the capitalist division of labor systematically relied on racism, see Aníbal Quijano, "Coloniality of Power, Eurocentrism, and Latin America" (2000).
17. As Coates observed: "The East was the Nazi Manifest Destiny. In Hitler's view, 'in the East a similar process will repeat itself for a second time as in the conquest of America.' As Hitler imagined the future, Germany would deal with the Slavs much as the North Americans had dealt with the Indians. The Volga River in Russia, he once proclaimed, will be Germany's Mississippi" (2014). See also: Sue Grand (2018: 84–102).
18. Hence, the ironic character of the fascist leadership, the phoniness, which Vladimir Safatle emphasizes and which indeed explains how disinhibition is possible (2021).
19. For an illuminating analysis of the transformation of the spectator in the age of individual media, see Gabriele Pedullá, *In Broad Daylight* (2012).
20. "Images are no longer only the medium by which we communicate our political activities, but have also become an end in themselves: the very stuff that politics is made of" (Bottici, 2014: 106).
21. Christian Fuchs' *Digital Demagogue* (2018) focuses on Trump, while his *Nationalism on the Internet* focuses on European cases.

Bibliography

Adorno TW (1991) Freudian Theory and the Pattern of Fascist Propaganda. In: JM Bernstein (ed.), *The Culture Industry*. London: Routledge, 132–57.

Aisch G, Pearce A, and Rousseau B (2016) How Far Is Europe Swinging to the Right? *The New York Times*, May 22. Available at: https://www.nytimes.com/interactive/2016/05/22/world/europe/europe-right-wing-austria-hungary.html (accessed September 13, 2021).

Albanese M and Del Hierro Lecea P (2018) *Transnational Fascism in the Twentieth Century: Spain, Italy and the Global Neo-Fascist Network*. London: Bloomsbury Academic.

Bernstein JM (2017) Adorno's Uncanny Analysis of Trump's Authoritarian Personality. In: *Public Seminar*. Available at: https://publicseminar.org/2017/10/adornos-uncanny-analysis-of-trumps-authoritarian-personality/ (accessed September 13, 2021).

Bernstein JM (2021) Fight Club: Enlivenment, Love, and the Aesthetics of Violence in the Age of Trump. In: D LaRocca (ed.), *Metacinema: The Form and Content of Filmic Reference and Reflexivity*. New York: Oxford University Press, 191–218.

Bottici C (2014) *Imaginal Politics: Images beyond Imagination and the Imaginary*. New York: Columbia University Press.

Butler J (2016) Trump, Fascism, and the Construction of "the people": An Interview with Judith Butler. Available at: https://www.versobooks.com/blogs/3025-trump-fascism-and-the-construction-of-the-people-an-interview-with-judith-butler (accessed September 13, 2021).

Butler J (2017) Reflections on Trump. In: *Society for Cultural Anthropology*. Available at: https://culanth.org/fieldsights/reflections-on-trump (accessed September 13, 2021).

Cammaerts B (2020) The Neo-Fascist Discourse and its Normalisation Through Mediation. *Journal of Multicultural Discourses* 15(3): 241–56. doi:10.1080/17447143.2020.1743296.

Canetti E (1973) *Crowds and Power* (trans. C Stewart). Harmondsworth: Penguin Books.

Coates T-N (2014) Hitler on the Mississippi Banks: Thoughts on Timothy Snyder's Bloodlands. *The Atlantic*, January 16. Available at: https://www.theatlantic.com/international/archive/2014/01/hitler-on-the-mississippi-banks/283127/ (accessed September 13, 2021).

Fanon F (2008) *Black Skin, White Masks* (trans. R Philcox). New York: Grove Press.

Finchelstein F (2014) Returning Populism to History: Returning Populism to History. *Constellations* 21(4): 467–82. doi:10.1111/1467-8675.12131.

Finchelstein F (2017) *From Fascism to Populism in History*. Oakland: University of California Press.

Fraser N (2019) Mass Psychology of Crisis. In: *Public Seminar*. Available at: https://publicseminar.org/2019/04/mass-psychology-of-crisis/ (accessed September 10, 2021).

Freud S (1949) *Group Psychology and Analysis of the Ego* (trans. J Strachey). New York: W. W. Norton.

Freud S (1965) *New Introductory Lectures on Psychoanalysis* (trans. J Strachey). New York: W. W. Norton.

Fuchs C (2018) *Digital Demagogue: Authoritarian Capitalism in the Age of Trump and Twitter*. London: PlutoPress.

Fuchs C (2020) *Nationalism on the Internet: Critical Theory and Ideology in the Age of Social Media and Fake News*. New York: Routledge.

Gentile J (2019) *Feminine Law: Freud, Free Speech, and the Voice of Desire*. London: Routledge.
Grand S (2018) The Other Within: White Shame, Native-American Genocide. *Contemporary Psychoanalysis* 54(1): 84–102.
Horkheimer M and Adorno TW (2002) *Dialectic of Enlightenment: Philosophical Fragments* (trans. E Jephcott). Stanford, CA: Stanford University Press.
Horney K (1924) On the Genesis of the Castration Complex in Women. *International Journal of Psychoanalysis* 5(1): 50.
Irigaray L (1985) *This Sex Which Is Not One* (trans. C Porter and C Burke). Ithaca: Cornell University Press.
Komporozos-Athanasiou A (forthcoming) *Speculative Communities: Living with Uncertainty in a Financialized World*. Chicago, IL: The University of Chicago.
Kristeva J (1984) *Revolution in Poetic Language* (trans. M Waller). New York: Columbia University Press.
Mathers M (2020) Trump "haemorrhaging" Twitter Followers in Wake of Election Defeat. *Independent*, November 26. Available at: https://www.independent.co.uk/news/world/americas/us-election-2020/trump-losing-twitter-followers-election-defeat-b1762502.html (accessed September 10, 2021).
Moreton-Robinson A (2015) *The White Possessive: Property, Power, and Indigenous Sovereignty*. Minneapolis: University of Minnesota Press.
Pedullà G (2012) *In Broad Daylight: Movies and Spectators after the Cinema*. Brooklyn, NY: Verso Books.
Pereyra Doval G and Souroujon G (eds) (2021) *Global Resurgence of the Right: Conceptual and Regional Perspectives*. Abingdon: Routledge.
Peters JW, Plott E and Haberman M (2020) 260,000 Words, Full of Self-Praise, from Trump on the Virus. *New York Times*, April 26. Available at: https://www.nytimes.com/interactive/2020/04/26/us/politics/trump-coronavirus-briefings-analyzed.html (accessed September 13, 2021).
Pinheiros Safatle V (2021) The Fascist Laugh: Propaganda and Cynical Rationality in Adorno. In: P-F Noppen and G Raulet (eds), *Théorie Critique de La Propagande*. Paris: Éditions de la Maison des Sciences de l'homme, 123–34.
Quijano A (2000) Coloniality of Power, Eurocentrism, and Latin America. *Nepantla: Views from South* 1(3): 533–80.
Schmidt R (2011) American Indian Identity and Blood Quantum in the 21st Century: A Critical Review. *Journal of Anthropology* 9: 1–9.
Shear MD, Haberman M, Confessore N, et al. (2019) How Trump Reshaped the Presidency in Over 11,000 Tweets. *New York Times*, November 2. Available at: https://www.nytimes.com/interactive/2019/11/02/us/politics/trump-twitter-presidency.html (accessed September 10, 2021).
Webster J (2017) Freudian Theory and The Pattern of Fascist Propaganda: Part 3. In: *Public Seminar*. Available at: http://publicseminar.org/2017/10/freudian-theory-and-the-pattern-of-fascist-propaganda/.
Whitebook J (2017) *Freud: An Intellectual Biography*. Cambridge: Cambridge University Press.
Zaretsky E (2018) The Mass Psychology of Trumpism. In: *London Review of Books*. Available at: https://www.lrb.co.uk/blog/2018/september/the-mass-psychology-of-trumpism (accessed September 10, 2021).
Žižek S (2018) *The Courage of Hopelessness: Chronicles of a Year of Acting Dangerously*. London: Penguin Books.

Part III

The Aesthetics of the People

8

Picturing the People

The Dilemmas of Democratic Representation[1]

Paula Diehl

People without a Picture

Two problems arise when exploring the representation of the people in modern democracy. First, should we talk about the people in the singular, as the expression of a political collectivity, or ought we talk about the people in the plural, as a more accurate understanding of the sociological and political differences that exist therein? Second, how can the unity and diversity of the people be represented without threatening the dynamics of political and democratic change in society while at the same time emphasizing the existence of the people as the sovereign of democracy?

Democratic theory has always asked itself the question whether "the people," as the subject of power, can take a form. The principle of popular sovereignty places the people at the center of the political imaginary (Diehl, 2015), transforming the people into a political subject. However, its iconographical rendering does not seem as successful (Falkenhausen, 1993). This is a significant issue since the constitution of a collective subject or a political unity is essential for a group's ability to act. In other words, in order for a people to become a subject, the individuals must form a whole. As a consequence, many authors have assumed that a process of identity construction is necessary (Laclau, 2005). The people *is* reliant and dependent on the identification of the individuals with the group, so that they can share a common imagination of the people. At the same time, the people *is* the result of conflicts, symbolic and discursive constructions within society. Only when the many organize themselves into a unity can a bond be established between individuals, and collective action becomes possible.

The problem can, however, be formulated in another way: the key to constructing a political subject is its representability. When the people[2] *finds* a representation of itself, it is possible for them to assert the principle of sovereignty and demand their own active role. In democracy it is certainly not a question of reflecting a preexisting identity of the people, as in Carl Schmitt's essentialist understanding of representation. On the contrary, the emphasis is on the construction of the unity of a people. Democratic representation does not equal personalization either, as Schmitt claimed (Diehl, 2015: 71). It is doubtless the case that the people can represent itself without necessarily being personalized; the case of mass events and protests demonstrate this. Moreover, in a broader sense, as a symbolic-performative process of constructing a political subject, I agree with Lisa Disch that "[i]t is only through representation that a people comes to be as a political agent, one capable of putting forward a demand" (2011: 104).

Given this, one has to wonder why democratic states, who effortlessly produce an iconography of the nation, cannot develop any pictorial symbol representing the sovereign people. While the nation is mostly portrayed through a female allegory, like Marianne for the French republic or Columbia for the United States—or through all kinds of symbols such as plants, flowers, and animals—for example, the eagle in the case of the United States and Germany, or the rooster in France—the people as the major actor in democracy is rarely the subject of state iconography. This fact is interesting, since the people still finds its place in the institutional symbolism of democracy, although not as an image, but in political speeches and declarations and, of course, in the most powerful form of symbolization: the people as the political sovereign in the constitution.

The famous preamble of the United States' constitution from 1787, ratified in 1788, even puts the people as the author of the text: "We the People of the United States, in Order to form a more perfect Union, establish Justice, insure domestic Tranquillity, provide for the common defence, promote the general Welfare, and secure the Blessings of Liberty to ourselves and our Posterity, do ordain and establish this Constitution for the United States of America" (The Constitution of the United States, n.d.). While the preamble is generally interpreted as lacking binding legal status (Orgad, 2010), it nonetheless fulfills a central symbolic function by introducing and validating the people performatively as both a political actor and the sovereign. The French constitution and the declaration of human rights from 1793 took a similar step, defining the people as "the source of sovereignty" so that the legitimacy of power was explicitly transferred to the people (Diehl, 2015: 204; Constitution du 24 juin 1793, n.d.). In 1789, the human rights declaration only states that "the nation" can be found in the "essence" of "the people." To this day, the people's representation in the constitution is the subject of democratic symbolism, whether it is mentioned as the explicit source of power, as the author, or as the authority that legitimizes the law. Yet, if the representation of the people plays such a crucial role in democracy, why does it lack any clearly recognized form for institutional representation?

The Indeterminacy of Democratic Symbolism and the Representation of the People

Democratic Symbolism in Claude Lefort

A first explanation for the absence of a pictorial representation of the people can be found in Claude Lefort's work. Lefort understands representation as the *mise-en-scène* of the political, that is, as the symbolization through which a society gives itself form and a structure by which human coexistence is itself determined. Furthermore, giving them a form implies giving them meaning (*mise-en-sens*) (Lefort, 1988: 11). Hence, the unfolding of political symbolization is not a minor question; rather, it is constitutive of the political *tout court*. Democracy, Lefort continues, is characterized by a specific form of symbolization. Freeing itself from the yoke of the absolutist embodiment of power, that is, the state and the nation embodied in the king, it instead elevates the people to the level of both sovereign and political actor.

Under absolutism, the people as a political actor did not exist; subsumed under the nation, they had no representation of their own, let alone an iconography. In a Hobbesian manner, the king's body absorbed the state and the nation, leaving little room for any creation of other political subjects besides the king himself (Diehl, 2015: 143). The state, which in the meantime had acquired a status as a legal person, would be absorbed and embodied by the king and symbolized accordingly. Hence, the image of the king's body was simultaneously the image of the state, of power, and of the nation that included the people.

Only after the revolutions of the eighteenth century would the people become sovereign. The principle of popular sovereignty thus established itself as the "main form of legitimation [*Hauptlegitimationsformel*]" (Kielmansegg, 1977: 373). It formed the "primary reference of democratic representation" and provided a normative orientation for political action and symbolic practices in democracy (Diehl, 2019: 411). The principle of popular sovereignty made possible a new structure of political representation, that is, a new arrangement of symbols, staging, and discursive production, by virtue of which the people could be represented as a political subject (Diehl, 2015: 35 a. 106). This marked a radical rupture, and nowhere was this break more evident than in France where, unlike in America, the revolution was in direct confrontation with the people, institutions, and the symbols of the *ancien régime* (Sennett, 1996: 277).

The Destruction of the Royal Body

Central to this new representational structure was the loss of the king's body. The king symbolically embodied political power before he was beheaded by the French revolutionaries on January 21, 1793. The pictorial testimony of this event is horrifying. Among countless depictions of the scene of the guillotine, there exists one of the most violent visual motifs of the French Revolution made by Louise-Jules-Frédérique Villeneuve: from the head, severed from the body, drips blood. In victory, it is held aloft. The engraving was made immediately after the beheading of Louis XVI and published in several copies (exact date unknown) (Duprat, 1992: 52). The picture bears the inscription "*Matière de réflexion pour les jongleurs couronnés*" ("*Grounds for reflection for the crowned jugglers*"). Underneath is a quote from the Marseillais, giving the act of violence the significance of a founding myth for the new republic: "que le sang impur abreuve nos sillon" ("That the impure blood waters our furrows"). Lefort interprets the beheading of the king as a radical symbolic rupture and a new beginning. Democracy is accordingly understood as ushering in a new form of representation that can no longer tolerate political embodiment in any individual (Lefort, 1988: 17).

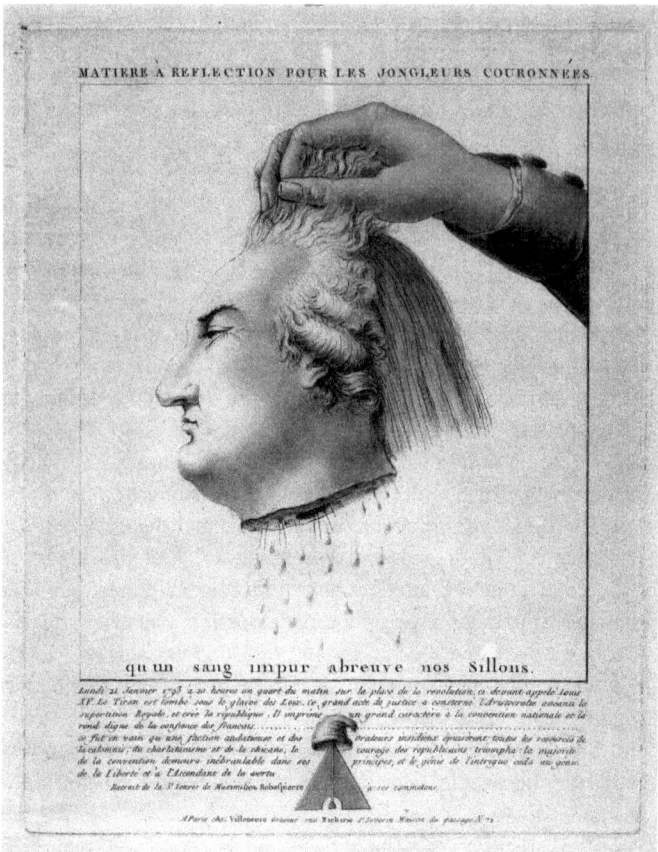

Figure 8.1 Unknown, *Matière à reflection pour les jongleurs couronnés*, 1793. © The Trustees of the British Museum, released as CC BY-NC-SA 4.0.

The effect of the new democratic structures of representation is not unproblematic, since the king's body cannot be replaced with another instance capable of symbolically including both power and the people. On the contrary, one of democracy's impositions lies in precisely the fact that the locus of power must symbolically be left empty (Lefort, 1988). The symbolic occupation of this space not only stands in direct opposition to the fact that popular sovereignty means the power of everyone and anyone, meaning that no claim of power made by any one person or particular group is possible. Moreover, the symbolical occupation of the place of power, that is, the embodying of the state and the people, would result in the end of the power of all and, *mutadis mutandi*, of democracy. The political representation of unity therefore loses a powerful pictorial presentation and must resort to visual processes that appear considerably more abstract than the royal body. Lefort speaks about the "disembodiment" of political representation, preventing any ultimate determination of society (1988: 18).[3]

Embodiment as Totalitarian Temptation

Recognizing such a disembodied society undermines any representation of it as an organic totality, even if the royal body survives as a phantasm (Manow, 2010). Only totalitarian movements produce "egocrats" that function as pictorial embodiments of the people (Lefort, 1981: 101). The pictorial cult surrounding totalitarian leaders is renowned for this. Their bodies constitute the place of power, absorbing the people and its will. Mussolini and Hitler are paradigmatic examples of leaders staging themselves as the embodiment of a united people. Both the pictorial and the mental images[4] of the body produced by the "egocrats" belonged to a repertoire that allow many layers of identification with the leader. For the representation of a people, this absorbing effect is especially important.

The imagery of Hobbes' *Leviathan* shows this symbolic absorption of the body, working as a visual presentation of the civil contract and the state. In Hobbes' model of representation, the Leviathan represents the transfer of the will of the individual to the sovereign.[5] The Leviathan becomes an anthropomorphic and masculine figure consisting of the innumerable bodies of individuals. The sovereign, here both as a person and as the state in the form of institutions, embodies not only power but also every individual. The multitude thus "are made one person," though it is "the unity of the representer, not the unity of the represented, that maketh the person one" (Hobbes, 1988: 109). The resulting person is not the people but the state or the "Common Wealth," and the individual does not become a part of the political subject, as is the case for Rousseau.

The case of totalitarian embodiment is more complex. Since totalitarian leaders no longer can banish the principle of the popular sovereignty from the political imaginary, they must find symbolic processes capable of absorbing the people as a political subject. It is therefore not a mere repetition of absolutist representation. Instead, as the historian Luisa Passerini has rightly pointed out, Mussolini's images created "a body of desire for the Italians," thereby making possible "a short circuit between power and the masses" (1991: 70). Like the Leviathan, Mussolini absorbed all individuals. But unlike the Leviathan, his body did not symbolize them as such, just the people as a whole. Totalitarian embodiment shifts the idea of popular sovereignty insofar as it shapes the will of the people by that of the leader. When the Leviathan does not produce a body of the people, the totalitarian short circuit creates a union of all in the body of the leader. It is easy, then, to agree with Susanne von Falkenhausen who speaks of a "legitimizing cycle between people and leader" (1993: 1022) in the totalitarian case. Popular sovereignty is absorbed by the leader and as a consequence is no longer the sovereignty of the people, but that of leaders.

The Dynamic Moment of the People and Its Symbolization

Lefort recognizes a second problem in totalitarian representation. Not only is embodiment unsuitable for democratic representation, the production of the people as a single body also endangers democratic symbolization, as well as a democratic understanding of the political. Following this approach, a democratic, symbolic, and pictorial rendering of the people is prevented by the fact that it remains too plural and transitory. Instead of any monolithic image, Lefort assumes the importance of transformation processes, including political and sociocultural change. The people is not a static entity but a transitory and variable sociohistorical product. Instead of an organic body of the people, Lefort employs the metaphor of the network, in which cooperation and friction between individuals and groups prevail. These groupings constantly change, forming fluid processes that cannot be represented. This is the opposite of totalitarian representation, which seeks to homogenize and fixate the people as the embodiment of unity (Lefort, 1981: 105).

In democracy, there is no such thing as an unchanging people. What is more, the symbolization of democracy is always faced with the problem of making its openness and motility representable (Diehl, 2015: 26). In a democracy, the consideration of social heterogeneity is fundamental. The political unity of the people becomes the object of dispute and must be permanently reconstructed. It is dependent "upon a political discourse and upon a sociological and historical elaboration, always bound up with ideological debate" (Lefort, 1988: 18). In any case, an organic representation of society as the body of a people is dissolved and instead processes and dynamics of social self-representation come to the fore (Diehl, 2015: 180). For Judith Butler it is precisely this indeterminate moment that makes every invocation and every image of the people contestable (2015: 164). So how can one even portray the people as a political subject when they are in a constant process of transformation? Lefort's answer: the people cannot be visually represented.

The Image of the People: The Attempted Iconography of the French Revolution

The effects of the democratic representational structure on symbolic practice and iconographic production are not as radical as its theoretical consequences. The French Revolution once again offers an exemplary illustration of this. One of the first postrevolutionary attempts at visualizing unity arose with the mass gatherings connected to revolutionary celebration.

The Crowd

Already in 1790, the crowd gathered for a ritual. The celebration of the revolution one year after the storming of the Bastille was organized under the motto of unity and was intended to facilitate the reconciliation of the nation. On a throne in the front sat the king who, just as during the *ancien régime*, was the audience of the spectacle. However, this was deceptive, since a fundamental change in meaning had occurred: the king himself had to swear an oath to the nation while it was the people who acted as witness. Here the presence of the people had not yet taken the symbolic form of sovereign, but it was at least represented as a collective subject seeking recognition from the king. This new meaning of the people was represented iconographically in part in the role as spectator, such as in the colored engraving of Charles Monnet who signed his picture with "Peintre du roi."[6] In the picture, the event seems distant but is cheered on by the people.

Five years later, the painter Charles Thévenin created a perspective that gave greater visibility to the people in the ritual.[7] In this oil painting one can still see the order in the stands, but the painter places another event in the foreground: soldiers and men dressed in bourgeois attire embracing one another. This is likely to be an affirmative gesture to establish unity, and it becomes a central component of the ritual in the staging of revolutionary celebrations, especially in its radical phase, between 1791 and 1794. The picture also clearly marks the presence of women. This visually expands the category of the "people" to include women, regardless of the fact that they had no political rights. In contrast to Monnet's representation, Thévenin's picture dissolves the separation between passive spectators and active participants. The gathering of the masses as people in the first celebration of the revolution in 1790 marked an important stage in the constitution of the people as a political subject: the sovereignty that once belonged to, and was embodied by, the king now belonged to the nation, as stated in Article 3 of the French declaration on the Rights of Man and the Citizen of August 1789: "The principle of any Sovereignty lies primarily in the Nation" (Declaration of Human and Civic Rights of August 26, 1789, n.d.). Even if one could not yet speak of the people as sovereign, the assembled crowd provided the first visual template that would shape the memory of the emerging democracy and inspire many painters.

Later, when the king was no longer alive, the radical revolutionary government made this type of popular representation a state task and practiced the choreographic organization of the people. The painter Jean-Louis David, himself a member of the National Convention, made several sketches of this staging, often inspired by Rousseau's idea of a collective body (2002: 158–68). Like a procession, the crowd was meant to stop at the major symbols of the republic, with the aim of bringing the many into a unity. The most famous of these paintings is probably *Fête de l'Être Suprême au Champ de Mars* by Pierre-Antoine Demachy. Demachy offers a panorama of what happened on June 8, 1794, showing the crowd in peaceful interaction. David's choreography is still recognizable, since the republican symbols are visible in the positions they take up amid the crowd. On the right side of the picture is the statue of Hercules, representing the people as sovereign; at the highest point, on the holy hill, the people finally come together under the tree of freedom adorned with the Phrygian cap. The organization of the masses brings the individuals together as a collective. Both Richard Sennett (1996: 296) and Judith Butler (2015: 160ff) have shown in what ways the plurality of symbolic expressions of the people creates fundamental conflicts.

In Demachy's *Fête de l'Être Suprême au Champ de Mars* a symbolic duplication can be recognized: the people as a crowd not only create their symbolization as a collective through their presence, but they encounter their own symbolization through Hercules; this encounter is the meeting of two different forms of symbolizing the people: the first draws its strength from the performativity of the presence that is represented. To this day, the gathering of the many is the most powerful symbolization of the people as a political subject. The second representation of the people in the picture draws its symbolic power from the tradition of allegory, which is suitable for abstract and ideal

Figure 8.2 Pierre-Antoine Demachy, *Fête de l'Être Suprême au Champ de Mars*, ca. 1794. © Musée Carnavalet, Histoire de Paris, released as CC0 1.0 Universal (CC0 1.0).

representation. Part of this tradition is the visualization of principles adopted from revolutionary symbolism on both sides of the Atlantic. In this way, freedom, equality, and justice were presented as central principles, but these representations also included the republic as a new form of government and the nation.

Demachy's painting, which shows the confluence of the people as a crowd and its symbolization in the form of Hercules, anticipates the distinction between the people as a political ideal and as a concrete social reality, something that Pierre Rosanvallon identifies in modern democracy. The people as a social fact *are* implicit in the crowd, while their idealization stands out clearly in the allegory of Hercules. Hence, when the people appear as a presence posed against the allegory of the people as sovereign in Demachy's painting, it is by no means a symbolic duplication. Rather, two images here meet, drawing attention to different dimensions of the meaning of the people. Demachy's painting poses the following questions to the viewer: How does the allegory of Hercules symbolize the people and what are its implications for the democratic imaginary? What is the relationship between the motif of Hercules and the visualized presence of the people?

The Failed Images of the People as a Political Subject

For a short period in French history, Hercules functioned as the official symbol of the people in *its* role as political sovereign. Yet Hercules had already appeared in US-American symbolism as early as 1776 when John Adams suggested that he would be part of the "US. Great Seal"—not explicitly as an iconograph for the sovereign people but as a representation of the unity of the nation. Hercules had to give way to the eagle and the inscription "E pluribus unum," even if in 1778 the Marquis de Barbis-Marbois chose the motif for his "Allegory of the American Union" (Herzogenrath, 2010: 11). In French history, however, the mythical figure became a symbol of the people as a political actor and sovereign, but only between 1793 and 1794 (Diehl, 2011).

After the king's beheading in 1793, the way was paved not only for the republic but also for the establishment of the principle of popular sovereignty. In this context, it is important to note that the Constitution of 1793 stipulated: "The sovereignty resides in the people; it is one and indivisible, imprescriptible, and inalienable" (Constitution du 24 juin 1793, n.d.). In 1792, the National Convention discussed the motif for the new state seal. Instead of the king, they chose a female allegory (not yet identified as Marianne). But in October 1793 the convention revoked this decision and opted for Jean-Louis David's proposal to depict the mythical figure of Hercules on the national seal as a representation of the people. This never came to pass, however. For not only did the Thermidorian government, which took office in 1794, oppose such a symbolic empowerment of the people, but even Robespierre remained ambivalent on the point, proposing instead the use of a pedagogical concept capable of taming the people.

What was the reason for such skepticism? Presumably, the disruptive factor lies less in the symbolization of the people itself and more in its symbolization as sovereign. In the French case, the Herculean motif contained a clear punch line: In monarchy, Hercules symbolized the sovereignty, power, and virtue of the monarchs. To choose precisely this motif for symbolizing the people was a revolutionary act, marking the people's possession of sovereignty. But portraying the people as the invincible Hercules was a delicate matter for government officials. It draws attention to the danger that the people actually can behave like the sovereign and, if necessary, eliminate its government with the use of force (Diehl, 2011: 152ff). France had been the showcase for such behavior, and the violent masses in September 1793 had not yet faded from memory. It is therefore unsurprising that the government, which ended the revolution's radical phase, pushed the figure of Hercules into the background. In fact, the way the radical government had previously handled the question was much more ambivalent. It emphasized the power of the people, but it also wanted to tame it through an educational program expressed in the visual politics of the revolution (Diehl, 2011: 157). The fear of the symbolization of the people as sovereign lies precisely in the fact that the actual people could actually behave as sovereign through this idealization and thereby question the power of the rulers.[8]

Two Dimensions of the People

Ideal People and the People of Society

Pierre Rosanvallon has drawn attention to two dimensions of the people in modern democracy, distinguishing between the people as a political abstraction and the people as a social reality, that is, a concrete grouping of individuals. According to Rosanvallon, there is a fundamental tension between these two dimensions that can be explained by way of the principle of popular sovereignty. Popular sovereignty creates a new political subject and founds a political and sociological imperative that is derived from the idea of the people as a principle of authority (*un régime d'autorité*) at the same time as it recognizes within this principle *un sujet exerçant*, an author, who can act (Rosanvallon, 2000: 15). Accordingly, the people are internally divided between a political principle and a social fact. This tension arises between the political moment of democracy and its social realization (Rosanvallon, 2000: 14). In its ideal dimension, the people *represents* the principle of unity; here Rosanvallon employs the expression *peuple-nation*. It is a question of an abstract people that must be symbolized in order to exist. The entire symbolic dimension of the French Revolution focused on the creation of a unitary body, which Rosanvallon interprets as the "principle and promise of democracy" (1998: 40).

In the second dimension, one finds the people as the people of society (*peuple-société*), that is, the set of concrete individuals, but for which no unity is created, since it is plural and historically variable (Rosanvallon, 2000: 40). As a social fact, the people is amorphous, elusive, and improbable (*sans formes, corps fuyant et improbable*) (Rosanvallon, 2000: 40). This people approximates Lefort's description of the disembodied society. It is plural in nature, constantly changing. For this reason it is "impossible to find," ergo unrepresentable (Rosanvallon, 2000: 419).

Might it, then, be possible to transpose Rosanvallon's distinction between the ideal and the concrete dimensions of the people onto Demachy's painting, where the visualization of the presence of the people meets its allegorical form? This would be a risky, but not an uninteresting, line of inquiry to pursue. We can understand Hercules as the idealization of the people without difficulty. The motif presents a singular actor that not only expresses sovereignty in an abstract sense but also gives symbolic form to the revolutionary program of popular sovereignty. Here the diversity of the concrete people is completely ignored in favor of the creation of a unified body. The image presents a united people capable of action. This is not the case with the image of the crowd. True, Rosanvallon expounds the thesis that the concrete dimension of the people cannot be represented owing to its malleability and plurality. The *representation* of the crowd— not only in Demachy's painting but in all visual forms—must then be understood as an expression of the ideal people. Judith Butler presents a similar argument: "Any photograph, or any series of images, would doubtless have a frame or set of frames, and those frames would function as a potentially exclusionary designation, including what it captures by establishing a zone of the uncapturable" (2015: 165). Any image *of* anything is, in other words, always just a selection of its possibilities and presupposes definite connotations and perceptual patterns. Even so, one might take the risky step of exploring the potential for plural symbolizations, something found in all images of the crowd, even if each image presents a frame and thereby already casts an interpretive gaze on the crowd.

The presence of the people and the portrayal of the people as the crowd have the potential of manifesting the plurality of society. Totalitarian symbolic expressions are exceptions here. And when it comes to such a kind of representation one can no longer speak of the crowd but, instead, must speak of the ordered masses of totalitarianism. In a democracy, on the other hand, the images of the crowd have the purpose of empowering the people symbolically, from out of which a political subject is created. The greater the inclusivity of these images, the more empowered the people will be. Behind the crowd one can surmise the plurality of the people and its "zone of unrepresentability." In Demachy's painting, this plurality is identifiable by the variegated dresses and gestures of the individuals, which serve to accentuate differences in both gender and social standing.

On the Relation between Unity and Plurality

Concerning the possible relation between the *principle* of unity of the people and the plurality of its social composition, questions still remain. Despite its centrality in the democratic symbolic order, the people *has* only for a short period been the object of institutional iconography. It looks as if giving the people a unified image and thus exalting it as a political actor would be a risky affair for those in power. At the same time, the symbolization of the people in terms of the presence of the crowd was supported institutionally in the very attempt at creating a governable unity of the people instead of the uncontrollable crowd. What characterized the postrevolutionary societies of both France and the United States was the notion that collective rituals and their civic religious effects had a pedagogical function. In both political traditions the gathering of the people belongs to the celebration of patriotic feeling and the staging of unity. July 14 in France and July 4 in the United States create an opportunity to celebrate patriotic unity through a mixture of popular festivity and political ceremony.

However, Rosanvallon has with good reason traced another tendency, one that is certainly inherent in modern democracy but that becomes all the more important with the growing social changes of the nineteenth century and the concomitant process of increased individualization: the recognition of social particularities. With that, the descriptive representation (Pitkin, 1972), which had guaranteed the representation of social classes under feudalism, returns in a new guise. Now the act of descriptive symbolization represents the diversity of society, giving it an image (Rosanvallon, 1998: 139ff). The intrinsic tension between the representation of the people as either unity or plurality is further accentuated. Here one must inquire into the relation between unity and plurality, as well as the relation between the act of creating a political subject and recognizing the heterogeneity of society. Is it at all possible to create a plural political subject? If so, what images are suitable in facilitating such a creation?

For Rosanvallon, the difference, even the distance, between the ideal of the People and a concrete people is first of all constitutive of democracies *tout court*. When it comes to the construction of the people as a political subject, though, this argument should be supplemented. Which is to say: not only do the ideal and the concrete people differ from each other, but they also interact. Democratic representation always contains the "actualization and presentation of what is most proper to the people, along with its images, that are invested in the citizen" (Böckenförde, 1983: 25).[9] This joins together the presentation of the political and the articulation of questions and demands addressed to the common. The constitution of the people as the political subject of democracy arises out of a dynamic process, from out of the interaction between the ideal and the concrete. It is because of this that the concrete people can understand itself as a political subject and constitute itself as one. Collective role models emerge with a normative character that are related to the present, the past, and the future—images and models that could belong to a pluralistic society. The people *create* its own presentations, transcending *its* own existence and thereby making possible the appearance of the ideal people. The political subject emerges always as the result of the interaction between the concrete and the ideal registers. And this interaction takes place within numerous and dynamic processes of construction—whether discursive, symbolic, or deliberative.

Three Relations between Unity and Plurality in Images

Political institutions rarely give rise to iconographical expressions of the negotiation between unity and plurality. However, in art any image of the people passes through the interpretive filter of the artist and therefore different relations between unity and diversity come to be expressed. The iconography of the people can mark out the relation between unity and plurality in one of three ways: (i) plurality as a precondition for the functioning of unity, (ii) plurality as a mark of unity, and (iii) the visualization of the people disclosing plurality as the dynamic moment of the people.

Plurality as a Precondition for the Functioning of Unity

The painting *The People of Chilmark* by the American artist Thomas Hart Benton from 1920 presents a group with different bodily shapes and genders. It is an attempt to visualize the diversity of society. The depicted bodies are engaged in different activities. However, on a second look one discovers that these different parts of society are not engaged in self-contained activities. Rather, a group characterized by the cooperation between the individuals is created. On a formal level, the following holds true: "the painting resolves an oversupply of visual information (. . .) into an integrated surface, one made dynamic by 'bumps and hallows' but held together by graceful rhythms" (Wolff, 2012: 171).

On a symbolic level, the image represents the interaction of the organisms with their environment, which "when it is carried to the full, is a transformation of interaction into participation and communication" (Wolff, 2012: 171). The art historian Justin Wolff goes so far as to say that the scene's protagonists do not even need to speak to one another, for their communication takes place in a "natural" way. Finally, the image depicts the rescuing of inhabitants of the island of Chilmark from a flood. In this situation, the collectivity is dependent upon the cooperative interplay between the different individuals. Plurality is here arranged as a unity, with each part performing a function within the whole, such that it appears to take place in an almost organic way. The motif of being shipwrecked is reminiscent of *The Raft of the Medusa* by Théodore Géricault, but instead, it presents a dynamic process along with the integration of the protagonists into a collection of individuals. Thus, in contradistinction to *The Raft*

Figure 8.3 Thomas Hart Benton, *People of Chilmark*, 1920. © Cathy Carver. Hirshhorn Museum and Sculpture Garden.

of the Medusa, *The People of Chilmark* manifests a living and active body. There are no dead corpses; the body is vital. The individuals appear as parts of an "integrated community" (Wolff, 2012: 174). Iconographically, unity is presented as a functional coordination of plurality.

At the level of political theory, the precursors to this conception are found in the combination of clockwork and the organ, finding expression in the model of the body machine.[10] This model was known since the early modern period and would influence democratic thought, as in the case of Jean-Jacques Rousseau. In *The Social Contract* the state is characterized as a body: all its parts interact with one another through a holistic principle, and sovereignty is distributed throughout the entire "political body" (Diehl, 2015: 197).

Plurality as a Mark of Unity

The second form of relation between plurality and unity can be observed in a painting by the Brazilian artist Tarsila do Amaral. The painting *Operários* ("The workers") from 1933 depicts a heterogeneous group and anticipates the notion of a diverse people in an immigrant society. To this very day, the image provides the visual model for the ideal conception of the Brazilian people and appears in school textbooks, advertisements, and book illustrations—among other things as the title image for the bestseller *O povo brasileiro* (*The Brazilian People*) by the anthropologist Darcy Ribeiro. The faces in the picture visualize different ethnicities, thereby emphasizing inclusivity. Apart from the different physiognomies, skin and eye color as well as gender, the clothes

Figure 8.4 Tarsila do Amaral, *Operários*, 1933. © Tarsila do Amaral.

also accentuate the diversity of the population in relation to class: the red headscarf of the farmer; the glasses as a sign of the intellectual in the middle of the image; or the choice between shirt or pullover among the male protagonists.[11] Symbolically, the portraits are framed by the smokestacks in the background, giving the different bodies one unitary identity as worker. From a Marxist perspective, this identity would secure the representation of the people.

During the 1930s Amaral was a member of the Communist Party and was in contact with Soviet intellectuals and artists. During this phase, she devoted herself to social critique. This explains why the people represented have a somewhat tired or sad disposition. None of them laugh—suggestive of Engels' descriptions of the inhuman working conditions of English industrialization during the eighteenth and nineteenth centuries. The conditions of the worker in Brazil during the 1930s were here the object of critique. The image homogenizes the faces by way of reductions in color and form and through this expresses its social critique (Amaral, 2006: 62).

In contradistinction to Benton's portrayal, Amaral's workers do not constitute an integrative or, for that matter, organic unity. In the foreground stands only their diversity, while their cooperation is altogether absent. What is culturally and physiognomically diverse, however, undergoes a process of homogenization through the representation of the working class. This homogenization of the people is the result of working conditions under capitalism. Here the people do not become a political subject, since this would require a symbolic-discursive articulation, as Ernesto Laclau, for example, has argued (Laclau, 2005). Notwithstanding this absence, on the specific relation between unity and plurality the image remains of interest, placing the heterogeneity of the people at the heart of the Brazilian national identity.

Plurality as the Dynamic Moment of the People

The third relation between unity and plurality in the iconography of the people belongs to a completely different medium, photography, and is dependent on its transmission through mass media. The photograph is particularly interesting because it shows the self-symbolization of the people as physical presence of different groups and individuals. When political movements and protests take to the streets, they always count on the mediating effect of those images that are produced by virtue of their presence. After the attacks in Paris on the editorial members of the satirical journal *Charlie Hebdo* on January 7, 2015, and on the kosher supermarket on the following day, the subsequent demonstration on January 11 manifested the central moment of recomposition of a traumatized society. 1.5 million people gathered on the Place de la République. They affirmed their collective belonging to French democratic society, which had now taken to the streets in a manifestation against intolerance. This mass demonstration was a part of the tradition of symbolizing collective unity, the echoes of which were with the *Fête Revolutionnaire* of 1790, thus reconnecting in a local way to the revolutionary tradition.

The first reaction to the attack came both from government officials and from the media. Both appealed to the unity of the French people and to republican values. The left liberal newspaper *Libération* entitled its edition from January 8 *Nous sommes tous Charlie*. To this day, the "we" is used as a way of showing solidarity within different protest movements. When the French government refused to grant the Jewish/German activist Daniel Cohn-Bendit an entry visa, the 68-movement organized itself and affirmed its solidarity with the phrase *Nous sommes tous des juif allemands* ("We are all German Jews"). It is a metonymical phrase: one part, the German Jews, becomes a symbol for all of the oppressed people, the ones with whom solidarity is to be shown. The component part *nous sommes tous* ("We are all") signals the identification of everyone with the oppressed. Thereby the identificatory object "the German Jews" or "Cohn-Bendit" becomes mutated into an "empty signifier," to use Ernesto Laclau's terminology (2005: 96, 98). The name Daniel Cohn-Bendit turns into a symbol that is sufficiently open to generate a form of identification between different groups and individuals. Cohn-Bendit becomes a symbol of oppression against which the mobilization of the individual is directed. For Laclau, the birth of the political subjects, the people, resides in such discursive equivalences (2005: 183). It is the identification with a common denominator that makes it possible for the individual to join with others.

Yet, on January 11, 2015, something else happened. The people could not unite around "Charlie" as an "empty signifier." The groups and individuals involved disagreed as to whether they should demonstrate in the name of the controversial publisher and further disagreed with what this meant for the status of Muslims in the country. On the internet the motto was quickly changed and appeared as "Je suis Charlie." This formulation served as the motto for the demonstration. The introduction of the individuating "I" in the history of collective symbolization in France is distinctive and remains an exception in its political culture. However, the images arising from this unfold a symbolic potential that can function as the source of democratization and as the reformulation of the symbolization of the people against the backdrop of increasing social diversity.

On the streets, the people demonstrated their heterogeneity through physical presence and by affirming their belonging to different identities within the republican unity. Many of the participants carried placards with variations of the motto "Je suis Charlie," but its use was additive.[12] When, as a motto for the demonstration, "Je suis Charlie" functioned in a way bordering an (albeit disputed) "empty signifier" for the people, the motto was supplemented with further differences. Below "Je suis Charlie" the protesters wrote on their homemade placards: "Je suis juive," "Je suis musulmane," "Je suis française" (all in a feminine form).

In many Parisian areas the authorities used traffic signs in order to repeat this symbolic procedure of supplementarity, but now in a masculine form with the addition "Je suis policier," as a reminder of the police officers who had been killed. Other images also displayed different national flags, representing the country of origin of Muslim immigrants. Other placards further reinforced the individual self-representation and sense of belonging to a myriad of other groups: "I am a Jew," "Muslim," "Catholic," etc., but also "Je suis Pd" ("I am gay"). Some even asserted "I am not Charlie." The novelty of this was that the participants of the event not only used the presence of the people as a means for a performative unity, but they used the occasion as a way of affirming diversity. Such a self-staging of the people can be understood as an "orchestration of the porous character of the people" (Butler, 2015: 165). Judith Butler's position is more radical than the argument presented here. According to her, the potentialities of democratic stagings also imply that it partly destroys the very framework of this

Figures 8.5 Collection of photos from Charlie Hebdo manifestations. © iStock.com/OnickzArtworks.

Figures 8.6 Collection of photos from Charlie Hebdo manifestations. © iStock.com/AdrianHancu.

Figures 8.7 Collection of photos from Charlie Hebdo manifestations. © iStock.com/OnickzArtworks.

performance. My argument runs in another direction, however, and acknowledges that a dynamic moment of democracy belongs to the connection between a conception of unity and the staging of plurality. While Rosanvallon stresses the difference between an ideal and a concrete people, and the tension that operates therein, in a somewhat superficial way, the discursive-symbolic innovation of the people of the Parisian demonstrations resides in the fact that both of the dimensions of the people interact with one another and are in fact co-constitutive. The opposition between the representation of the people as a unity and the representation of the diversity of society operates here by way of a dialectical relation. This dialectic can, with reference to John Grant, be described as "simultaneously dependent on and antagonistic towards each other." Grant has used this mechanism in order to explain a differently layered problem—the problem surrounding the imaginary of sovereignty and the imaginary of democracy, but his description is also enlightening when it comes to an understanding of the symbolization of the people as unity and diversity in modern and global societies. Interdependency and antagonism "are therefore productive insofar as they contribute to the terrain of political contestation" (Grant, 2014: 584). This opens up the perspective for Lefort's conception of society as both dynamic and open, without having to relinquish the possibility of creating a political subject.

Concluding Remarks

The iconography of the people points to the difficulties of representing the people as the political subject of democracy. In institutional iconography, the people is rarely represented. First, this is due to the fact that the act of giving a material presence to the people as a political subject remains marked by ambivalence on the side of the governing order, since the concrete people can easily constitute a counterpower to it. Second, the images of the people operate within a zone of tension between the representation of unity and plurality, a tension constitutive of democracy *tout court*. Images of the people are expressions of the political imaginary. At the same time, they are the principal symbolic means for a political intervention in the imaginary—which is to say, they materialize different understandings of democracy, as well as different conceptions of inclusion and exclusion, giving expression to varied figurations of the citizen and of the people. When society is given form through staging and symbolization, and therefore the political order acquires meaning, as Lefort's theory of democracy advances, then the forms and ways in which the political subject of a democracy, that is, the people, is visualized is not a question that is exclusive to art history or the cultural sciences.

Images are an extraordinary means for the representation of the people. However, each visualization is at the same time a reduction and fixation of the represented object. Despite this, the many attempts to represent the people remain incomplete. Nonetheless, all attempts are testaments to the transformation of the political and are inseparable from the history of political ideas and its concepts. These images of the people, whether pictorial or mental, belong to the political imaginary. And when we confront them, a new perspective on political institutions and on political culture opens up; for it is these images that show us what was and is thinkable and imaginable in the political field. Visual variations of the representation of the people in a democracy manifest the different political concerns with the necessity of constituting the people as a unitary political subject, on the one hand, and the ever more pressing need of recognizing its plurality on the other. Against this background, the images of the people's presence and the representation of its diversity on the 11th of January 2015 are manifested: they mark a dialectical relation between a people's unity and popular diversity, between what Rosanvallon calls the "ideal people" and the "concrete people." *E pluribus unum* thereby receives a completely new meaning.

Notes

1 This chapter is a reworked version of "Die Symbolisierung des Volkes in der Demokratie: Eine ikonografische Spurensuche" published in *Leviathan: Berliner Zeitschrift für Sozialwissenchaft*, 2018, 34, 23–47. Translation from German by David Payne, Alexander Stagnell, and Gustav Strandberg.
2 In English, the concept of "the people" is notoriously ambiguous with regard to its grammatical number, something which is not the case in German which offers a more clear-cut distinction between *das Volk* and *die Völker*.
3 Similarly, Judith Butler argues that the visualization of the people always comes up against the limits of what can be represented (2015: 165).
4 For the difference between pictures and images, see Mitchell (1983).
5 Bredekamp interprets this moment as a contract of everyone with everyone, but one can certainly here follow Hanna Pitkin and recognize in this an act of pure authorization (1972: 39).
6 The painting from 1790 bears the title *Féderation générale des Francais* and can be found in La Bibliothèque National in Paris.
7 The painting by Charles Thévenin (1764–1838) *La Fête de la Fédération*, le 14 juillet 1790, au Champ-de-Mars, was created in 1795 and can be found in the Musée Carnavalet in Paris.
8 For Butler, this is not just a tension but an opposition between popular sovereignty and state sovereignty (2015: 170).
9 All translations are made by the chapter's translators if nothing else is indicated.
10 For an account of the historical development of this metaphor, see Stollberg-Rilinger (1986).
11 Brazilian art history does not acknowledge these differences and emphasizes the homogenizing representation of the image (i.e., Amaral, 2006).
12 Similar images could be seen at numerous websites and blogs. By now they are hard to find. Here is an example: France Info, "La France a-t-elle manqué son rendez-vous avec l'islam?" (Caro, 2015).

Bibliography

Amaral AA (2006) A gênesis de Operários de Tarsila. In: *Textos Do Trópico de Capricórnio: Artigos e Ensaios (1980-2005), Vol. 1*. São Paulo: Editora 34, pp. 57–62.
Butler J (2015) *Notes toward a Performative Theory of Assembly*. Cambridge, MA: Harvard University Press.
Caro I (2015) La France a-t-elle manqué son rendez-vous avec l'islam ? *Franceinfo*, January 11. Available at: https://www.francetvinfo.fr/faits-divers/attaque-au-siege-de-charlie-hebdo/la-france-a-t-elle-manque-son-rendez-vous-avec-l-islam_793219.html (accessed September 10, 2021).

Constitution du 24 juin 1793 (n.d.) Conseil Constitutionnel. Available at: https://www.conseil-constitutionnel.fr/les-constitutions-dans-l-histoire/constitution-du-24-juin-1793 (accessed September 8, 2021).
Declaration of Human and Civic Rights of 26 August 1789 (n.d.) Conseil Constitutionnel. Available at: https://www.conseil-constitutionnel.fr/sites/default/files/as/root/bank_mm/anglais/cst2.pdf (accessed September 10, 2021).
Diehl P (2011) Symbolrecycling als politische Strategie: Das Beispiel von Herkules während der Französischen Revolution. In: H Bluhm, K Fischer, and M Llanque (eds.), *Ideenpolitik. Geschichtliche Konstellationen Und Gegenwärtige Konflikte*. Berlin: Akademie Verlag, pp. 141–62.
Diehl P (2015) *Das Symbolische, Das Imaginäre Und Die Demokratie. Eine Theorie Politischer Repräsentation*. Baden-Baden: Nomos.
Diehl P (2019) Temporality and the Political Imaginary in the Dynamics of Political Representation. *Social Epistemology* 33(5): 410–21.
Disch L (2011) Toward a Mobilization Conception of Democratic Representation. *The American Political Science Review* 105(1): 100–14.
Duprat A (1992) *Le roi décapité: Essai sur les imaginaires politiques*. Paris: Les éditions du CER.
Falkenhausen S von (1993) Vom "Ballhausschwur" zum "Duce": Visuelle Repräsentation von Volkssouveränität zwischen Demokratie und Autokratie. *Die neue Gesellschaft Frankfurter Hefte* 40(11): 1017–25.
Grant J (2014) Becoming One': Visions of Political Unity from the Ancients to the Postmoderns. *Constellations* 21(4): 575–88.
Herzogenrath B (2010) *An American Body|politic: A Deleuzian Approach*. Lebanon: University Press of New England.
Hobbes T (1988) *Leviathan* (trans. CB Macpherson). Harmondsworth: Penguin Books.
Kielmansegg PG (1977) *Volkssouveränität: Eine Untersuchung Der Bedingungen Demokratischer Legitimität*. Stuttgart: Ernst Klett Verlag.
Laclau E (2005) *On Populist Reason*. London: Verso.
Lefort C (1981) *L'invention Démocratique: Les Limites de La Domination Totalitaire*. Paris: Fayard.
Lefort C (1988) The Question of Democracy. In: *Democracy and Political Theory*. Cambridge: Polity Press, 9–20.
Manow P (2010) *In the King's Shadow: The Political Anatomy of Democratic Representation* (trans. P Camiller). Cambridge: Polity.
Mitchell WJT (ed.) (1983) *The Politics of Interpretation*. Chicago: University of Chicago Press.
Orgad L (2010) The Preamble in Constitutional Interpretation. *ICON* 8(4): 714–38.
Passerini L (1991) *Mussolini Imaginario*. Rome: Editori Laterza.
Pitkin HF (1972) *The Concept of Representation*. Berkeley: University of California Press.
Rosanvallon P (1998) *Le Peuple Introuvable: Histoire de La Représentation Démocratique En France*. Bibliothèque des histoires. Paris: Gallimard.
Rosanvallon P (2000) *La démocratie inachevée: histoire de la souveraineté du peuple en France*. Paris: Gallimard.
Rosanvallon P (2011) *Democratic Legitimacy: Impartiality, Reflexivity, Proximity* (trans. A Goldhammer). Princeton: Princeton University Press.
Rousseau J-J (2002) *The Social Contract: And, The First and Second Discourses* (trans. S Dunn). New Haven, CT: Yale University Press.

Sennett R (1996) *Flesh and Stone: The Body and the City in Western Civilization*. New York: Norton.
Stollberg-Rilinger B (1986) *Der Staat Als Maschine: Zur Politischen Metaphorik Des Absoluten Fürstenstaats*. Berlin: Duncker & Humblot.
The Constitution of the United States (n.d.) National Archives. Available at: https://www.archives.gov/founding-docs/constitution (accessed September 8, 2021).
Wolff JP (2012) *Thomas Hart Benton: A Life*. New York: Farrar, Straus and Giroux.

9

Aesthetic Forms of the Political

Populist Ornaments, Cultures of Rejection, Democratic Assemblies

Stefan Jonsson

Seeing Populism and People through Art

At the peak of Clinton-era optimism, sociologist Immanuel Wallerstein went against the tide. Rejecting what back then was a widely shared belief in globalization as a benign process debouching into a borderless cosmopolitan future, Wallerstein instead argued that the global system was headed toward self-destruction. This outcome was visible in the figures, he explained: the first decades of the new millennium would see the fall of the "crazy fantasies of neoliberal capitalism" and the coming of a "dangerous, chaotic and unpleasant time" (Wallerstein, 2003). This period would be marked by struggles between crowds seeking to democratize society from below and authoritarian counterreactions that would put democratic institutions under tremendous pressure.

Twenty years later, few would dispute the truth of Wallerstein's prediction (1998). According to several theorists, democracy's future today hinges on the ability of political institutions and civil society to handle political passions erupting in collective street protests or at alt-right rallies (Balibar, 2015; Bertho, 2009; Mouffe, 2005; Therborn, 2014). In such and other contexts we witness an assault on established political parties and institutions, which are accused of betraying the hard-working rank and file.

Yet, a big No to politics-as-usual does not warrant a sweeping ascription of a common identity, "populist," to everyone behind the rebuff. There are as many reasons to reject politics-as-usual as there are areas in which politics-as-usual has failed— from infrastructure and minimum wages to health care and climate change. This is why the term "populism" should be used with caution. As our political elites grope for words in order to confront the unpleasant face of today's political life, populism often becomes their *cri de guerre*, naming an enemy against which we must mobilize democratic institutions, liberal values, and civic virtues. To be sure, such reactions are welcome and needed as a defense against the world's Bolsonaros, Erdogans, Trumps, Modis, Salvinis, and Orbans. But are they sufficient? The rhetoric elicited in response to these autocrats shows that populism is a label emerging from the embattled center of politics, a warning against invasion by political outsiders.

As a theoretical term, "populism" invites ideological confusion and tends to obscure political nuances and historical contradictions so as to support a statist liberal parliamentarism and a ratio-critical or deliberative notion of democracy, often in support of neoliberal dogma in relation to which most if not all extra-parliamentary alternatives now can be portrayed as delusive or dangerous or, in a word, populist. As argued by Chantal Mouffe, Pierre Rosanvallon, and Jacques Rancière, political institutions are being hollowed out by such neglect of alternative movements, whose critique of sitting parties and politicians make up a "popular surplus" constituted by voices and passions with no representation in democratic institutions. As history shows, this surplus should not be underestimated; it has often ensured a vital renewal of the democratic system, and sometimes it has spelled its collapse (Mouffe, 2013; Rancière, 2014; Rosanvallon, 2008).

Yet, by describing this popular surplus *tout court* as "populism," centrist politicians and commentators put all dissent in one bag, from socialism and feminism to eco-fascism and radical nationalism. As Enzo Traverso points out, this strategy works only for as long as the debate confines itself to political rhetoric and style. On this level there are indeed strong similarities.[1] Traverso speaks of "a rhetorical procedure that consists of exalting the people's 'natural virtues' and opposing them to the elite—and society itself to the political establishment—in order to mobilize the masses against 'the system'" (2019: 15–16).

As Traverso argues, however, the fact that "we can see such rhetoric among a great variety of political leaders and movements" all the way from Venezuela's Chavez to Hungary's Orban is reason enough to avoid discussing populism as a question of political style (2019: 16). Were we instead to scrutinize the programs and policies of the movements grouped together as populist, we would find that some advocate for persecution of migrants whereas others promote poverty alleviation, reduced fuel prices, and anti-racism. So why group them together in the first place? Traverso asks.

While this conclusion is true and sound, Traverso's argument is still flawed in that it presumes that there is "a political *style* which can be shared by currents of both left and right" (2019: 19). As I will argue, the styles of the movements placed under the umbrella of populism are just as different from one another as are their respective political programs. More than that, these styles, or what I prefer to call their aesthetic dimensions, are indicative of the political substance of the movements themselves. As I will explain presently, the aesthetic dimension refers to the embodied, affective, sensory, and performative aspects of political action and organization. Instead of dismissing such phenomena as irrelevant to the real politics of populist movements, we should treat them as significant symbolic forms. For instance, the visual appearance, affective appeal, embodied practices of a political movement disclose fundamental political ideas: the nature of collective action; political identity; community; political boundaries; agency, and revolutionary events, to mention the most obvious ones.

My critique of the category of populism is thus more far-reaching than Traverso's. While he states that the concept of populism can be used coherently only on the level of political style, I argue against using populism as an overarching descriptor even on that level. This enables us to better recognize that the "popular surplus" that inevitably accompanies, supplements, and challenges all systems of democratic representation contains multiple political tendencies and cultures. I will discuss two such tendencies, which often stand opposed to one another in the contemporary political landscape: cultures of rejection and cultures of protest (including the protest by feet which we call migration).

My initial step in this investigation is to consider two categories that often crop up as contradictory yet mutually supporting items in mainstream debate and commentary: the fascist and the migrant. To note, I am not concerned with "fascist" and "migrant" as empirical referents. I approach them as imaginary categories, or ideologemes, the circulation of which serves to uphold a (neo)liberal view that manifests itself in the debate on populism and its roots. The subsequent section discusses a comparable polarity between incompatible notions of the "popular" in Germany's Weimar Republic (1919–33). I will here rely on two cases. The first one presents a nationalist and essentially fascist configuration of the people, prevalent in right-wing ideas and writings on the popular masses. The second case, by contrast, features a collectivity endowed with a capacity for self-presentation and democratic performativity. Against this historical background, I return in the final section to our present conjuncture and explore how the two cases of a fascist aesthetics and a democratic aesthetics help map the contemporary political landscape in a way that clears the foggy ideas of populism and allows us to make meaningful distinctions between cultures of rejection and cultures of protest. As for the former, I demonstrate how cultures of rejection reestablish the contours of the people by relying on aesthetic and ideological configurations of the earlier period. As an example of the latter, I discuss the protest assemblies of the Occupy movement in 2011 and the migrant opera *Bintou Wéré* (2007), these two showing how collectives performatively establish popular and political agency in cultures of protest.

Two theoretical assumptions frame this interpretation. First, I propose that we distinguish right-wing authoritarianism, collective democratic protest, and migration and migrant activism as movements of *political emergence*, that is, movements emerging outside democratic institutions and portending profound reorganizations of political order, but not yet fully recognizable as political entities since they have weak political representation.[2] Second, I submit that the current social sciences—with their established methodologies and patterns of specialization—is often unable to comprehend political emergence (Jonsson, 2020: 204–22). Meanwhile, visual art, art activism, literature, and film are preoccupied by the very same movements of political emergence. Aesthetic works—from postcolonial novels and art biennales to banlieue rap music and street actions for refugees—have produced deep insights into the nature of collective mobilizations and protests (Jonsson, 2021). I suggest that we stand to gain from an effort to merge social scientific research with aesthetic analysis. Such an undertaking would contribute to what Mills in 1959 called the "sociological imagination," and it also answers recent calls by sociologists and political scientists to reflect on the potential of literature and the arts to overcome the epistemological limits of the social sciences (Mills, 1959; Edling and Rydgren, 2015; Lepenies, 1988; Kompridis, 2014).

Returning to my abovementioned remarks, I should underline that I use aesthetics not in its conventional, watered-down sense, as referring to some exclusive quality or worth of certain texts, images, or objects usually called high art, but rather in its rigorous epistemological meaning: as understanding acquired through sensory perception and imagination, that is, how we make *sense* of the world and how the world is made intelligible or *sensible* through acts of hearing and seeing, as in fiction, poetry, visual arts, film, or theater, but also in masks, songs, slogans or graffiti. Such presentations enable us to comprehend political emergence because they register sociopolitical transformation through voice, embodied experience, and subjective expression in ways comparable to the testimonial mode of the participant and the witness. Put differently, the *aesthetic act* conveys political emergence and political transformation in their sensory, affective, performative, and participatory dimensions.

In interrogating this problem, we bridge a divide inherited from modern and modernist distinctions between the aesthetic domain and the domain of politics (Bürger, 1974; Huyssen, 1986). The challenge is to demonstrate the ability of aesthetics to expose a feature of the political process that has received insufficient attention in the social sciences; before collective actors emerge as subjects and objects of *political* representation they always appear as subjects of *aesthetic* self-presentation through the simple fact of *claiming voice and presence*, by *being seen and heard* in the polity (Rancière, 2004). Cultures of rejection and cultures of protest may be seen as approximative designations of such claims, both being part of the democratic surplus generated by and in political emergence. As political emergence is primarily accessible through aesthetic mediations, the latter can provide knowledge about political participation and experience that have been overseen in political science and theory.

Fascist/Migrant

Given these preliminaries, let me now suggest how the two ideologemes of the fascist and the migrant indicate specific forms of political emergence and how they elucidate the category of populism. In mainstream political rhetoric, media punditry, and social imaginary the migrant and the fascist are ominously coupled. We increasingly hear statements to the effect that migrants, if admitted in too great quantities, will generate reactions of white identitarianism. In Europe this is a scenario that conjures up dark memories of the past when white or European culture rejected "otherness" by perfecting fascist and quasi-fascist systems of control, detention, deportation, and extermination of supposedly alien populations. When German chancellor Angela Merkel stated in 2015 that the "refugee crisis" of that year was "a historic test for Europe" (2015), or when the president of the European Commission Jean-Claude Juncker shortly after contended that the migration challenge, among other events, had brought "Europe" to the brink of "an existential crisis" (2016), or when Hillary Clinton later asserted that "Europe needs to get a handle on migration because that is what lit the flame" (2018), they tacitly confessed a shared fear of populism and its nationalist, authoritarian, or racist subspecies.

Apparently, this fear stems from a worrying question: Can Europe's white-majority populations tolerate contingents of migrants without compulsively repeating past crimes that would undercut the self-image of peace, human rights, and international cooperation by which the continent's leaders have laboriously sought to redress Europe's past in the postwar era? However, the ways in which the question is posed, implicitly blaming migration for the rise of racism, should prompt an even deeper worry: Are not Europe's leaders, in their efforts to prevent a return to fascism by preventing migrants from coming to Europe, already endorsing measures that repeat the old authoritarian agenda? It is unacceptable to blame the presence of Judaism in Europe for the rise of Nazism in the 1920s and 1930s. It should be just as unacceptable to blame the presence of migrants for the rise of xenophobia and neofascism in the early 2010s and 2020s.

All of which goes to say that debate on Europe's so-called migration challenge is a contorted affair, rich in fear-mongering and false dilemmas.[3] Preservation of welfare systems is wrongly pitted against refugee solidarity. Migration is insidiously launched as an explanation of fascism. This debate shows that the political future of Europe and North America hinges on how the presence of migrants is understood. If they are today seen as exceptional problems, tomorrow they will be nationalistic, racist, or fascist. If migration and the presence of migrants are understood as normal, the future can be envisioned as in some sense cosmopolitan and transnational, which is not to say that it will be free from exploitation.

How to explain this dichotomy that stages fascism and migration as opposite and mutually dependent terms in Europe's social imaginary? While the former indicates a political subjectivity that is enclosed in a "walled identity," the latter indicates an equally recurrent subjectivity that is somehow fugitive and illicit (Brown, 2010: 41). What I want to stress is that both are cultural figurations of "the popular," but with diametrically opposed political valences, so much so that we are tempted to ask whether ideas of the popular collective perhaps always split into a double with two incarnations, one immobile, the other mobile, the fascist being sealed up in a homogeneous identity, the migrant deprived of identity and forming a blank screen for projected stereotypes and prejudices. Meanwhile, we should also note that the fascist and the migrant are two contemporary modes of appearance of class. In the global economy, they mark two positions to which neoliberal capitalism assigns members of the contemporary working classes, or what some theorists call the precariat (Bourdieu and Accardo, 1993; Standing, 2011; Schierup et al., 2015; Schierup and Jørgensen, 2016). Whereas the "domestic" segment of the working classes occupies socioeconomic tiers with access to welfare and labor-market security and defends this position in increasingly nativist and racist terms, the "foreign" segments, the migrants, are often pushed into extreme precarity.

In this way, the two ideologemes of fascist and migrant help explain the rise of populism by showing how its rhetorical tools enforce this division of the global working classes. However, theories of populism rarely account for the breadth and depth of the richly articulated web of subjective expressions, social practices, and political discourses that make up the repellant interface between the groups. We may heuristically understand these expressions, practices, and discourses as together forming a public disposition of recent date: a "culture of rejection," that is, the privileged groups' modes of living, acting, and communicating so as to safeguard their social position and cultural beliefs as against perceived threats, intruders, and injurious transformations. Cultures of rejection name the lived socio-spatial and digital contexts and interactions in which the violent tropes and antagonistic stereotypes that suffuse populist discourse gain acceptance.[4] To describe the polarizing patterns that characterize today's white-majority societies in terms of "cultures of rejection" is to attend to the importance of the cultural and aesthetic level in people's reactions to social change and economic insecurity, and it is on this level that we can trace the coming into being of new political identities.

Let me turn to two cases of political emergence in the past, in which we can observe how conflicting ideas of the popular, or the people, were registered as a contrast between an authoritarian or populist aesthetic and a democratic aesthetic.

Fascist Ornaments/Collective Vision

"Power struggle has entered new forms," German writer Ernst Jünger wrote in his introduction to a selection of photographs published in 1933 by Edmund Schultz. The book was called *Die veränderte Welt* ("The world transformed") and carried the subtitle *Eine Bilderfibel unserer Zeit* ("A picture album of our time"). It consisted of thematically arranged photographs accompanied by striking captions. The objective was to show how the world was changing because photography and mass media provided new forms to which politics now had to adapt. And politics, according to Jünger, was always about a "struggle for power" (1933: 9).

"Intensification of optical and acoustic means provides the political will with unexpected possibilities," exclaims a caption in the book (Schultz, 1933: 33). On the one hand, the advent of photography made a certain kind of politics obsolete. "Today, a reasonable objection against a politician is that he looks ugly on photo," Jünger asserted (1933: 9). Moreover, he implied that the parliamentary system was outdated because its reality made for boring cinema. On the other hand, photographic media favored a different set of political forms. The pictures chosen by Jünger and Schultz left no room for doubt as to the kind of politics that harmonized best with recent optical and acoustic inventions. "The will to dress in uniform," reads one caption. Next to it are photographs depicting, respectively, a workers' parade in Moscow and SA-militia under the Swastika (Schultz, 1933: 36). Such were the new forms of mass power favored by new mass media.

One section in their picture album was entitled "The changing face of the mass" (*Das Veränderte Gesicht der Masse*) The selected photos show marching masses and working masses; they portray masses in combat, in the factory, and on the beach, while also depicting sporting, playing, mourning, and parading masses. The photographs show the different faces of the masses. But they also reveal how the camera is not merely a neutral medium which registers masses already present on the social field, but an active force that groups people together in new designs. The point was often to render the crowd as an oceanic force of nature, yet one that had to be dammed, controlled, and directed (Schnapp, 2002: 272, see also 2006).

Die veränderte Welt is just one among countless similar publications that described interwar society as dominated by the masses. As I have argued elsewhere, the masses that we encounter here express the difficulty to give a coherent political, narrative, or visual representation of society in a situation of social disintegration and conflict (Jonsson, 2013). Roughly speaking, this difficulty was resolved in two ways, one which may be called, in shorthand, the fascist ornament, the other one investigating collective vision. The first way is demonstrated by Jünger and Schultz's book; it invites readers to look upon society from a distance, as an object, or a representation, with the result that its population readily appears as a "mass ornament," as Siegfried Kracauer called it, and which he identified as a precursor of the fascist mass (1995). Thus, when Jünger and Schultz point at "the face of the mass," they refer least of all to the individual faces in the mass but, rather, to the greater collective face that subordinates each of them to the larger figure made up by the people under their leader. When speaking of "the changing face of the mass," they meant that the mass looks different depending on the regime that commands it. The point was that the masses have to be commanded, molded, shaped, edited, framed, and presented as one entity under the leader. The political problem raised by the masses was therefore also an aesthetic one. Or, as Joseph Goebbels contended in 1929: "Leader and mass, that's no more of a problem than painter and paint. To form a mass into a people and the people into a state has always been the deepest meaning of true politics" (Goebbels, cited in Theweleit, 1987: 2: 94).

It is strange that Jünger and Schulz could have devoted so many pictures and pages to the changing face of the masses without ever asking whether this face also had eyes to see with. How can we picture a seeing collective? Weimar Germany, a laboratory for aesthetic and ideological experiments, produced fascinating answers to such questions too. Parallel to the story of the manipulation of the masses by fascist leaders, there is a story of how the masses got eyes of their own, thus claiming their own perspective on the world and the ability to act as a political and historical subject in their own right. A key person in this context was Willi Münzenberg, the media genius of the German labor movement in the interwar period. In 1924, Münzenberg founded a weekly magazine, *Arbeiter-Illustrierte Zeitung* (AIZ). It aimed to break bourgeois indoctrination of the labor movement. Like all popular media of the period, AIZ featured the photographic image, which was believed to possess unique properties for instruction and propaganda, and all the more so if one wanted to reach an audience with little education or literacy. AIZ encountered serious problems, however. The editors had to rely on existing photo agencies, all of which were private and commercial enterprises. Furthermore, the photographs available from these agencies rarely touched upon the everyday working life that the AIZ sought to cover.[5]

Münzenberg's solution was to create a pool of photographers supplying the magazine with the pictures it needed. In March 1926 AIZ launched a competition among its readers for the best photographic renderings of working-class life (Münzenberg, 1926). The response was overwhelming—so much so that in the fall of the same year the magazine created an amateur organization for the camera-owning part of the working class, the German association of worker photographers (Vereinigung der Arbeiter Fotografen Deutschland), which at its height in

1931 counted more than 100 local branches. The organization launched its own forum which soon became an ambitious magazine in its own right. It is in this magazine, *Der Arbeiter-Fotograf*, that we, issue by issue, can follow how the mass grows eyes of its own that brings into being hitherto unknown ways of viewing and representing society.

The process may be observed on several levels. First, *Der Arbeiter-Fotograf* offered education and advice on the technical skills and equipment that workers needed to produce their own images. Second, *Der Arbeiter-Fotograf* provided its readers with a *sociological* inventory, naming the hidden corners that the worker photographer should capture. This category comprised not only the factory, demonstrations, and political meetings but also inconspicuous phenomena such as the potato harvest and the playground. This ambition also demonstrates a *political* tendency: to show the unseen and to depict what has for long been pushed outside the frame. *Der Arbeiter-Fotograf* also contains articles on how proletarian photographers can influence politics in a more direct sense, for instance, by documenting police violence and the right-wing militias. This, in turn, also contains the seeds of a new kind of *journalism*. The magazine explains how worker photographers should form proper reporter teams and news organizations in order to get the news out first. On yet another level *Der Arbeiter-Fotograf* expressed an ethical thrust, an intention to humanize the worker by emphasizing his or her beauty and dignity. Finally, the magazine contained an aesthetic didactic, with famous photographers such as Laszlo Moholy-Nagy, Tina Modotti, and John Heartfield held up as models to be emulated.

Der Arbeiter-Fotograf thus offered an entire curriculum for to-be-photographers. The ambitious aim was captured in a nutshell by Franz Höllering, editor of the magazine, as he spoke of "the conquest of the machines of observation" (1928: 3–4). Once accomplished, this conquest would yield a new eye, or mode of vision, which no longer observed the lower classes from afar, as a "mass ornament," but which was an organ of the masses themselves. Attaining its own instrument of visual perception, the mass would cease being a mass and transform itself into a seeing collective. The result was a new mode of political and aesthetic figuration, what Edwin Hoernle in one article called a "class-eye" (1930), or what Moholy-Nagy called a "socialism of vision" (1971: 185 [orig. 1922]). This attempt to grow new visual organs may be seen as a decisive phase in the history of democratic aesthetics, or the people's quest for form that allows them to see and make themselves seen in ways that they themselves can recognize and approve of.

Cultures of Rejection/Aesthetics of Assembly and Migration

I have staged a confrontation: an authoritarian aesthetic versus a collective and revolutionary one. Some examined "the face of the mass": Jünger & Schultz's *Die veränderte Welt* is an example. Others sought to investigate "the gaze of the mass": the masses endowed with a subjectivity and perceptual apparatus of its own, as in *Arbeiter-Fotograf*. Leaving aside the question as to possible parallels between the political crises of the 1930s and the populist moment of our own present, I will now explore whether this distinction can illuminate our contemporary situation.

The historical examples I have offered are both similar and different. The similarities: both appeal to an idea of the people; both show how people become "political beings" through aesthetic mediation; both show that the being of the people differs depending on the aesthetic approach that is adopted (cf. Jonsson, 2008). This brings me to the differences: whereas populist aesthetics show the emergence of the people as predetermined, or conjured forth, by an already established form of power that is stamped out in the form of a leader, democratic aesthetics show political emergence as something that is formless and plural, a mode of life prepared to assume any and all forms and speak with multiple voices, and which therefore cannot be assimilated into any figure of identity.

As I have discussed earlier, contemporary cultures of rejection appear historically persistent in the ways in which they circumscribe *the people*. This happens in at least four interrelated forms that can be traced back to the nationalist and authoritarian imaginaries of earlier periods. First, diverse populations are cut up and framed as separate and homogenous peoples, on the presumption that the respective members of each people identify with one another in so far as they all identify with a dominant political fiction whose hero and expression is the leader. Second, aesthetic expressions in cultures of rejection circle the male and female body in recognizable ways. Aesthetic expressions here draw on a tradition—in the visual arts, film, and literature—in which feminized images serve as allegories of a people in need of protection by a weaponized masculinity.[6] Aesthetic works of this brand also utilize female allegories in value struggles over women's pursuit of personal autonomy and sexual freedom (Abu-Lughod, 2013; Scott, 2007). Should women be mothers or professionals? How should they dress? Who should they marry and at what age? Some of these struggles tend toward the fascist will to bind the female body to the reproduction of the race. A third obvious feature of today's cultures of rejection is that they excel in well-known imagery of the stranger or migrant: the public sphere is flooded by caricatures of enemies within and enemies without. We encounter in these contexts an authoritarian aesthetic register that cannot do without its designated outsiders, the rejection of which establishes the self-identity of the people.

Finally, and least surprising, current cultures of rejection draw on a reservoir of nationalist symbolism. This gives them a taint of nostalgia, amounting to the reinvention of an imagined past purged of elements of impurity and conflict. For instance, when European neofascists evoke the era of the strong welfare state, they present it as an organic outgrowth rooted in a consensual agreement among an ethnically homogenous citizenry. Whereas, in fact, all welfare reforms won between 1930 to 1970 were the outcome of particular forms of class struggle.[7] Contemporary populism also draws on numerous other points of identification derived from national traditions, which in many countries has led to heated struggles over the correct way to represent the cultural heritage (Jonsson and Willén, 2017).

In this way, cultures of rejection recode and repurpose what has been preserved in the archive of nationalism and democracy. It happens through a process that Robin Wagner-Pacifici has called "political semiosis": each new political rupture or event is purloined by a rhetoric that relates it to ideas and values in the nation's past and to the effect that each such event is made to appear as a crisis of the very identity of "the people" or "the nation" (2017). If a formula is needed, the aesthetic forms made manifest in cultures of rejection concern the enforcement of identity in situations where the ethnos appears to be threatened and the *oikos*—the household or homeland—to be under siege.

If authoritarian tendencies in contemporary culture pull the idea of the people toward a neofascist worldview and thus toward particularism, other aesthetic expressions stretch the idea of the people in the direction of universality. Here, meaning is attributed to popular forces that are plural, and multivocal, and that therefore cannot be assimilated into a figure of identity. These forces today often materialize in the form of collective protest and migration and migrant movements, and they are often rendered in aesthetic works that promote community formation across boundaries. I will offer a brief example from each of these two spheres.

As for the sphere of collective protest, consider the Occupy movement, which started as a local occupation of Zucotti Park near Wall Street in New York City. This movement invented a new form of democratic dialogue, or perhaps we should say that it returned to older modes of assembly, which short-circuited established modes of political representation. Strictly speaking, the Occupy movement was the emergence of people in public space—"bodies in assembly," to quote Judith Butler—who claimed the urban topography, instituted spontaneous assemblies, and reinvented democratic dialogue (2015: 66–98).

Without leaders or programs, this movement was to be heard and seen only on location. Yet, these locations multiplied in rhizomatic fashion to all parts of the world. In conventional political theory, such a movement may seem incomprehensible, insisting, as it did, on multiplicity (rather than policymaking and majority rule) as the content of democracy. In order to comprehend its political nature, we must approach it from an aesthetic angle and scrutinize its methods of making new things audible and visible. As Bernard Harcourt has pointed out, the most striking aspect of the Occupy movement was its unorthodox yet strictly regulated conduct of political dialogue. Harcourt explains:

> The apparatus of general assemblies, "human microphones," and hand signals contributed to the effort. The "human mic," as a form of expression, communication, and amplification, has the effect of undermining leadership. It interrupts charisma. It's like live translation: the speaker can only utter five to eight words before having to shut up while the assembled masses repeat them. The effect is to defuse oratory momentum, or to render it numbingly repetitive. The human mic also forces the assembled masses to utter words and arguments they may not agree with—which also has the effect of slowing down political momentum and undermining the consolidation of leadership. Somewhat prophetically, these creative measures reinforced the leaderless aspect of the movement itself. (Harcourt, 2013: 59)

The "human microphone" is an aesthetic device that configures meanings within an assembled collective. What from a habitual political perspective appears to be this device's enervating slowness and impracticality in fact draws into focus a set of fundamental political mechanisms, determining whose voices can be heard and by whom, which tend to be neglected or ignored in politics and political science. These mechanisms are usually not discussed as proper political matters and must in fact *not* be interrogated as such, because they are the very mechanisms that constitute the arena in which political matters are settled. In exposing these mechanisms, aesthetics—as the "human microphone"—also exposes the exclusion at the heart of every political system.

This example shows that if we were to take aesthetics seriously in matters of democracy, we would imagine society as a social force field as yet undivided between leaders and people, individuals and masses: a public space without center. In this way, aesthetic figuration symbolically displaces power by imagining the people as a power in itself, owning the capacity to *do things together* rather than in *exercising power over others*.

A society without individuals, masses, or fixed identities would be a society that dispels every *form* of sovereignty, except that power which everyone has in common with others. In order to imagine such a process, we have to assume a level of the social—society degree zero, we may call it—at which we can identify the stirrings of collective intentionality and political emergence. This level is rarely visible, and difficult to conceptualize, because it precedes all forms of conceptual and political representation. As the example illustrates, it is a transient "space" created by speech and action characterized by dialogic equality between people who claim political agency through their own assembly. In such assemblies, the agent does not derive its identity from the symbolic order of a constituted political community. Rather, and because such established forms of representation are being challenged or annulled, the democratic subject is emancipated from any identity that seeks to capture it.

Such an agent, animated by lack and multiplicity rather than communitarian loyalty to an imagined people, recognizes plurality as an inescapable condition and resource. Therefore, it is also an agency that may offer an idea of universal democracy which has no place in the existent world of political communities. It is only through aesthetic mediation, moored in the embodied, affective, and performative aspects of human action, that this idea of democracy becomes imaginable as a possibility or utopia. Aesthetics is therefore a central concern for democratic thought. To the attempt by cultures of rejection to make democracy depend on the bounded national identity of an exclusive "people," democratic aesthetics responds by figuring a subject who is open to the outside.

Toward a Populism without Borders

This finally brings us to the second sphere of the culture of protest and the question of what we may learn about populism and democracy from migrant movements. This question is important also because it demonstrates a blind spot in most studies of so-called transnational populism, which have failed to incorporate a discussion of migration in its analysis of existing efforts to construe "a transnational *people*," as Benjamin Moffitt puts it (Moffitt, 2017; cf. De Cleen, Moffitt, Panayotu, Stavrakakis, 2020; Panayotu, 2017). But now, who would constitute a transnational people, if not migrants and their movements? Indeed, any serious acknowledgment of migration today is tantamount to the recognition of an emerging social movement of international or global makeup (de Genova, ed., 2017; Mezzadra and Neilson, 2013; Jonsson, 2020; Schierup, Delgado Wise and Ålund, 2022). As Michael Hardt and Toni Negri (2019) argue, it would be a class characterized by multiplicity rather than unity: "the migrants' lines of flight constitute an internationalist power. [. . .] Rest assured that the ruling authorities recognize the menace." "Migratory aesthetics" has become a term for artistic and literary practices that enable community formation across boundaries. It registers how foreign bodies and beings appearing at the borders of the self-enclosed nation ask to be seen and heard in public life. In this way, as migration "enters" into art, the boundaries of the people expand (Petersen, 2017).

In order to grasp this process, I will discuss Manthia Diawara's recent film, *An Opera of the World*, commissioned by the Documenta 14 (2017). A Malian-American filmmaker, Diawara in his visual essay circles around Wasis Diop's opera *Bintou Wéré: A Sahel Opera*, with a libretto by Chadian poet and novelist Koulsy Lamko (2017). At its premiere in Bamako in 2007, the production gathered an ensemble of leading West-African performers who staged an epic of migration through a repertoire of modern and traditional West-African song, music, and storytelling.

"Who is the hero in today's world? Might it be the migrant?" Diawara asks. The opera's plot is centered on the destiny of Bintou Wéré. A pregnant teenage girl, she joins other recruits from the jobless and landless class of the Sahel on a trek North, as they see no other way forward in life than to risk crossing the border into Europe. Bintou has been sexually abused by most of the men in the group of travelers, who all claim fatherhood of the unborn child. They quarrel over whether the child will be better off in Europe or in Africa. The desperate hopes accompanying this trail of migrants bring forth strange projections. At one point, Bintou points at the moon over the horizon, exclaiming: "Look, there is Europe!"

In his film Diawara interviews Alexander Kluge, who argues that Diop's opera appropriates the preeminent form of European high art and brings it back to "its *plebeian* origins" (emphasis added). Interestingly, Diop's search for the social roots of the opera form leads him toward the socioeconomic destitution and political messianism that surround the topic of migration in the popular imaginary of contemporary West Africa. The result is remarkable: *migration turns out to be the popular origin of political change*. Through the medium of the opera, a group of miserable West-African migrants transforms themselves into secret missionaries of coming social movements.

Bintou Wéré may be seen as a culmination of a postcolonial tradition of West-African narratives that probe the experience of living in a society in which failed national projects of development elicit social unrest, as well as migratory movements toward the North. By taking the political implications of migration as its basis for a new community, the opera captures the significance of contemporary protest and resistance for the renewal of a democratic agency that strives to move beyond national and/or imperial frames. At the core of *Bintou Wéré* is thus a political emergence; the process whereby political exclusion, ontological negativity, and objective historical constraints are transformed into agency, a potential for action and change. *Bintou Wéré* shows how an aesthetic presentation transforms the objective circumstances of a situation into a site of becoming: the victims become the future.

The final tableau of the opera is an exact rendering of this process. Having sold off her infant to cover the trafficker's fare, and now mounting the shaky ladder to cross the electrified fences into Melilla, the EU's outpost on the African continent, Bintou Wéré is halted and killed midway in her upward movement toward the distant moon, or Europe. The secret term that underlies the democratic aesthetic of cultures of protest comes to the fore in this scene: what is embodied by Bintou's corpse, a dead migrant brutally affixed to the border, is the collective and political being of the people itself, but in the form of its own negativity, as nonbeing or waste. This becomes even more clear as the dead Bintou Wéré is suddenly transubstantiated in the opera's concluding *lamentatio*, as the choir of mourners, incarnating generations of Sahel migrants, resurrects her memory and testifies to her undying, persistent agency.

In this way, the opera's aesthetic figuration is inseparable from Pan-African resistance and protest. The opera of our world turns out to be an opera about unstoppable popular movement, the mobility of the poor. Is this not the unthinkable core of many of the best dreams and worst nightmares of our historical moment? Theories of politics and populism, including those of *transnational* populism, have yet to fathom this option: the people as a multiple, boundless, and moving being. Were we to engage seriously with such a notion of the people, we would have to admit that every truly consistent conception of populism must look like this universe of African migrants: a populism without borders.

Notes

1 On such similarities and populism defined as political style, see Benjamin Moffitt (2016). See also Kurt Weyland on populism as a strategically deployed combination of style, charisma, and mass appeal (2001).
2 My approach is inspired by Keith Sawyer's *Social Emergence* (2005), Pierre Nora on historical emergence (1972), and Raymond Williams on emergent sociocultural formations in *Marxism and Literature* (2009).
3 For an overview, see Peo Hansen, *A Modern Migration Theory* (2021).
4 See the ongoing research project, http://www.culturesofrejection.net/. See also Benjamin Opratko, "Die Kultur der Ablehnung" (2020), and Harder and Opratko, "Cultures of rejection at work" (2021).
5 For close analysis of *Arbeiter-Fotograf*, see Jonsson, *Crowds and Democracy*, ch. 4, and Wolfgang Hesse, ed., *Die Eroberung der beobachtenden Maschinen: Zur Arbeiterfotografie der Weimarer Republik* (2012).
6 For classical studies: Joan B. Landes, *Visualizing the Nation* (2001) and Theweleit, *Male Fantasies*.
7 For an example, consider right-wing appropriations in Sweden of the progressive social democratic notion of the "people's home" (*folkhemmet*).

Bibliography

Abu-Lughod L (2013) *Do Muslim Women Need Saving?* Cambridge, MA: Harvard University Press.
Balibar É (2015) *Violence and Civility: On the Limits of Political Philosophy* (trans. GM Goshgarian). New York: Columbia University Press.
Bertho A (2009) *Le Temps Des Émeutes*. Paris: Bayard.
Bourdieu P and Accardo A (eds) (1993) *La Misère Du Monde*. Paris: Editions du Seuil.
Brown W (2010) *Walled States, Waning Sovereignty*. New York: MIT Press.
Bürger P (1974) *Theorie der Avantgarde*. Frankfurt am Main: Suhrkamp.
Butler J (2015) *Notes Toward a Performative Theory of Assembly*. Cambridge, MA: Harvard University Press.
Clinton H (2018) Hillary Clinton: Europe Must Curb Immigration to Stop Rightwing Populists. Available at: https://www.theguardian.com/world/2018/nov/22/hillary-clinton-europe-must-curb-immigration-stop-populists-trump-brexit.
De Cleen B, Moffitt B, Panayotu P, and Stavrakakis Y (2020) The Potentials and Difficulties of Transnational Populism: The Case of the Democracy in Europe Movement 2025 (DiEM25). *Political Studies* 68(1): 146–66.
De Genova N (ed.) (2017) *The Borders of 'Europe': Autonomy of Migration, Tactics of Bordering*. Durham, NC: Duke University Press.
Edling C and Rydgren J (eds.) (2015) *Sociologi genom litteratur: skönlitteraturens möjligheter och samhällsvetenskapens begränsningar*. Lund: Arkiv förlag.
Hansen P (2021) *A Modern Migration Theory: An Alternative Economic Approach to Failed EU Policy*. Newcastle: Agenda Publishing.
Harcourt BE (2013) Political Disobedience. In: WJT Mitchell, BE Harcourt, and M Taussig (eds.), *Occupy: Three Inquiries in Disobedience*. Chicago, IL: The University of Chicago Press, 45–92.
Harder A and Opratko B (2021) Cultures of Rejection at Work: Investigating the Acceptability of Authoritarian Populism. *Ethnicities*. doi:10.1177/14687968211012437.
Hardt H and Negri A (2019) Empire, Twenty Years On. *New Left Review* 120: 72–84.
Hesse W (ed.) (2012) *Die Eroberung Der Beobachtenden Maschinen: Zur Arbeiterfotografie Der Weimarer Republik*. Band 37. Leipzig: Leipziger Universitätsverlag.
Hoernle E (1930) Das Auge des Arbeiters. *Der Arbeiter-Fotograf* 4(7): 152.
Höllering F (1928) Die Eroberung der beobachtenden Maschinen. *Der Arbeiter-Fotograf* 3(10): 3–4.
Huyssen A (1986) *After the Great Divide: Modernism, Mass Culture, Postmodernism*. Bloomington: Indiana University Press.
Jonsson S (2008) *A Brief History of the Masses: Three Revolutions*. New York: Columbia University Press.
Jonsson S (2013) *Crowds and Democracy: The Idea and Image of the Masses from Revolution to Fascism*. New York: Columbia University Press.
Jonsson S (2020) A Society Which is Not: Political Emergence and Migrant Agency. *Current Sociology* 68(2): 204–22. doi:10.1177/0011392119886863.
Jonsson S (2021) The Art of Protest: Understanding and Misunderstanding Monstrous Events. *Theory & Event* 24(2): 511–36. doi:10.1353/tae.2021.0024.
Jonsson S and Willén J (eds.) (2017) *Austere Histories in European Societies: Social Exclusion and the Contest of Colonial Memories*. London: Routledge.

Juncker J-C (2016) *State of the Union 2016*. Bratislava. Available at: https://ec.europa.eu/priorities/state-union-2016_en.
Jünger E (1933) Eintleitung. In: E Schultz (ed.), *Die Veränderte Welt: Eine Bilderfibel Unserer Zeit*. Breslau: Wilhelm Gottl. Korn Verlag, 5–9.
Kompridis N (ed.) (2014) *The Aesthetic Turn in Political Thought*. New York: Bloomsbury Academic.
Kracauer S (1995) The Mass Ornament. In: T Levin (ed.), *The Mass Ornament: Weimar Essays*. Cambridge, MA: Harvard University Press, pp. 75–88.
Lamko K and van der Plas E (2017) *Bintou Wéré – African Opera*. Amsterdam: Netherlands Prins Claus Fonds.
Landes JB (2001) *Visualizing the Nation: Gender, Representation, and Revolution in Eighteenth-Century France*. Ithaca: Cornell University Press.
Lepenies W (1988) *Between Literature and Science: The Rise of Sociology* (trans. RJ Hollingdale). Cambridge: Cambridge University Press.
Merkel A (2015) Person of the Year: Angela Merkel – The Transformation of a Cautious Chancellor. Available at: https://www.ft.com/content/ffb1edb2-9db5-11e5-b45d-4812f209f861.
Mezzadra S and Neilson B (2013) *Border as Method; or, the Multiplication of Labor*. Durham, NC: Duke University Press.
Mills CW (1959) *The Sociological Imagination*. Oxford: Oxford University Press.
Moffitt B (2016) *The Global Rise of Populism: Performance, Political Style, and Representation*. Stanford, CA: Stanford University Press.
Moffitt B (2017) Transnational Populism? Representative Claims, Media and the Difficulty of Constructing a Transnational "People." *Javnost - The Public* 24(4): 409–25. doi:10.1080/13183222.2017.1330086.
Moholy-Nagy L (1971) Constructivism and the Proletariat. In: R Kostelanetz (ed.), *Moholy-Nagy*. London: Penguin, 185.
Mouffe C (2005) *On the Political*. London: Routledge.
Mouffe C (2013) *Agonistics: Thinking the World Politically*. London: Verso.
Münzenberg W (1926) *Arbeiter-Illustrierte Zeitung*. Berlin: Neuer Deutscher Verlag.
Nora P (1972) L'événement monstre. *Communications* 18: 162–72.
Opratko B (2020) Die Kultur der Ablehnung. *Tagebuch*. Available at: https://tagebuch.at/politik/die-kultur-der-ablehnung.
Panayotu P (2017) Towards a Transnational Populism: A Chance for European Democracy (?) The Case of DiEM25. Populismus Working Papers No. 5. Thessaloniki.
Petersen AR (2017) *Migration into Art: Transcultural Identities and Art-Making in a Globalised World*. Manchester: Manchester University Press.
Rancière J (2004) *The Politics of Aesthetics: The Distribution of the Sensible* (trans. G Rockhill). London: Continuum.
Rancière J (2014) *Hatred of Democracy* (trans. S Corcoran). London: Verso.
Rosanvallon P (2008) *Counter-Democracy: Politics in an Age of Distrust* (trans. A Goldhammer). Cambridge: Cambridge University Press.
Sawyer RK (2005) *Social Emergence: Societies as Complex Systems*. Cambridge: Cambridge University Press.
Schierup C-U and Jørgensen MB (eds) (2016) *Politics of Precarity: Migrant Conditions, Struggles and Experiences*. Leiden: Brill.
Schierup C-U, Munck R, Likić Brborić B, et al. (eds) (2015) *Migration, Precarity, and Global Governance: Challenges and Opportunities for Labour*. Oxford: Oxford University Press.

Schierup C-U, Delgado Wise R and Ålund A (2022) Global Migration Governance: Positionality, Agency, and Impact of Civil Society. In: A Pecoúd and H Thiollet (eds.), *Handbook on the Institutions of Global Migration Governance*. Northampton, MA: Edward Elgar, 1–22.
Schnapp JT (2002) The Mass Panorama. *Modernism/Modernity* 9(2): 243–81.
Schnapp JT (2006) *Staging Fascism: 18 BL and the Theater of Masses for Masses*. Stanford, CA: Stanford University Press.
Schultz E (ed.) (1933) *Die Veränderte Welt: Eine Bilderfibel Unserer Zeit*. Breslau: Wilhelm Gottl. Korn Verlag.
Scott JW (2007) *The Politics of the Veil*. Princeton, NJ: Princeton University Press.
Standing G (2011) *The Precariat: The New Dangerous Class*. London: Bloomsbury Academic.
Therborn G (2014) New Masses? Social Bases of Resistance. *New Left Review* 85: 7–16.
Theweleit K (1987) *Male Fantasies, 2 Vols* (trans. E Carter and C Turner). Minneapolis: University of Minnesota Press.
Traverso E (2019) *The New Faces of Fascism: Populism and the Far Right* (trans. D Broder). London: Verso.
Wagner-Pacifici RE (2017) *What Is an Event?* Chicago, IL: The University of Chicago Press.
Wallerstein I (1998) *Utopistics: Or Historical Choices of the Twenty-First Century*. New York: The New Press.
Wallerstein I (2003) Kapitalismens död är nära . . . . Available at: https://www.dn.se/arkiv/kultur/kapitalismens-dod-ar-nara/.
Weyland K (2001) Clarifying a Contested Concept: Populism in the Study of Latin American Politics. *Comparative Politics* 34(1): 1–22. doi:10.2307/422412.
Williams RL (2009) *Marxism and Literature*. Oxford: Oxford University Press.

10

The Undivided People

On the Hypothesis of Radical Democracy in Peter Weiss' *The Aesthetics of Resistance*

Kim West

Has *The Aesthetics of Resistance* (1975–81), Peter Weiss' three-volume opus about the anti-fascist struggle in Europe in the late 1930s and early 1940s, finally become a novel of our time? Written in the "divided world" of the final years of Cold War détente, the novel's hypothesis was vastly ambitious: it sought to show that, in spite of everything, it was still possible to construct a radically democratic and therefore anti-fascist political subject, and that cultural history *in its totality* could be enlisted for that task, setting the persistence of an "undivided people" against the fractured social and political world of the author's own present.

In this chapter I will attempt to trace how the hypothesis of radical democracy is inscribed into *The Aesthetics of Resistance* across all levels of the text, from diegesis to narrative to graphic form. I will then pose the question of the possible actuality of such a hypothesis in our historical present, four decades after the writing of Weiss' book, on the other side of the global neoliberal regime that replaced the macropolitical configuration against which Weiss outlined his political position. How do we read this book in a time when we see the political resurgence of fascism in nations across the world, and when new figures of populism are claiming to be the rightful heirs to the project of emancipation?

Ultimately, *The Aesthetics of Resistance* is a text that urges its readers to confront issues of historical continuity and responsibility, and therefore of practice: if the history that the novel narrates is the history of "us"—and this, I will argue, is its central tenet, *even today*—then what might this entail for the understanding of "us," with respect to the forces that define today's social world?

An Antagonistic Universal

The Aesthetics of Resistance tests the hypothesis of the undivided people in the divided world by setting it to work as an antagonistic universal. In itself it is an empty universal, which assumes form in and through the conflicts that arise when its validity is invoked against the limitations of any particularity. There is, the book asserts, an undivided people, both de jure and de facto: both as a popular capacity for equal and groundless self-realization and as the antagonisms that ensue when the different attempts at realizing this capacity in social, political, and cultural practice are confronted with the limits of the divided world.

The book is consistently at work on the levels of both situated, historical specificity, and universal potentiality. There is a narrator who guides the reading, ensures narrative continuity, and serves as a diegetic mediator for the many dialogues and theoretical excursions that make up a large part of the book's volume—but there is also a deindividualized, impersonal, elusive voice, an *anyone* who is always on the verge of unsettling the text's narratological stability. The book shifts between a series of closed, claustrophobic spaces, in which the anti-fascist resistance cells seek refuge from the enemy's violence—but these spaces are always in some kind of connection, however remote, with the internationalist horizon of the socialist liberation struggle. And the events that the book narrates, with rigorous faithfulness to historical data, all take place on set dates, between September 22, 1937, and the end of the Second World War—but each of these moments opens onto a historical abyss, onto chasms of time where all chronology is suspended in a great contemporaneity. We must "create unity": so reads the book's governing imperative. The movement from fragmentation to assembly generates its fundamental conflict.

> Just as this room we were talking in was accidental and could be located in any country whatsoever, so too would my writings address people who might be found anywhere, whatever their background, internationalism would be the criterion of my affiliation. [. . .] Granted, I could see the advantages of belonging to a country, a city, but for my purposes there was no such point of departure, I would have to start with the shapeless, the unattached and seek connections beyond the borders of states and tongues. Perhaps we had meant something along these lines when calling our discussions of art and literature political. If ever we became implementers in that area, our activities would be steered by our intention to bridge gaps, to find something that might be common to us, who were cut off from being at home anywhere. (Weiss, 2005: 117f)[1]

Peter Weiss devoted the full decade of the 1970s to writing *The Aesthetics of Resistance*, inscribing the problem of his own time, the problem of the divided world, into the story of the anti-fascist struggles of a group of young German workers during the 1930s and 1940s. Against the political fragmentation that the book describes—the fatal schism between social democrats and communists, the collapse of the popular fronts under the pressures of anti-communism, the Spanish catastrophe, Stalin's crimes, the disintegration and annihilation of the German resistance movement—Weiss set the story of the protagonists' education, of their insatiable search to grasp art, literature, language, and philosophy, to comprehend cultural history in its totality as something that concerned them, something in relation to which they could understand themselves as elements of an "us," beyond the forces of fragmentation.

The book's portraits of these teenage autodidacts—full-time factory workers wholeheartedly devoted to political struggle—push against the limits of the credible. They seem only partly troubled by the divisions that would normally have defined their world, by the barriers that were set up against persons from their social and economic conditions, by the limits that would have determined their existence in the shape of not having access to books and artworks, of physical and mental toil after days of manual labor and political organization. They read, among other things, Dante:

> We had come no further than Francesca da Rimini and Paolo Malatesta, spending a lot of time reinterpreting Gmelin's translation in a Reclam paperback and Borchardt's in the Cotta pocket edition, comparing the German tercets with the Italian terza rima, which Heilmann read aloud to us on the basis of his knowledge of Latin and French. (I: 67)

There is no reason to doubt Weiss' own knowledge of the merits of different German Dante translations or of the subtleties of the terza rima: he had long nurtured plans to write a play of his own based on the *Divine Comedy*, which is inscribed as a central intertext in *The Aesthetics of Resistance*, whose three-part structure reflects the orders of the three realms in Dante's epic poem.[2] But would such a text-critical, philological, and in-depth reading actually be within the realm of the possible for a group of young socialist proletarians in Berlin in 1937, under the full pressure of the Nazi regime? One is tempted to answer: "Yes, in principle, *but* . . ."—in order then to conclude that there are any number of reasons why it would not be very likely. Weiss erases this "*but.*" *Yes, in principle*: *The Aesthetics of Resistance* narrates what the protagonists are capable of, the undivided capacity that they embody, as that capacity comes up against the limits of the divided world. The book evokes the immeasurable knowledge the protagonists *could have* access to in an equal society, *as* this knowledge enters into contradiction with the social conditions of the workers, with the reality of labor, with the fragmentation of politics and the violence of repression.

> We could compare the start of [Dante's] journey with somnolence, we were familiar with the abrupt sagging of something within reach, the start of a dream, the moments when the grabhook dangling from the crane might hit your skull, the drive belt of the machine might rip off your arm. (I: 68)

This contradiction—where the validity of the universal is invoked against the limitations of the particular—is never fully controlled within the logic of the book's diegesis. Generally, Weiss resolves it through the form of the dialogue: the narrator remembers—often in some detail—conversations he has participated in or overheard; through the knowledges, experiences, and positions of the different interlocutors, narrated in indirect address, a vast body of learning is folded into the story. This narratological device is often pushed to the limit: the narrator remembers how someone talks about her recollections of a conversation; one of the interlocutors in this memory-inside-a-memory herself remembers something or recalls a dream in which she had a conversation with someone else, and so on. Reading these passages, it is often difficult to keep track of the mediations, to trace the bifurcations and extensions at the level of enunciations, and at the same time to follow the comprehensive recollections, arguments, and debates at the level of the enunciated.

> There were also Bedouins here, in front of their tent, Australian aborigines with spears and boomerangs, tattooed inhabitants of houses on stilts from the Solomon Islands, artfully woven sentry huts from Samoa were to be seen, Japanese gardens, temples and ritual objects from Burma, Korea, Tibet, Eskimo igloos, totem poles of the prairie Indians, but the sight etched deepest in my memory was the family of the Pygmy people. I asked my father about our street in Bremen because I wanted to compare his impressions with my own recollections, which, stemming from the first few years of my life, were sharper, clearer than the image that Pflugstrasse had left in me. Now we were doubling back across the Weser Bridge, toward the Alte Neustadt, along the pontoons under St. Martin's Church lay the steamboats, including a side wheeler, which all went to Hemelingen and Delmenhorst, to the harbor and to Vegesack. (I: 84)

In the paragraph from which these three sentences are drawn, the narrator remembers how he, on his way to Spain to join the International Brigades, visits his parents in the Czechoslovakian city Warnsdorf. There, he asks his father to tell him about the family's earlier home in Berlin, and together they recall how once, during a walk, they visited that city's geological museum. This memory evokes the memory of another museum visit, in the family's previous hometown, Bremen. The first sentence—"There were also Bedouins . . ."—relates to this visit, at an ethnological museum, a memory that gives Weiss an opportunity to introduce the problem of European imperialism, which will then become a major theme in the book. In the second sentence—"I asked my father about our street in Bremen . . ."—we return to the protagonist's conversation with his father in Warnsdorf, where he compares the different degrees of intensity of his memories from Berlin and Bremen. In the third sentence, finally—"Now we were doubling back across the Weser Bridge"—"we" are *inside* the father and the son's memory (which is consequently a memory inside a memory inside a memory) of a perambulation around Bremen, which will soon open toward the book's description of the father's experiences in the Bremen Soviet Republic during the German revolutionary year of 1919—the moment of the fateful split between social democrats and communists, another of the book's major themes.

The combined effect of this complex narratological arrangement—and the quoted passage is a striking but not exceptional example—is that utterances gradually drift away from their connections to speaking subjects, toward an impersonal *anyone* whose voice is not that of an external, omniscient narrator, but someone who is at once an individual (since the voice remains in principle attached to a specific speaker), collective (since voices belong to the different interlocutors who are mediated through the narrator's words), and anonymous (since the narrative tends toward a state where utterances can no longer be ascribed to enunciating subjects). And all of this, these different layers of statements and voices-inside-voices, these strata of reminiscences and recollected exchanges, form an undivided unity on the book's pages. All of them have the same status on the surface of the text, where they are juxtaposed without marks that guide the reading, admitting no differences in degree between various mediations, diegetic layers, or historical contexts. As a rhetorical and formal composition, then, *The Aesthetics of Resistance* enacts the principle of unity, which in turn implies a specific mode of reading. We will return to this.

Readings in Resistance

It is also from the same contradiction that we can deduce the principle for the great counter-reading that is the heart of *The Aesthetics of Resistance*. The first obstacle that the protagonists encountered when they sought to comprehend cultural history in its totality as a history that concerned them was that it did not concern them.

> If we want to take on art, literature, we have to treat them against the grain, that is, we have to eliminate all the concomitant privileges and project our own demands into them. In order to come to ourselves, said Heilmann, we have to re-create not only culture but also all science and scholarship by relating them to our concerns. (I: 33f)

It is this strong, nearly violent imperative that generates the readings of the Pergamon Frieze and *The Raft of the Medusa*, of Angkor Wat and Adolph von Menzel's *Iron Rolling Mill*, for which Weiss' novel is justly famous. The "resistance" in *The Aesthetics of Resistance* is perhaps above all this: the immeasurable ambition in asserting that all cultural objects can "concern us," that is, potentially everyone, in seeking to understand those objects against themselves as the creations of an undivided people, in which an undivided people can recognize the history of itself.

In order to do so, Weiss must establish a critical mode of reading, which replaces these cultural objects in the social contexts that the objects themselves repress: the reality of domination and class relations which remains outside of the world represented on the surface of images, which is excluded from the community manifested in sculptural figures and forms. The Pergamon Frieze, *The Magic Mountain*, and *Iron Rolling Mill* are representations of gods, patriarchs, and industrialists, but they are also creations conditioned by the systems of production out of which they emerge and by the social relations that those systems presuppose and reproduce.

To read those works as objects that "concern us" must therefore entail showing how that reality is, in spite of everything, present in the works, how those repressed contexts and relations can actually be read as elements in their compositions, in such a way that the works, according to their inner logic, transcend the scope of their signatures, reject the ranks of their motifs, address others than their intended receivers. This was the question that Brecht posed, in his poem about a reading worker from 1935: Who was it that built the wonders of the world? In the annals of history only the names of emperors and tyrants are recorded. Were they the ones who carried the rocks, whose bodies were worn out by the strain of the labor? (see Brecht, 2006: 63). "In many works," Heilmann remarks, "no matter whether princes, prelates, or speculating patrons had laid claim to ownership, the artist, following his own sense of truth, overcoming biases and boundaries, had always included the element of classlessness" (I: 73). But such classless elements, these inscriptions of social totality, can also be negatively present: the repression itself leaves traces in the work it defines, as Adorno explained, the world's antagonisms return in the artwork as immanent problems of form (2004: 6). In what may be the strongest passage in the famous reading of the Pergamon Frieze that opens *The Aesthetics of Resistance*, Weiss restores this reality to the aesthetic arrangement of the work, enouncing and dramatizing the antagonism which is registered in the tense composition of the sculptural assemblage.

In the book's opening scene, the narrator and his two friends Coppi and Heilmann—who will all soon be dispersed in exile, resistance, and war—are at the Pergamon Museum in Berlin, facing the altar's vast frieze. Studying the bodies that lunge at them from the stone, "crowded into groups, intertwined, or shattered into fragments," the protagonists imagine how the "master sculptors" once stood in the marble quarries, pointing to the finest boulders. "Shielded and fanned by palm branches" they had been "eying the Gallic captives toiling in the sultry heat [. . .], transporting the gigantic ashlars on long wooden sleds down the twisting paths." The masters had studied "the rippling of the muscles, the bending and stretching of the sweating bodies," and then, "[u]p in the gardens of the castle [. . .], in the gentle breeze wafting up from the sea," they had recalled "the lugging and shoving, the stemming of shoulders and backs against the weight of the stone." Filled with these impressions they had seen "the figures of the frieze slumbering in the marble coffins," and then slowly carved out the limbs, searching them out, seeing forms emerge. "With the plundered people transferring their energies into relaxed and receptive thoughts, degradation and lust for power produced art" (I: 10).

On one level, this anecdotal account of the physical work, the production process that must have preceded the artistic interventions of the sculptors, appears merely to dramatize a hierarchical relation that was already implicitly and allegorically present in the frieze's representation of the struggle between gods and giants. But to draw attention to this relation, to expose this divided world, this relationship of domination and exploitation is also to expose a wrong and, consequently, to break open a space where an undivided people may stake its claims.

> Since our goal was to eliminate injustice, to wipe out poverty, [Heilmann] said [. . .], we could imagine that this site would some day demonstrate the expanded and mutual ownership intrinsic in the monumentality of the formed work. (I: 9)

Aesthetics against Abstraction

This is also one way of understanding "aesthetics" in *The Aesthetics of Resistance*: as a critical attitude, directed against the abstraction of the sensible and social totality in which every cultural object is necessarily an element. This is what Fredric Jameson seems to suggest when he in his reading of Weiss' book writes that a "true 'aesthetics' of resistance therefore will not seek to 'correct' bourgeois aesthetics or to resolve its antinomies or dilemmas: it will rather search out that other social position from which those dilemmas do not emerge in the first place" (2007: 415). Such an aesthetic would therefore seek to place itself on this side of the dichotomies that delimit the field of what Jameson calls "bourgeois aesthetics": the dichotomies between immanent form and social context; between formal composition and social relations of production; between the noble artist's "relaxed and receptive" senses and the "subaltern" worker's physical exertion, enclosed space, and limited time.

But to search for a location on this side of such dichotomies is also to search for a position from which other social and cultural forms may become legible as abstractions. The structure that sustains the repression of the artwork's social totality is the same as the one that represses the absurdity and the violence of the division of labor in all domains. It is, *The Aesthetics of Resistance* shows, in aesthetic experience that the divided world can be apprehended as divided. For us, Heilmann continues, there is "something peculiar" about even the most fundamental truths. "If we state principles of physical orders, they involve the division of labor into doers and drivers, a split as old as science." It is in the interest of the rulers to present the world's social order as a necessary consequence of the world's natural order—a necessity that is as unyielding as the laws of logic. "Only by realizing that we are on a rotating sphere and by forgetting all the connected things that are taken for granted can we grasp the horrors that mold our thinking" (I: 34).

When the novel's protagonists seek to appropriate cultural history as a history that concerns them, it is therefore more than culture they must seek to grasp. The knowledge toward which their education points must be an undivided knowledge, from which nothing may be excluded in principle. Anything else would give support to the logic of the divided world, would confirm the "horrors that mold our thinking" by inscribing its structure in a social hierarchy. This principle is the basis of the argument for a unitary culture, which is yet another of the book's major themes: the repeated confrontations with the divisive elitism of oligarchic orders; with the worker movement's self-defeating anti-intellectualism and populism; with communism's betrayal against the openness to change and self-critique that, Weiss held, was one of its essential components.

> At the round table covered by a lace tablecloth, in the weak glow of the lamp with its parchment shade, we spoke about the continual attempts to portray the intellectuals as a parasitic group and to sever them from the working classes and throw them in with the bourgeoisie. The effect of this manipulation, apparently guided by the intention of foregrounding our autonomy, hampered our ongoing development toward scientific thought (2020: 101).[3]

Such "ongoing development" is by necessity a political process. The "social position" that Jameson evokes, on this side of the dichotomies of "bourgeois aesthetics," is not freely accessible. To "seek to attain it" is the same as entering into conflict, as attempting to realize an undivided capacity, but therefore also to be forced to confront all that is opposed to such realization; it is to try and appropriate knowledge, but also knowledge's social conditions. "While we acquired culture," the narrator's father says, "that overall mechanism, of which culture had been a component, had to be destroyed" (I: 163). Just as politics cannot be thought without culture, since it is in the experience of culture that social totality can be perceived, that an undivided people may identify itself as undivided—so culture cannot be understood without politics, since its realization at once presupposes and implies social change.

> Culture was resistance, [Hodann] said, upheaval against the painfully dominant. The force of the resistance could be measured by the degree of the oppression. As long as the drive to oppose existed, culture existed. Where there was silence, subjugation, there culture withered, there only ceremony and ritual remained. (Weiss, 2006: 978)[4]

What *The Aesthetics of Resistance* proposes as a verification of Weiss' radically democratic hypothesis is, on the most fundamental level, the notion of a politics that answers to the experience of culture, a *cultural politics* that does not suspend its both parts in a common synthesis but can recognize "the two forces in their unique characteristics and equivalence" and "bring their parallel courses, their simultaneous creations together to form a common denominator" (II: 63). It is a notion that is incompatible with the dialectical scheme with which the revolutionary experiments of the historical avant-garde have often been theorized: culture and politics should not be transcended in the shared realization of a new world; instead, they can feed off each other, nurture one another, "form a common denominator" only to the extent that they both maintain their autonomy.

The Undivided Montage

In *The Aesthetics of Resistance*, Weiss employs a range of stylistic and narratological techniques in order to create a form that can respond to the immeasurable claims of this "cultural politics," reflecting and embodying the book's governing imperative to *create unity*. It is, for example, a novel that features a great number of characters, but very few first names: the countless individuals that pass through its pages are, with some exceptions, referenced only by surnames. It is also a novel without one single digit: all years, numbers, times, and ages are detailed in letters, sometimes with unwieldy results. Surnames, that is, family names: the novel's characters figure semantically as members of families, as links in lineages, whose wholes transcend them. And the absence of numerical signs in favor of alphabetical ones, the use of words rather than symbols contribute to the book's conflation of linguistic levels, generating the tightly held typographical image that the reader encounters on every page.

A number of other decisions at the level of linguistic detail contribute to the book's singular, strictly unitary semiotic and syntactic system. *The Aesthetics of Resistance* employs a limited range of punctuation marks: there are no quotation marks, no dashes, no colons, no parentheses. These semiotic exclusions also assist in leveling the book's linguistic field, placing all signs and statements on one common surface, which in turn has wide-ranging effects on the syntax of the text. No graphic markers can indicate hierarchies or logical relationships between different levels of utterance, no punctuation marks can announce relations of superiority or subordination between principal clauses and subordinate clauses, can signal that a certain phrase is commenting or commented upon, is quoted or referenced, inserted or parenthetical. These linguistic limitations, which sometimes evoke the lipogram technique, generate the book's often tightly wound sentences in which references can drift out of reach and clause elements become difficult to identify.

Among these techniques, the most conspicuous one is the book's infamous abstention from using line breaks and column and chapter partitions: the book's 1,000 pages consist of 89 undivided paragraphs, generally about 10 pages long, organized into 6 giant text blocks. Together, the techniques through which the book's unified semiotic system is established unsettle every "normal" connection between book and reader. The absence of graphic markers that can structure the reading, the lack of partitions that can announce pauses and intervals, indicating varying rhythms and intensities, rupture all possible concord between the book as a material sign system and the reader as a physical organism. If punctuation marks are pulse and breath, if the graphic disposition of a well-written novel corresponds to the physical constitution of a healthy reader, then *The Aesthetics of Resistance* is something else. Its taut linguistic totality implies a tense reading body, turning reading into a confrontation with the reader's physical limits. This contributes to the book's remarkable rhetorical, even pathological force.[5]

At the level of narrative structure, the book's unitary logic is reflected and embodied in a composition technique we might call *the undivided montage*. At this level too, it is evident that Weiss' radically democratic hypothesis can only be set to work as an active contradiction, as antagonism in writing. The book is generally based on the more or less drastic juxtaposition of separate semiotic elements, where it is the pronounced difference, the sustained distance between those elements that generate the significance of the whole. In this sense, the book's composition conforms to the "traditional" logic of montage: two or more elements acquire a new significance by being combined, while this new significance is at the same time drawn from the sustained integrity of the elements, whose qualities of otherness are not reduced. Such juxtaposition is a major narratological principle in *The Aesthetics of Resistance*, operative at different scales: historical tracks run in parallel, diegetic layers are superposed, relations of analogy or parallax are established between passages of political exposition or of art critical ekphrasis.

The vast Engelbrekt complex, which takes up almost the entire second part of the book's second volume, in itself combines a range of such techniques. At least four diegetic and historical tracks run parallel or intersect: an account, from the perspective of the narrator, of how Bertolt Brecht during his period of exile in Stockholm enlists a group of collaborators in the preparation of a play concerning the fifteenth-century Engelbrekt uprising, seen as a point of origin of Swedish class conflicts; a detailed description of the historical context and the social conditions of this uprising, from a workers' perspective; an account of the macropolitical conflicts in Europe around the period of the outbreak of the Second World War, taking place concurrently with the Brecht group's work on the Engelbrekt material; and a comprehensive account of the historical development of Swedish social democracy, from the "first study circles" around the mid-nineteenth century to the communists' breakout at the time of the Russian Revolution and to the Saltsjöbaden corporatist agreement, in 1938.

At the macro-level of the narrative, this montage sets up a number of correspondences, the main one of which is the analogy between Engelbrekt's inability or unwillingness to realize the egalitarian potentials of his uprising, in favor of a concord with the aristocracy, who warmly welcomes his reforms and then immediately assassinates him; and the social democrats' inability or unwillingness to realize the egalitarian promise of the workers' movement, in favor of a concord between trade unions and corporations and an expulsion of all radical elements. In the crosscutting of the montage, the devastation that overcomes Europe during the fall of 1939, at the same time as Brecht's working group is trying in vain to assemble the Engelbrekt material into a functioning play, appears as the ultimate consequence of this disintegration of egalitarianism. And what serves as a counterforce to this division in the montage is the narrator's development, as he gradually overcomes his fragmented existence as a lawless immigrant worker and an anonymous disciple to the authoritarian Brecht and instead begins to achieve a positive identity as a writer. Indirectly, by placing these separate diegetic elements on equal footing, the montage asserts that it must be possible to read all of these stories as one and the same: as the story of how an undivided people, in its search to realize itself as undivided, is confronted with the limits of the divided world.

But there are also passages in *The Aesthetics of Resistance* where the elements of the montage remain separate, while they are integrated into syntactic and narratological wholes in which they should grammatically and stylistically have belonged to one and the same semantic field, in one and the same field of reference. These are important passages in the book: those disorienting, demanding sentences where a political discourse may suddenly open toward a mythological chasm; where the narrator's own present may violently interfere with a narrated past; where historical layers may shift and slide over into one another without indications or demarcations. For Jameson, these passages are manifestations of an oneiric logic, and it is evident that Weiss is here engaged in a refashioning of the surrealist legacy that was long central to his work (2007: 399f).

> And yet something that is cruel can never contain beauty, said Coppi's mother, and shouts came up the courtyard shaft, windows were slammed, doors banged; despite the blackout ordered for the air-raid drill the janitor had discovered a gleam of light, there was a trampling in the staircase, we sat still, listening as stifled fear and fury, bottled-up disgust, repressed frenzy were suddenly vented, to erupt in scolding and raging and then just as quickly peter out. Somebody sneaked down the stairs, Phoibe, the glorious, radiant one, aimed her burning torch at the face of the flinching winged giant, and Asteria, her daughter, the bright goddess of the stars, grabbed the hair of the serpent-legged opponent, who had been yanked down by the hound, and, unhindered by the fallen man's hand on her arm, she plunged the sword through his clavicle, piercing deep into his chest. (I: 43f)

Here, however, the late Weiss' artistic and literary turn becomes evident. Unlike the surrealist montage, where the unexpected combinations would tend to refer back to the liberated imagination of a mythologized—and patriarchal—artist subject, in *The Aesthetics of Resistance* the undivided montage serves a critical function. The subject for which it seeks to assert the possibility of a history—a history that concerns it, and therefore us—is a potentially universal one, and the political and historiographic operations of the montage consequently imply another, radically democratic social configuration.

The undivided montage, we might say, adds a further stage to the semiotic operation of the "traditional" montage. Where the latter is based on the juxtaposition of separate elements, so that the sustained division between the elements gives the whole its new significance, something else, and something more, takes place in these passages: the significance is generated from the tense, irreducible contradiction of combination-in-separation—the passages are still montages, in that sense—but at the same time this relationship is inscribed into constructions that are grammatically and stylistically opposed to such division. An imperative dimension is added, a *must*—the elements *must* belong to one and the same whole, even though the very condition of the meaning of the whole is that they are held apart—which is addressed to the reader through the formal organization of the sentences, through the narratological arrangement of the text. The undivided montage says: it must be possible for these histories to be one history, their common totality must be conceivable, their subject must be an undivided people.

History Is Not Over

The Aesthetics of Resistance functions critically by urging its readers to identify with the historical subject whose existence it asserts. The book's possible actuality is related to the question it demands us—its readers—to ask: Can the history it narrates be "our" history, and if so what would that imply for the understanding of "us," in relation to the forces that define today's social world? The answer to that question cannot be given in advance: any response must itself be historically mediated. It is a political and therefore antagonistic task.

The Aesthetics of Resistance is not primarily a historical *allegory* of the political situation that characterized its author's world during the period in which the book was written. Nor does it operate critically by constructing a *utopian* ideal that can stand against political reality, in order to guide political action. Instead, it proposes a radically democratic position, incompatible with *populism* and only realizable in conflict, in the shape of an identification that, against new forms of domination, asserts the continued existence of the undivided people.

Allegory

When Weiss wrote *The Aesthetics of Resistance*, he was still seeking to respond to the problem he had described in his "Ten Working Points" from 1965: the divided world of the Cold War, split into a socialist eastern and a capitalist western bloc, themselves fractured by internal contradictions. There were direct continuities between the macropolitical conflict that characterized Weiss' situation as he was writing the novel and the cataclysmic struggle that the novel describes: the Cold War division was a consequence of the great showdown between the Allied powers in Europe at the end of the Second World War; the economic system whose class logic and endemic crises had facilitated fascism's rise was still expanding, morphing toward global dominance.

At the political horizon of Weiss' book was the notion of a reconciliation of these divisions, a resolution of these contradictions. If the world of "actually existing socialism" could overcome its fragmentation—that is, if Soviet communism could undergo some sort of democratic, anti-Stalinist reform, of the kind that had appeared possible during the early years of the Khrushchev era (Spufford, 2011)—then socialism could once again "grasp the lion's paw" (III, 1002), become an effective international force for liberation and egalitarian change, and so contribute to the resolution of the contradictions of the other capitalist world (through class struggle). The relation was one of continuity, of ongoing conflicts, of unresolved problems and persisting patterns of domination, not one of allegory. In the temporally elusive final sentences of the book, the narrator anticipates how, once, "much later," he *would come to have* seen the figures of resistance continue their long struggle, witnessing how miners would come to have climbed up out of the deep in order to engage in a battle that had begun already on the battlefields of the giants and the titans, how the soldiers of the Viet Cong would come to have taken up arms where the republican fighters in Spain were once gunned down:

> bearded faces would for some seconds fight their way up from the multitude, brown, scarred faces with small lamps over their foreheads, yellow faces under bast helmets, young, even childish faces would storm forward, in great numbers. (III: 1001f)

The history of the liberation struggle is one and the same, in other words, just like the history of oppression. But it can be argued that with *The Aesthetics of Resistance*, Weiss failed to identify his own time's most decisive political event, that process through which, beginning in the 1970s, his antagonist would come to be reshaped, even endowed with a "new spirit." Weiss remained faithful to a traditional Marxist analysis, according to which fascism was an expression of the crises of capitalism in its imperialist phase, so that he could see a direct link between the US "world order" of his own present and the Third Reich. But while he was busy exposing the implications of that continuity, a process of ideological and economic restructuring was initiated, which would soon come to render such analytical models insufficient, if not plain wrong. Neoliberalism, not a renewed fascism, was the governing form for the right's counteroffensive after the upheavals of the late 1960s, and in anticipation of capitalism's full globalization with the dissolution of the Eastern Bloc around the end of the 1980s.

Read as a book that speaks primarily to the moment of its own writing, *The Aesthetics of Resistance* can in this respect appear somewhat misdirected, outdated, out of kilter with the development of capitalism: it speaks a language of proletarian and class struggle that no longer seems to have real resonance or application; it levels accusations of exploitation, dispossession, oppression, and fascism against an enemy who is no longer interpellated by such calls and who no longer answers to such names. In a sense, the book was published at once too late and too early.

Today, on the other side of this historical process, after three decades of global neoliberal hegemony, the situation is of course different. Perhaps, *The Aesthetics of Resistance* has for the first time become a novel of the present. The new language of power—a language which, it was said, was supposed to be incompatible with grand narratives and totalitarianism—turns out to have served to divert attention from those authoritarian structures that lay, and had always laid, at the basis of the new international division of labor. If "America First" was a slogan for Nazis and Klansmen in the 1920s, 1930s, and 1940s, it could now be the promise and the principle of an official state policy (Churchwell, 2018).

The divided world has changed and mutated but is also inert and persistent. In relation to this structural continuity, and with respect to the violence that has been unleashed against the language of emancipation, the antagonist universalism of Weiss' Marxism seems like necessary pragmatism. The hypothesis of the undivided people in the divided world is placed on a level of abstraction beyond the late twentieth century's struggles for ideological hegemony but does not belong to the order of utopian abstraction.

Utopia

The Aesthetics of Resistance has often been associated with the genre of the *Bildungsroman*. For Fredric Jameson, Weiss' book is a "proletarian *Bildungsroman*, a pedagogy of the subaltern," in which a young German worker, forging his path through history's vicissitudes, gradually "learns a politics of resistance" and "appropriates a whole aesthetic culture." The nameless narrator, Jameson means, serves as a substitute for the reader, as a mediator through which the reader can establish a relation of "imagined sympathy" with the historical and political position that the narrator represents (2007: 383; see also Scherpe, 1983: 100f).

This is a fairly traditional way of engaging with the novel, and it is apparent that the text itself supports such an interpretation: Weiss in fact did place himself in the tradition of the *Bildungsroman* when he constructed his story about the protagonists' educational journey and the narrator's gradual development toward an identity as a writer, by way of experiences of violence, resistance, and exile. But in one fundamental sense, *The Aesthetics of Resistance* is incompatible with that genre. The *Bildungsroman* draws its dynamic from its protagonist's development toward a higher degree of insight, and therefore self-knowledge, and by extension freedom. Its basic pattern is the sequence of evolution, individuation, and emancipation. That pattern can be endlessly varied, but the movement must lead from ignorance toward knowledge.

Such a dynamic does not animate *The Aesthetics of Resistance*. Why not? Because from the very start, from the book's first pages, the protagonists potentially know everything, and this potentiality, this undivided capacity, is what the novel narrates, in its confrontations with the limits of the divided world. In the narrative there is no movement from unknown to known: its driving principle is the conflict between the undivided people's immeasurable capacity—for which history in its totality can be a history that "concerns them"—and the forces with which this capacity enters into opposition, through the different attempts to realize it in practice. This is what gives the text its singular, contradictory character of being at once dynamic and static, heading toward something and always already there.

The whole is therefore not a distant, either attainable or unattainable, goal in *The Aesthetics of Resistance*; it is not anticipated in the novel's early parts in order then to be redeemed in the later ones. It is present all the time, as the ether through which the protagonists move, but which they have not yet assimilated. And as we have seen, Weiss employs a range of narratological and stylistic techniques for channeling this ether into the diegetic space—through other voices, through readings of artworks, etc.—at the same time as the novel remains constricted by the protagonists' limited perspectives.

The structure of the novel therefore does not admit teleology or eschatology. Its governing logic is neither the journey toward a goal nor does it set up the vision of some final paradise of redemption beyond history's antagonisms, some utopian world of social harmony that can serve as an ideal for political imagination and practice. All there is is an empty abstract universal—the idea of an undivided people—which is defined and given content in and through the conflicts that arise when its validity is asserted against the limits of the divided world. The universal of the undivided people is an antagonistic universal, which is only significant as contradiction, which only exists practically as ongoing conflict.

In this respect we can note that *The Aesthetics of Resistance* marks its distance from a messianic tradition within the revolutionary left, where the total social upheaval is understood as an event that transcends history's continuum and logic, and so can only be grasped through figures of grace and redemption. In this sense there is not only an evident kinship but also a decisive difference, between the critical principle that animates Weiss' readings of cultural objects in *The Aesthetics of Resistance*—to treat history "against the grain" (I: 33), as Heilmann said—and Walter Benjamin's famous formulations about "brushing history against the grain," in his "On the Concept of History" from 1940 (1996: 392).

If the idiosyncratic "historical materialism" that Benjamin develops in his later texts remains inscribed in a scheme of transcendence and redemption—where the dialectical image's "flash"-like representation of history's true heterogeneity should give rise to an "awakening" that liberates a coming community from the continuum of dominant history (1999: N3.1)—then the hypothesis of the undivided people in *The Aesthetics of Resistance* is, on the contrary, consigned to a dimension of historical and practical immanence: its political objective exists within its conceptual horizon; its moment of transcendence—the immeasurability of the undivided—is something that can only be manifested negatively, in the form of the contradictions that emerge when its validity is asserted against the limits of the particular.

The politics that can be derived from *The Aesthetics of Resistance*, and its great account of the left's attempts to overcome the world's divisions, from the revolutionary years around 1920 to the oppositions of the Cold War, thus differs from Benjamin's vision of an at once historical and extra-historical "revolutionary violence" (2021). Weiss' politics has a closer vicinity to Raymond Williams' "long revolution," that is, a radically democratic search to extend the field of social and cultural self-determination, through an ongoing, antagonistic work of creating and recreating the institutions that define a social and political reality. But to engage in such work in the name of the undivided people, Weiss insists, must also entail remaining categorically opposed to all populism, whether it refers to a predefined people or one belonging to a coming age.

Populism

Several authoritative, early commentaries of *The Aesthetics of Resistance* read the book as a contribution to the work of mourning of the left's historical failure, in a way that did not evidently correspond to the complex, antagonistic continuity that the text proposed. For a critic such as the Hungarian philosopher Ferenc Fehér—whose article on *The Aesthetics of Resistance* as "The Swan Song of German Khrushchevism" was published at the peak of dissident literature, in 1983—the living trauma of Soviet violence was still the determining historical and political experience, so that Weiss' attempt to establish a nuanced critical relation to the "divided world" of actually existing socialism could only appear as pro-Soviet apologetics (Fehér, 1983: 168f).

For readers with an American perspective, such as Andreas Huyssen—in an important text from 1985—and to some extent Fredric Jameson, whose reading was not published until 2005, the book could only be a contribution to the debate about the postmodern epochal shift and the end of the "great narratives." *The Aesthetics of Resistance*, Huyssen held, was an attempt to salvage "the memory of the avant-garde" by rejecting its connection to "absolutist revolutionary claims," in order to try, "in an almost Benjaminian mode," to "harness the expressive powers of the art of past ages to the articulation of a space of resistance in the present" (1986: 136). And in Jameson's reading, Weiss' book is also imbricated in the tragic memorialization of a postmodern and "postrevolutionary" era, where it can contribute to creating a "new historicity" for a reunited Germany, but also for a left that has lost its world-historical calling (Jameson, 2007: 380f).

Today, four decades after the publication of the final volume of *The Aesthetics of Resistance*, and some thirty years after the fall of the wall and the collapse of the Soviet Union, we instead find ourselves in a "post-traumatic" situation with respect to the lost projects and utopias of the "short century," as Eric Hobsbawm spoke of it. If the political subjects who bore the most severe symptoms of the trauma—the proletariat and the working class—no longer constitute social movements, forming the base for a progressive political project, then perhaps we no longer need the therapeutic protective barrier of a historico-philosophical epochal shift in order to be able to read Weiss' book and to think the implications of his hypothesis of the "undivided people." The long distance to the disasters of the short century seems paradoxically to make it less difficult to imagine a continuity between the tradition of conflicts that *The Aesthetics of Resistance* narrates and a possible contemporary project of emancipation.

In this sense it might not be implausible to see a connection between Weiss' position and the different endeavors today to reinvent the political project of the left by setting a radically democratic subject against "third way" social democracy, whose assimilation of the neoliberal program is one major cause of the ongoing crisis of the large social democratic parties, in Sweden, in Europe, and beyond. Chantal Mouffe, a prominent representative of such a position, argues that this assimilation has today passed beyond the point of no return, and that any notion of a radicalization of social democracy "from within" is therefore bound to fail; at the same time, she claims, neoliberalism is today, after the "great recession" of the 2010s, in a historical crisis, where its hegemonic formation risks being overtaken by authoritarian forces. This, she holds, places us in a "populist moment," a transitional phase where it could be possible to rechannel the "floating signifiers" of politics into a new, more democratic formation, through the construction of a "left populist" subject, defined negatively by its opposition to "oligarchy" (Mouffe, 2018; see also Laclau, 2015).

Such an attempt to recreate a radically democratic politics by setting up a confrontation between an abstract "people," established through a fundamentally arbitrary "chain of equivalences," and an "oligarchy" as its constitutive other can, at first glance, appear, if not synonymous, then at least compatible with the hypothesis of the undivided people in Weiss. But at the same time populism is, as we know, something against which *The Aesthetics of Resistance* consistently delimits itself: it is what the autodidactic worker students in the Coppi family's kitchen cannot afford to permit themselves; it is what the narrator's father cannot accept when he describes the worker movement's struggle for dignity and justice; it is what the communist and Spain fighter Rogeby warns for when he discusses the right's attempts to control and to stifle the radical implications of the project of popular education.

Perhaps this is the greatest provocation of *The Aesthetics of Resistance* for a contemporary reading, its most untimely element, where it lays itself bare to accusations of mythologization and essentialism: that it claims that the "undivided people" is not only defined negatively. The undivided people is an empty universal that only becomes distinct once its validity is asserted against the limits of any particularity: this is the operation we have followed through *The Aesthetics of Resistance*, at the different levels of the text, from diegesis to narrative to graphic form. But the undivided people is also—Weiss throws the full weight of his book behind this assertion—a subject that can understand itself as undivided, through the mediation of art and culture. Culture, the book argues, is that through which an undivided people can identify itself as undivided in a divided world.

What characterizes a culture that can serve such a purpose? *The Aesthetics of Resistance* can in some ways be understood as one single, vast answer to that question. And we know what that answer is: what is characteristic of such a culture is that its objects can be read as the expressions of social totality, even though they represent specific social categories, even though they repress that totality at the levels of composition or motif, of mode of production or style. A culture that can be the culture of an undivided people is a culture that can be an object of critical appropriation, of a reading "against the grain," on account of which it is something that "concerns us," that is, potentially everyone.

According to its concept—the concept that the critical readings in *The Aesthetics of Resistance* must invoke—such a culture must therefore be understood as a culture that does not in principle exclude anything. And if it does not in principle exclude anything, if it is not delimited by any defining, determining barriers, then it must consequently define itself only from within its own conditions: it must be autonomous, in the strict sense of the word. Such a concept of an autonomous culture is in itself empty, since nothing *a priori* delimits its possible reach, but it may become distinct when it is invoked as a principle in particular cases, for example, in the counter-readings of critical appropriation, through which cultural objects can be understood as the expressions of an undivided people—just as the "undivided people" is in itself empty but can become distinct when its validity is asserted against the limits of the divided world, a validity that can itself find support in the experience of autonomous culture.

Culture and politics mirror each other, in other words, transform each other into their respective selves, confront one another with the image of their highest potentiality: this circular, mutually reinforcing logic describes, at the most fundamental level, the relation of cultural politics in *The Aesthetics of Resistance*. The question today is if it may be possible, from within such a relation—from which any populism is by definition excluded—to think a renewed project for radically democratic change.

Notes

1. Henceforth quoted as I, followed by page number.
2. See, for example, the discussion about *Divina Commedia* as a model for *The Aesthetics of Resistance*, in Klaus R. Scherpe (1983: 102).
3. Henceforth quoted as II, followed by page number.
4. My translation from the Swedish edition of *Motståndets estetik*. Henceforth quoted as III, followed by page number in reference to this edition.
5. There are elements of a reading of the pathos figures in *The Aesthetics of Resistance* in Robert Buch (2008), but Buch's analysis focuses on the text's "depictions of suffering and violence," not on its formal structure and rhetorical operations.

Bibliography

Adorno TW (2004) *Aesthetic Theory* (trans. R Hullot-Kentor). London: Continuum.
Benjamin W (1996) On the Concept of History. In: H Eiland and M Jennings (eds.), *Selected Writings, Vol 4: 1938-1940*. Cambridge: Belknap Press, 389–400.
Benjamin W (1999) *The Arcades Project* (trans. H Eiland and K McLaughlin). Cambridge: Belknap Press.
Benjamin W (2021) *Toward the Critique of Violence: A Critical Edition* (trans. PD Fenves and J Ng). Stanford, CA: Stanford University Press.
Brecht B (2006) Questions from a Worker Who Reads. In: R Grimm and C Molina y Vedia (eds.), *Poetry and Prose*. London: Continuum, 62–3.
Buch R (2008) The Resistance to Pathos and the Pathos of Resistance: Peter Weiss. *The Germanic Review: Literature, Culture, Theory* 83(3): 241–66. doi:10.3200/GERR.83.3.241-266.

Churchwell SB (2018) *Behold, America: A History of America First and the American Dream*. New York: Bloomsbury Publishing.
Fehér F (1983) The Swan Song of German Khrushchevism, with a Historic Lag: Peter Weiss' *Die Asthetik des Widerstands*. *New German Critique* 30: 157. doi:10.2307/487837.
Huyssen A (1986) Memory, Myth, and the Dream of Reason: Peter Weiss's *Die Ästhetik des Widerstands*. In: *After the Great Divide: Modernism, Mass Culture, Postmodernism*. Bloomington: Indiana University Press, 115–40.
Jameson F (2007) A Monument to Radical Instants. In: *The Modernist Papers*. New York: Verso, 380–419.
Laclau E (2015) Populism: What is in a Name? In: DR Howarth (ed.), *Ernesto Laclau: Post-Marxism, Populism and Critique*. London: Routledge, 152–64.
Mouffe C (2018) *For a Left Populism*. London: Verso.
Scherpe KR (1983) Reading the Aesthetics of Resistance: Ten Working Theses. *New German Critique* 30: 97–105.
Spufford F (2011) *Red Plenty: Inside the Fifties' Soviet Dream*. London: Faber and Faber.
Weiss P (2005) *The Aesthetics of Resistance, Vol I* (transl. J Neugroschel). Durham, NC: Duke University Press.
Weiss P (2006) *Motståndets estetik: Roman* (transl. U Wallenström). Stockholm: Albert Bonniers Förlag.
Weiss P (2020) *The Aesthetics of Resistance, Vol II* (transl. J Scott). Durham, NC: Duke University Press.

Part IV

The People beyond the Political

11

Fragmentation of the Idea of the People

The Afro-Brazilian Event

Muniz Sodré

Can we speak of an event that belongs to, and defines, a people? If yes, then what would the nature of such an event be? The drafting of the American constitution? The storming of the Bastille? The fall of the Berlin Wall? A clearly punctual point, an origin in history, that gives to the people its sacramental unity and its proper historicity. Let us not speculate on the abstract relation between people and event but, rather, draw attention to a specific manifestation of their relation, what we can refer to as the Afro-Brazilian event of the people. In contradistinction to the Western "events" mentioned earlier, which at least purportedly entailed a demos rising up and taking power, the Afro-Brazilian event, that is, the forced displacement of African peoples to South America by way of slavery, constituted, from out of fragmented ethnicities, a Brazilian "people." In modern Western thought, the people comes into its own once it has become a demos, that is, the sovereign subject of political life. At the same time, the people as demos is said to be irreducible to the question of ethnos, the latter term of which becomes the defining feature of what is "other," "premodern," "non-western." Significantly, though, as I shall explore in this chapter, the Afro-Brazilian event manifests another way of forming a people that fundamentally problematizes the Western presuppositions surrounding the categorial difference between ethnos and demos, where the event proper to the forming of the Brazilian people arises not from the irruption of the unity of a demos through revolutionary political action but through the composite explosion of multiple ethnicities resulting from the traumatic event of African slave ships arriving to the shores of Brazil.

The Simulacrum of the Event, or on the Event That Never Took Place

In 1818, King João VI of Portugal commissioned the French artist Jean-Baptiste Debret to paint his public acclamation as the first monarch of the United Kingdom of Portugal, Brazil, and the Algarves, and, indeed, the first crowned monarch in the Americas.

Debret's etching (1818) is, we can say, the first official simulacrum of Brazilian history: the sovereign appears surrounded by the people who in reality did not exist as such. In a way, this scene can be regarded as the first expression of "populism" in Brazil: while there was no "people" under the Portuguese monarchy of Brazil, it could be rhetorically or pictorially simulated.

This type of simulation has various outlines. One is the painting *The First Mass in Brazil* (*A Primeira Missa No Brasil*), painted between 1859 and 1861 by Victor Meirelles (1832–1903). The purpose was to create a heroic figuration of the people through an exaltation of nature. The painting was based on the account given by Pero Vaz de Caminha, who wrote the first official report of the discovery of Brazil in 1500. Painted in Paris, at a time when the Brazilian National State was asserting itself in the shadow of the Second Kingdom, the painting was inspired by the work of Horace Vernet, author of the image of the mass celebrating France's colonization of North Africa. Its ideological leitmotif ratifies the structuring power of Europeans in the colonies: in front of the Catholic Friar Henrique de Coimbra performing mass, kneeling Portuguese and natives, perched on tree branches, make up the audience, or we may say, "the people."

In *Independence of Brazil* (*Independência do Brasil*), also known as *The Cry of Ipiranga* (*O Grito do Ipiranga*), Pedro Américo (1843–1895) was commissioned by the Brazilian emperor Pedro II (1888) to celebrate, some sixty-six years later, the moment when independence was proclaimed by Pedro I, on the banks of the Ipiranga stream. The picture was painted in Florence, where Pedro Américo was enjoying a scholarship paid for by his commissioner. Here, too, the people is not shown (only the figure of a cattleman [*boiadeiro*] unaware of the act). The image is instead populated with various military men on horseback. Compared to actual accounts of what happened, the

Figure 11.1 Jean-Baptiste Debret, *Vista do Largo do Palácio no dia da aclamação de D. João VI*, 1818. © Public Domain/Alamy Stock Photo.

Figure 11.2 Victor Meirelles, *A primeira missa no Brasil*, 1859–61. © Public Domain/ Alamy Stock Photo.

picture dissimulates more than it simulates: Dom Pedro II was actually riding a mule, not a brave steed, and the stop he made beside the stream was due to diarrhea, at least according to historiographical *doxa*.

Already in the middle of the republican regime, the painter Aurélio de Figueiredo (1854–1916), incidentally Pedro Américo's brother, presents on canvas his vision of the Brazilian people (*The Last Ball of the Monarchy* [*O Ultimo Baile da Monarquia*] or *The Illusion of the Third Kingdom* [*A ilusão do Terceiro Reinado*] [1905]), staged as a white elite, dressed in fine clothes: marquises; viscounts; viscountesses; barons; counselors, political, and military personalities, as well as the emperor, the princess, and her consort. In fact, the almost 3,000 guests, in attendance for what was also called the "Fiscal Island's Ball," represented the cherry on top of the hegemonic social order of the time; no darkly pigmented individual appears in the image, even though it is known that there existed a brown (*pardo*) elite within the Second Kingdom. The canvas was meant to allegorically celebrate the transition from empire to a republican constitution, already emerging as a full-blown simulation of modernity that was wary of African descendants.

Unlike the act of dissimulation, simulation does not hide the real but, rather, produces a fictitious reality. In patriotic fictions of a populist nature—most explicit in the image of the public acclamation for the Portuguese King João VI—the subject of populism abstractly "loves" the people (by a kind of affective outpouring), positioning himself as in touch with the divine. At the heart of all forms of populism there is always a perverse appeal to familiarity. Essentially, in fact, this simulation lies at the very core of the concept of a people—a reality that can only be supposed, that only exists as the result of a political invention. The immediate reality of a people is that of

Figure 11.3 Horace Vernet, *Première messe en Kabylie*, 1854. © Musée cantonal des Beaux-Arts de Lausanne.

Figure 11.4 Pedro Américo, *Independência do Brasil ou O Grito do Ipiranga*, 1888. © Museu Paulista da USP, released as Creative Commons (CC)—CC BY-SA 4.0.

Figure 11.5 Aurélio de Figueiredo, *O Ultimo Baile da Monarquia ou a Ilusão do Terceiro Reinado*, 1905. © Public Domain/Alamy Stock Photo.

a demographic aggregation of individuals gathered together within the one national territory (an indeterminate number of people in a region) or that of the mass, which is a pre-political figuration alien to any claim to the truth of space and representation.

Precisely, a spatial and representative "truth" is consonant with the idea of the nation, which while indeterminate is intellectually understandable as a stable community rooted in territory, history, culture, and, even, psychical identifications. It would not be incorrect to designate this stability as "political" also, provided that we broaden the semantic or even mythical scope of this word so that it branches into the meaning of *human identity*, that is, the binding complex that links an individual to a continuous frame of reference, where an individual's own biography intersects with the group with which she lives. For these very reasons, the influential French Orientalist and philologist Ernest Renan preferred, during the nineteenth century, to define the nation as a "spiritual principle."

Under the aegis of republican ideology, what has always produced political effects, in the modern sense of this word, is the fiction of the people. But the fictitious, if not the factitiousness of this supposed political unity of a demographic whole, presents a conceptual problem. In fact, the idea of "people" (etymologically, a translation from the Greek *demos* to the Latin *populus*) does not have the transparency that is commonly assigned to it. It also belongs, like the nation, to the broad scope of the concept of collective identity. Moreover, it contains socially hierarchical differences: *populus* refers to the Romans invested in the political and legal power (the patriciate), distinct from *plebs*, who are the common people, without civic privileges.

On *Demos* and *Ethnos*

In ancient Greece, the generic agglomeration of settlers or occupants of a region was *ethnos*, that is, a collective identification with particular sources that serve as the bases for communitarian belonging. These sources—archaic, symbolic, and religious—are the most durable, the most rooted, the least "chosen." They are the *differentiae specifica* marking out the consciousness of one human group from another on the basis of customs, language, beliefs, etc. These original units were called *genos*, later aggregated into *fratrias* which, in turn, resulted in tribes or *demos*, the name of each of the ten different tribes (*phylia*) into which Attica, the region around Athens, was subdivided. Reunited after the Reformation of Clisthenes (508 B.C)—already with a principle of "choice" or identity—the tribes politically asserted the power (*kratos*) of differences: demos/*kratos*, democracy. In this constellation, demos and ethnos (the mythical and clanic subjectivation of tribes constituted by family groups or *fratrias*) coincide. This is because, even if conducted by the aristocrats of the tribes (the *eupatrids*), subjectivation is guided by the democratic traction implied in citizenship. People is then a dynamic form; more than *being*, it is a *becoming*—a process producing its own subject.

Western modernity introduces a distinction: *a people* is people conceived as demos (and not as ethnos). Thus, the political principle of democracy is now assumed to be that which transforms the population (a huddled or aggregated people into the subject of sovereignty, or into a particular form of autonomy that opposes state power). As Rancière writes, "[t]here is politics from the moment there exists the sphere of the appearance of a subject, *the people*, whose particular attribute is to be different from itself, internally divided" (1999: 87). A people is not something unified or indivisible. Rather, and when thought rhetorically, it has a metonymic function: although a division or a part of a human mass, the people as a category intends to designate the whole.

Let us accept that people are defined in principle as a collective form of subjectivation. Politically, this notion is of great importance because it already favors the hegemonic identity actively protected by the state. State power manages to perpetuate itself thanks to the aura of potency surrounding the people, seen as an essence of freedom guaranteed by laws and rights. As a concept, it is a product of the moral philosophy of the Enlightenment. Connecting the people with the nation was a strategy for developing and consolidating the power of the liberal state. In this coupling, as Gérard Mairet stresses,

> it is the people who are dominant, to the point that one could not, today as yesterday, nourish a political ambition for oneself or for all if one did not take it for granted that the people are sovereign. The people appears, in effect, as the obligatory referent, the source and norm of all politics since the "ideals," as they say, of the glorious French Revolution resounded in Europe and in the world. (. . .) The people is not, therefore, a population, it is a principle, and the ideology of the people is the systematic set of meanings of all kinds deduced from this principle. (Mairet, 1997: 311)

It is, therefore, a sociopolitical construction that "stages" the demos, in the manner of a dramatic play, seeking to "naturalize" through narratives and myths the link between the social agent and his active part in the polis. This is the basic fiction that legitimizes elections in parliamentary democracies, but which also makes parliamentarianism something more than a mere mechanism of representation. It should be understood: if the people is the collective subjectivity that legitimates state power, then it is important to reflect on the scope of this form of subjectivation in parliamentarianism itself in order to know the type of demos politically implied therein.

From a politico-anthropological point of view, the modern privileging of the demos over the ethnos belongs the concept of *humanity*, an exclusively Western construct. As a Renaissance idea, it emerges at the decisive moment in modern history that Fernand Braudel referred to as the "long sixteenth century," when the increasingly dominant actions of Europeans are intensified on a planetary scale. This idea of humanity attributes to man one and the same rationality, which, according to Gaston Bachelard, is nothing but a "statistical synthesis," since it studies him "from a general point of view, disregarding the fluctuations of this study." But this idea—an ideological façade for the legitimation of the plunder of markets in Southeast Asia, of precious metals in the Americas and labor-power in Africa—is conceptually consolidated to the extent that it helps sustain the way Europeans know themselves as "wholly human men" and others as *anthropos*—a way of abstracting and universalizing the ethnos—that is, incomplete. In other words, while the demos is humanly whole, the ethnos is only halfway up the evolutionary ladder of humanity. The word "ethnicity," derived from this, ends up being incorporated into academic terminology to classify forms of life alien to European reality.

The *human being* is thus defined from the inside out, rejecting otherness on the basis of hierarchical standards established by Christian cosmology and implicitly endorsed by secular philosophy. From this stems the epistemic judgment that the *Other* (*ethnos, anthropos*) is not imbibed with rational plenitude, and therefore ontologically inferior to the Western human. The "anthropological fairs"—a kind of theme park of people and customs considered exotic—held in Europe from the second half of the nineteenth century to the first decades of the twentieth century are notorious. In them, the racist spectacle of the difference between demos and ethnos was produced as entertainment.

This is the same idealist anthropology responsible for the naturalization of concepts, such as private property, market mechanisms, labor, and capital processes that Marx subjected to decisive critique. Marxist analysis dismantled the conceptual framework that supports the fiction of the "people" and shows that the ideal reference of this idea appears when the traditional community is historically broken up and replaced with the emergent concentration of the uprooted masses in urban areas. As Jean Baudrillard writes, "Marxist analysis unmasked the myth of the People and revealed what it ideally concealed: the salariat and the class struggle" (1975: 57). But this myth is politically durable, modified in different ways according to variations in national realities, always harnessed as a way to validate the nature of state power or a particular political ideology, as in the case of the use of *Volk* in German National Socialism. The Russians approached things differently: in their period of exaltation of internationalism, they bypassed the use of the idea of the people, transferring political power to the *proletariat*, understood as "the subjectivized body of communism" (Badiou, 2016: 23). The proletariat thus designated the mass above national borders. Generally speaking, for specific ruling elites, at certain moments within particular histories, the principal strategy is the construction of an overarching identity and, at the same time, exercising within this space of domination other autochthonous forms of subjectivation.

The ruling elite denies the concrete possibility of other understandings of the people, which try to bypass the idea of race and which thereby follows a historicity unrecognized by the West. In this sense, there is no French or German ethnicity, since "ethnic," as race, is always in the Other.[1] The case of Brazil is notable since, constituted in, with, and through the arrival of the slave diaspora, its history discloses a different identity formation and civilizing pattern. Although having arrived under the sign of ethnos, of race, the black race, a variety of "nations" had in fact landed on its shores—but such a variety could not be captured under the classificatory term of nation, since these collective groupings were far removed from the construct of "European nation" and closer to ethnicity. It is in this sense that the phrase of the abolitionist Joaquim Nabuco still resonates today: "The blacks gave Brazil a people." Here we will do well to emphasize that this entire process fundamentally undermines the assumptions and procedures by which Western thought understood the being of a people, an ethnos, and a nation. The passage of the Blacks is shown in its heterogeneity, in its resistance to any abstract capture under a generic and homogenizing race. Blackness is thereby granulated, fragmented in and through an array of localized differences, thus giving to Brazil its singularity on the basis of plurality. We shall explore this in the following section.

On the Afro-Brazilian Event

In order to understand the categorial distinction between demos and ethnos, and the manner in which this distinction operates in the construction and invention of the people in modernity, it will be useful to make some observations on what could be called the Afro-Brazilian event. While referring to the modern demos, Alain Badiou understands the *organization* or *discipline of the event* as "the possibility of an efficacious fragmentation of the Idea into actions, proclamations and inventions attesting to a *fidelity to the event*. All in all, an organization is something that declares itself collectively adequate to the event and the idea alike, in a duration which has once again become that of the world" (Badiou, 2012: 69). In principle, this organization or discipline of the event is antithetical to the *deterritorialization* exercised by the West against Africa, and which has been responsible for the destruction of socioeconomic structures and the desacralization of original forms of life. The organization or discipline of the event "reenacts" the (immemorial) African origin, as well as the (memorial) resistance against its violation, as a consequence of transatlantic slavery (the first to be based exclusively on racial criteria), therefore, of the *slave diaspora*, responsible for the migration of several million Africans to Brazilian territory over the centuries.

Let us recall that from the sixteenth- and throughout the following century, the so-called nations of the Bantu linguistic group were mainly in Salvador, the capital of Brazil at that time. Coming mainly from subequatorial Africa were the Ambundo and the Bacongo, who predominated in Bahia, while the Ovimbundu had a stronger presence in São Paulo, Minas Gerais, and Rio de Janeiro. The cultural marks left by the Bantu are unmistakable in Catholic brotherhoods, in traditional religions synthesized in the Angolan and Congolese *candomblés*, and in popular games. But from the second half of the eighteenth century, when the slave trade favored supra-equatorial Africa (the

Mina Coast, the Bay of Benin, and other places), the slave masses were sourced from regions that today correspond to parts of Nigeria and Benin (ex-Dahomey), where "nations" or "city-states" such as Anagó, Oyó, Ijexá, Ketu, Ifé, and others extended. All this constituted a complex system of civilization, alternatively designated by the generic "Yoruba," "Nagô," or even "Sudanese" (it is worth remembering that the word "Sudan" comes from the Arabic "assuad," meaning black), whose cultural practices were better delineated in the Brazilian region of Bahia.

This complex network of places of belonging nonetheless indicates a bias toward supremacy on the part of the Nagôs and the Jejes, the latter being a term used by Yoruba speakers to refer to the Fon people. But this indication of ethnic supremacy never really erases the strong civilizing marks of all the other African ethnicities: to trace the "bantuisms" that multiply in Brazilian speech is to come across etymons coming from languages such as kicongo, kimbundo, umbundu, quioco, ronga, and others. "Candomblé," the generic designation for Afro-Brazilian cults, is a Bantu word. One can thus point to something in Brazil's history that corresponds to a civilizing paradigm which nonetheless is distinct from the European model that is centered on the powers of capitalist organization and the rationality of signs. It is a paradigm that is properly African, realized in Brazil through the Bantu and Nagô. The Brazilian author Jorge Amado's novels rely on the specificity of this event as a way of speaking about the singularity of the Brazilian people by amplifying their blackness by a process of *mestizament*.

If we pay attention, for example, to the Nagôs, who made up the largest number of migrants in the last of the big slave shipments to Brazil, we can see that they correspond to a complex set of cultural ties whose origins go back to Nigeria and Benin (ex-Dahomey), comprising "nations" known as Egbá, Egbádo, Ijebu, Ijexá, Ketu, Sabé, Iaba, Anagô, and Eyó, and which themselves incorporate traces of the Adja, Fon, Huedá, Mali, Jegum, and others known in Brazil under the generic name of Jeje. In historical and geographical terms, these nations came from the Mina Coast (an area that today includes Benin, Nigeria, and Togo) and began arriving at the port of Salvador, in Bahia, at the end of the eighteenth century. The slaves were used as African currency for the acquisition of tobacco produced in the Bahian Recôncavo. Nagô became a generic name for the diversity of these cultural relations and in fact was equivalent to the word "Yoruba," designating the speakers of this language, which at certain times had wider significance and extension in Africa. The insistence on the name "Nagô" is due to the intense trade between Bahia and the Western African coast, therefore, to the maintenance of permanent contact between the elements of the slave diaspora and their regions of origin.

African historiography is lavish in its accounts of interethnic wars—for example, of how the Nagô city of Ketu was conquered and razed to the ground by King Ghezo (1818–58), of Dahomey (today Benin), who sold captives to the Portuguese in order to make his kingdom prosperous—and of the warlike incursions of the slavers on that continent. The singularity of the Africanization process of Salvador-Bahia—an important stage in the Afro-Brazilian event—has been emphasized by various foreign chroniclers in the past.

It is known that a large part of those Africans brought as slaves were political prisoners, many of whom were well educated. While from Europe came convicts, from Africa came princes, princesses, and priests, such as Otampê Ojaró, twin daughter of Alaketu (king of Ketu), founder of the first liturgical community of Ketu in Bahia, succeeded by her Brazilian daughter Iya Akobiodé. An African elite was formed here through an implicit symbolic pact between individuals of different ethnicities, despite the hostilities between Creoles (born in Brazil) and Africans of the Mina- or the Slave-Coast.

But does all this human movement constitute a demos? Or does it simply refer to the forced displacements of an ethnos?

In returning to Badiou, the original *event* contains the idea of *trauma* (in our case, the slave diaspora) and of *restoration* (the continuation of the Origin). As for *organization*, it is an attempt to "preserve the characteristics of the event (intensification, contraction, and localization), when the event as such no longer possesses its initial potency. In this sense organization is, in the subjective latency where the Idea holds itself, the transformation of eventual power into temporality" (Badiou, 2012: 70). This "event-keeping" evidently implies a group memory, which can be described, in the manner of the sociologist Maurice Halbwachs—disciple of Bergson and Durkheim—by traits of (i) *collectivism* (a synoptic view of individual memories), (ii) *presentism* (the representation of the origin depends on the here and now), and (iii) *spatiality* (representations depend on the construction of a specific territory) (Halbwachs, 1992). Impregnated by a structuring affective atmosphere, memory focuses mainly on a way of being and thinking that is directly affected by territory, which, in the case of the Nagôs, gives rise to specific community bonds that are indicative of a singular "people." Not that there are only groups of afro-descendants, there are also the indigenous, the river dwellers, the *caboclos*, the whites. In contemporary Brazil, the current designation of "Indians" for the native or the autochthonous parts of the population is ambiguous. It is common that they themselves reject this characterization, preferring to identify themselves as "indigenous peoples" internally comprised of multitudinous languages: Tupinambá; Mundurucu, Krenaks, Pataxó, Guarans, and others—in total 305 peoples and 274 languages.

This brief account of the traumatic Afro-Brazilian event of slavery confirms Badiou's understanding of the event as the possible fragmentation of an idea, in our case, the idea of the people. The idea of the people is thus fragmented into actions, statements, and inventions, becoming reduced to just a linguistic issue. However, if we instead pay closer theoretical attention to how the actions, statements, and inventions of peoples (diverse forms of collective subjectivation) fragment the idea of the people, then might it in fact be possible to find new paradigms for thinking the category? It is important not to forget the traumatic aspect of the Afro-Brazilian event. Thus, in attesting to the possibility of the coexistence of *peoples* in the same national territory, this traumatic event also signals a collective *fear*—a fear of the ruling groups or stratums facing the force of diversity, which is none other than the experience of contingency that belongs to being human. To legitimize their historic domination, the rulers and governing classes nationalize the idea of the "people" by speaking of the *Brazilian* people in an elaborate discourse of monocultural synthesis, that is, of a "national people," a "national culture," etc.—something that is clear when speaking of concepts such as the Brazilian "syncretic culture" or Brazil as a "racial democracy." These discourses endeavor to depict an image of conciliatory, non-conflictual unity in the face of a sociohistorical reality made up of traumatic contradictions and suffering through diversity. In the Brazilian case, identity is ambiguous: there are different "peoples" that as a whole share various linguistic memories but through one common language.

It is within this ideological mask—forged by the incapacity of the ruling bureaucracies to grasp the historical reality of peoples—that populisms of various kinds arise and unfold. Populism is the cousin and brother-in-law of cross-eyed nationalism—a nationalism that exhausts itself in chanting the national anthem and peddling phobias and petty resentments against everything that is "other." The fiction of a national people empties the peoples of its historicity and produces a nationalism that is, as Samuel Johnson said, "the last refuge of the scoundrel [quote modified]" (quoted in Boswell, 1906: 615) (in Old French, the word for "scoundrel," *canaille*, designates both the despicable individual and the lower social stratum)—that is, a nationalism that is based on "the remnants" of a fictional people.

"People" has thus lent itself to diverse and fluid classifications, ranging from meanings once attributed to the "lumpenproletariat" to the identification of a new fraction of the "middle class," on the fringes of the institutional mechanisms of representation. At stake is a movement in the rational idea of people that favors a nebulous population mass, statistically redefined and fixed by the expanded market. Moreover, today we live in a historical moment in which the weakening of political liberalism coincides with the strengthening of social media. While the people was a fabrication of a classical political phenomenon, the mass is a fabrication of the mediatization of the social sphere. The power exercised over it no longer derives from state apparatuses but essentially from business organizations which accumulate and concentrate exorbitant amounts of information on "users."

For a critic such as Baudrillard, the mass is no longer "objectifiable (in political terms: no longer is it representable), and it annuls any subject who would claim to comprehend it (in political terms: it annuls anybody who would claim to represent it). Only surveys and statistics (like the law of large numbers and the calculus of probabilities in mathematical physics) can account for it, but one knows that this incantation, this meteoric ritual of statistics and surveys has no real object, especially not the masses whom it is thought to express" (Baudrillard, 2007: 31–2). In other words, the contemporary mass is neither subject nor object but a simple simulation effect, like the people in historical pictorial representations of the past. If we today have to think the people as a dangerous and void category, the Afro-Brazilian and similar traumatic events can certainly show how the meaning of ethnos unveils other practices of being-together beyond the categories of people, states, nation, and race.

Translation Cecilia Schuback

Note

1 Affirmation may sound contradictory when considering the fiction of the Aryan race by the Nazis, but the Nazi logic is in its intrication still quite clear. In order to affirm itself as unique, as the "only one," it has to be *the* "Other" of all "others." The elimination project of exterminating all the "others," all other races, was necessary for its affirmation of the only and superior *Volk*, as well as race.

Bibliography

Badiou A (2012) *The Rebirth of History* (trans. G Elliott). London: Verso.
Badiou A (2016) Twenty-Four Notes on the Uses of the Word "People." In: *What Is a People?* New York: Columbia University Press, 21–31.
Baudrillard J (1975) *The Mirror of Production* (trans. M Poster). St. Louis: Telos Press.
Baudrillard J (2007) *In the Shadow of the Silent Majorities, or, The End of the Social* (trans. P Foss). Los Angeles: Semiotext(e).
Boswell J (1906) *Life of Samuel Johnson, Vol. 2*. New York: E. P. Dutton and Co.
Halbwachs M (1992) *On Collective Memory* (trans. LA Coser). Chicago, IL: University of Chicago Press.
Mairet G (1997) *Le Principe de Souveraineté: Histoires et Fondements Du Pouvoir Moderne*. Paris: Éd. Gallimard.
Rancière J (1999) *Disagreement: Politics and Philosophy* (trans. J Rose). Minneapolis: University of Minnesota Press.

12

A Politics of the People and a Politics of the Popular

From the Russian Revolution to *Gramsci's Ashes*

Tora Lane

In her oft-quoted text on populism, Margaret Canovan argues that "populism is the shadow cast by Democracy itself" (1999: 3), for the simple reason that an appeal to the people is the ground for the very legitimacy of modern democracy. Which is to say, the *sine qua non* of modern democracy is the support from the voices of the common people, the *vox populi*. Today this means periodic general elections. But can we assume that, throughout its history, democracy has been conditioned by the same idea of the people, and that today appears to be invoked by contemporary examples of populism (on the left or the right)? On a terminological level, it seems that both democracy and populism refer back to the people. One question is whether the ideas of the popular and the people should remain distinct. It is my contention that what today remains of the notion of vox populi in contemporary forms of populism is the superordination of the notion of the popular over the people. While the idea of the people is largely understood as a self-sustaining group with the capacity to represent itself, the idea of the popular has a quantitative determination, referring to popularity, for example, popular support and popular vote.

There is an inherent ambiguity in the word "popular." According to its Latin roots, whatever is popular is "of the people" (as opposed to the elites), that is, it designates what belongs to a people. Historically, the ideas and associations attached to the popular have transformed markedly, increasingly acquiring the meaning of whatever is "liked by many." Today, this has reached the point where "liked by many" has become synonymous with being "of the people (as opposed to the elites)."[1] To the extent that democracy is conditioned by the people, then any modification in the meaning of democracy's operating term (demos, or the people) will alter the nature of democracy as such. Here, the term "populism" is itself instructive. The very use of the word "populism" for two radically different movements—the Russian *Narodniks* at the turn of the nineteenth century, who sought to educate the largely rural masses, and today's populist parties, simply aiming for the broadest popularity in periodic elections—reminds us that, through an ambiguous *populology*, the same political vocabulary deployed during the history of democracy can be used to denote quite diffuse and different political appearances.[2] The question I wish to pose in this chapter is the following: While the political vocabulary used to designate the principal political subject in democratic life may remain the same, how might we approach the conceptual difference that seems to be at play between, on the one hand, ideas of the people and the popular, on the other?

In order to discuss this difference between the people and the popular, I will trace back the idea of the people in modern democracy to its revolutionary legacies. My point of departure here will be Hannah Arendt's notorious critique of the French Revolution where the idea of the people was coterminous with the downtrodden masses. In *On Revolution* (1963), among other places, Arendt provides a historical account of the people that ties the category to revolutionary politics—a tradition of revolution where a reckoning with the "social question," and theretofore with society in its totality, paved the way for totalitarianism and the figure of the popular leader as the point of fusion of the masses. At the same time, we should not forget that the ideology of the people incubated in the French Revolution also contained a utopian moment; the people as the carriers of the possibility of another history. As Marx argued, the French Revolution problematized the relation between the people and history. In modernity, precisely, the changing valences of the people mirrored the profound structural and economic changes society was itself undergoing. Albeit in different ways, Marx understood the people as both a transformative and historical force, politically working in opposition to the processes of massification of the people in modern (capitalist) society. Arguably, Marx's wager was lost once the idea of the people was transformed into popular politics, which no longer represents either historical transformation or a radical reconstruction of society in its totality. Contemporary forms of populism today indicate that the modern concern with radical social transformation, led by the people, has now been replaced with popular appeals to the people. Today, this is often carried out by way of an appeal to popular opinions or by stoking up affects such as resentment. We may ask, then, whether or not we are facing a new form of ideological apparatus today that works on and promotes immediate articulations of popular sentiments that potentially differ from totalitarianism.

In order to capture how the idea of the people and the underlying ideology of democracy has changed—specifically with respect to how the people as a category has framed and today frames a relation to history—I will draw upon two historical examples: the Russian Revolution and postwar Italy. Here I shall turn to literary and essayistic reflections on the politics of these very distinct historical moments. For they not only offer a different insight into the workings of ideology, but they also show, despite similarities in political vocabulary, how the workings of political ideology differ experientially. To begin with, I will consider Lenin's concept of the people and the utopian project of revolutionizing Russian society, alongside the literary response to the Russian Revolution in the writings of the Russian-Soviet author, Andrey Platonov, who sought to write the revolution from the perspective of the Russian people themselves. Through Platonov's writings, we can grasp the double character of the revolutionary legacy, which, on the one hand, serves as a pedagogical project for transforming "the people" into the modern political subject of democracy, and on the other, as a utopian opening into a question of the experience of the people as the nameless other of society. In stark contrast to the soviet revolutionary experience, and in order to elaborate on how the category of the people changes in postwar politics, I shall discuss Pier Paolo Pasolini's understanding of his own contemporaneity: the postwar Italy of *Gramsci's Ashes*, the title of a collection of his poems. In the title of the poem, Pasolini refers not to the literal remains of Gramsci the historical figure but the ashes from the "attempts to remake life [that] end up among the ruins" (2014a: 167), that is, the ashes of the utopian moment of the revolutionary ideology of the people. By way of his reflections on the remnants of fascism in postwar Italy, Pasolini allows us to consider a "mutation" in politics, a transformation of the idea of the people in popular culture, led astray by developments in media technology. By bringing these writers together, I will pose the question whether we should insist on drawing a distinction between, on the one hand, a revolutionary utopian ideology of the people and, on the other, a post-utopian and thereby postrevolutionary ideology of the popular. These different ideological tendencies, I would propose, present us with contrasting promises and threats in the history of democracy.

Revolution and the Concept of the People

In *On Revolution* Hannah Arendt argues that the appearance of the masses on the streets during the French Revolution, marking the birth of modern mass democracy, laid the foundations for totalitarianism. According to Arendt, it was owing to an understanding of the people as masses that made possible their cruel and total exploitation as a uniform and headless political body under totalitarian rule. In other words, according to Arendt, the origins of totalitarianism are to be sought in the legacy of the French Revolution, having itself developed a proto-totalitarian leadership, which acquired its legitimacy in the name, and with the blind support, of the people as the downtrodden and unhappy masses, whose communal will became law. Arendt writes: "It is by no means merely a matter of misguided theory that the French concept of *le peuple* has carried, from its beginning, the connotation of a multiheaded monster, a mass that moves as one body and acts as though possessed by one will" (Arendt, 1963: 94). Arendt criticizes this configuration of politics, and ultimately democracy, because of the way it takes as its starting point a particular ideological conceptualization of the people as the entire social body.[3] Politics in Europe thus came to be framed as social engagement, which, according to Arendt, was often ideological and hypocritical. What, according to Arendt, it should have been concerned with was the development of a proper public sphere where matters of the people could be dealt with in a distinguished and disinterested manner by "free men." More so, addressing the social question, alongside Rousseau's sense of the general will, meant following a movement from the particular to the universal. The history of modern politics, from the French Revolution up to and including the event of the fall of totalitarianism, was according to Arendt the tragic historical realization of the false ideology of the people, whose flaw laid in the universalization of *a* particularity, not only a people but the people as masses. What this led to was a concentration of unprecedented levels of power in the hands of a leader, who in speaking through decree is said to enact the general will (in the terms of a specific ideology at a particular time). The leader represents the people, while hearing and heeding their will in an almost immanent relation; both leader and the figuration of the people are then raised as transcendent political principles. According to Arendt, the people were to trust their leader, often in flagrant opposition to their own thoughts and experiences. Two different forms of totalitarianism (Soviet and National Socialist) would designate two different kinds of ideologies of the people that amounted more or less to the same outcome—the elimination of the particular (e.g., other races or classes) in the face of the universal (the German or the Soviet people), which was solely an ideological construction.

Considering the ambiguization and the continual renegotiation of the revolutionary legacy today, one of our tasks today is to distinguish between two different ideas of the people which appeared in the two European forms of totalitarianism. The utopian moment that begins with the experiences of a people as the other of society would indeed seem to distinguish the socialist revolutionary legacy from Nazism or fascism. At the time of the emergence of a fascist ideology in Germany, the mass of the people was already considered a political force, the principle of its own mythical formation in the name of race. The function of ideology in this case was to strengthen the force of its own cultural belonging. Thus, Hitler in *Mein Kampf* calls upon the German people in their quality of becoming and being *more* German, of purging themselves of any foreign influence, both in culture in general and in their personal conduct specifically.[4] The notion of the people in Bolshevism is quite different. It is much closer to the revolutionary legacy of the people as a utopian transformation of the "no ones" into the all, as the *Internationale* heralds. Translated into the Russian context of Bolshevism, the dominant strands of Marxist thought on the people can be summarized as follows: (i) the spontaneous forces of popular uprising will evolve into a critique of capitalism once the political consciousness of the proletariat has fully matured; (ii) an imagined people coextensive with a different form of (premodern) communality or *Gemeinwesen*, possessing within it the universalism of a classless society. For Lenin, though, this second idea surrounding the specificity of the Russian people was not crucial. And although the Bolsheviks anticipated the hegemony of the proletariat, the people of the revolution did not in any straightforward way necessitate the universalization of a particularity, in contradistinction to the Nazi mythologization of Germany and the German people.

The People in the Russian Revolution

Arendt's thoughts are certainly relevant for understanding how the idea of the people operated during the Russian Revolution. Yet, it does not entirely account for how the people were put into question during the revolution and under concrete pressures of economic modernization, and how the idea of the people in spite of its totalizing movement still opened up for an inclusion of the experience *of the people*. Although Lenin's concept of the people conforms in several respects to Arendt's critique—insofar as he considers the people as the downtrodden masses in need of ideological transformation, the transformative process of which came to be dictated by the party in a way that led to totalitarianism—equally the revolution also marked a fundamental transformation of Russian society that not only meant the transformative inclusion of the nameless masses in existing forms of society but also the transformation of society in view of the people, which went beyond the blind alleys of totalitarianism by opening up the possibility of thinking the people in their otherness. The word "people" in Russian, *narod*, can designate people in general and peoples, communities and nations, in particular, and was less frequently used alongside the term *natsional'nost'* to define different peoples of the Russian empire and subsequently USSR.[5] And as for the *Narodniks*, an early revolutionary movement engaged with educating and bringing political awareness to the people, "the people" denoted the vast majority of the Russian population, as well as others who had not yet entered the social stratifications of modern society, such as the newly emancipated peasants of rural Russia.

Lenin's formulation of the revolution as electrification plus the power of the Soviets also indicates his preoccupation with the backwardness of rural Russia in contradistinction to the development of the larger cities after Peter the Great's modernizing Europeanization of Russia, and the party's attempts at integrating the peasantry into the continuous modernization of Russia. Lenin was initially reluctant to recognize this vast majority of the Russian people as revolutionary subjects. Since class struggle was understood to be the principal motor of historical change, for the Bolsheviks the proletariat was the political subject par excellence. Thus the Bolsheviks' notion of the formation of a revolutionary political body of the people was predicated specifically on the proletariat and its role in the historical transformation in both the forces and relations of production.[6] Famously, Marx had interestingly argued in the 1882 second introduction to the Russian translation of the *Communist Manifesto* that it was possible that the peasant's *obshchina*—deriving from the Russian word *obshchii* (common) and designating the peasant commune—could form the basis of communist society in Russia. Lenin, however, was not interested in the communal life of the peasant but was in fact highly critical of what he called *narodnichestvo*, understood as a kind of *Schwärmerei*, an enthusiastic devotion to the people. And in a discussion of the German word *Gemeinwesen*, Lenin prefers the translation *kommuna* to *obschina*,[7] untainted as it is by the connotations of the people, indicating instead a form of communality linked to modern industrial life, joining together the French revolutionary tradition and the Communist Party.

Yet circumstantial issues would mark a discursive shift. After the 1905 revolution, it was crucial for the successful realization of a communist revolution and the formation of Soviet society that Lenin adjusted his view by following Trotsky and asserting that the peasants could play an active part in the revolution. For the purposes of effective leadership (*opiraias' na krestianskuiu stikhiiu i rukovodia eiu*), revolutionary action would require support from the rural population. This led to the maxim, "the revolutionary-democratic dictatorship of the proletariat and the peasants" (Lenin, 1967b: 378–9), implying, as he further writes, the inclusion of all people. Here we find the basic Leninist formula that would prove decisive in how he and the party would relate to the people. The people was the site of spontaneous forces. In order to attain the requisite revolutionary consciousness, the proletariat needed special guidance and awareness of their own conditions. The common root for all revolutionary forces was, according to Lenin, the experience of exploitation, and the people became political once they had realized their common cause (and also their common good) of overthrowing the structural conditions of exploitation. This all depended on their collective ability to organize themselves as a united movement. By 1917, and with the publication of *State and Revolution*, Lenin's equation that the people = peasants + workers is supported by a quote from Marx claiming that the abolition of capitalism required a "real people's revolution." Here it seems that Lenin's reference to the people was, just like much of his politics, strategic. The idea of the people was but a tool for bringing about the revolution, couched in terms of a historical necessity. To compound this sense of a pragmatic deployment of the idea of the people, after the revolution, Lenin showed little interest in the people as a principle for the formation of communist culture. Instead, Marxist-Leninist vocabulary adopts a quasi-scientific language based on the necessity of historical laws, with specific focus on the laws of Soviet modernization. After the revolution, when the Bolsheviks embarked upon an unprecedented project of "People's Enlightenment," the purpose of the postrevolutionary situation was as much about forming a uniform political "body of the people" as it was to modernize Russia. Education of literacy went hand in hand with the ideological formation of the Soviet people as a united political subject with the requisite proletarian consciousness (a central question for Lenin and the Russian Revolution). Yet, while the revolution led to an unprecedented process of political and ideological formation of the Russian people, this formation was itself motivated by the "social question" as the historical need to include the people in the modernization of Russia. It was a historical moment that opened up for a new experience of the people (or, perhaps, more accurately, it was the experience of the people that opened up for a new experience of history).

The Experience of the People According to Platonov

In order to explore the Russian Revolution as an opening for a new experience of the people, I shall now turn to the writings of Andrei Platonov, a unique voice in the depiction of the experience of a revolutionary people. A writer of proletarian origin, Platonov was able to develop a literature that engaged with the revolutionary cause by adopting the perspective of the people. This literary engagement did not follow the dictums of Proletarian or Socialist Realism. Rather, Platonov testifies to a form of immanent critique, congenial with his concern of depicting the consequences of politically forming the people from out of their own experiences *as if* these experiences were communicated through their own consciousness and language, and not as the axioms of a political language used to instruct them (e.g., Socialist Realism). The language of these experiences is absurd and grotesque, depicting the dismal consequences of the people's own understanding of how communism might be realized. In the story of *Chevengur*, for example, we are told, communism already exists since the leader, Chepurnyi, has sanctioned a mass liquidation of whatever and whoever could be called bourgeois in the city. In *The Foundation Pit* the story of the death of an orphan child is told through the protagonists of the revolution, who are unable to save her. What Platonov's literature insistently returns to is the possible retrieval of forms of experience that, in spite of the terrifying implications of the party's ideological machinery, were proper to the people at that time. One could say, paradoxically, that the consequences of the revolution Platonov depicts testify to how the people's own understanding of events was in question during the revolution—where people's lived experiences serve not as a model for historical understanding but as what escapes all models of understanding history. In other words, what we see is how the political pedagogical project of the formation of the people goes fundamentally awry. It is by understanding what drives all misunderstandings, and the alienation of which these misunderstandings are indicative, that we ultimately can understand what is at stake when Platonov poses the question of the people at this particular historical conjuncture.

Platonov writes about a people who, through revolution, came to initiate something new in society, the novelty of which evaded the historical formation within which Lenin had sought to induct them. This novelty can be thought as a turning toward the commonality of the people as a different experience of existence, as an interest in how people experience *being* a people. In Platonov's novels, "the people" is not only a name for the nameless and what is unrepresentable; in being nameless, one experiences something that specifically belongs to the people. In his writings, Platonov often returns to the story of the orphaned child as an exemplary figure of the revolution, as well as a certain mode of existing for the people, which the revolution was supposed to call into question. The orphaned child is the nameless one, deprived of personal history, and completely exposed to the forms of sharing that society offers. It is therefore no wonder that in *The Foundation Pit* the orphaned child, Nastia, is called the beloved child of the revolution, while in the novel *Chevengur*, we follow the revolutionary fight and search of the main character, Sasha Dvanov, who is himself a nameless orphan; the surname of the family who took care of him serves as a name for the nameless experience he carries within him:

> No matter how much he read and thought, some kind of hollow place always remained ever within him, an emptiness through which an undescribed and untold world passed like a startled wind. At seventeen Dvanov still had no armor over his heart, neither belief in God nor any other intellectual. He did not give a stranger's name to the nameless life which opened before him. However, he did not want that world to remain untitled; he only waited to hear its own proper name, instead of a purposely conceived appellation. (Platonov, 1978: 43)

This passage depicts an event that takes place just before the revolution. However, it nonetheless shows how Platonov examined the revolution in terms of the experience of life by those people whose life was "nameless." What is at stake for the character Dvanov in his entry into the world of revolution is the possibility of hearing the proper name of this "undescribed and untold world" that passes through the emptiness. He does not want to give it "a stranger's name," and it cannot be heard as "a purposely conceived appellation," in other words, not in any of the pre-given political categories. In a way, the nameless is his own proper name for people; people cannot be conceived as something proper and distinct but are recognized as an initial and nameless strangeness of being in-between different forms of sharing. This namelessness is an emptiness in which some untold world passes like a startled wind, and while Platonov does not explicitly say so, we can read this emptiness of the nameless as the very possibility of a utopian opening toward the experience of the people, where the untold world passes like a startled or, rather, anxious (*trevozhnyi*) wind—that is, a new beginning. In other words, the people carry with them an alienation or strangeness to the world that the nameless (anonymous) people name. It would be this that contains the positive new beginning of the revolution.

The forms of being-together in the world, to which the existential opening of this nameless experience leads, can be found in a beautifully poignant scene at the end of the story *Dzhan* (*The Soul*). There, the young man Nazar Chagataev transfers the people of *Dzhan*, who are not a people in any generic sense of the word, from their remote place of habitation, Sary-Kamysh in the valley of Ust-Yurt, to Chardzhou, further travelling to Tashkent. His task is to save them from starvation in their remote lands and offer them a life of abundance in Soviet civilization. Once they arrive, the young girl Aidym, who belongs to the community of *Dzhan*, understands that the people, who are to be saved by way of their relocation to civilization, have lost their sense of communality. In other words, the people could be saved as living human beings but not as people, with their sense of communality. As we read:

> We're Dzhan, replied the old man, and it emerged from his words that every little tribe, every family and chance group of gradually dying people living in the empty places of the desert, the Amu-Darya and the Ust-Yurt, called themselves by the same name: Dzhan. It was their shared name, given to them a long time ago by the rich beys, because dzhan means soul and these poor, dying men had nothing they could call their own but their souls, that is, the ability to feel and suffer. (Platonov, 1978: 141)

It is not only the people of *Dzhan* but people in general that are able to feel and suffer. An ability, though, that modernization seems to undo. Platonov here returns to a paradox in the revolution of thinking the people as both a vehicle for modernization and a lost form of communal sharing. It is a paradox that remains unsolved. The problem with the difficulty of both attaining socialism and affirming the experience of the people at the same time is that the experience of the people is not only left untranslated when couched in political categories, which had promised to educate—and thereby liberate—the people, but that forms of sharing were vanquished by a life that now understood itself as possessing the world—by naming. Thus, modernization, which was meant to liberate people, ultimately meant eliminating forms of being that made possible the people's exposure to, and sharing in, the world. Yet, in the immediate aftermath of the Russian Revolution, this transition toward modernity appeared as an open wound in need of care, a wound everyone ignored after having been blinded by political slogans, slogans that did nothing other than to alienate.

One of the strange paradoxes of the Russian Revolution is how it could both indicate the "people" as an ideological formation and affirm the alterity of a people in the guises of the exploited proletariat and the immiserated peasants. By delving into the people's utter estrangement after the revolution, Platonov managed to hold onto what ultimately evaded the communist narrative and the conditions of its own logic, namely, to hold in common the actual and erring experiences of the people. At the point where a pre-political experience of life and an entry into the common political body of a communism to come—fatal, grotesque, catastrophic, but at the same time carrying with it an undefined promise—meet,[8] Platonov takes up the viewpoint of the people themselves. In so doing, we can say that he provides a foothold for thinking through Arendt's critique of the totalizing feature of the ideology of the revolutionary people. Platonov goes further, however, by showing how these totalizing features are bound up with modernization itself. This is to say, the ideological instruction of the people goes hand in hand with the modernization of Russia and with political indoctrination. In all this, there remained, nonetheless, a utopian moment wrapped up in these revolutionary processes that invoked the experiences of the people for the sake of human emancipation. This was none other than a bearing witness to the experience of being nameless, of being completely exposed to existence. It is in this that Platonov finds the germ of a socialist revolution. Within the revolutionary tradition, especially in the context of modern European democracy, the name of the people denotes also this idea that politics is and should be conditioned by the historical development of society in its entirety. Therefore, Platonov, in a movement that goes beyond Arendt's critique, invites us to understand the historical moment of the revolution as a utopian idea of a people being exposed to the world as the basis for a future experience of communality, as well as marking the possible destruction of the political and ideological formation from which this possible experience arises.

The People in Postwar Culture

In Europe, from the latter part of the twentieth century onwards, politics can be characterized in terms of its "afterness." The period, we can say, marks the gradual subsidence of the revolutionary ideologies of history. Which is to say, our world is post-ideological, post-totalitarian, postmodern and perhaps, more precisely, post-utopian, both in the West and the East. It goes without saying that this period, traceable from the end of the Second World War onwards, has marked a massive expansion of popular culture in light of late Fordism, pop music, and large-scale consumerism. Here we see the transformation of the revolutionary legacy and the idea of the people that nurtured it. In the final part of my examination, the question will be whether within this recent transformation of the idea of the people and in the people themselves, we face an additional problem surrounding the idea of the popular within processes of modernization today. I suggest here that by following the thoughts of Pier Paolo Pasolini on the destiny of the people and of culture in postwar Italy, we are able to trace the roots of the problems of contemporary populism surrounding how politics has abdicated its utopian impulse. In his writings, Pasolini establishes a dialogue with Antonio Gramsci, the founder and leader of the Italian Communist Party. Pasolini specifically focuses on Gramsci's thoughts on the possibility of transforming society through a people's revolution. As already mentioned, in the collection of poems, *Gramsci's Ashes* (1957), Pasolini turns to Gramsci, while remembering "keen, naïve attempts / to remake life" (2014a: 167):

the close of a decade where
we saw our keen, naive attempts
to remake life end up among the ruins
and a sodden, sterile silence . . . (Pasolini, 2014a: 167):

In the long poetic suite, the Gramscian belief in the people's revolution has vanished. What remains is a "sterile silence," "a deathly peace as unloved as our destinies." While for Pasolini Gramsci stood for a revolutionary time that had passed, Gramsci remained an important reference point in thinking through the fascist takeover of the popular revolutionary moment in modern democracy. The historical necessity of the revolution was no longer a blind conviction. Instead, Gramsci warns us about the forces that may appear when the established grounds of society are shaken: monsters are born because, as Gramsci famously writes, "the old world is dying and a new is struggling to be born." Pasolini addresses Gramsci as someone with whom he shares a love of the people; someone who nurtured ideals and illusions, which, while giving light and hope, were already hopelessly naive. Gramsci was thus correct and wrong at the same time. Pasolini writes about "self-contradiction," being both with Gramsci and against him:

drawn to a proletarian life
from before your time, I take for religion
its joyousness, not its millennial
struggle—its nature, not its
consciousness. /. . ./ (2014a: 175, 177)

Common in the understanding of the people found in the writings of Gramsci, Pasolini, and Platonov is the sense of a historical (rather than an existential) negativity. What distinguishes the people is an exposure to a life experienced as dispossession. Pasolini identifies with the people because "every day of my life I fight / just to live." However, in contrast to the people, Pasolini possesses history and is possessed by it. Ultimately, Pasolini recognizes in his times a loss of history as a loss of the people's revolutionary force. He goes so far as to describe this loss of the people as a "genocide," the extinction of the people as a category in the real. More important still, for Pasolini, this loss indicates a mutation in politics. And it is this mutation that may allow us to understand today's transformation of the idea of the people by means of the superordination of popular culture. On the basis of the drift into the popular, the utopias that nurtured the revolutionary irruption of the people have been emptied and vanquished, even if the basic political divisions of modern democracy are preserved. In the essay "Unhappy Youths," Pasolini stresses that the proletariat and the bourgeoisie have become one and the same, the result of which is that "*we believe that history is not and cannot be other than bourgeois history* [italics in original]" (1983: 16). This means that the people no longer presents the possibility of an opening into history, by virtue of the irruption of an alterity breaking the continuum of identity. The bourgeoisie remain in power, in possession of the world, and have abandoned the old world of the humanist tradition that was meant to be its distinguishing mark. The "new children" "wake up old"— inhabiting a world renewed by its own repressions.[9] It will "contradict itself, in order to go on"; and lead to "the day you shall wake up old, without any love of books or life, / without any love of books or life,/ /. . ./" (Pasolini, 2014b: 391).[10]

In this mutation of politics, popular culture plays a crucial role, sublimating the opposition between the old and the new. In popular culture, as well as popular media, anyone can be anything. All categories are homologized, possessed as cultural simulacra. This is not a manifestation of the emancipatory force of popular culture. On the contrary, as Pasolini writes in "A Study of the Anthropological Revolution": "Power decides that all must be the same." While a film shown at a cinema theatre was considered a collective appeal to the people,[11] the media that answers to post-utopian mass culture is the TV screen, where private and public blur, and simulacra reign. The popularization of culture and the means of cultural (re)production, he argues, does not mean the inclusion of the people, but instead an ambiguous homologization of society. It is the time of "the Automaton as All." Pasolini's critique is in several ways reminiscent of Horkheimer's and Adorno's reflections on the Cultural Industry. More striking though is the resemblance to what Guy Debord called the "society of the spectacle," when existing social relations are not questioned but are continuously destroyed and reproduced on screen or, as Fredric Jameson writes in *Postmodernism. The Logic of late Capitalism* (1992), when the media becomes the ultimate form of fetishism in consumer society. It is in the reproductive and fetishizing character of popular culture that Pasolini finds a "new fascism" different from its previous iterations. In Pasolini's terms, everyone is turned into a floating figure of the bourgeoisie, desiring to possess his own conditions and to possess what everyone else desires—the lives and archetypes broadcast on screen. It is a time when everyone is educated and educates themselves via the screen, becoming full paid up members of the consumer bourgeoisie, while they live the same alienated and atomized social life, neither as equals nor as individuals.

The mutation of politics in Pasolini's terms can also be read as a mutation of the idea of the people in modern European democracy. Reading it in this way would not undo the problems Arendt addresses, but instead would transform the very terms of the problematic, from the revolutionary people to the popular. In Italian postwar society (like elsewhere), the popular subsumes the people as a dominant mode of cultural expression. Thus we can see that while in its immediate and immanent expression— that is, the direct self-representation of the people—popular culture would seem to have short-circuited the problem Arendt raises between, on the one hand, the people as a force of opposition against cultural hegemony and, on the other, the political representation of the people (i.e., the ideological formation of the people), this would only serve to side-step the question of the role of the people as other in and of history. Rather, following Arendt's critique we can see that we now face an idea of the popular that is equally totalizing, without it either taking up the social question or opposing the process of modernization. The popular is thus bereft of the utopian idea of the other. The idea of the "end of history" can itself be read as the end of the very idea of making an intervention in history. Or in Pasolini's terms, history has now become but an automaton—a closed automatic and immanent body of reproductions and mutations that feed on the lost tradition of its meanings. It is a "void of history" or a "void of power," when nothing really matters; the overcoming of history is also the overcoming of the history of the people or even of mankind (as per the humanist tradition) as an instance of the free and direct expression of a people. It shows that history is understood in terms of the evolutions of its mediatic forms in the ever new developments of technology, with popular culture as a manifestation of the technological progress of consumer society that is liable to express precisely the ideology of technical progress.

What Pasolini ultimately invites us to think about is the fetishization of politics itself and its history through the multifarious popular appeals made to the people. It is to Pasolini's credit that he shows how the political categories of today have been appropriated while feeding on a lost tradition of engaging with history. And through Pasolini's reading of the development of politics in postwar Italy, we can also understand how in contemporary populism the ideology of the popular is the antipode of the politics of the people. What drives modernization today has more to do with forms of technology or technologies of expression than with the irruption of the people in its relation to history and politics. In this way, politics appears as an emptied form, an idea devoid of actual content. What does this mean for us today? I take it that today the point is not to retrieve an idea of the people but, rather, to think the consequences of the loss of a politics that can positively and transformatively affect the course of history. Otherwise we are in the hands of blind technological development, bringing with it an ever-increasing sphere of exploitation, both of people and earth. Perhaps, through thinking the difference between a politics of the people and a politics of the popular in a history that we take to be the same, we can also open up a thought of difference today, in the homogenizing course of history, a thinking of difference either in terms of the nameless life of Platonov or the "uncertain morning" in Pasolini's *Resistance and Its Light* (2001: 63–6).

Notes

1 Interestingly, in German and Russian, there is a more obvious distinction. Popular in the sense "of the people" is in German *völkish* and in Russian *narodnyi*, while in the sense of "liked by many," these two languages retain the Latin root: *populär* and *popul'iarnyi*, respectively. The vast difference between these two meanings of the popular can be exemplified when we consider, on the one hand, a historical form of populism, such as for instance the late nineteenth-century prerevolutionary Russia, *Narodniks* movement, and, on the other, contemporary forms of right-wing populism.
2 The ambiguization of language in general and of political terms in particular opens up for a reflection on whether or not we are witnessing the "Fascism of ambiguity," today as Marcia Schuback Sá Cavalcante has recently argued in *Fascismo de Ambiguidado*, forthcoming in English 2022.
3 She contrasts the French experiment with the American Revolution, where politics was understood as a sphere of public excellence and happiness, working with the purpose of founding political authority. This critique holds equally in *The Origins of*

Totalitarianism as it does in *On Revolution*. In the former she speaks of the "nameless masses" of the Russian Revolution, who were "not citizens with opinions about, and interests in, the handling of public affairs" (Arendt, 1973: 6) as democracy was, in the Greek sense, originally about, the traces of which could, according to Arendt, still be found in the American revolution. In other words, a feature that particularly distinguished the French from the American Revolution was what Arendt calls "the social question," the engagement with poverty, with poor people as the principle of politics (1963: 178).

4   As Lacoue-Labarthe and Nancy showed in the "Nazi Myth," the forming principle in the Nazi Reich was that of race, which turned the idea of the (German) people into a mythified origin and organic growth, by contrast, the dynamics of transformation of the people in the making of them into modern political subjects is in Russia entirely different and not predicated on the notion of the people (Lacoue-Labarthe and Nancy, 1990).

5   In the Soviet system of official representation, the people was an important category. We find it to begin with in the people's commissariats, *narodnye kommisariaty*, and in many similar formations, and here it refers to all Soviet citizens, but it can also mean nationhood, as designating the different nations within the Russian-Soviet empire, alongside with the word *natsional'nost'*. The difference between two commissariats that were established at the time of the revolution can perhaps well illustrate the difference. There was the People's Commisariat for Education (*Narodnyi kommisariat prosvescheniia*), in fact an inversion of the old ministry of the people's education, *Ministerstvo narodnogo prosvescheniia*, and it was indeed to handle the question of people's education (*narodnoe prosveschenie*), that is, the education of the people as masses. There was, however, also the People's Commissariat of the Nationalities of the Russian SFSR, who were to handle the issues of the different nations or peoples within the territory of RSFSR. Interestingly enough, Stalin was the first People's Commissariat of the Nationalities (see Hirsch, 2005).

6   In his early writings, as for instance in "What the Friends of the People are" from 1894, Lenin had argued vehemently against the *Narodniks*, because, as he saw it, the people was antagonistic to the revolutionary cause of the proletariat since they lacked class consciousness and therefore could not understand the "social organization of production" and would therefore be liable to enter the capitalist forms of property and production—not the revolutionary overtaking of the means of production. The *Narodniks* had been unsuccessful in their attempt to mobilize the people and form a political awareness, and Lenin coined the phrase "we take another road" ("my idem drugim putem").

7   See for instance Sergei Karza-Mura, *Sovetskaia Tsivilizatsiia* (2004). And generally, Lenin was against what he calls *obschinnost'*. See for instance, "Ot kakogo nasledstva my otkazyvaemsia?" (Lenin, 1967a).

8   As becomes very clear from the short story "Rubbish Wind" (*Musornyi veter*), about the attempts made by Albert Lichtenberg to resist Nazi Germany. According to Platonov, there was no appeal made in Nazism to the people as the poor or as the working forces of society (Platonov, 1999).

9   See also a similar theme in "The Poetry of Tradition" (Pasolini, 2014b).

10 This critique also goes for the 1968 Student revolt in Italy; in fact, there is a case for arguing that his critique is triggered by it. And what Pasolini criticizes the leftist movement of 1968 for is that it bases its political distinction between the people and the bourgeoisie on a situation that does not only hold no more but that also does not

really correspond to their own conditions. Through its idealism, it preserves the idea that there is a political continuation on the level of political ideology.
11 This idea can be found in the works and writings in a series of film theorists and directors, as for instance Walter Benjamin in *Art in the Age of Mechanical Reproduction*, Dziga Vertov, and, following him, Andrei Tarkovsky and Jean-Luc Godard.

Bibliography

Arendt H (1963) *On Revolution*. London: Penguin.
Arendt H (1973) *The Origins of Totalitarianism*. New York: Harcourt Brace Jovanovich.
Canovan M (1999) Trust the People! Populism and the Two Faces of Democracy. *Political Studies* 47(1): 2–16. doi:10.1111/1467-9248.00184.
Hirsch F (2005) *Empire of Nations: Ethnographic Knowledge & the Making of the Soviet Union*. Ithaca: Cornell University Press.
Jameson F (1992) *Postmodernism, or, The Cultural Logic of Late Capitalism*. Durham, NC: Duke University Press.
Kara-Murza SG (2004) *Sovetskaja civilizacija ot načala do Velikoj Pobedy*. Moskva: Èksmo.
Lacoue-Labarthe P and Nancy J-L (1990) The Nazi Myth. *Critical Inquiry* 16(2): 291–312. doi:10.1086/448535.
Lenin VI (1967a) Ot kakogo nasledstva my otkazyvaemsia? In: *Polnoe sobranie sochinenii, Vol. 17*. Moscow: Gos. Izd. Polit. Lit, 505–50.
Lenin VI (1967b) *Polnoe Sobranie Sochinenii, Vol. 17*. Moscow: Gos. Izd. Polit. Lit.
Pasolini PP (1983) Unhappy Youths. In: Stuart Hood (trans.), *Lutheran Letters*. Manchester: Carcanet New Press, 11–16.
Pasolini PP (2001) *Roman Poems* (trans. L Ferlinghetti). San Francisco: City Lights Books.
Pasolini PP (2014a) Gramsci's Ashes. In: Stephen Sartarelli (ed.), *The Selected Poetry of Pier Paolo Pasolini*. Chicago, IL: The University of Chicago Press, 166–87.
Pasolini PP (2014b) The Poetry of Tradition. In: Stephen Sartarelli (ed.), *The Selected Poetry of Pier Paolo Pasolini* Chicago, IL: The University of Chicago Press, 388–92.
Platonov A (1978) *Chevengur* (trans. A Olcott). Ann Arbor: Ardis Publishers.
Platonov A (1999) Rubbish Wind. In: Robert Chandler (trans.), *The Return and Other Stories*. London: Harvill Press, 71–87.

13

Facing People

Ramona Rat

Exploring the notion of the people from the premises laid out by the notable twentieth-century philosopher Emmanuel Levinas, in an effort to potentially salvage its meaning from substantialization and practices of exclusion, calls for rethinking the notion through an ethical relation to the other. Indeed, at first glance, to consider the ethical relation to the other when discussing *the people* seems to provide a necessary counterpoint to contemporary nationalist discourses with xenophobic undertones, to which the meaning of this notion is threatened to succumb. However, the answer to this problem is not so straightforward. Primacy given to the Other when tackling the question of community and the political, while seemingly having a counteractive effect on the abovementioned problems, also carries its own risks, as pointed out by Jean Luc Nancy and Alain Badiou, who, in different ways, have raised concerns regarding conceptions of the Other. Both Badiou and Nancy recognize the risks involved in the "other" as an ethical category, more precisely when it becomes a mere empty concept or a given label that refers back to the self. An emphasis on the concept of the other, "the Other," only reinforces a Same/Other dialectic, which through a negative determination leads back to the Same. Moreover, it may also imply the designation of the other as "the Other," its assignation to a category allocated by the Same (cf. Nancy, 2000; Badiou, 2001).[1] It is indeed not difficult to see the significance of this critique for the notion of the people: a category of "the Other" would allow assigning an identification in the form of "the Other people," which, in its turn, could lead to further categorization and the very problematic us-them division, echoing an enclosed conceptualization of the people, and thus finding its way back to the same xenophobic views that we were trying to avoid in the first place. This raises the question: How can we engage the ethical relation to the other in thinking the notion of the people, without turning the other into a mere ethical abstraction or creating a category of "the Other" and thus reinforcing an us-them division?

Taking up this question from a Levinasian perspective is particularly interesting since the abovementioned risks, as Badiou points out, often arise through "recognitions of the other" made in the name of Levinas, although sometimes "strikingly distant from Levinas' actual conception of things" (2001: 20). Indeed, Levinas is well-known for his efforts of thinking the other outside categorization.[2] However, the way in which this can be successfully reflected in the notion of the people remains a question that he never really addressed in a direct way.

It is perhaps tempting to view the notion of the people as being encompassed within Levinas' thoughts on the political and societal relations, or to frame it in the form of the "Jewish people" or "the people of Israel," evoked in Levinas' confessional writings, also echoing his interest in the communal, societal, and political.³ This political side of Levinas' philosophy, amply discussed by his commentators, is guided by the question of justice, "inseparable from the political" (Levinas, 1986/1988: 171),⁴ and introduced by what Levinas calls "the third."⁵ While the ethical relation to the other is frequently considered a relation between "the two of us" (Levinas, 1982/1998: 106), "the third" (not to be confused with a single empirical third person) signifies precisely the necessity to consider the larger, sociopolitical context of society. In a way, it would make sense to resort to this sociopolitical aspect of Levinas' philosophy, if we were interested in the political understanding of the notion of the people in connection to "the third." However, in order to explore this notion in connection to the ethical relation to the other, we need to venture in a different, less explored direction. Levinas' thoughts on the ethical relation to the other need to be carried beyond the restrictions of a dyad, yet without turning this relation into the question of justice and the "third." This will eventually lead us to a notion of *people* that resists a unifying determination, by considering it with the help of the movement of *facing*, anchored in Levinas' later work. In order to faithfully follow a Levinasian approach, our exploration will emphasize the necessity to embrace paradoxes and the significance of indeterminacy. Provided that Levinas does not seem to be specifically interested in analyzing the notion of the people as such (neither as *peuple* nor as *gens*), the aim here goes beyond an exegesis. Apart from an interpretation of Levinas, what is proposed here is an attempt at a Levinasian interpretation of the notion of the people as a way to address its meaning through the relation to the other.

"People" and the Intertwining of Ethics and Justice

Although examining the political side of Levinas' philosophy per se is not the focus here, Levinas' insistence on the intertwining of ethics and justice is a pivotal part of his philosophy, and thus, it needs to be taken into account in order to understand the larger picture of his thoughts on the relation to the other. To put it simply, for Levinas there is a central difference between the ethical relation to the other and the societal relationship where the question of justice and the political comes into play. While in an ethical relation, the other is unique and incomparable, justice and the political field need symmetry and possibility for comparison in the light of equity and equality (Levinas, 1984/1996: 168). Nevertheless, such a difference between the ethical and the political does not mean separation, nor mutual exclusion. On the contrary, in order to avoid an abstracted "ethereal sociality of angels" (Levinas, 1982/1994: 47),⁶ that is, an isolated dyad of the self and the other, the context of the political, a concrete society, needs to be considered. Here comparing the incomparable becomes necessary. Levinas refers to "the third" as that which "disturbs" the "intimate" I-you relation several times (Levinas, 1954/1998: 19, or 1986/2001: 214), and by this emphasizing further the necessity of considering the larger societal and political context. This disturbance of the relation to the other does not annul the relation but, instead, constitutes an "essential ambiguity" (Levinas, 1996/2001: 230), which was referred to earlier as the intertwinement of ethics and justice.[7] There is a double purpose imbedded in this ambiguity: On the one hand, by means of the ethical relation to the other, where the other is unique and incomparable, it guards against a possible totalization resulting from a fusion of the self and the other into the same category under a common denominator. On the other hand, by means of the political and societal context, the intertwinement assures concreteness, thus it assures that the relation to the other does not turn into mere abstraction, an abstract Other, or an abstract dyad, outside the rest of the world.

When exploring the meaning of the notion of the people through the Levinasian relation to the other, the ambiguity of the ethical and the political, with its double purpose of resistance to a totalizing fusion and of giving concreteness to the relation to the other, has to be considered. Thus, bearing in mind Levinas' emphasis on a resistance to fusion, we need to be cautious about the universality that the word "people" possibly carries, a universality in the etymological meaning of "turned into one" (from the combination of Lat. *unus* and *vertere*). This unification under one becomes especially pronounced when the definite article (*the* people) is used. But even framing it in terms of *a* people or *my* people can implicate a unifying determination, this time through a negative definition: the unifying designation of *a* people as opposed to another people, *my* people as opposed to your/their people, etc. Even when "people" is referred to in its plural form (peoples), meaning more than one distinct people, there is a unifying determination involved by means of the same type of negative definition. Although perhaps in a different context these forms could be considered as particularizations, from a Levinasian perspective, they indicate a unifying attempt, a fusion, under a determined identity assigned to their meaning. It is this unifying character of the notion of the people, and thus universalization of the relation to the other, that we should be cautious about, if we want to adopt a Levinasian approach.

Seemingly opposite to the risk of fusion and totalization, the word "people" also implies plurality, in its basic understanding as more than one person. This would lead us away from the dyadic intimate relation to the other and toward Levinas' abovementioned efforts of assuring the concreteness of the relation to the other, which cannot be considered in isolation. In order not to fall into abstractions we need to keep in mind that the other is among others, in a plurality, and that the relation to the other is in the world, in a *populated* world. This is clearly pointed out by Levinas himself in the lecture "Dying for . . ." from 1987:

> The *there* of being-there is world, which is not the point of geometrical space, but the concreteness of a populated place in which ones are *with* the others and *for* the others. (Levinas, 1987/1998: 213)[8]

However, in this quotation there lies much more than a mere demand for concretization. The "people" of the "populated place" reveals the coincidence of the relation "with" the others and "for" the others. Here we get a glimpse of the true potential in problematizing the notion of the people from a Levinasian perspective: *people* is not only that which gives concreteness to the relation to the other by preventing an ethereal relation with an abstract Other, as "the third" does, but, more importantly and with the same move, it brings forth the ethical relation to the other, the "for the others" itself, within this concreteness, instead of "disturbing" it, as "the third" does. This enriched meaning given to the notion of the people is promising in that it seems to reach beyond a sociopolitical understanding through the "third" and carry in itself the essential ambiguity of resistance to fusion through a common denominator while keeping the concreteness of its plurality. This is a direction of interpretation we need to explore further.

Levinas' Critique of Collectivity Formed around Something in Common

Surpassing fusion through a common denominator, which seems to be crucial in unfolding the role of the ethical relation to the other when thinking the notion of the people, is echoed in Levinas' critique of collectivity formed "around something in common." Although as his work matures his terminology changes, the core of this critique is constant, and it is found from the early stages of his oeuvre, as, for example, in the following quotation from *Time and the Other*:

> It will be thought that, in its relationship with the other, the subject tends to be identified with the other, by being swallowed up in a collective representation, a common ideal. It is the collectivity that says "we," that, turned towards the intelligible sun, towards the truth, feels the other at its side and not in front of itself. This collectivity necessarily establishes itself around a third term, which serves as an intermediary. [. . .] It is a collectivity around something in common. (Levinas, 1947/1987: 93)[9]

In this quotation, Levinas puts into question the understanding of the relation to the other on the basis of "something in common." Now, denouncing a notion of community defined and determined on the grounds of a "collective representation," a shared common something (a *something* that could take the form of a common characteristic, territory, believes, values or even the idea of community itself), a community that ultimately runs the risk of essentialization, is not specific only to Levinas. We find a similar critical view against an essentialized notion of community in, among others, Bataille (1985; 1988), Nancy (1991), Blanchot (1988), and later in Agamben (1993) and Esposito (2009). In Levinas' case, this critique is threefold: first, a critique of grounding collectivity on a third term (*un troisième terme*), an intermediary term or the "something in common" that Levinas emphasizes at the end of the quotation; second, a critique of determining community through a unifying "we," which also translates into building collectivity around something in common (that *something* is the "we" itself); and third a critique of understanding the relation to the other as a simple side-by-side type of relation ("feels the other at its side and not in front of itself"). These three aspects of his critique remain important to Levinas in all stages of his philosophy, albeit in different forms. The first two aspects are reinforced by his objections to a community of genus, for example, in *Totality and Infinity* (Levinas, 1961/1969: 194), *Otherwise than Being* (Levinas, 1974/1998: 87), his essays "Uniqueness" (Levinas, 1986/1998: 192–3) or "Diachrony and Representation" (Levinas, 1985/1987: 110). The critique of the side-by-side type of relation, sometimes referred to as "standing alongside" each other, is also kept alive throughout the years, for example, in *Otherwise than being* (Levinas, 1974/1998: 182).[10]

Levinas' above-described three-folded critique, although expressed slightly differently throughout his oeuvre, underlines the same main idea: when defined through a mediating common ground, community (or "collectivity") becomes communion, a fusion of the self with the other. In such communion, the self and the other are both identified through the same common denominator of the "we" or of the *something* in common (a third intermediary term, or a "collective representation"). By stretching Levinas' argument a bit further, we can add that the members of a community that becomes a communion are just that, "members," incorporated in a totality formed by their communion. As such, these "members" (or *we*) stand alongside each other, equally and in symmetry, the same *in front of* a common shared *something*, and defined as *those who share that something*. *We*, united through communion, are facing that shared *something* which ultimately is the very *we*. This implies an essentialized conception of community closing up upon itself.

Thus, after a closer examination, it becomes clear that Levinas' three-folded critique reflects his objections to an enclosed conception of community. This seems to be consistent with Levinas' earlier mentioned efforts to refuse totalization that led us to deem any definite or indefinite article, possessive or demonstrative pronoun placed in front of the word "people" problematic. Consequently, in order to respect Levinas' objection to an enclosed conception of community expressed by his three-folded critique, the definite article "the" from the notion of "the people," which in this context encloses through its unifying determination, must be abandoned. The same goes for the indefinite article "a" and the possessive or demonstrative pronouns (*my* people, *their* people, *this* people, etc.). Accordingly, from this point on, we will be referring simply to the notion of *people*.

Nevertheless, Levinas' abovementioned critique is not a mere destructive endeavor, but it prepares the terrain for emphasizing the importance of the face-to-face relation to the other when thinking community: "[collectivity that says 'we'] feels the other at its side and not in front of itself," says Levinas, meaning that this "in front of itself" might rescue community from enclosing upon itself in communion. Instead of a side-by-side collectivity, Levinas proposes "the I-you collectivity," which is the "face-to-face situation," a relation "without mediations" (Levinas, 1947/1978: 94–5, 1947/1987: 93–4).[11] This could mean that, when thought through the ethical relation to the other, the notion of *people* does not refer to "members" of a collectivity which says "we" or face a common *something* (a *something* that ultimately is itself), but instead, it needs to involve, in some way, a face-to-face relation. Further clues in this direction can be found in Levinas' Talmudic reading from 1986, "The Pact":

> A veritable pact is thus concluded, and in the presence of the people as a whole, of a society—as I keep emphasizing—in which everyone looks at everyone else. (Levinas, 1982/2007: 71)

Here quickly unfolds the difficulty of thinking *people* as face-to-face: "[E]veryone looks at everyone else" suggests a different kind of face-to-face than a simple dyad, the "intimate society" (Levinas, 1954/1998: 20) that is usually associated with the Levinasian ethical relation. This time, plurality beyond duality needs to somehow find its way in the ethical relation to the other while its contextualization, necessary to avoid pure abstraction, is not simply given by the contemporaneity introduced through the third. At the same time, as an ethical relation to the other, it has to refuse fusion through a common denominator. Thus, it cannot be the "ones" and "others" that are face-to-face, which would imply the fusion through a common denominator given by the category "one" and the category "other." Moreover, while reading the quotation here, we cannot overlook the apparent problem given by the phrasing "people as a whole": Does not "people as a whole" indicate precisely the kind of unifying fusion that Levinas wanted to avoid by involving a face-to-face type of relation in the first place?

As we can see, there are indeed several difficulties that we are confronted with here. Yet, along with these, an interesting and important detail is revealed in the quotation here, through the expressions: "everyone" and "everyone else." Even though in *Totality and Infinity* Levinas arguably insists on the Same/Other division, here it is not the "ones" (same) that look at the "others," which would reinforce the division, but it is the *every-one* looking at the *every-one else*. It is the fragmentation into *every-one* and *every-one else* that might offer the key for introducing plurality into the face-to-face relation, without reinforcing an us-them division that the Same/Other (or, in this case, Ones/Others) dialectic would imply. Here, fragmentation is different from division, where the plurality is still composed by mere parts of a unifying totality. If we interpret the plurality of *people* in this sense, as fragmentation, then the "wholeness" of "people as a whole" needs to be different from the universality as "turned into one." Then, the question is, how can we think this "wholeness"? Some help in this direction comes, just a few pages later, when Levinas specifies that *people* "*opens on* to the whole of humanity" (Levinas, 1982/2007: 74, my emphasis). Although the formulation continues to be problematic (Levinas is still using the universalizing expression: "the whole of humanity"), here we find signaled an openness of the "wholeness" of *people*, which might indicate Levinas' effort to listen to his own, abovementioned, critique of community enclosed upon itself in communion.

Perhaps this aspiration for an accordance between his critical approach of collectivity as communion and his effort to develop an understanding of *people* that are face-to-face is reflected in Levinas' persistent attempt to reconcile the distinction between a face-to-face community and society. "[A] community whose members are practically face to face should keep its interpersonal relationship when its members look towards humanity. The distinction between community and society testifies only to a social thought that is not yet mature," says Levinas (1982/2007: 74). His attempt at dissolving this distinction points toward the importance of maintaining the face-to-face relation to the other in the larger societal setting, yet without transforming this societal setting in an idyllic and abstract society of the face-to-face. Striving for an ideal, unattainable, and abstract face-to-face relation would conflict with Levinas' efforts of avoiding an "ethereal" relation and would contradict his very reason for emphasizing the necessity of a "populated place." Thus, his endeavor is quite different from expressing a nostalgia for a lost community, that Nancy, inspired by Bataille, rightly deems "ridiculous" (1991: 17). This is not the striving for a lost "more mature" or "better" model of community or society. Instead, it is an effort to conceive plurality while remaining faithful to the ethical relation to the other that the face-to-face relation signifies. Here, a notion of *people* is awaiting to come forth: *people* refusing fusion and "turning into one," just as a face-to-face relation does, yet *people* beyond a dyad, in a plurality through fragmentation, as an open wholeness where the adherence to each other is not given by "something in common."

Thinking "People" through the Movement of Facing

The insufficiency of a bond given by "something in common" between people reveals itself clearly in the feeling of "not belonging" while among people, a feeling of solitude that perhaps we are all familiar with, and that Levinas also points out:

> [E]veryone has the impression of being simultaneously related to humanity as a whole, but also solitary and lost. (Levinas, 1982/2007: 68)

Paradoxically, there seems to be a sense of being lost, a feeling of solitude and "not belonging" in the midst of belonging. However, this solitude and sense of being lost, of "not belonging," does not seem to have the same meaning as isolation or breaking loose from all bonds and undoing any trace of belonging altogether. In lack of any kind of belonging, the ethical relation to the other would be ripped out from concreteness and ultimately turned into nothing more than abstract and empty concepts, like the category of "the Other" that Nancy, and Irigaray, among others, vehemently criticize (Nancy, 2000; Irigaray, 1991). As we have seen, a Levinasian defense against this abstraction is given through emphasizing the importance given to the concreteness of the relation to the other, to which the very notion of *people*, of a "populated place," testifies. In this sense, there needs to be a "belonging" to this populated world that gives concreteness and resists pure abstraction, yet, not in the way that provides a common denominator or brings symmetry, as "the third" would. There is a "belonging" that is also a "not belonging" to anything specific, not even a "we" that would turn people into *the* people, into an enclosed unity of auto-determination. This "belonging" through "not belonging" resembles another, previously mentioned paradox where people are together in plurality through the very fragmentation of *people* into "every-one" and "every-one else." To embrace these paradoxes seems to be necessary for thinking *people* with Levinas. So, instead of a futile attempt at solving the paradox, we should try to understand the way in which it may transform both the meaning of "belonging" and of "not belonging," and thereby further shaping the meaning of *people*.

From the start, we can observe that a more Levinasian terminology corresponding to the "belonging—not belonging" constellation is given by the expression "relation without relation" through which Levinas famously describes the relation to the other (Levinas, 1961/1969: 80). The self *in relation to* . . . yet not *relative to* . . . the other, conveyed by the phrasing "relation without relation" ensures that neither the self nor the other are defined in relative terms (the self as non-other, the other as non-self), where the other is defined through the self, or vice-versa. At the same time, this relation "without relation" prevents the relation itself from coming into the foreground and converting the self and the other into interchangeable "terms" of the relation, simple members. The importance of this non-relativeness of the relation to the other is consistent throughout Levinas' writings, but the way in which it is depicted differs somewhat among the various phases of Levinas' work. Perhaps the most notable change occurs when his notion of substitution is introduced. In Levinas' later works, the ethical relation to the other comes forth through the notion of substitution, and not so much as the face-to-face relation that prevails in Levinas' early and mid-works.

Without going into details,[12] substitution can be seen as Levinas' way of de-essentializing subjectivity. The self becomes self not through itself but through the other, yet not as a relative definition (i.e., self as non-other). However, the non-relativeness of the "relation without relation" is maintained without an emphasis on the autonomous self that would enter into a relation with the other, as a face-to-face relation from Levinas' early work seems to do. Levinas himself acknowledges this shift of focus, moving from underlining the importance of the autonomy of the self in *Totality and Infinity* to focusing on the emergence of the self in its relation to the other in *Otherwise than Being* (Goud, 2008: 23). Thought in terms of substitution, the core of the self doesn't belong to itself. This should not be seen as a coincidence or a fusion of the self with the other; the self still emerges as a self and does not become an other.[13] Instead of an alteration, according to Levinas, substitution signifies a movement of de-position (1974/1998: 126), a "null site" (*non-lieu*) (e.g., 1974/1990: 24, 1974/1998: 10), where the self is out of place from itself. The self doesn't find itself in itself, nor in the other, but, paradoxically, in this very movement of losing itself, through its not belonging to itself.

It is not hard to notice that Levinas' more mature expression of the "relation without relation," has a very similar configuration when compared to the "not belonging" at the core of "belonging" involved in the meaning of *people* that we are trying to articulate. Similar to the relation to the other expressed by the notion of substitution, the meaning of *people* seems to involve a movement of de-position, where people are de-posed from their belonging to *the* people. Just as the de-position characteristic of substitution leads to a de-essentialization of the subject, there is a de-essentialization involved in the meaning of *people*, as shown in connection to Levinas' threefold critique of a collectivity formed around "something in common." It seems that the meaning of *people* resonates well with the way Levinas describes the relation to the other in his later work, through substitution. In comparison to the face-to-face relation, which, given its dyadic character, remains hard to reconcile with the plurality implied by the notion of *people*, substitution has a much more undetermined, dynamic character through the movement of de-position. As such, it doesn't seem to carry the same solidity as the dyad of the face-to-face does. Accordingly, we need to rethink the previous understanding of *people* as a "face-to-face situation," in terms that are more consistent with the movement of substitution.

Although the face-to-face relation somewhat fades out from Levinas' later work, the *face* of the other remains very important and is often evoked even in *Otherwise than Being*. In light of this, it seems reasonable to embrace the significance of the "face" even when renouncing the "face-to-face" as an articulation of *people*. The face remains significant for the notion of *people* not only because it is consistently used throughout Levinas' work but also due to its role in assuring the concreteness of the ethical relation, through the physical face.

The physical face, which, in its Levinasian meaning, is not reduced to the face as a body part, but it is the whole body (e.g., Levinas, 1961/1969: 262; 1982/1985: 97; 1984/1996: 167), gives concreteness by "presenting oneself in person" (Levinas, 1961/1969: 262). However, it is not reducible to this appearance; it points beyond itself, without a *something* or a *somewhere* where this beyond leads. As Levinas underlines, the face (*visage*) is not limited to the physical face, but neither is it an abstraction, an "angelic" face. Instead, it is both "visage and visible" (Levinas, 1974/1998: 160). The face, Levinas explains, does not represent a withdrawal into an inaccessible hidden world; it is not a representation, nor a sign or an indication of something other than itself, but rather it is like a "trace of itself," "a trace in a trace of an abandon" (1974/1998: 94). In this alliance between elusiveness and presence, the face of the other, in its manifestation, is the very impossibility of manifestation. We can see how a similar paradox unfolds here as the loss of self at the core of itself, or as "belonging" through "not belonging." And, similarly to these cases, there is a de-position, a movement opened up by the face. The face invites for a movement, for a turning toward the face. In fact, this movement, or "orientation," is emphasized by Levinas already in *Totality and Infinity*. Even though there, the notion of substitution is not yet developed, and the Same/Other distinction is still quite dominant, it is already clear that the core of a Levinasian perspective is not about dichotomies but about "orientation."[14] No wonder that Levinas gives a central importance to it:

> The priority of this orientation over the terms that are placed in it (and which cannot arise without this orientation) summarizes the theses of the present work. (Levinas, 1961/1969: 215)

This means that the notion of *people*, approached from this angle of Levinas' work, does not submit to a simple priority given to the Other or a Same/Other dichotomy, where the Same or the Other become defined (negatively) through their counterpart, risks about which the Nancyian or Badiouian critique alerts us. Instead, it is the priority of "orientation" that becomes important for the meaning of *people*.

If we think this priority of "orientation" through Levinas' later works, which has been shown earlier to be more appropriate for exploring the meaning of *people*, we can find it reflected in the de-positioning movement of substitution. This movement makes the dynamic character implicit in "orientation" even more pronounced, and in order to remain faithful to the importance of the "face" (but not the face-to-face), we can rethink the movement of orientation as a movement of *facing*. At times, when describing the ethical relation to the other, Levinas himself uses the expression "en face de . . ." (e.g., 1987 1961/1990: 244; 2011: 94), which can be translated as "facing." We can borrow this expression with the intention to capture more adequately the de-positioning movement of orientation, while trying to break free from the problematic dyad of the face-to-face. Seen as a de-positioning movement, *facing* is a much better fit than the face-to-face relation, which, as shown earlier, was Levinas' proposal of an alternative to the enclosed side-by-side community. Following a Levinasian approach, yet not directly following Levinas, the movement of *facing* can help us rethink the understanding of *people* in terms that are less problematic than the face-to-face dyad, and more consistent with Levinas' later work.

The English word "facing," through its plasticity, could suggest both people who are facing and people who are faced. This double aspect serves remarkably well the paradoxical character of *people*, where the wholeness, the belonging together of *people* consists in its very fragmentation, not belonging. Fragmentation, as pointed out earlier, is very different from division, where the one is divided into its parts. Accordingly, *people* as *facing* is different from a conglomeration of members ("terms" of the relation) included in a totality of *the* people. With its emphasis on movement and the instability of de-position, *facing* has the potential to avoid categorization, and thus it avoids designating people through the category of "the Other" and perpetuating a Same/Other, us-them division. As a movement, an orientation, *facing* does not solidify in a simple mirroring of oneself in the other, nor in a negative determination by contrasting that which is faced; it is more of a lack of determination at the core of identity. Consequently, the notion of *facing people* proposed here does not imply an auto-reflection (people facing itself) that would only lead to an enclosement upon itself, to fusion and a turning into one, that Levinas so clearly criticized. It is neither the splitting into One and Other (one people facing other people), where *people* becomes categorized as "the One" or as "the Other" and follows the articulation of a dichotomic thinking. It is impossible, or rather has no sense to determine or define who is facing and who is faced. Instead, the sense, the orientation, reveals itself as the very movement that *facing* entails. It is the movement at the core of *facing* that prevents the congealment of *people* into a united one or its categorization into "the One" and "the Other." Taking into consideration the importance of this paradoxical and ambiguous indeterminacy of *facing*, the meaning of *people*, approached from the perspective of a Levinasian ethical relation to the other, cannot lead to *establishing* an ethical meaning of *people*. *Facing people*, through its movement and ambiguity, not only prevents an established meaning of *people* but also resists the designation of people (a group of people, a community, a nation, etc.) as "the Other." Understood in this way, the notion of *people* allows for a relation to the other, as *facing*, without compromising either the concreteness (through the plurality of fragmentation and the concreteness of "the face") or the uniqueness (by refusing fusion and entering categories, even the category of "the Other") required by a Levinasian approach to the ethical relation to the other.

As we can see, in order to answer our initial quest in trying to bring forth the meaning of *people* from a Levinasian perspective, and at the same time evade an enclosement in abstraction, categorization, and the very problematic us-them division, paradoxically, certain distance needed to be taken from the emblematic Levinasian face-to-face relation to the other, and preference was given to the relation to the other as *facing*. Inspired from the core of Levinas' philosophy, where the primacy is given to orientation and not the relation or its terms, *facing people* implies the primacy of the de-positioning movement of *facing*. In this way, it offers the possibility of engaging the relation to the other in thinking the notion of *people*, yet not by giving primacy to the Self or to the Other, or *the* relation/dialectics that these might constitute, risks that Nancy and Badiou warned us about. Understanding *people* as *facing people* not only reinforces the resistance to the Same/Other dichotomy and to categorization, but it also resists attaching a determined ethical meaning to the notion. This instability, or ambiguity, which might be seen as a weakness, proves to be a strength. Thinking the notion of *people* through the movement of *facing*, together with the paradoxes and indeterminacy that it brings, doesn't endow it with a meaning that is ethical or defined according to certain established ethical categories, such as "the Other." Instead of settling upon a certain meaning, when approached in terms of *facing*, the notion of *people* opens up towards its meaning, its sense, its orientation, through the movement of facing.

Notes

1 Nancy's and Badiou's thoughts carry complexities that are not addressed here, and analyzing their philosophy as such is not the purpose of this investigation. Similarly, it is less important whether Badiou's or Nancy's overall interpretation of Levinas is just or not, the point here being to bring forth possible problems that should be considered when thinking the other in connection to the notion of the people.
2 Perhaps most illustrative and well-known in this sense is his comment from an interview in 1982: "The best way of encountering the Other is not even to notice the color of his eyes!" (1982/1985: 85).
3 As Oona Eisenstadt (2018) points out, Levinas' so-called "confessional" writings are recognized by most readers as related to the question of the political. One also needs to note that making a distinction between the "confessional" and "philosophical" texts within Levinas' oeuvre can be a topic of debate and entering this debate exceeds the purpose here. Instead, let us here follow Levinas' own remarks according to which his confessional and philosophical texts are separated, even though they contain "infiltrations" from one another (cf. Mortley, 1991: 13). One of these "infiltrations" is recognized in the present text by engaging Levinas' Talmudic reading "The Pact" in connection to both his early and later philosophical writings.
4 It is this understanding of the notion of justice, given by Levinas in his later writings, after *Totality and Infinity*, that this text will follow.
5 The present text will consistently refer to "the third" as the translation of Levinas' expression *le tiers*. Nevertheless, several kinds of "thirdness" can be recognized in Levinas' work: "the third" (*le tiers*), "the third person" (*la troisième personne*), "the third man" (*le troisième homme*), and even "illeity" (*illéité*) or "he-ness," from the grammatical third person. For a discussion on the different kind of thirdness in Levinas' work, see Robert Bernasconi (1999).
6 The abstraction of the relation to the other in the form of an "ethereal sociality" also represents Levinas' critique of Buber's *I-you* relation (cf. Levinas, 1982/1994: 47).
7 Perhaps the most famous Levinasian quotation that reflects this ambiguity in relation to "the third" is: "The third party looks at me in the eyes of the Other" (Levinas, 1961/1969: 213).

8   Translation altered according to the French original (Levinas, 1987/1993: 210).
9   Levinas presents this critique by using very similar formulations in *Existence and Existents* (1947/1978: 94–5). The context of both of these discussions is a critique of Heidegger's *Miteinandersein*. However, Levinas' more specific critique of Heidegger is not of interest here and will not be examined closer.
10 Through the expression "alongside of..." Levinas sometimes underlines the ontological attachment of the self to the things of the world, that is to say, the self is *alongside of* the other and of things. This idea appears for ex. in *God Death and Time* (1976/2000), see especially: "An Obligatory Passage: Heidegger." At the same time, "alongside" is also used when Levinas indicates the third which is alongside the other (cf. 1974/1998: 16, 83), meaning which is closer to the side-by-side relation referred here.
11 Levinas adds that he is "taking this ['I-you' collectivity] not in Buber's sense" (1947/1987: 93–4), and by this Levinas means that it is not a mere abstraction of the relation to the other.
12 Substitution becomes a key concept in Levinas' later work, and, unsurprisingly, it is a much-discussed topic among commentators. For Levinas' more focused discussion on this notion, see especially the chapter "Substitution" from *Otherwise than Being* and the essay "Substitution" (Levinas, 1968/1996).
13 When Levinas famously formulates the meaning of substitution as "I is an other," "Je est un autre" (Levinas, 1974/1990: 187), he immediately adds that this is not to be understood in the Rimbaudian sense, where I *becomes* an other. This is not a form of alienation according to Levinas.
14 Robert Bernasconi (1988) brings to our attention Levinas' expression "priority of orientation" and discusses it in connection to Buber's "primacy of relation," where the focus is on the "primacy" and not on the relation as such.

Bibliography

Agamben G (1993) *The Coming Community* (trans. M Hardt). Minneapolis: University of Minnesota Press.

Badiou A (2001) *Ethics: An Essay on the Understanding of Evil* (trans. P Hallward). London: Verso.

Bataille G (1985) Labyrinth. In: *Visions of Excess: Selected Writings, 1927–1939* (trans. A Stoekl). Minneapolis: University of Minnesota Press.

Bataille G (1988) *Inner Experience* (trans. LA Boldt). Albany, NY: State University of New York Press.

Bernasconi R (1988) Failure of Communication' as a Surplus: Dialogue and Lack of Dialogue between Buber and Levinas. In: R Bernasconi and D Wood (eds.), *The Provocation of Levinas: Rethinking the Other*. London: Routledge, 100–35.

Bernasconi R (1999) The Third Party. Levinas on the Intersection of the Ethical and the Political. *Journal of the British Society for Phenomenology* 30(1): 67–87.

Blanchot M (1988) *The Unavowable Community* (trans. P Joris). Barrytown, NY: Station Hill Press.

Eisenstadt O (2018) Levinas's Jewish Writings. In: ML Morgan (ed.), *The Oxford Handbook of Levinas*. New York: Oxford University Press, 549–72.

Esposito R (2010) *Communitas: The Origin and Destiny of Community* (trans. T Campbell). Stanford, CA: Stanford University Press.

Goud JF (2008) "What one asks of oneself, one asks of a saint": A Dialogue with Emmanuel Levinas, 1980–1981. *Levinas Studies* 3: 1–33.
Irigaray L (1991) Questions to Emmanuel Levinas. On the Divinity of Love. In: R Bernasconi and S Critchley (eds.), *Re-Reading Levinas*. Bloomington: Indiana University Press, 109–18.
Levinas E (1947/1978) *Existence and Existents* (trans. A Lingis). Dordrecht: Kluwer Academic Publishing.
Levinas E (1947/1987) *Time and the Other and Additional Essays* (trans. RA Cohen). Pittsburgh, PA: Duquesne University Press.
Levinas E (1954/1998) The I and the Totality. In: MB Smith and B Harshav (trans.), *Entre Nous: On Thinking-of-the-Other*. New York: Columbia University Press, 13–39.
Levinas E (1961/1969) *Totality and Infinity: An Essay on Exteriority* (trans. A Lingis). Pittsburgh, PA: Duquesne University Press.
Levinas E (1961/1990) *Totalité et infini*. Paris: Le Livre de Poche.
Levinas E (1968/1996) Substitution. In: AT Peperzak, S Critchley, and R Bernasconi (eds.), *Emmanuel Levinas: Basic Philosophical Writings*. Bloomington: Indiana University Press, 79–97.
Levinas E (1969/1990) Judaism and Revolution. In: A Aronowicz (trans.), *Nine Talmudic Readings*. Bloomington: Indiana University Press, 94–119.
Levinas E (1974/1990) *Autrement Quêtre, Ou, Au-Delà de l'essence*. Paris: Le Livre de Poche.
Levinas E (1974/1998) *Otherwise than Being, or, Beyond Essence* (trans. A Lingis). Pittsburgh, PA: Duquesne University Press.
Levinas E (1976/2000) *God, Death and Time* (trans. B Bergo). Stanford, CA: Stanford University Press.
Levinas E (1982/1985) *Ethics and Infinity* (trans. P Nemo). 1st ed. Pittsburgh, PA: Duquesne University Press.
Levinas E (1982/1994) Apropos of Buber: Some Notes. In: *Outside the Subject*. (trans. MB Smith) Stanford, CA: Stanford University Press, 40–8.
Levinas E (1982/1998) Philosophy, Justice, and Love. Remarks recorded by R. Fornetand A. Gómez. In: MB. Smith and B Harshav (trans.), *Entre Nous. Thinking-of-the-Other*. New York: Columbia University Press, 103–22.
Levinas E (1982/2007) The Pact. In: GD Mole (trans.), *Beyond the Verse: Talmudic Readings and Lectures*. London: Continuum, 67–84.
Levinas E (1984/1996) Peace and Proximity. In: AT Peperzak, S Critchley, and R Bernasconi (eds.), *Emmanuel Levinas: Basic Philosophical Writings*. Bloomington: Indiana University Press, 161–70.
Levinas E (1985/1987) Diachrony and Representation. In: RA Cohen (trans.), *Time and the Other and Additional Essays*. Pittsburgh, PA: Duquesne University Press, 97–120.
Levinas E (1986/1988) The Paradox of Morality: An Interview with Emmanuel Levinas. In: R Bernasconi and D Wood (eds.), *The Provocation of Levinas: Rethinking the Other*. Warwick Studies in Philosophy and Literature. London: Routledge, 168–80.
Levinas E (1986/1998) Uniqueness. In: MB Smith and B Harshav (trans.), *Entre Nous: On Thinking-of-the-Other*. New York: Columbia University Press, 189–96.
Levinas E (1986/2001) The Proximity of the Other. In: J Robbins (ed.), *Is It Righteous to Be? Interviews with Emmanuel Lévinas*. Stanford, CA: Stanford University Press, 211–18.
Levinas E (1987) *Hors Sujet*. Montpellier: Fata Morgana.
Levinas E (1987/1993) Mourir pour . . . . In: *Entre nous: essais sur le penser-a-l'autre*. Paris: Grasset, 204–14.

Levinas E (1987/1998) Dying for . . .In: MB Smith and B Harshav (trans.), *Entre Nous: On Thinking-of-the-Other*. New York: Columbia University Press, 207–18.

Levinas E (1996/2001) Responsibility and Substitution: Interview with Levinas Conducted by Augusto Ponzio. In: J Robbins (ed.), *Is It Righteous to Be? Interviews with Emmanuel Lévinas*. Stanford, CA: Stanford University Press, 228–33.

Levinas E (2011) *Œuvres complètes Tome 2. Parole et silence et autres conférences inédites*, Paris: Grasset.

Mortley R (ed.) (1991) *French Philosophers in Conversation: Levinas, Schneider, Serres, Irigaray, Le Doeuff, Derrida*. London: Routledge.

Nancy J-L (1991) *The Inoperative Community* (trans. P Connor). Minneapolis: University of Minnesota Press.

Nancy J-L (2000) *Being Singular Plural* (trans. RD Richardson and AE O'Byrne). Stanford, CA: Stanford University Press.

Epilogue

14

On "People"

Brief Theoretical Notes

Michael Marder

Presented in fourteen theses, the brief theoretical notes that follow are meant to put "people" under a microscope. Which senses are tucked into this all-too-common word, senses we are perhaps only vaguely (if at all) aware of? How do we choose among its at times incompatible significations? What comes to the fore and what recedes to the background? Is there a way to restore to "people" its semantic and conceptual dynamism in the twenty-first century?

i. The term "people" lies at the intersection of collective determinacy and indeterminacy. Much hinges on whether this noun is preceded by the definite article, the indefinite article, or no article at all. And on whether it is treated as a noun or as a verb.

ii. *The* people is a category of belonging: often to a geopolitical locale (e.g., "the people of Florida" or "the people of Ghana") but also to a tight-knit group with a strong leader, an inner circle, or a clique (e.g., "the people of Putin"). The stress is on the exclusivity of membership. Avowedly plurinational states, such as Bolivia, rightly insist that a more accurate expression to use is "the peoples," as in "the peoples of Bolivia."

iii. *A* people hints at particular belonging within a field dotted with multiple belongings, refusing to privilege one or another among them. It requires a certain degree of indifference and detachment: the gaze of a historian, a diplomat, or those who feel a sense of non-belonging to "their" people. Overviewed with this panoramic gaze, peoples are multiple multitudes, the category of quantity doubly accentuated.

iv. *People* may indicate non-geographical affinities, for instance, those based on tradition, as in "People of the Book," or it may refer to people "in general," everyone and anyone—what in German is signaled by *das Man*. It is noteworthy that, in its generality, *people* is asexual; it erases sexual differences. *People* borders on a crowd, throngs, or multitudes without much in common, amassed or massified.

v. *People* is not only a noun but also a verb. A people peoples: to people is to populate a territory. This activity entails the reproductive functioning on a demographic scale and an ecological relation to the land that comes to sustain (or not!) a general population increase as it is being peopled. In the reproductive vein, *people* (from the Latin *populus*) overlaps with *proletariat* (from the Latin *proletarius*: "producing offspring"). The paradox is that the procreative upsurge is signaled by a word that has erased the very sexual difference this upsurge entails. The act of peopling adds a biological or a biopolitical dimension to the cultural sense of tradition, national identity, or a more restricted group membership.

vi. In its verb form, *people* alludes to *over*population, that is to say, to the depletion of resources, depriving a land that has been peopled of the material conditions for sustaining life. While *populus* is a "collective term for Roman citizen body," *populari* means "to lay waste to," "to pillage," "to devastate" (Cornell, 2016). Populonia, one of the names of the goddess Juno, is "she who protects against devastation"—hence, the protector of one people from another, or, more poignantly, of the land and the people from itself (Banier, 1738: 195). Military connotations go hand in hand with those of environmental destruction.

vii. *People* are, obviously, also the commoners, as opposed to nobility, the poor and progressively impoverished masses, the plebs. These constitute a vast portion of the population, overflowing even the conceptual confines of a class.

viii. *People* is, therefore, a contested site of meaning, vacillating between the individuation of a group and the de- or non-individuation of its members, between privilege and equalization, sexual difference and indifference, population and devastation, a verb and a noun. If "people" (or "popular identity") is an empty signifier, as Ernesto Laclau contends, that is because, in the term itself, polar opposites join together in an immediate fashion, with the effect of rendering the word nearly meaningless (2005: 96). It is overdetermined, not underdetermined. As a key concept of political theory and practice, *people* acquires its meaning through a set of largely implicit political choices. In other words, in any given historical, cultural, linguistic, and geographical context, *people* is meaningful only thanks to the essentially political operations of highlighting and bringing to the fore some of the antithetical determinations it contains at the expense of others.

ix. The protocols, politically circumscribing time and again the semantics of *people*, must be in place in order for the term to retain a modicum of meaning. It is necessary to dip back into the indeterminacy of the word with the view to renewing its determinations. Conflicting significations must be mobilized against its contemporary hegemonic sense. For example, instead of a purely biologist movement of degrowth (*decrescita*, *décroissance*) predicated on the idea that there are too many people in the world today, it is prudent to deploy another sense of people and peopling as devastation, or laying waste, that emphasizes a qualitative, rather than a quantitative, approach to and pressure upon the natural environment.

x. People speak; a people does not. Therefore, some people speak for a people in the process of representation, which is actually that of substitution, of slipping a part in the place of the whole (synecdoche). The Preamble to the US Constitution, with its famous beginning "We the people of the United States," was drafted by Gouverneur Morris and a few others in the final days of the Constitutional Convention of 1787 without as much as a discussion on the Convention floor. Drawing legitimacy from "the people," rather than the thirteen states, it created a whole that had not yet been in existence at the time of this formulation and that exceeded by far not only the actual authors of the phrase but also their generation (Brookhiser, 2014: 91–2).

xi. *People* is a speculative concept par excellence, and as such, it holds the seeds of its own demise. Peopling a territory is a long-term strategy of depopulating it due to the exhaustion of its resources. This is not to mention that plans to people a territory are typically rooted in willful blindness, the refusal to recognize as people—and as a people—its already existing human inhabitants.

xii. There are various, internal and external, ways of negating the people. *Depopulation* is provoked by short- or long-term demographic trends that counteract those inherent to peopling. To *unpeople* a place is to perpetrate acts tantamount to genocide; not by chance, this word sprang up in the English language in the early part of the sixteenth century, when the colonial unpeopling of the Americas was underway. (Its recorded usage peaked in the first third of the eighteenth century before declining and virtually vanishing in the end of the nineteenth.)

xiii. The categories of belonging go both ways: the people is of *X*, while *Y* is of the people. So does the apparatus of negation. For the Jewish people, the equivalent of excommunication (*ḥerem*: ban, ostracism), to which Baruch Spinoza was subject, is the infrequently applied procedure, announcing that *one is no longer of the people*. There are different ways to be ejected from the people, and the effects of the ejection are equally varied. The one whose belonging is instantaneously revoked is denied basic rights and community support. In other instances, the sense of non-belonging may be chronic—less dramatic, albeit no less insidious. The position of modern cosmopolitanism departs from the usual immiseration hypothesis. Instead, for a true cosmopolitan, to become people—each for her- or himself and all of us together—we need to be without the people.

xiv. In a precise turn of her verse, Russian poet Marina Tsvetaeva calls the condition of those rejected by the people "being spat out by the people into the night [в ночь, выхаркнуты народом]" (2014: 171). Asking *who are* we? ("Кто—мы?"), Tsvetaeva seems to give a retort to the US Constitution's Preamble: we *are not* the people, or, more accurately, we are a part of the people that attains a terrifying nocturnal freedom when it is cut loose from the people, whose own untroubled breathing we obstruct. We are the sputum of the people. Why? Perhaps, because we do not correspond to its reproductive function or vision of territorial domination with its combination of military conquest and environmental devastation? Perhaps, because we see through the sleight of hand that allows a privileged part to speak for the whole? Because we eschew belonging that is indistinguishable from possession?

Bibliography

Banier A (1738) *The Mythology and Fables of the Ancients, Explain'd from History, Volume 3*. London: A. Millar.

Brookhiser R (2014) *Gentleman Revolutionary: Gouverneur Morris, the Rake Who Wrote the Constitution*. New York: Free Press. Available at: http://www.myilibrary.com?id=899198 (accessed September 10, 2021).

Cornell T (2016) Populus. In: *Oxford Research Encyclopedia of Classics*. Oxford: Oxford University Press. doi:10.1093/acrefore/9780199381135.013.5248.

Laclau E (2005) *On Populist Reason*. London: Verso.

Tsvetaeva M (2014) *Popytka Revnosti*. Moscow: Eksmo.

Contributors

Chiara Bottici is Associate Professor of Philosophy at the New School for Social Research, New York.

Maria Brock is a Marie Skłodowska-Curie action research fellow at the University of Malmö.

Mark Devenney is Professor of Critical Theory at the University of Brighton.

Paula Diehl is Professor of Political Theory, History of Ideas, and Political Culture at Kiel University.

Karl Ekeman is a doctoral research fellow in Rhetoric at Engaging Vulnerability, Uppsala University.

Jenny Gunnarsson Payne is Professor of Ethnology at Södertörn University, Stockholm.

Stefan Jonsson is Professor of Ethnic Studies at REMESO, Linköping University.

Tora Lane is Associate Professor of Aesthetics and Research Leader at the Centre for Baltic and Eastern European Studies at Södertörn University.

Oliver Marchart is Professor of Political Theory at the University of Vienna.

Michael Marder is Ikerbasque Research Professor of Philosophy at the University of the Basque Country, Vitoria-Gasteiz.

David Payne PhD in Political Theory, lectures and researches at Södertörn University. He is also International Research editor for Södertörn University, Sweden.

Jacques Rancière is Professor Emeritus of Philosophy at Université Paris-VIII.

Ramona Rat is a senior lecturer in philosophy at Södertörn University, Stockholm.

Muniz Sodré is Professor Emeritus at the School of Communication, Federal University of Rio de Janeiro.

Alexander Stagnell is a postdoctoral research fellow in Rhetoric at Université Libre de Bruxelles.

Gustav Strandberg is a philosopher, writer, and translator based at Södertörn University.

Samo Tomšič is visiting professor of philosophy at the University of Fine Arts Hamburg and research associate at the Humboldt University Berlin.

Kim West is a critic, researcher, editor, and translator based at Södertörn University.

Clare Woodford is Senior Lecturer at the Centre for Applied Philosophy, Politics, and Ethics, University of Brighton.

Index

Adorno, T W   11–12, 123–32, 181
aesthetics, definitions of   17–18, 162–73, 181–2
affect/affectivity   5, 13, 17, 32, 94–103, 104 n.6, 107–20, 124–5, 130, 210
Althusser, L   9, 19, 33, 41 n.3
ambiguity
  fascism of   220 n.2
  of the people   7, 14, 15, 19, 33
  of the popular   209
  of populism   6
  and relation to the other   225–6, 237 n.7
antagonism/antagonistic   4, 13, 15, 18, 40, 43–5, 48, 54, 56, 63, 66–70, 72, 79, 80, 83, 103, 108, 110, 156, 176–81, 184, 189
anti-populism   5–7, 16, 44–9, 56, 56 n.5, 71. *See also* populism; liberalism
antisocial   38, 94–103
anxiety   17, 102–3, 114, 131
Arendt, H   35, 93, 210–12, 219, 221 n.3
articulation
  democratic mode of   52, 55, 70, 80, 82, 88
  populist mode of   45, 55, 56, 61, 83, 110, 118, 152
  as strategy   60, 63, 67, 70
authoritarian/authoritarianism   21 n.17, 45, 46, 48, 56 n.6, 82, 93, 97, 109, 117, 118, 128, 130–1, 160, 163–5, 167–9, 188, 191
autonomy   4, 5, 7–9, 11, 51, 116, 168, 183, 202, 230
  of politics   82

Badiou, A   14, 16, 65, 73 n.3, 203, 204, 206, 223, 233
belonging   8, 13, 14, 35, 127, 153, 154, 202, 205, 212, 229–32, 239, 241
Benjamin, W   189, 222 n.11
Bildung   10

Bosteels, B   14
Bourgeoisie   7, 11, 35, 36, 39, 49, 104 n.8, 127, 132, 145, 166, 182, 214, 218–19, 221 n.10
Brazil   18, 33, 152, 197–207
Brecht, B   1, 11, 180, 184, 185
Butler, J   12, 14, 20 n.2, 116, 119, 128, 144, 145, 148, 154, 157 n.3, 157 n.8, 169

Canovan, M   2, 5–7, 45, 209
capitalism   43, 50, 51, 53–4, 94–8, 100–1, 104 n.7, 104 n.8, 104 n.11, 105 n.19, 105 n.20, 116, 130, 131, 152, 160, 164, 187, 212, 214
citizenship   202
class
  social   11, 49–54, 66, 67, 152, 164, 166, 180, 99–100, 105 n.18 (*see also Lumpenproletariat*)
  struggle   39, 67, 68, 70, 73 n.2, 168, 184, 187–8, 190
common, the   2, 4, 10, 14, 36, 38, 40, 109, 119, 139, 149, 160, 170, 177, 183, 201, 206, 209, 213, 217, 226–30
common sense (*sensus communis*)   49, 62–4, 104 n.11
communism   103, 111, 187, 203, 214, 217
community   2, 10, 14, 17, 20 n.3, 39, 40, 61, 65, 66, 81, 85, 103, 113, 114, 126, 130, 151, 161, 169–71, 180, 189, 201, 203, 206, 216, 223, 226–9, 232, 241
constitution   9–10, 20 n.1, 70, 76, 138, 140, 145, 149
  of the First French Republic   140, 147
  of the Republic of Brazil   199
  of the US   140, 197, 241
contingency, recognition of   63–7, 69, 71, 72
critical thought

contemporary   12–15, 21 n.16
people as a limit category of   8–12, 16, 19
crowd/crowds   17, 124–6, 129, 134 n.9, 144–9, 160, 165
culture   5, 37, 40, 129, 162–72, 182, 183, 188, 191–2, 201, 206, 211, 212, 214, 217–20
Culture wars   108, 111, 115

Dean, J   13, 73 n.3
Deleuze, G   73 n.3
democracy   1, 2, 9, 15–17, 20 n.1, 30, 43, 45, 55–6, 59–73, 75–80, 93, 97, 139–49, 155, 156, 168–70, 206, 209–11, 217–19, 221 n.3
   deliberative   161
   illiberal   109
   liberal or representative   1–2, 5, 7, 46–8, 50–4, 79–81, 122
   radical   45, 49–53, 56, 59, 64, 69–72, 176, 202
demophobia   16, 43–5, 49
Demos   1, 14, 15, 36, 38, 39, 52, 60, 62, 65, 66, 69, 70, 197, 201–4, 206, 209
difference
   against identity   97–9, 103, 184, 220
   logic of   63, 64, 69, 89 (*see also* equivalence, logic of)
   sexual   96, 239, 240
disagreement   38
   as opposed to antagonism   68–9
disavowal   16, 75, 79, 82–3, 86, 88
disgust/disgusting   17, 107–19
dis-identification   5, 33, 36, 41 n.4, 65–9. *See also* identification
diversity, as opposed to unity   81, 84, 139, 148–57, 206

elite, people *vs.*   5, 32, 44–9, 54, 79, 83, 103, 110, 111, 114, 161, 199, 204
emancipation   3, 11–16, 18, 19, 33, 36–40, 60, 64, 71, 72, 97–9, 176, 188, 190, 217, 219
equality   16, 33–4, 37, 38, 40, 52, 55, 59–73, 80, 100, 107, 108, 146, 170, 224
equivalence, logic of   50–3, 61, 63, 64, 66, 89. *See also* difference, logic of

ethics/ethical   4, 5, 19, 55, 56, 224–6
Ethnos   4, 5, 31, 66, 169, 197, 201–7
event   168–9, 189, 197, 204–6, 211
exclusion, as condition for belonging   4, 13, 14, 35, 52, 61, 63, 71, 96, 100, 103, 105 n.15, 156, 170, 172, 223

Fanon, F   132
fascism   3, 11–14, 17, 18, 21 n.17, 45, 60, 62, 94, 122–33, 133 nn.2–5, 134 n.18, 162–9, 176, 187, 188, 211, 212, 218–20, 220 n.2
Fassin, E   13, 102, 103, 105 n.14, 105 n.22
feminism   37, 97, 111, 118, 123, 134 n.12, 161
form/forming/formed
   the people as   1–2, 4–6, 8, 9, 18, 36, 66–7, 127, 139, 140, 153, 166, 202
   the political as   77, 86, 140
   as unity   183–5
Foucault, M   12, 73 n.3, 86–8, 103 n.1, 104 n.9
France   32–3, 38, 45, 61, 71, 140–1, 147, 149, 153, 198
Fraser, N   16, 45, 49–51, 53–4, 131
freedom   5, 7, 11–12, 55, 62, 66, 100, 145–6, 188, 202
French Revolution   9, 12, 17, 103, 141, 144–8, 202, 210, 211
Freud, S   11, 16–17, 67, 123–7, 131–2
friend/enemy or 'us' and 'them'   5, 89, 98, 103, 130, 223, 228, 232

gender   107–12, 116–18, 125, 128, 149–51
   anti-gender   108–10
government   1, 31, 47, 70, 82, 87, 93, 122, 145–7, 153
Gramsci, A   49, 51, 53, 62, 66, 69, 211, 217–18

Hall, S   57 n.6
Hegel, G W F   3, 9–12, 16
hegemony/hegemonic   33, 49–53, 60–72, 80, 109, 117–18, 131, 188, 191, 199, 202, 212, 219
heterogeneity   4, 13, 43, 56, 98, 144, 149, 151, 152, 154, 189, 204

homogeneity 13, 44, 75, 78–9, 81–9, 97, 98, 144, 152, 164, 168, 204, 220
human 201, 203
humanity 111, 203, 228–9
human Rights 37, 55, 108, 140, 164

identification 5, 17, 33, 34, 65–72, 82, 95, 117, 124, 139, 153, 168, 186, 201, 207
   with leader 125–6, 128, 129, 131, 143
identity
   of the people 14, 30, 55, 81, 82, 85, 88, 89, 98, 139, 152, 160, 168–9
   popular 5, 55, 84, 164
   principle of 2, 11–13, 30, 31, 61, 67, 68, 71, 202, 203, 225
ideology 18, 95, 107, 117–18, 122, 129, 131, 132, 162, 201–3, 210–12, 217, 220, 222
imaginary 18, 139, 143, 146, 156, 163, 164, 171
imagination 130, 131, 139
   the sociological imagination 162–3
institutions 20 n.3, 54, 57, 122, 123, 133 n.7, 141, 143, 150, 156, 160–2, 168

Jameson, F 104 n.8, 182, 185, 188, 190, 219
justice 10, 44, 51, 78, 140, 146, 191, 224–6

Kaltwasser, C R 5–7, 20 n.6, 21 n.10, 21 n.11
Kant, I 3, 4, 8–9, 11, 12, 16, 21 n.14
Katsambekis, G 21 n.16
Kioupkiolis, A 21 n.16

labor 105 n.21, 127, 134 n.16, 178, 180, 182, 188, 203
   organized 50
   power 99
   precarious 49, 97
Lacan, J 101, 102, 103 n.1, 104 n.5
Laclau, E 14–16, 20 n.6, 20 n.9, 21 n.12, 44, 51, 53, 55, 59–73, 75, 89, 139, 152, 153, 191, 240
   and Mouffe 14, 15, 51, 118

leader 105 n.18, 122–32, 143, 166, 168, 210, 212, 214, 239
Le Bon, G 16, 17, 124, 126
Lefort, C 55, 69, 75–8, 81, 85, 87–9, 140–4
Lenin, V I 70–1, 210, 212–15, 221 n.6, 221 n.7
Levinas, E 19, 223–34
LGBTQ+ 51, 53, 97, 107, 111, 113, 114, 116, 117
liberalism 7, 44, 45, 49, 52, 54–6, 59, 80, 81, 94, 99, 100, 104 n.2, 207
libidinal
   bond 17, 123, 125–8
   economy 98, 101–2
Lumpenproletariat 99–100, 105 n.18, 105 n.19

Macciocchi, M A 19
Marx, K 10–11, 20 n.1, 20 n.5, 54, 93, 98–101, 104 n.8, 203, 210, 213, 214
Marxism/Marxist 11, 30, 33, 37, 39–41, 70, 71, 112, 188
   Post-Marxism 16, 71
masses, in relation to the people 11, 14, 15, 17, 18, 29, 34, 48, 49, 94, 99, 104 n.2, 124–6, 128, 131, 143, 145, 147, 148, 161, 162, 165–7, 169, 170
media
   mass 5, 16, 43–5, 153, 165, 211, 219
   social 109, 116, 129–31, 207
migrant, the figure of the 17, 50–3, 97, 102, 111, 115, 151, 154, 161–4, 168–72, 185, 205
migration 48, 162–4, 167–71
morality 10, 84
   slave morality 96–7, 101
Mouffe, C 3, 12, 16, 49, 51–7, 80–2, 107, 109, 110, 160, 161, 191
   and Laclau 14–15, 66, 68, 70
Mudde, C 5–7, 20 n.6, 21 n.10, 21 n.11, 44, 48, 76, 79
Müller, J-W 7, 79, 80, 82, 83

name, of the People 5, 31, 39, 44, 190, 217
Nancy, J-L 14, 223, 226, 229, 233
   and Lacoue-Labarthe, P 221 n.4

nation/national 6, 14, 15, 30, 109–11, 118, 120–2, 140, 141, 144–6, 148, 152, 154, 169–71, 197–207, 232, 240
nationalism/nationalist 3, 13, 47, 52, 56 n.4, 94, 107, 109–12, 117, 161–4, 168
negativity 14, 17, 83, 98, 99, 172
Negri, A 1, 14, 40
    and Hardt, M 73 n.3
neoliberalism/neoliberal 32, 34, 38, 44–53, 56 n.2, 56 n.5, 75, 77, 80, 86–9, 93, 95–9, 103, 104 n.10, 104 n.13, 109–11, 115, 160, 161, 164, 176, 187, 188, 191
Nietzsche, F 11, 100–1
nonidentity 11–12, 14, 98, 103, 168–70, 206, 219, 232. *See also* identity
Nussbaum, M 113–14, 116, 117

ontology 5–7, 15, 20 n.8, 29, 30, 59, 60, 65–9, 71, 72, 172, 203, 234 n.10

Pascal, B 101
Pasolini, PP 211, 217–20
people
    as *hyle* 1–2, 6–7, 9, 10, 18, 146–9
    as Idea 18, 83–5, 146–9, 157, 168–70, 189, 201, 203, 206, 207, 210–12, 214, 217–19, 226
    prejudices against 4–5, 7–12, 48–50
    relevance as an emancipatory term 13–16, 18, 19, 31, 33–4
Platonov, A 210, 214–17
Plebs 14, 61, 71, 201
pluralism 7, 45, 52, 54, 70
plurality, and the one 6–7, 12, 15, 145, 148, 149, 157–62, 170, 204, 225–6, 229–30, 232
popular, as opposed to the people 209–11, 217–20, 240
populism 3–7, 12–17, 19, 31, 32, 39, 43–6, 48, 49, 56, 56 n.4, 56 n.5, 61, 63–4, 75, 77, 79–82, 86–8, 93–104, 107–19, 160–3, 164, 168, 176, 182, 186, 190–2, 198, 199, 207, 209, 210, 217, 220
    characteristics of 4–5, 15, 17, 20 n.6, 20 n.7, 20 n.10, 79–81, 83–5, 94, 97–9, 102, 105 n.14, 107, 110–11, 172 n.1, 207
    Left-wing 16, 19, 45, 49–55, 56 n.3, 94, 97–8, 103, 104 n.2, 104 n.3, 161, 191
    Right-wing 19, 21 n.17, 36, 45, 46, 52, 56, 93–5, 97–8, 100, 103, 104 n.2, 108–12, 117, 122–3, 161
    as thin centered ideology 20–1 n.10, 79, 83
    transnational 14, 170–2
    as a vague and essentially contested term 5–6, 43, 21 n.11, 76, 94, 160–1, 209
proletariat/proletarian(s) 11–14, 35, 39, 40, 61, 98, 167, 178, 187–8, 190, 203, 212–18, 240
propaganda 5, 166
    fascist 17, 126–8, 131
proper 61–72, 113, 115, 149, 170, 197, 211, 215–16
    in relation to the improper 14, 34–9
protest/protesters 17, 98, 105, 117–18, 140, 153–4, 160–3, 169–72
psychology/psychological 16–17, 49, 95, 115–16, 122–32
Public Sphere 168–70, 211

race 13, 67, 127, 168, 204–12
Rancière, J 14–16, 29–41, 43–56, 59–72, 75, 161, 163, 202
rational/rationality 9, 11, 16, 29, 32, 68, 83–8, 114–15, 118, 203, 205, 207
    irrational, irrationality 4, 10, 16, 29, 49, 114–15, 132
Real, the 78, 199, 218
reason 4, 7, 10, 11, 62, 78, 87, 118
representation 12, 17, 46, 62, 65–6, 77, 81–2, 85–7, 105, 111, 139–57, 161–70, 180–1, 189, 201–2, 206–7, 219, 221, 226–7, 231, 240
resentment/*ressentiment* 5, 13, 17, 37–8, 93–103, 107, 111–14, 207, 210
resistance 3, 95, 98–9, 103, 108, 115, 171–2, 177, 182–3, 187, 204, 225–6, 233
revolution/revolutionary: 1, 11–12, 18, 30, 34, 37–8, 56, 71, 98–9, 141, 161, 167, 179, 183, 189–90, 197

American   146, 197, 220–1 n.3
French   9, 17, 55, 103, 144–9, 153, 202, 218
Russian   70, 185, 209–17, 221
rhetoric/rhetorical/rhetorically   19, 51, 84, 86, 110–11, 115–17, 122, 127–8, 160–4, 169, 180, 184, 198, 202
Rimbaud, A   30
Rosanvallon, P   14, 104 n.2, 146–9, 155, 157, 161
Rousseau J-J   2–5, 9, 11–12, 15, 18, 143, 145, 151, 211
Russia   4, 110, 118, 134, 203, 209–20, 241

Salecl, R   110, 117, 120
Scheler, M   100–1
Schmitt, C   82, 105 n.22, 139
Schuback Sá Cavalcante, M   220 n.2
sensible/sensibility/sensibilities   11, 13, 16, 17, 36, 38–9, 60, 62, 65, 69, 72, 78, 163, 181
sexuality   107–10, 114, 116, 119, 125
signifier(s)   30, 43, 52–4, 65, 103
   empty   14–15, 38, 54, 61, 65–7, 70, 89, 118, 153–4, 240
   floating   38, 191
socialism, socialist   3, 32, 44, 54–5, 94, 103, 126, 161, 167, 177–8, 187, 190, 214, 216–17
sovereignty   1–2, 17, 52, 55–6, 79–84, 110, 139–48, 151, 156, 170, 202
state   1, 6, 9–10, 15, 31, 34, 44–6, 60–1, 68, 70, 80, 87, 96–7, 122, 141–3, 147, 151, 166, 168, 177, 188, 198, 202–3, 207, 239
Stavrakakis, Y   5, 6, 15, 43, 46, 56, 171
struggle   15, 30, 34, 36–7, 39–41, 47, 48, 51–3, 63, 82, 97–8, 103, 108, 117–18, 160, 165, 168, 176–8, 181, 187–8, 191, 203, 213, 218
   emancipatory   16, 37, 71, 97–8, 177 (*see also* emancipation)
   hegemonic   65–72 (*see also* Hegemony/hegemonic)
subject(s), subjectivity   8–12, 17, 34–5, 40–1, 51, 57, 60–2, 67, 69, 71, 87, 97–105, 107, 111, 115, 117, 153, 163–4, 167, 179, 197, 199, 203, 207, 226, 230
   democratic   69–70, 170, 191
   political   30–1, 39, 68, 139–41, 143–6, 148–50, 152–3, 156, 176, 190, 210, 213–14
subjectivation   14, 33–4, 68, 202–3, 206
symbolic   50, 61, 65, 77–9, 81–2, 85–6, 96, 104, 110, 127, 130, 139–50, 152–6, 161, 170, 202, 206

totalitarianism/totalitarian   81–2, 85–6, 88, 133 n.2, 143–4, 148, 188, 210–13, 217
totality   53–4, 143, 176–7, 180–6, 189, 191, 210, 232
transcendental, questioning of the people   5, 8, 9, 11
Traverso, E   21 n.17, 161
Trump, D   31–3, 50–1, 53, 89, 94, 96, 105 n.18, 111, 118, 122–3, 126–31, 133–4, 160
truth   97–9, 105, 109, 122, 129–30, 181–2, 201, 226

unity   1–2, 5–6, 10–15, 18–19, 61, 75, 78, 81, 83–8, 98, 109, 139, 142–6, 148–56, 171, 177, 179–80, 183, 197, 201, 206, 229

violence   4, 9, 14, 94–7, 99–100, 104–5, 116, 122–3, 127, 141, 167, 177–8, 182, 188, 190

Wallerstein   I 160, 175
Weiss, P   18, 176–92
woman/women   37, 51, 53, 96–8, 102, 108–11, 115–18, 145, 168
worker(s)   13, 17, 32, 34, 36–41, 47, 50–2, 70, 73, 100, 152, 165–7, 177–8, 184–5, 214
worker Movement   182, 191

Žižek, S   13, 25, 60, 65, 73–4, 133, 136

www.ingramcontent.com/pod-product-compliance
Lightning Source LLC
Chambersburg PA
CBHW062135300426
44115CB00012BA/1936